IN THE SHADOW OF POWER

In the Shadow of Power

States and Strategies in International Politics

ROBERT POWELL

PRINCETON UNIVERSITY PRESS

PRINCETON, NEW JERSEY

Library of Congress Cataloging–in–Publication Data

Powell, Robert, 1956–
    In the shadow of power : states and strategies in international
politics / Robert Powell.
        p.   cm.
    Includes bibliographical references and index.
    ISBN 0-691-00456-0 (cl. : alk. paper). — ISBN 0-691-00457-9 (pbk. : alk. paper)
    1. International relations.   I. Title.
    JZ1242.P68   1999   99-12207
    327.1′01—dc21

This book has been composed in Times Roman and Times Roman Bold

The paper used in this publication meets the minimum requirements of
ANSI/NISO Z39.48-1992 (R1997) (*Permanence of Paper*)

http://pup.princeton.edu

Printed in the United States of America

1 3 5 7 9 10 8 6 4 2
1 3 5 7 9 10 8 6 4 2
(Pbk.)

Contents

Preface

A decade ago I wrote a book about nuclear deterrence theory. That book and this one are related in a very general way. Much of nuclear deterrence theory is about trying to understand the strategic logic of a stylized environment in which the states have secure, second-strike capabilities. Much of international relations theory is about trying to understand the strategic logic of a stylized environment in which states exist in a more general Hobbesian state of nature. The previous book tried to advance our understanding of the first environment. This book tries to advance our understanding of the second.

Because this book focuses on threats to use force and states' responses to them, the analysis might at first seem to be irrelevant to many other issues in international relations and politics more generally where the use of military force is not at issue. I do not believe this to be the case. Some aspects of the strategic problems states face when responding to threats may be special, but many are not. There are, for example, some close parallels between the strategic problem facing two states who are bargaining about revising the territorial status quo and two litigants who are bargaining about the terms of an out-of-court settlement. Working through some of the strategic problems underlying states' responses to threats will give us a deeper appreciation of a broader range of concerns that arise in the shadow of power, where it is the use of power—be it military, legal, or political—that is at issue.

Finally, there is an important difference between my earlier book on nuclear deterrence and this one. This book does not presume any special training in game theory. The body of this book should be accessible to anyone who has a basic background in international relations theory. Separate appendixes at the end of the book do provide formal analyses for interested readers, but I have tried very hard to make the body of the book a self-contained whole that can be read without referring to the technical appendixes.

Acknowledgments

Many colleagues and friends have given freely of their time and good advice. I am grateful to James Alt, Henry Brady, Elaine Chandler, Ruth

Collier, George Downs, Jeffry Frieden, Charles Glaser, Joanne Gowa, Ernst Haas, David Lake, Robert Powell Sr., Leo Simon, Alastair Smith, Shannon Stimson, Kenneth Waltz, Barry Weingast, and Ethan Zorick. Bruce Bueno de Mesquita, James Fearon, Robert Keohane, and James Morrow provided exceptionally detailed and helpful suggestions at critical points in the development of the manuscript.

Because I have tried to write this book so that it could be used in a first-year graduate course in international relations theory, it was especially important to have comments from graduate students. Matthew Benke, Kevin Donovan, and Robert Rauchhaus were willing to tell their professor that he was at best confusing and probably confused about some things, and the manuscript has benefited greatly from their reviews. Kevin Donovan also served as my superb research assistant throughout most of the project. He saved me from making several stupid mistakes as well as some subtle ones.

Finally, I owe a special debt to Ken Waltz. I took my first course in international relations theory from him almost twenty years ago—it was the semester *Theory of International Politics* was published. As this book makes clear, we agree about some things and disagree about others. But it is also true that this book would never have been written had he not been my teacher.

I would also like to thank the Institute on Global Conflict and Cooperation and the National Science Foundation for their financial support. Chapters 2, 3, and 6 are drawn from articles (Powell 1993, 1994, 1996a, 1996b) published in the *American Political Science Review, Games and Economic Behavior, International Organization*, and *World Politics*.

IN THE SHADOW OF POWER

1

States and Strategies

How does the shadow of power affect state behavior? How, for example, does the distribution of power affect the likelihood of war? Is war less likely if there is an even distribution of power or if one state preponderates? Or, is there any relation at all between the distribution of power and the risk of war?

How do states cope with shifts in the distribution of power among them? Thucydides ascribed the cause of the Peloponnesian War to the rise of Athenian power: "What made war inevitable was the growth of Athenian power and the fear which this inspired in Sparta." But the profound shift in power that took place between Britain and the United States in the century after the War of 1812 did not lead to war even though it was at times fraught with conflict and tension. Why do some shifts lead to war and others not? When is a declining state tempted to launch a preventive war against a rising state, and when does it heed Bismarck's counsel that "preventive war is like suicide from fear of death" by trying to accommodate a rising state?

If one state threatens another, how do other states react? Do they tend to balance against the threat by aligning with the threatened state as republican France and czarist Russia did against Germany in 1894? Or do states tend to bandwagon by joining in with the state making the threat as Prussia, Austria, Russia, and Spain did at various times during the Napoleonic Wars? Or do states try to avoid conflict by not taking sides as the United States did for the first three years of the First World War?

How do changes in military technologies affect the prospects for peace? Is war more likely if technology gives the offense an advantage over the defense, as was believed to be the case in the summer of 1914? Or do the states, recognizing the greater technological danger, take steps to offset it as states tried to do before the First World War by concentrating their troops farther back behind the frontier? And, if it such steps are unavailable, do states compensate for the greater technological danger by moderating their behavior so that the overall risk of war remains largely the same?[1]

These were important questions before the end of the cold war and they remain so afterward. China's rapid economic growth since Mao's death has begun to raise security concerns about East Asia. The demise of the Soviet Union has left a power vacuum in resource-rich Central Asia and has sparked talk of another round of the "Great Game." And, some ponder the effects of the possible reemergence of Russia as a Great Power.

Much of international relations theory seeks to understand how states interact in the shadow of power by trying to abstract away from many of the details of international politics and foreign policy. These analyses focus instead on attempting to understand the strategic logic of a simple, stylized model of the international system. This stylization strives to distill the essence of some of the strategic problems states actually face—or at least important aspects of them—into a simpler analytic setting where it is easier to see how states deal with these problems, how these efforts interact, and what the outcomes of these interactions are.

In this stylization, a small number of states interact in a Hobbesian state of nature. Each state is assumed to be a rational, unitary actor and to have control over a limited amount of resources. These resources can be used in one of two general ways. A state can allocate resources toward the satisfaction of its immediate ends or toward the means of military power. Because these states exist in a condition of anarchy or a Hobbesian state of war, there is no supranational Leviathan to impose order and to protect the states from each other. There is nothing to stop one state from trying to further its interests by using its military means against another state if the former believes that doing so is in its best interest. However, a state's ability to achieve its ends through the use of military force against another depends in part on the relative amounts of resources the states have devoted to the military. The more a state allocates to the military, the stronger it becomes *ceteris paribus*

---

[1] See, of course, *The Peloponnesian War* for Thucydides' account and see Kagan (1969, 1974, 1981, 1987) for a modern treatment. Allen (1955), Bourne (1967), and Campbell (1974) provide an overview of the relations between Britain and the United States. Levy (1987, 103) quotes Bismarck's view on preventive war. Kennan (1979, 1984) discusses the Franco-Russian relations and A. Taylor (1963, 325–44) offers a brief summary. Schroeder (1994a, 1994b) and Schweller (1994) examine balancing and bandwagoning. Jack Snyder (1984a, 113) notes France's efforts to decrease its vulnerability by locating its railhead disembarkation points far enough back from the frontier. Nalebuff (1986) studies the possibility that states moderate their behavior when the technological risks are higher.

and the more likely it is to prevail in any conflict. Thus, allocations to the military, which are assumed to have no intrinsic value and bring no direct gain to a state, may bring important indirect gains by providing a state with the means of protecting the resources it already has or of taking resources from others.

Variants of this stylization and efforts to understand it can be found in Thucydides' account of the Peloponnesian War; in E. H. Carr's ([1939], 1954) study of the twenty-years' crisis between the two world wars; in Quincy Wright's ([1942], 1965) compendium on war; in Martin Wight's (1946) examination of power politics; in Hans Morgenthau's early attempt to "present a theory of international politics" ([1948], 1967, 3); in Edward Gullick's (1955) endeavor to systematize balance-of-power theory; in Morton Kaplan's (1957) application of "systems theory" to international politics; in John Herz's (1950) and Herbert Butterfield's (1950) early explications of the security dilemma; in Kenneth Waltz's (1959) third image of the causes of war; in Arnold Wolfers's (1962) theorizing about discord and collaboration; in Raymond Aron's (1966) "determination to offer a general theory, starting from the specific features of international relations" (Hoffmann 1987, 53); in Hedley Bull's (1977) striving to understand international order and an anarchical society; in Robert Keohane and Joseph Nye's (1977) work on power and interdependence; in Robert Jervis's (1978) elaboration of the security dilemma and its relation to the offense-defense balance; in Waltz's (1979) attempt to construct a structural theory of international politics; in Bruce Bueno de Mesquita's (1981) start on formalizing the expected-value calculations leading to war; in Robert Gilpin's (1981) explanation of hegemonic war; as a point of departure for Keohane's (1984) efforts to understand international cooperation and the role of institutions; in Robert Axelrod's (1984) study of cooperation; and, albeit often less explicitly so, in a myriad of other analyses. Indeed, this stylization has now become part of what Thomas Kuhn (1970) would call the "disciplinary matrix" of international relations theory.

In this stylized environment, a state can respond to threats to its security in at least three general ways. It can reallocate the resources already under its direct control in what Waltz calls "internal balancing" (1979, 168). A state can try to resolve conflicts and diffuse threats through bargaining and compromise. Or, it can try to draw on the resources of others by allying with them.

This book tries to advance our understanding of the strategic logic of this stylized environment and of international politics more broadly by examining each of these three responses. More fundamentally, the analysis tries to illuminate some of the basic mechanisms through which states pursue their ends and conflicts of interest play themselves out. These mechanisms are too general and too spare to explain particular outcomes in any degree of specificity. These mechanisms instead provide a kind of template for thinking about the ways that states—or, more broadly, actors—interact in the shadow of power.

This examination suggests that many widely made arguments about the ways that states interact in this environment and about the outcomes of this interaction are at best incomplete and need to be qualified: Neither a balance nor a preponderance of power is necessarily more peaceful. There is no general tendency to balance. Anarchy does not imply that states are concerned about relative gains and that these concerns in turn impede cooperation.

The following chapters indicate instead that the relation between the likelihood of peace and the distribution of power depends on the distribution of benefits associated with the existing international order. War is least likely when the international distribution of benefits reflects the underlying distribution of power. The greater the disparity between the distribution of power and the distribution of benefits, the more likely war. Whether states balance, bandwagon, or stand aside while others fight depends in a complicated way on many different factors, which include the cost of fighting, the extent to which military forces cumulate when combined together in an alliance, and the relative aggressiveness of potential coalition partners.

The remainder of this chapter serves three ends. First, the analysis of the three responses to threats emphasizes the importance of commitment issues, the effects of asymmetric information, and what will be called the "technology of coercion."[2] The next section introduces these ideas. The subsequent section then provides an overview of each of the following chapters. These chapters use a series of game-theoretic models to examine the strategic problems and trade-offs states face when responding to threats.[3] This modeling-based approach raises a methodological question, which the final section of this chapter addresses: What is the role and usefulness of formal models in the study of international politics?

[2] See Fearon (1995b) for a discussion of the importance of commitment issues and informational asymmetries in theories about the causes of war.

[3] As elaborated more fully below, the general discussion and analysis of these models does not presuppose any previous knowledge of game theory. The technical analysis of the models is confined to the appendixes.

Commitment Issues, Informational Problems, and the Technology of Coercion

Commitment issues, informational asymmetries, and the technology of coercion play key roles in defining the strategic problems states face, and this section introduces these terms. A *commitment problem* exists among a group of actors if they could make themselves better-off by being able to commit themselves to following a particular course of action but are unable to do so. This situation occurs when, loosely speaking, individually sensible decisions lead to outcomes that are collectively inferior. More precisely, commitment problems exist if each actor's acting in its own self-interest leads to an outcome that leaves everyone worse-off.

The prisoner's dilemma is a classic example of a commitment problem, and it has been widely used in international relations to illustrate problems as diverse as the Concert of Europe (Jervis 1985), the failure of cooperation in the July 1914 crisis (Van Evera 1985), arms races (Downs and Rocke 1990), trade agreements and wars (Conybeare 1985, 1987; Yarbrough and Yarbrough 1992), international banking (Lipson 1985), alliance politics (G. Snyder 1984), and the effect of alliances on trade (Gowa 1989, 1994; Gowa and Mansfield 1993). In the prisoner's dilemma, two players, say *I* and *II*, must choose between the two alternatives of "cooperating" and "defecting." Suppose for example that the actors are states and that each state can decide to build up its arms or not build. These choices are illustrated in figure 1.1 where *I*'s choices are denoted by rows and *II*'s choices are represented by columns. If, for instance, *I* decides to build and *II* does not, then the outcome would be in the upper-right cell of the matrix. The four cells of the matrix show all of the possible combinations of the states' decisions and, implicitly, the outcomes associated with these decisions.

The numbers in the cells reflect the way the states rank the possible outcomes. In a prisoner's dilemma, an actor's most preferred outcome is for it to defect while the other actor cooperates. In the arms-race context, this means that each state's most preferred outcome is for it to build while the other does not because this is assumed to lead to a favorable shift in the distribution of power. The next best outcome is for neither state to build, as this leaves the distribution of power unchanged and avoids the added economic burden of spending more on the military. The third-best outcome is for both states to build. This, too, leaves the distribution of power unchanged but now entails spending more on arms. And, the worst outcome for a state is not to build when the other does, as

State II

	Build	Not Build
Build	2,2	4,1
Not Build	1,4	3,3

State I

Figure 1.1 The decision to build armaments as a prisoner's dilemma

this leads to an unfavorable shift in the distribution of power. Using the numbers 1 through 4 to depict this ranking and letting larger numbers correspond to more favorable outcomes then gives the entries in the cells in figure 1.1 where the first number in a pair represents *I*'s ranking.

To see that the states face a commitment problem in the prisoner's dilemma, consider what they will do. If the actors are unable to commit themselves to not building, then each builds. This follows from the observation that if *II* builds (i.e., chooses the left column in figure 1.1), *I* obtains a payoff of two by building and a payoff of one by not building. *I*, therefore, prefers to build if it expects *II* to build, as this prevents an unfavorable shift in the distribution of power.

In fact, *I* also does better by building even if *II* does not build (i.e., if *II* plays the right column). If *I* builds while *II* does not, the distribution of power shifts in *I*'s favor. By contrast, *I* does save money if it does not build, but it foregoes the opportunity to shift the distribution of power in its favor. The assumptions that we have made about state preferences in this simple example then imply that *I* prefers the former outcome to the latter.[4] In numbers, *I* obtains 4 if it builds and 3 if it does not. Thus, *I* prefers to build even if *II* does not build.

---

[4] What to assume about state goals and preferences has recently been the subject of intense debate in international relations theory, and will be discussed more fully below in chapter 2.

In sum, *I* does better by building regardless of what *II* does. A similar argument shows that *II* also prefers to build regardless of what it expects *I* to do. Consequently, each state builds and receives a payoff of two as long as the states are unable to commit themselves to refraining from building. However, each state would have done better if both had been able to deny themselves the option of building as each would have received a payoff of three. The fundamental problem facing actors caught in a prisoner's dilemma arises because they are unable to commit themselves to a course of action that would benefit both of them.

A commitment problem also lies at the center of the security dilemma (Butterfield 1950; Herz 1950; Jervis 1978; Glaser 1992, 1997). A security dilemma exists when one state's efforts to increase its security also has the—perhaps unintended—effect of reducing another state's security. In an effort to restore its initial level of security, the second state may then take steps that diminish the effectiveness of the first state's efforts to enhance its security. This, in turn, prompts the first state to take additional steps and so on. In a security dilemma, one state's efforts to increase its security may trigger a spiral of hostility leading to war. In this situation, both states would be better-off if the first state could somehow commit itself to refraining from using its greater military capability offensively. If such a commitment could be made, then the first state's initial efforts to increase its security would not spark a spiral by threatening the second state.

The second feature that often characterizes the strategic problems states face is *asymmetric information*. Information is asymmetric or incomplete when different actors know or believe different things about a situation. These asymmetries typically take the form of uncertainty about states' goals (or, more formally, their preferences) or capabilities. For example, each state may know how much it values prevailing in a crisis but be unsure of how much another state values prevailing. Information is asymmetric in this case because each state knows its own payoff to prevailing but not that of the other state. States may also have different beliefs about their capabilities and therefore about their chances of prevailing. When each state believes that it is well prepared and, lacking complete information about the other side, also believes that the other side is comparatively less well prepared, then both states will overestimate their chances of prevailing. Conversely, each state may believe itself to be unprepared for war while fearing that the other is. In this case, the informational asymmetry leads both states to underestimate their chances of success and thereby facilitates a peaceful resolution of a dispute.[5]

Informational asymmetries about states' goals abound in international politics. Uncertainty about the scope of Hitler's ultimate ends was a crucial aspect of the strategic problem facing Britain in the 1930s. Britain was generally willing to revise the Versailles Treaty in Germany's favor (Gilbert 1966) but unwilling to let Germany dominate the continent. However, Britain was unsure whether Hitler's aims were limited or not. As Alexander Cadogan, the new permanent under-secretary in the British Foreign Office put it shortly after Germany annexed Austria: "I am quite prepared to believe that the incorporation in the Reich of Austrian and Sudentendeutsch may only be the first step in a German expansion eastwards. But I do not submit that this is necessarily so, and that we should not rush to hasty conclusions."[6] This informational asymmetry led Britain to make a series of concessions to Germany throughout the 1930s in the hope that Hitler's ends were limited and that these concessions would appease him. But each concession led to a new demand and, ultimately, war when Britain became convinced that Hitler's aims were unlimited.

Asymmetric information about goals also played a critical role in the Agadir crisis, which raised the specter of war between Britain and Germany in the summer of 1911 and subsequently led to an intensification of the arms race (Barlow 1971; Barraclough 1982; Kennedy 1980; Stevenson 1996; A. Taylor 1963; S. Williamson 1969). In May of that year, France tried to enhance its position in Morocco by occupying Fez, an occupation which, if prolonged, would violate the Algeçiras Act. Earlier that spring the French ambassador to Berlin had warned his government that violating that act would lead Germany to demand a Moroccan port in compensation, and the crisis grew out of the bargaining over Germany's compensation.

German Foreign Minister Alfred von Kiderlen-Wächter exacerbated tensions when he tried to demonstrate Germany's resolve by order-

---

[5] Much work in international relations has been done on the effects of misperception (e.g., Jervis 1977; Levy 1983; Stein 1982), and the concepts of misperception and asymmetric information are related. Both approaches posit actors that may have different beliefs about a situation. But there is also an important and complementary difference in emphasis. The former usually focuses on psychological processes and cognitive limitations, which may lead to a distorted view of a situation. The latter, by contrast, focuses on the uncertainty that arises simply because actors know different things about a situation and not because they process information differently.

[6] Quoted in R. A. C. Parker (1993, 135).

ing the gunboat *Panther* to Agadir. But what drove the crisis forward was "Kiderlen's failure to spell out his objectives to the other Powers" and their lack of information about those objectives (Stevenson 1996, 183–92). The problem was that if

> (as the German evidence suggests) he [Kiderlen] wished to abandon Morocco and get the best possible Central African compensation, all three capitals could perhaps be satisfied. If he wanted a political presence in the sultanate he might be able to drive London and Paris apart. But if he intended to inflict on France a humiliation that would jeopardize its Great-Power status, the entente would come back into play. (Stevenson 1996, 184)

This uncertainty led Britain to interpret Kiderlen's disproportionately large demand for all of the French Congo as an attempt to humiliate France and ultimately as a threat to the entente between Britain and France. As a result, British Foreign Secretary Grey began to take a firmer line with Germany; Lloyd George, with Grey's approval, publicly warned in his Mansion House speech that Britain's interests had to be taken into account; and a war scare between Britain and Germany followed.

Asymmetric information about capabilities also pervades international politics. When Russia declared war on Turkey in April 1887, both Britain and Russia were confident of a Russian victory. "In June it looked as though the Russians would conquer all of Turkey-in-Europe within a month; then they ran against the *hitherto unknown* fortress of Plevna, barring the road further south, and failed to take it until 11 December" (A. Taylor 1963, 245, emphasis added). By the time Russia reached Constantinople in January, its army was exhausted and the Ottoman Empire had been given "another forty years of life" (A. Taylor 1963, 245). Two decades later the Russo-Japanese war resulted in part from Russia's underestimation of Japan's military strength and a general unwillingness to make concessions that arose from it (Fearon 1995b, 398–400; Lebow 1981, 244–46; Nish 1985, 240–41; Richardson 1994, 292; White 1964, 95–146). "A widespread view in Port Arthur was that the Japanese army would not dare to attack because of its poor calibre" (Nish 1985, 241).

Britain's decision to fight on alone in the summer of 1940 also seems to have been based at least in part on asymmetric information about Germany's capabilities. British leaders mistakenly "believed that the German war machine was approaching maximum efficiency" and was therefore vulnerable to economic pressure and strategic bombing

(Reynolds 1985, 160).[7] More generally, asymmetric information under-lies Geoffrey Blainey's discussion of the causes of war. He argues that uncertainty about the distribution of power is a major cause of war: "Wars usually result when the fighting states *disagree* about their relative strength" (1973, 122) and are overly optimistic about their prospects for success.[8]

Informational asymmetries create strategic problems when two condi-tions hold. The first is that the missing information must matter. That is, at least one actor would alter its behavior if it knew what another actor knows. Uncertainty does not matter if resolving that uncertainty would not affect the actors' actions. Second, when one actor knows something another does not, the former must have some incentive to misrepresent or, more bluntly, lie about what it knows (Fearon 1995b, 395–401). Oth-erwise, each actor could simply ask the other actors to disclose what they know.

A simple bargaining model, which will be studied at length in chap-ter 3, illustrates these two conditions. Suppose that a satisfied state and a dissatisfied state are bargaining about revising the territorial status quo. The situation is depicted in figure 1.2. The line between the satisfied and dissatisfied states' capitals represents the territory to be divided. The sat-isfied state currently controls the territory to the right of the status quo q, and the dissatisfied state controls the territory to the left of q.

Assume further that the satisfied state knows that the other state is dissatisfied with the present territorial division and will go to war to change it unless a compromise is found. But, the satisfied state is unsure as to how much it has to concede to the other state to satisfy its minimal demands and thereby avert a war. To keep the example simple, assume that there are two possibilities: the dissatisfied state's demands are either moderate or extensive. If the dissatisfied state's demands are moderate, then its demands would be satisfied if it controlled the territory to the left of m. That is, while this state prefers to control more territory than less, it is unwilling to use force to expand its border beyond m. If, by contrast, the dissatisfied state's demands are extensive, then it has to control the territory to the left of e before it becomes unwilling to use force to acquire more territory. Finally, suppose that the satisfied state

---

[7] For other discussions of British intelligence, see Hinsley et al. (1979–90) and Wark (1985).

[8] Morrow (1989) and Bueno de Mesquita, Morrow, and Zorick (1997) analyze this prob-lem formally.

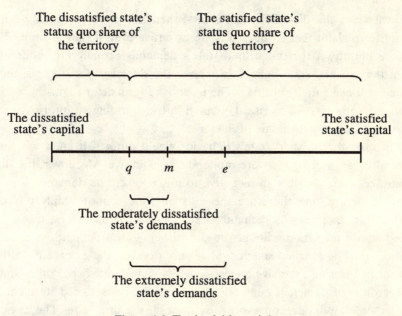

Figure 1.2 Territorial bargaining

is willing to withdraw to *m* or *e* to avoid war but prefers holding the line at *m* if that would be enough to appease the other state.

In this situation, the presence of asymmetric information matters. If the satisfied state knew what the dissatisfied state knows, i.e., whether the dissatisfied state's demands are moderate or extensive, then this knowledge would affect the satisfied state's behavior. If, for example, the satisfied state knew that its adversary's demands were moderate, then the satisfied state would agree to withdraw to *m* but not to *e*. Moving back to *m* would be enough to meet the dissatisfied state's minimal demands and eliminate the risk of war. If, by contrast, the satisfied state knew that the dissatisfied state's demands were extensive, the satisfied state would withdraw to *e* to remove the danger of war.

The fact that the satisfied state would change its behavior if it knew what the dissatisfied state knows does not in and of itself create a strategic problem. If the dissatisfied state has no incentive to misrepresent the scope of its demands, then the satisfied state could simply ask its adversary whether its demands were moderate or extensive. If the answer was moderate, then the satisfied state would pull back to *m*; if the dissatisfied state declared that its demands were extensive, the satisfied state would retreat to *e*. If, however, the satisfied state is going to react in this way to whatever the dissatisfied state says, then this gives the latter an incentive to claim that its demands are extensive even if they are not. Put more bluntly, if the dissatisfied state's demands actually are moderate but the satisfied state believes whatever the dissatisfied state says, then the latter can gain by bluffing. The incentive for an actor to misrepresent what it knows is also a critical element in transforming an informational asymmetry into a strategic problem.

In sum, the satisfied state's behavior would differ if it knew whether its adversary's demands were moderate or extensive. Moreover, the dissatisfied state also has an incentive to misrepresent its demands if they are moderate, and therefore the satisfied state cannot simply rely on what the other says its demands are. In these circumstances, the satisfied state's uncertainty about the dissatisfied state's demands creates a trade-off. The satisfied state could be sure of obtaining a peaceful settlement by offering extensive concessions that would satisfy the other state regardless of its actual demands. Alternatively, the satisfied state could offer only moderate concessions by drawing the line at m. The advantage of this is that if the dissatisfied state's demands really are moderate, it would accept this new territorial division and the satisfied state would not have to give up as much. The obvious disadvantage to making moderate concessions is that if the dissatisfied state's demands actually are extensive, then standing firm at m means war. The satisfied state, therefore, faces a trade-off. It can increase the chances of a settlement by offering more, but, because it has offered more, the agreement will be less attractive. This kind of trade-off is typical of situations in which there is asymmetric information and will play a crucial part in the analysis in the following chapters.

Along with commitment issues and informational asymmetries, the *technology of coercion* helps define the strategic arena in which states interact and the problems they face there. The technology of coercion is, roughly speaking, the analogue of a production function in microeconomics. A production function describes the technological relation between inputs and outputs; it specifies, for example, how much more labor it takes to produce one more unit of output. *The technology of coercion describes the relation between what an actor does and how those actions exert coercive pressure.* The technology of coercion thus defines at least implicitly what it means to be powerful in a particular situation. The greater an actor's coercive capabilities, the more powerful it is.

Changes in this technology can have important effects on the outcome of state interactions. Two examples illustrate the point.[9] First, the
balance between offense and defense has long been thought to have a
significant effect on states' interaction. The offense has the advantage
when "it is easier to destroy the other's army and take its territory than
it is to defend one's own. When the defense has the advantage, it is easier to protect and to hold than it is to move forward, destroy, and take"
(Jervis 1978, 187). Jervis (1978), Quester (1977), Van Evera (1998), and
others argue that offensive advantages make war more likely and the
international system less peaceful. Christensen and Snyder (1990) also
suggest that the offense-defense balance affects the alliance behavior of
states. When states believe that the offense has the advantage, as in the
summer of 1914, alliances are tighter and states are more likely to be
dragged into a war by an adventurous ally. By contrast, alliances are
looser and the members of an alliance work harder to ensure that the
other members of the alliance bear most of the cost of resisting an opposing alliance when the defense is perceived to have the advantage, as
in the 1930s.

The second example of the effects of a change in technology is the
nuclear revolution. The advent of secure, second-strike nuclear forces
created a condition of mutually assured destruction (MAD), in which
both the United States and the Soviet Union could launch a massive,
society-destroying second strike after absorbing a first strike from the
other. This technological development made it impossible for a state to
defend itself and in so doing changed the way that states exert coercive pressure on each other. Before the nuclear revolution, the use or
threatened use of force during a confrontation was a contest of military strength in which each state tried to defend itself while destroying
the other's military capabilities. By rendering defense impossible, the nuclear revolution transformed the way that coercive pressure is brought
to bear. Because each state remains vulnerable to a society-destroying
attack from the other regardless of the verdict on the battlefield, the
means through which coercive pressure can be applied changes from a
contest of military strength into a contest of resolve (Schelling 1966).
Each state now tries to influence the other during a crisis by trying to
hold on longer in the face of a growing risk that events will go out of

---

[9] McNeill (1982) offers a broad historical survey of some of the effects of military
technology.

control.[10] One consequence of this change in the technology of coercion, it is argued, is that it makes major war much less likely (Jervis 1984; Waltz 1990).

The two previous examples, like most of this book, focus on the use or threatened use of military force to exert coercive pressure and on the effects that changes in that technology have on these efforts. Nevertheless, the broader term "technology of coercion" is used instead of the perhaps more direct, but also more limited, term "military technology." The former generalizes the latter by describing how actors can exert coercive pressure on other actors in settings where the use of military power is not a significant concern. This broader notion, along with commitment issues and informational asymmetries, may be useful in characterizing political situations in international relations and politics more generally where coercion and the exercise of power are very much at issue but in which the use of military force is not.

Three Responses to Threat

Once we begin to think about international politics in terms of commitment issues, informational problems, and the technology of coercion, what patterns should we expect to see? The following chapters address this question by examining three ways that states can respond to threats in the context of the simple stylization of the international system described above. Chapter 2 focuses on internal balancing and the guns-versus-butter problem underlying it. When a state tries to further its ends and maintain its security by relying on its own limited resources, what determines how much of these resources it devotes to the means of military power? How do the states' decisions interact, and when do these interactions sustain a peaceful outcome and when do they break down in war?

A commitment issue lies at the center of the guns-versus-butter problem. Because states are unable to commit themselves to refraining from using force against each other, they face a fundamental trade-off between the resources they devote to satisfying their immediate ends and those they allocate to the means of military power. The more a state allocates to the military, the less it can devote to satisfying its immediate wants. However, allocating more to the military today makes that

---

[10] For discussions of the nuclear revolution, see Brodie (1946, 1959), Herz (1959), Schelling (1966), Jervis (1984), and Powell (1990).

state stronger tomorrow. Being stronger, in turn, makes it easier for that state to defend the resources it has and, if it wishes, to capture additional resources. Conversely, the more a state devotes to satisfying its immediate wants, the less it can allocate to the military and the weaker it will be in the future. Should another state then decide to attack, this military weakness means a higher probability of defeat and, in the event of defeat, fewer future resources to devote to its immediate ends. The specter of war, therefore, gives rise to a trade-off between the present and the future. The more resources a state devotes to satisfying its current wants, the fewer resources it can expect to have in the future.

This trade-off would disappear if the states could commit themselves to refraining from using military force against each other. If such commitments were possible, no resources would have to be spent on deterring or defending against an attack. Instead, each state could devote those resources toward satisfying its ends, and this reallocation would make each state better-off. The states' inability to deny themselves the option of using force makes all of them worse-off. This is a commitment problem.

The analysis of the guns-versus-butter trade-off highlights three issues. First, the analysis clarifies the circumstances in which internal balancing can maintain the peace and why it may break down in war. The second issue is the effect of changes in the technology of coercion on the guns-versus-butter trade-off. The analysis helps explain how changes in the offense-defense balance and in the cost of fighting affect the states' military allocations. As will be seen, shifts in favor of the offense lead to larger allocations whereas higher costs lead to smaller allocations.

The third issue that the guns-versus-butter trade-off highlights is the effect of relative-gains concerns on the prospects for international cooperation. Waltz argues that when states are considering a cooperative agreement in a system in which they are unable to commit themselves to refraining from using force against each other, then those states "are compelled to ask not 'Will both of us gain?' but 'Who will gain more?'. . . Even the prospect of large absolute gains for both parties does not illicit their cooperation so long as each fears how the other will use its increased capabilities" (1979, 105).

The claim that states must be concerned with their relative gains has led to a heated debate about the effects of these relative-gains concerns on the ability of states to realize mutual gains through international cooperation.[11] The analysis of the guns-versus-butter problem suggests that the effects of the relative-gains concerns have been vastly overstated and generally do not impede cooperation.

Chapters 3 and 4 focus on states' efforts to respond to threats through bargaining and compromise. To foreshadow the discussion, suppose that a satisfied and a dissatisfied state are bargaining about revising the territorial status quo. If the states had complete information about each other, then the satisfied state would know the other state's payoffs. In particular, the satisfied state would know how much it has to offer the other state in order to satisfy its adversary's minimal demands and thereby remove the threat of war. The satisfied state thus faces a simple, if stark, choice. It can either make the needed concessions or fight.

Asymmetric information complicates the situation. If the satisfied state is unsure of what it takes to meet the other's minimal demands, the satisfied state faces a trade-off. The more it offers, the greater the chance of appeasing the other state and the smaller the probability of war. But the more the threatened state offers, the less it will have in the event that its offer is accepted.

Chapter 3 examines how changes in the distribution of power and the technology of coercion affect this trade-off and the likelihood of war. The balance-of-power school argues that the probability of war is smallest if there is an even distribution of power among the states (Claude 1962; Mearsheimer 1990; Morgenthau 1967; Wolfers 1962; Wright 1965), whereas the preponderance-of-power school claims that the risk of war is smallest if one state has a preponderance of power (Blainey 1973; Organski 1968; Organski and Kugler 1980). The analysis in chapter 3 qualifies these claims and shows that neither a balance nor a preponderance is necessarily more peaceful.

War is least likely when the international distribution of benefits reflects the underlying distribution of power. The larger the disparity between these distributions, the more likely war. Consequently, the risk of war is low *if* there is an even distribution of power and *if* there is also an even distribution of benefits but not *if* the distribution of benefits favors a particular state. Similarly, the risk of war is low *if* one state has a preponderance of power and *if* that state also receives a preponderance of the benefits but not *if* there is an even distribution of benefits.

---

[11] This debate will be reviewed in more detail in chapter 2. For a sampling of it, see Grieco (1988a, 1993); Grieco, Powell, and Snidal (1993); Keohane (1993); Powell (1991, 1993, 1994); and Waltz (1979).

Changes in the technology of coercion often have simple overall effects on the likelihood of war, but the simplicity of the overall effect masks a complicated interaction of opposing factors. Consider, for example, the consequences of a shift in the technology of coercion, which makes fighting more costly. Chapter 3 shows that this shift affects the bargaining between the satisfied and dissatisfied states in three ways. First, the dissatisfied state is less likely to use force because fighting is more costly, and this tends to make war less likely. But, the satisfied state, knowing that its adversary is less likely to use force, tends to offer smaller concessions, and this factor makes war more likely. However, fighting is also more costly for the satisfied state and this tends to produce larger concessions, which makes war less likely. As we will see, the net effect of an increase in the cost of fighting is a lower risk of war. But when we look closely at the mechanism through which states exert coercive pressure on each other, it is not at all obvious that things should work out in this simple way.

A shift in the offense-defense balance also influences the bargaining in opposing ways. Larger offensive advantages incline the satisfied state to make larger concessions. But these advantages also make the dissatisfied state less likely to accept any specific offer because the larger offensive advantages raise the expected payoff to attacking. The overall effect of larger offensive advantages is to make war more likely.

Thucydides attributed the Peloponnesian War to the rise in Athenian power, and chapter 4 generalizes the model developed in chapter 3 to examine how two states cope with a shift in the distribution of power between them. Suppose that the distributions of power and benefits initially favor one of the states. As long as the distribution of power remains constant, then the distribution of benefits will continue to reflect the underlying distribution of power and there will be peace. But what happens if the distribution of power begins to shift in favor of the other, weaker state? As the weaker state becomes stronger, it becomes increasingly dissatisfied with the existing distribution of benefits and begins to demand that the status quo be revised in its favor.

These demands confront the declining state with a clear, albeit unpleasant, choice if there is complete information. If the declining state knows the rising state's payoffs, the declining state also knows how much it has to concede in order to meet the rising state's minimal demands. The stark choice facing the declining state is either to make those concessions or fight. Asymmetric information makes the choice less stark but more complicated by creating a familiar trade-off. The more the declining state offers, the greater the chances of at least temporarily satisfying the rising state's demands, but the less satisfying the agreement will be.

As will be seen, the declining state deals with this trade-off by making a series of concessions. It concedes little to the rising state in the early phase when the rising state is still relatively weak and unlikely to be willing to use force. But as the rising state becomes stronger, the declining state grants more concessions. Throughout the shift in power, the declining state decides how much to concede by balancing the marginal gain of reducing the probability of war by offering slightly more with the marginal cost of having granted slightly more and therefore being a little less satisfied with any settlement. In general, the declining state's concessions are enough to satisfy the rising state if that state is relatively irresolute and unwilling to use force. In this case, the status quo is revised in favor of the rising state and the shift in power passes without war. However, the declining state will not concede enough to appease the rising state if that state is resolute and more willing to use force. In these circumstances, the shift in the distribution of power ends in war. And, the more willing the rising state is to use force, the sooner war comes.

These results clarify some existing claims about the effects of a shift in the distribution of power and contradict others. Drawing on Thucydides' ideas about the causes of the Peloponnesian War, Gilpin (1981) develops a theory of hegemonic war. (A hegemonic war is a war that determines which state will dominate the international system and thereby be able to define the international order and the distribution of benefits associated with that order.) He argues that different rates of economic growth produce shifts in the distribution of power among states. As a once weak state becomes stronger, it becomes increasingly dissatisfied with the existing distribution of benefits. Eventually the disparity between the distributions of benefits and power becomes so great that the rising state resorts to force to effect a more favorable distribution.

This argument explains one reason why the distribution of power may change, but it is less clear about why the declining state would wait for the rising state to become so dissatisfied that it would go to war. If the declining state would rather satisfy the rising state's demands than fight, why does it not try to do so by making concessions to the rising state in order to avert war? If, alternatively, the declining state would rather fight than satisfy the rising state's demands, why does it wait for the rising state to become stronger? Why does the declining state not attack the rising state while the latter is still relatively weak?

Viewing the shift in the distribution of power in terms of asymmetric information and the trade-off it creates provides an answer. Unsure of the rising state's willingness to use force and of how much it would take to satisfy its demands, the declining state does try to alleviate some of the mounting pressure by making a series of concessions. But the declining state is also willing to accept some risk of war and so does not offer enough to be certain of satisfying the rising state. Whether or not the shift in power ends in war depends on how willing the rising state actually is to use force.

We can see this pattern in the series of concessions Britain made to the United States during the nineteenth century as the distribution of power shifted in favor of the latter. In disputes over Maine, Texas, Oregon, Nicaragua, Venezuela, and other non-territorial issues, Britain came to accept the westward expansion of the United States and acquiesced in the rise of American power. When at century's end the United States wanted to build, fortify, and control a canal across the isthmus of Panama—all of which directly contravened the Clayton-Bulwer Treaty of 1850—Britain "granted every significant demand of the United States" (Allen 1955, 603). Although the British admiralty thought that construction of a canal, let alone the fortification and American control of it, was detrimental to British interests, Britain acceded to all of these things in the Hay-Pauncefote Treaty of 1901, which superceded the Clayton-Bulwer Treaty and "amounted to a major concession to the growth of American power" (Bourne 1967, 348; also see Friedberg 1988, 169–74).

Viewing the strategic problem confronting a declining state during a shift in the distribution of power from the perspective of asymmetric information also contradicts some of the claims of the power-transition school. That school argues that the most dangerous time during a shift in the distribution of power occurs at a transition, i.e., when the rising and declining states are roughly equal in power (Organski 1968; Organski and Kugler 1980). However, what the declining state concedes to the rising state at any point during a shift is determined by weighing the marginal gain of a lower probability of war against the marginal cost of a slightly less favorable agreement. As will be shown, whether the distribution of power is even or not has little bearing on these marginal calculations. Shifts in the distribution of power may be dangerous, but there is nothing especially dangerous about the point at which the rising and declining states are equally powerful.

A third way that a state can deal with threats in the shadow of power is by aligning with others, and chapter 5 examines this response. Do threatened states tend to balance by aligning with other threatened states or bandwagon by aligning with the source of the threat? Walt (1987) and Waltz (1979) believe that states generally balance, whereas Schroeder (1994a, 1994b) concludes from his study of European politics that states bandwagon or wait while others fight more often than they balance.

Alignment decisions are extremely complex. Consider the simplest situation in which there are three states, S_1, S_2, and S_3, and S_1 is threatening to attack S_2. At a minimum, S_3 has three options. It can bandwagon by joining the threatening state S_1, balance by aligning with S_2 against the would-be attacker, or wait by not joining either S_1 or S_2.

Each of these alternatives has advantages and disadvantages. Waiting, at least initially, avoids the immediate cost of fighting, but it also entails a risk that the confrontation between S_1 and S_2 will result in an unfavorable shift in the distribution of power against S_3. This latter factor encourages S_3 to enter the fray. Once S_3 has decided to enter the conflict, it can maximize its chances of being on the winning side by joining the stronger of the two potential coalition partners. This consideration makes S_3 more likely to join the stronger state. But there is an opposing factor. If S_3 aligns with the stronger state and that coalition prevails, then S_3 will be in a weaker and more vulnerable position with respect to its coalition partner than it would have been had it aligned with the weaker state. How these competing pressures play themselves out and which, if any, generally dominates the others is unclear.

The analysis in chapter 5 suggests two broad conclusions. The first is a note of caution. The model used to study these issues is intended to be as simple as possible. Even so, the model shows that a large number of important assumptions must be made about the technology of coercion and, in particular, about the ways that alliances and war affect the distribution of power. Unfortunately, little empirical or theoretical evidence exists to guide us in making these assumptions. The results of the analysis are therefore tentative and must be interpreted carefully. Of course, this caution also applies to other investigations of balancing and bandwagoning. These assumptions must be made in any analysis whether formal or not. Formalization only makes them explicit. Second, the analysis does not support the claim that states generally balance. Bandwagoning and waiting are more common. But which of these three behaviors occurs depends in a complicated way on the distributions of power and benefits, the technology of coercion, and the states' relative resolve.

The Role of Formal Models

Chapters 2 through 5 use a series of game-theoretic models to examine the three ways that states can respond to threats, but these chapters do not analyze the games formally. Rather, the models help fix ideas and make the analysis of these responses more precise than would otherwise be possible. The discussion in these chapters emphasizes the insights and intuitions that emerge from the models about the strategic problems states face, the trade-offs these problems create, and the ways that states resolve these trade-offs. This discussion does not presume anything more than a passing familiarity with some basic game-theoretic concepts like a game tree, a strategy, and an equilibrium, which are reviewed in appendix 1.[12] A technical analysis of the games is provided in appendixes at the end of the book, but the following chapters are self-contained and can be read without referring to those appendixes.

Although this study does not emphasize the technical details of models, it does pursue an approach based on a series of models, and this raises a general question about the role and usefulness of models in studying the complex problems that characterize international politics. Suppose we take the goal of international relations theory to be that of explaining and, to the extent that it is possible, making predictions about the empirical world. Given this goal, what is to be gained from looking at very simple models—models that are much too simple to capture the historic richness and detail of the actual decisions that leaders and others make? How do models, especially formal mathematical models, help explain? What are some of the relative advantages of a modeling-based approach over other kinds of approaches?

This section addresses these questions by first describing what the *modeling enterprise* is and how it works. This enterprise is not necessarily based on formal, mathematical models, and, indeed, most of the efforts to analyze the stylized model of the international system described above have not relied on formal models. Nevertheless, the models developed in this volume are mathematical, and this section's second task is to discuss some of the general advantages and disadvantages of formalization. There are, however, different kinds of mathematical models, and each brings different strengths and weaknesses. The third task is to describe what game theory brings. Finally, this section concludes by

---

[12] Morrow (1994b) provides a comprehensive introduction to game theory.

examining some of the factors that need to be kept in mind when evaluating the game-theoretic models developed in the following chapters.

The Modeling Enterprise

The modeling enterprise is a process. It is a way of trying to use a series
of simple models to understand complicated things. At its best, the enterprise consists of an iterative procedure in which research moves back
and forth or iterates between a modeling realm and a more empirical
realm in what Roger Myerson (1992) calls a "modeling dialogue." Understanding grows with each round of iteration even if that understanding is simply a clearer sense of what we really do not understand very
well. As Robert Jervis puts it, "Good theories do not spring full-blown
from the minds of a few scholars. Rather, they develop as people test
them and examine their internal dynamics and causal linkages" (1979,
303).

Although models may be very simple and highly stylized, they are
generally inspired by an empirical problem. *Models are a constrained, best
effort to capture what the modeler believes to be the essence of a complex
empirical phenomenon or at least an important aspect of it.* A good model
provides at least a partial picture of a causal mechanism. Indeed, the
modeler may believe that several causes are at work but nevertheless
designs a model to focus on only one facet of a problem. A good model
need only explain how *some* things are related to *some* other things and
why.[13]

Two kinds of constraints limit a model. The first is tractability. A model
is a tool and a tool must be simple enough to use. The second constraint
is the modeler's current understanding of the problem at hand. When
constructing a model, the modeler tries to build in what she believes the
essential cause or causes to be in order to see if they actually can explain
at least part of the outcome.

Once a model has been specified, deductions can be derived from it.
The specification and analysis of a model as well as the derivation of
hypotheses is work conducted in the modeling realm. The dialogue then
moves to the empirical realm where the deductions are evaluated or

---

[13] Dessler (1991) emphasizes the need to focus on causal mechanisms in international
relations theory. Elster (1989) gives a brief overview of the role of mechanisms in the
social sciences more generally, and Miller (1987) offers a more comprehensive treatment
of mechanisms and causal theories.

scrutinized empirically. Data and history help discipline the model. In principle, the model might get everything right in the sense that all of the deductions are borne out empirically. In practice, this almost never happens, especially in the social sciences. At best, the model gets some important things right and some things wrong. At worst, the model seems to get everything wrong.[14]

What does one do with an analysis that gets some important things right and others wrong? One reading of Karl Popper (1959), which Imre Lakatos (1970, 103–163) calls naïve falsificationism, might suggest that the model should be abandoned since some of the deductions derived from it have been falsified. The modeling enterprise takes a different tack. The fact that the model got some important things right is taken as a sign that the model is tapping into and capturing important aspects of the underlying causes. This directly contributes to our understanding of those causes.

The fact that the model got some things wrong also contributes to our understanding, albeit indirectly. A model is a distillation of the modeler's best current understanding of the causal factors underlying the phenomena being modeled. When that model gets important things wrong or, worse, everything wrong, it at least tells the modeler that his or her current understanding of the phenomena is inadequate. To the extent that the model also reflects the current understanding present in the existing literature, the model's deficiencies also show more generally that the current understanding expressed in the literature is also inadequate. When models get things wrong, they contribute to our understanding by helping to outline the limits of our understanding and thereby motivating us to rethink the issues and search for new ideas.

New ideas can come from the modeling realm. Models, especially in the early stage of the modeling enterprise, often contain assumptions the modeler believes to be very restrictive but that greatly simplify the analysis. In these circumstances, the modeler, of course, hopes to learn something substantively interesting from the simple model. But she also expects to be better able to deal with less restrictive models after first learning how the simpler model works. Models are tools, and sometimes it helps to master a simple tool first even if the ultimate goal is to learn

---

[14] In a trivial sense, a model is certain to get some things wrong. Models make simplifications and thus incorrectly describe the thing that is being simplified. The more important issue is whether these simplifications significantly distort the analysis of the problem at hand.

how to work with a more complicated tool. Thus, when a simple model goes astray and gets things wrong, it is natural to ask if some of these restrictive assumptions can be relaxed in light of what has been learned from the simple model.

Indeed, a modeler often expects that the simple model will go astray and will want to try to relax some of these restrictions even before moving back to the empirical realm. Lakatos describes this process well:

> Few theoretical scientists engaged in a research programme pay undue attention to "refutations." They have a long-term research policy that anticipates these refutations. This research policy, or order of research, is set out—in more or less detail—in the *positive heuristic* of the research programme . . . which lists a chain of ever more complicated *models* simulating reality. . . . (1970, 135)

The Italian economist and sociologist, Vilfredo Pareto, put the same point more concretely.

> It was a fortunate circumstance for the foundation of celestial mechanics that in Kepler's time observations of the planet Mars were not very exact. If they had been he would not have detected an ellipse in the curve traversed by that planet and so would not have discovered the laws of planetary movement. It was also fortunate that he elected to study the movements of Mars rather than those of the Moon, which is subject to much greater disturbances.
>
> What at the time was the work of chance must now be done by the method of successive approximations. Every now and then scientific theories of economics and sociology are challenged as disregarding certain particulars. That, instead, is a merit. One must first obtain a general concept of the thing one is studying, disregarding details, which for the moment are taken as perturbations; and then come to particulars afterwards, beginning with the more important and proceeding successively towards the less important. (1935, 322–23)

Treating states as rational unitary actors is an example of a restrictive assumption that may be relaxed over time. Although the stylization of the international system described above and the models developed below assume states to be rational unitary actors, this assumption does not mean that domestic politics is unimportant. Rather, this assumption reflects, first, the hope that we can learn *some* interesting things by assuming that states are rational unitary actors and, second, that studying these kinds of models will also help us relax this assumption in interesting ways in subsequent work.[15] For example, models that take states to be rational unitary actors suggest that asymmetric information is often crucial to explaining why interstate bargaining breaks down in war.[16] In light of this unitary-actor finding, Schultz (1996) and others are trying to explain the "democratic peace" by breaking down the unitary-actor assumption and explicitly modeling some aspects of democratic domestic politics.[17] The goal of this work is to understand how democratic institutions affect the likelihood of war by changing the informational asymmetries that exist between states during a crisis.

The need to start with simple, if restrictive, assumptions—to walk before we can run, as it were—explains why modelers sometimes do not find the criticism that this or that model is too simple to be very helpful. Modelers often think in terms of a series of models that evolve through a modeling dialogue. They already know that the current model is in some sense too simple and that making it more general is a good idea. The problem is to figure out *how* to do so in an interesting and fruitful, yet tractable, way.

New ideas can also come from the empirical as well as the modeling realm. In international relations, there are often only a few cases and a myriad of factors that could be at work. A detailed historical knowledge and deep sense of the cases coupled with an understanding of a model's successes and failures may suggest which factors actually are at work and should be examined more closely. Factors once thought to be irrelevant or unimportant may now take on greater significance.

Armed with these new ideas, the modeling enterprise moves back to the modeling realm where these ideas are incorporated in new or modified models. New deductions are derived, and the dialogue moves back to the empirical realm where these deductions are evaluated. Ideally these new models get more right than the previous ones. But these new models will almost surely continue to get some things wrong, and another round or iteration will begin with a search for new ideas.

---

[15] Chapter 6 discusses some of the formal work that is already being done on domestic politics.

[16] See Fearon (1995b) and chapter 3 below for a discussion of this.

[17] The "democratic peace" puzzle is used to explain the empirical observations that democratic states do not seem to fight each other even though they seem to be, on the whole, as likely to engage in war as non-democratic states. The volume of work on the problem is now quite large. For surveys and contributions to it, see Ray (1995), Rousseau et al. (1996), and Russett (1993). For other efforts to break the unitary-actor assumption, see Downs and Rocke (1994, 1995) and Bueno de Mesquita et al. (1997, 1998).

The iteration that defines the modeling enterprise occurs whether the models are mathematical constructs or employ ordinary language. Indeed, much of the existing work in international relations theory moves back and forth between non-mathematical but nevertheless theoretical models and arguments and the empirical realm of historical case studies and, less frequently, larger statistical studies. Christensen and Snyder's (1990) study of alliance dynamics exemplifies this iterative procedure.

In an effort to explain some variation in alliance behavior, they add the offense-defense balance to Waltz's (1979) theory. Based on this modification, they conclude that alliances will be tighter if there are large offensive advantages. Tighter alliances in turn imply that states run a higher risk of being dragged into a war by an ally because they are "chain-ganged" together. If, by contrast, the defense has the advantage, alliances will be looser and states are more inclined to "pass the buck" by letting others pay the costs of maintaining the alliance.

Moving to the empirical realm, Christensen and Snyder find that these conclusions turn out to be exactly backward in the two historical cases they consider. Alliances were tighter before the First World War and looser before the Second World War. But the defense had the advantage in the former, and the offense had the advantage in the latter. Given these findings, Christensen and Snyder move back to the theoretical realm where they modify their formulation by stipulating that it is the decision-makers' *perception* of the offense-defense balance that matters, and then they return to the empirical realm where they find that this modification does seem to fit the cases of the First and Second World Wars. This fit, however, is not terribly compelling because these cases also motivated the modification (Christensen and Snyder 1990, 145), and Morrow (1993) argues that this formulation does not account for the failure of Austria and France to ally against Prussia during the 1860s. Morrow then moves back to the theoretical realm where he draws on Altfeld's (1984) model in an effort to explain alliance behavior.

In sum, the modeling enterprise is an iterative procedure or dialogue in which research moves back and forth between a more theoretical realm and a more empirical realm. Models do not drive this process; ideas about possible explanations of empirical phenomena do. However, one can often trace this iterative procedure in the literature in which one sometimes finds a series of related models where each model focuses on a new facet of the problem by trying to relax an assumption made in a previous model.

This description is, of course, an idealization of the modeling approach. It often falls short in practice because there is too little dialogue. Sometimes work stays in one realm or the other too long. Albert Einstein once observed about the relation between Euclidean geometry and experience, "In so far as geometry is certain, it says nothing about the actual world, and in so far as it says something about our experience, it is uncertain."[18] His observation about mathematics applies equally well to any logical deduction. Work that remains in the modeling realm too long can begin to mistake logical deductions for empirically established explanations and become substantively sterile. By contrast, work that remains too long in the empirical realm can begin to mistake descriptions of specific factors and taxonomies of different kinds of factors for causal explanations.[19]

Some Advantages and Disadvantages of Formal Models

If the modeling enterprise, whether it be based on mathematical or non-mathematical models, iterates between a more theoretical realm comprised of models and abstractions and a more empirically oriented realm, what are some of the specific advantages that formal, mathematical models offer? Mathematical models give us "a clear and precise language for communicating insights and notions" (Kreps 1990, 6). They help us discipline our thinking about what we are trying to model. Formal models provide a kind of accounting mechanism that enables us to think through some issues more carefully than ordinary-language models can. Accounting schemes make a firm's financial situation more transparent to those both inside the firm and outside it. Formal models make arguments more transparent both to those making them and to those to whom the arguments are made.

This improved transparency comes from two sources. First, models must be fully specified or closed before they can be analyzed. Closing a

---

[18] Quoted in Frank (1947, 177).

[19] Of course, individuals may specialize in working primarily in one realm or the other. Mastering the skills and knowledge needed to work in either realm may require a substantial investment, and this tends to encourage specialization. If this division of labor does occur, then those specializing in more modeling-oriented work and those specializing in more empirically oriented work need to be able to communicate with each other in order to engage in a dialogue. Research as a whole needs to move back and forth, whether it be through an internal dialogue within an individual or an external dialogue among different individuals.

model often reveals that important but previously unappreciated assumptions have to be made in order to support an argument. Models help make critical assumptions more explicit. Second, the links from assumptions to conclusions are clearer in formal models. Indeed, the derivation of conclusions frequently takes the form of mathematical proofs or demonstrations. These clearer linkages in turn make it easier to trace the effects of changing one or more of the assumptions.

The benefits to more transparent arguments are at least threefold. First, greater clarity provides a check on the internal logic of existing arguments. These checks are obviously important when they reveal that an argument is wrong or, as more commonly happens in international relations theory, incomplete. And, much recent formal work in international relations theory—as well as the following chapters—shows that many widely accepted "conclusions" do not follow from the assumptions said to imply them. These arguments are generally not wrong. Indeed, they reflect a deep sense of international politics, and the assumed causes are almost certainly linked to the conclusions said to follow them. But formalization shows that other important and previously unappreciated assumptions often must be added to the arguments in order to complete them.

These additional assumptions in effect narrow the range of conditions in which the original arguments should be expected to hold. In the language of statistics, these assumptions specify what to "control" for when testing the arguments. Having an idea of what to control for may in turn make it easier to find empirical regularities in case studies as well as large data sets. Indeed, it is remarkable how few robust, well-established empirical regularities we have in international relations—the absence of war among democratic states is one of the very few—and part of the reason for this lack may be that the hypotheses we have been testing have been too broad because we have not known what to control for.

Checking the internal logic of an argument is also important even if in the end the check simply confirms the argument. If this happens, especially if simple models are used to do it, the formal analysis may seem trivial or superfluous. It may appear that the model exists for the sake of having a model—reflecting a kind of "modeling mania"—and just tells us "something we already knew." The model is simply putting old wine in new bottles.

This charge misses an important point. We do not know that an existing argument satisfies the accounting standards formalization imposes until it has been modeled, and, as just noted, recent formal work has shown that many seemingly simple and straightforward arguments do not hold up very well when we try to model them. Some old wine turns out to be vinegar when we try to put it in new bottles.

The second benefit of formalization is that the more explicit statement of assumptions and the tighter deductive links between assumptions and conclusions facilitate the derivation of new and directly testable hypotheses. An excellent example of this is Fearon's work (1994). He uses an asymmetric-information formulation to derive new hypotheses about the factors that make deterrence more likely to work. He then shows that these hypotheses fit the existing data better than other prevalent arguments do. More specifically, Fearon's asymmetric-information model of a crisis leads to the hypotheses that measures of a defender's interest in protecting a protégé *which are known before any direct threat against the protégé is made*—for example, the level of trade between the defender and protégé—should make threats to this protégé less likely. But these *ex ante* indicators should be negatively related to the likelihood that a challenger will back down *after it has already made a threat*. These are certainly new, non-obvious hypotheses, and they fit Huth and Russett's (1988) data better than the existing alternatives do.

A third, broader potential benefit of formalization is that analyzing a model and then asking what accounts for the outcome sometimes leads to new insights and new ways of thinking about a large set of issues. For example, the models in the following chapters do make some specific predictions. But the models are very spare and the mechanisms they highlight are too general to explain particular outcomes in any degree of detail. Too much has been left out. But these template-models, along with the broader notions of commitment problems, asymmetric information, and the technology of coercion, provide insights and a framework for approaching a wide range of issues. These insights and the framework supporting them are most powerful and most useful when they go beyond the formal models that inspired them and help us think through complicated real-world problems which may at present be too hard to model very well.

In sum, mathematical modeling provides a language that makes it possible to define our terms more precisely and less ambiguously and

to show that certain precise assumptions lead to other precise conclusions. It also allows us to stretch our analyses and to unify them; once we have worked our way through the logic that assumptions A imply conclusions X, we may see how assumptions A′ lead to conclusions X′ by the "same basic argument." It allows us to appreciate how critical are certain (often implicit) assumptions: If A leads to X, but a slight change in A to A' leads to not X, then we can appreciate that X or not X depends on the seemingly slight differences between A and A'; hence X is not a very robust conclusion. Taking logical deductions back to the real world, where the satisfaction of assumptions A or A' is a matter of some controversy, our developed intuition concerning what assumptions lead to which conclusions, together with a sense of how closely the real world conforms to A or A', gives us the courage to assert that X will or will not pertain with very high probability. (Kreps 1997, 63–4)

This form of reasoning is used throughout the following chapters to examine several important and very influential arguments in international relations theory.

The advantages of formalization come at a price. Requiring arguments to satisfy a different set of accounting standards may make it impossible, at least in the short run, to study some important ideas and insights because no one can figure out how to investigate them with arguments that meet the new standards. Indeed, because what we "know" is partly a function of the standards by which we evaluate arguments, imposing a different set of standards may mean that at least at the outset we "know" less that we thought we did. "Model-building, especially in its early stages, involves the evolution of ignorance as well as knowledge; and someone with powerful intuition, with a deep sense of the complexities of reality, may well feel that from his point of view more is lost than is gained" (Krugman 1995, 79). Whether more is lost than gained, whether truly important insights can be distinguished from those that only seem impressive, and whether the former can ultimately be incorporated in the modeling enterprise is a judgment that can be made only over the long run after much work has been done.[20]

What is clear, however, is that many widely accepted arguments in international relations theory appear to be incomplete and in need of qualification when they are subjected to the accounting standards and greater transparency of a model. Many "conclusions" do not follow from the stated assumptions, and completing the argument sometimes reverses the conclusions or at least qualifies them by narrowing the range of

---

[20] For an excellent example of this evolution of ignorance and the costs and benefits of mathematical models, see Krugman's (1995) discussion of Albert Hirschman's and Gunar Myrdal's rejection of efforts to formalize their ideas and what Krugman calls the "fall and rise of development economics."

circumstances in which they hold. Chapter 2, for example, shows that an anarchic environment does not imply a concern for relative gains. Chapter 3 indicates that despite the claims of the balance-of-power and preponderance-of-power schools, neither an even distribution of power nor a preponderance of power is necessarily the most stable distribution. Chapter 4 demonstrates that contrary to the arguments of the power-transition school, power transitions are not the most dangerous phase during a shift in the distribution of power. And, chapter 5 suggests that anarchy does not imply that states generally balance.[21]

Although each of these arguments seems convincing and has been widely accepted, each turns out to be incomplete for one of two basic reasons. In some cases, the argument focuses on one or a few intuitively plausible factors that point in the direction of the purported conclusion. Because these factors do point in the direction of the conclusion, the argument sounds persuasive. But usually there are other equally intuitive factors that point in the opposite direction and would render the argument much less compelling *if they were taken into account*. However, these opposing factors often remain hidden in ordinary-language arguments because the accounting standards by which this kind of argument is judged frequently do not force opposing factors to the fore. The second related reason that these arguments turn out to be incomplete is that even if the arguments at least initially recognize a fundamental trade-off, they often fail to carry it through the entire analysis.

Formalization helps overcome these problems. Satisfying the accounting standards inherent in specifying a formal model often exposes previously opposing factors and unappreciated trade-offs. (This commonly happens, to the consternation of the modeler who now must contend with a more complicated formulation than was anticipated.) The greater precision of a formal model and the deductive structure underlying it

---

[21] Of course showing that a conclusion does not follow from a particular set of assumptions does not imply that the conclusion is wrong as a statement of empirical fact. States may be more likely to balance than bandwagon, or an even distribution of power may be more peaceful than a preponderance of power regardless of what a particular model says. If so, then, to the extent that the model also reflects the literature's current understanding of these issues, the model's failure also suggests that the understanding reflected in the literature is incomplete. This, indeed, is one of the ways that we learn from the modeling enterprise even when a model gets important things wrong. (As already noted, unfortunately it has been very difficult to establish many robust empirical regularities in international relations. As elaborated below, the empirical support for the claims that states generally balance or that a particular distribution of power is more peaceful is mixed at best.)

also make it easier to trace the implications of this trade-off through the entire analysis and, sometimes, to weigh the relative strength of the competing factors and to predict how these trade-offs are resolved empirically.

Game-Theoretic Models

Game theory is a particular kind of mathematical modeling used for studying situations in which a group of actors are strategically interdependent in the sense that each actor's optimal course of action depends on what the other actors will do.[22] These situations are difficult to analyze because deciding what option is best depends on a complex chain of beliefs about beliefs about beliefs about beliefs, and so on. To illustrate these complexities, suppose two actors, A and B, are in a strategic setting in which each actor's optimal action depends on what the other does. In such circumstances, A decides what to do on the basis of what it believes B will do. But what B does depends on what it believes A will do. A's decision, therefore, is really based on its belief about what B believes A will do. But then what B does is really based on its belief about A's belief about B's belief about what A will do, and so on. These chains of beliefs about beliefs make strategic interdependence complicated.

Game-theoretic models help us discipline our thinking about strategic interaction in at least two important ways. The first results from defining a game. Specifying a game tree requires us to describe who the actors are, the order in which they make decisions, what alternatives each actor has to choose from when deciding what to do, and, finally, what each actor knows about what others have done when deciding what to do.[23] These requirements make the assumptions being made about the actors' strategic environment more transparent.

Second, games are generally analyzed in terms of their perfect equilibria. Solving a game for its perfect equilibria disciplines our predictions about how the game will be played, just as defining a game disciplines our thinking about the strategic setting. Equilibrium analysis

---

[22] Kreps (1990) provides an accessible overview of what game-theoretic work in economics has achieved, and much of what he says applies to political science as well.

[23] See appendix 1 for a brief discussion of game trees and Morrow (1994b, 58–65) for a more extensive treatment.

forces us to look at the situation being modeled from the perspective of each and every actor and to ensure that the prediction makes sense from all of these perspectives.

A perfect equilibrium is a set of strategies—one for each actor—that satisfy two conditions, and meeting these two requirements is what effectively forces us to look at the situation from each actor's position. The first condition is that the set of strategies must be self-reinforcing. That is, no actor can benefit by deviating from its strategy given that that actor believes that all of the other actors are playing according to their strategies. If this condition did not hold, then at least one actor would want to do something other than what he was predicted to do and the prediction as a whole would not make sense. Strategies that satisfy this condition are called *Nash equilibria.*

The second condition is what makes an equilibrium "perfect." This requirement is important because self-reinforcing strategies beg a prior question. A set of strategies is self-reinforcing if no actor can increase its payoff by altering its strategy *given* that the other actors follow their strategies. But is it reasonable in the first place for an actor to believe that the other actors will play according to the posited strategies? One situation in which it is unreasonable is if the threats and promises implicit in another actor's strategy are inherently incredible. Suppose, for example, that the strategy an actor is presumed to follow relies on a threat which would not be in that actor's own self-interest to carry out if the time came to do so. If other actors know this, then it no longer makes sense for them to assume that the first actor will follow its posited strategy and carry out its threat.

The doctrine of massive retaliation espoused by the Eisenhower administration during the 1950s is a classic example of a set of strategies that are self-reinforcing if believed but are also inherently incredible. In its simplest form, the doctrine said that the United States would launch a massive nuclear attack against the Soviet Union if the Soviet Union precipitated a second Korean War or threatened any other American interest whether that interest be a vital or peripheral American concern. *If* the Soviet Union believed this threat, then it would not want to challenge the United States. And, as long as this threat deterred the Soviets, it would not have to be carried out and, therefore, making it would have been in the United States' interest. Accordingly, the American strategy of threatening massive retaliation and the Soviet strategy of not challenging the status quo are self-reinforcing. Neither state has any reason to change its strategy *if that state believes the*

other will follow its strategy. However, if following through on this strategy would cost the United States more than was at issue in a crisis—as
certainly became the case as the United States became increasingly vulnerable to a Soviet nuclear retaliation—then the Soviet Union would
have a good reason to doubt that the United States actually would
carry out the threat and the doctrine of massive retaliation would be
incredible.[24]

Insisting that a set of self-reinforcing strategies also be perfect helps
resolve this issue formally. Perfection requires that following through
on the threats and promises implicit in each actor's strategy be in that
actor's self-interest. Thus, no actor has any reason to doubt that any
other actor will not play according to its posited strategy.

Assessing Models

Three considerations need to be kept in mind when evaluating game-
theoretic models and, especially, those developed below. The first relates
to the art of modeling. The accounting mechanism embodied in game
theory is very limited and can easily be overwhelmed by trying to incorporate too many factors in a single formalization. Adding more and
more elements to a model may bring some advantages. It may appear
to make that model more general and better able to capture the complexities of an empirical situation. These benefits, however, must often
be weighed against some significant costs. Incorporating many factors in
a game can readily render the model utterly intractable. Including too
much can make a model too complicated to analyze. Even if the model
can be analyzed formally, it may still be difficult or impossible to understand the role of one or two factors if too many other factors have been
included. Although less general and less representative, a simpler model
that has been well designed to focus on one or two factors may actually
prove to be more useful and insightful. The art of modeling is finding a
formulation that strikes an acceptable balance between these costs and
benefits. The need to strike this balance suggests that the most important
criticism of a model is not that it is simple or leaves much out. Rather,
the important issue is whether what a model leaves out seems likely to

---

[24] Although he did not use the language of game theory, this is the basic logic behind
Kaufmann's (1956) criticism of massive retaliation. See Powell (1990, 12–32) for a more
extensive discussion of this example.

affect the conclusions that are being derived from it, and, if so, how these factors might be incorporated in an interesting and tractable way.

This judgment should also be made comparatively. A model may be too simple in some absolute sense and one may hope to relax some restrictive assumptions as the modeling enterprise continues. But how does the present model compare to existing alternatives? Formal models in international relations theory do surprisingly well by this comparative standard. Many ordinary-language analyses in international relations theory are described in the context of complicated historical cases. But when one strips away this descriptive richness to examine the underlying causal structure, that structure often turns out to be very simple: The more threatening a state is, the harder other states will try to counter or balance against it. A preponderance of power is more peaceful because a very weak state is unlikely to prevail if it resists the demands of a much stronger state. An offensive advantage raises the payoff to attacking relative to being attacked and this makes war more likely. If waiting while others fight can rapidly lead to an adverse shift in the distribution of power, states will be less likely to wait and will appear to be chain-ganged together. Formal models look very stark in comparison to the descriptive and historical detail of many ordinary-language analyses. But this apparent contrast between "rigor and richness" is often a matter of presentational style and not causal complexity. When one looks at the underlying causal arguments, formal models in international relations theory frequently are at least as rich causally as ordinary-language analyses. Indeed, the accounting mechanism inherent in the formalization may make it possible to see more complex causal relations.

Second, formal models are often criticized because so many assumptions have to be made in order to specify the model, and the conclusions usually depend on which assumptions are made. This may make a formal analysis appear to be much less robust than an ordinary-language analysis. This criticism is, however, a bit like shooting the messenger because one does not like the message. If assumptions are important, they are important whether we recognize it or not. Formalization does not make these assumptions important; it only helps us see that they are. And, failing to take important assumptions and the conditionality inherent in them into account may lead to explanations and claims that are too broad and do not hold up when the modeling dialogue moves back to the more empirical realm to consider new case studies or statistical analyses.

The third consideration centers on the broader contribution that models and, especially, game-theoretic models can make and on a criticism of this contribution. As discussed above, formal analyses at their best do much more than show that existing arguments fail to go through because they are wrong or incomplete. The best models suggest new insights and new ways of looking at things. These insights are most useful when they go beyond the models that produced them and help explain or illuminate a wide range of substantive problems. Once seen, these ideas often seem quite intuitive. Indeed, they almost have to be intuitively clear if they are to be widely applied. But, ironically, the fact that the insights are intuitively clear—at least in retrospect—leaves them vulnerable to the charge that the models were unimportant and not really essential to generating the insights in the first place. One could have come up with these intuitive ideas without laboring through a formal analysis.

This criticism is correct in principle but seems to be wrong as a matter of fact. In some instances the accounting mechanism embodied in a formal model provides a simpler way of working with a complicated set of issues. This is precisely what models have to offer and why people use them. But any formal argument can be translated into ordinary language. One can translate an equation into English. Thus, any conclusion derived from a formal model can in principle be derived from an ordinary-language analysis. But what is possible in principle frequently does not occur in practice. As much of the recent formal work in international relations theory shows, formal models have often proved to be an important source of new insights. Perhaps these insights could have originated in ordinary-language analyses, but the fact is that they did not.

Some Templates

The following chapters are part of modeling dialogue. They use a series of game-theoretic formalizations to try to discipline and deepen our understanding of international politics by examining three ways that states can respond to threats. The models are very spare and, indeed, almost certainly too spare to explain any particular outcome in any degree of specificity. Instead, the models are intended to provide a kind of template that helps us organize our thinking about specific problems and more general issues. This template offers a framework and point of departure for the analysis. It identifies critical assumptions and explores some basic issues. But just as the present models qualify some of the existing arguments in international relations theory, future work will undoubtedly qualify some—if not all—of the conclusions derived from the present models by showing how different assumptions may lead to different conclusions. This is the way that the modeling enterprise works, and the rest of this book tries to lay some of the foundation for that future work and for the next round of the modeling dialogue.

2

Guns, Butter, and Internal Balancing in the Shadow of Power

A state's resources are limited and how it allocates them is critically important. The Republic of Sienna lost its independence when it was besieged in 1554 because it had spent so much on fortifications that it could not raise a relief army (G. Parker 1988, 12). Toward the end of their reigns, Elizabeth I of England and Phillip II of Spain were devoting as much as three-quarters of all governmental revenues to paying for wars past and present, and this limited their ability and that of their successors to pursue their ends effectively (Kennedy 1987). The political history of the second half of the seventeenth century turned on the larger resources that Louis XIV had and on the capacity this gave him to "eclipse any rivals, simply by putting larger and better-trained armies into the field" (McNeill 1982, 124). Similarly, Britain's economic preeminence during much of the nineteenth century underwrote its mastery of the seas during that period, just as its relative economic decline in the latter part of the century undermined it (Friedberg 1988; Kennedy 1976, 1987). Economic constraints were even more acute in the 1930s when Britain began to rearm against Germany (Kennedy 1983; R. Parker 1981; Peden 1979; Shay 1977).

Resource limitations also constrained the United States and the Soviet Union during the cold war. The "New Look" national security policy of 1953 reflected President Eisenhower's belief that the United States had to limit its military spending. If the United States became a "garrison state" in response to the perceived Soviet threat, he feared, "then all that we are striving to defend would be weakened and, if long subjected to this kind of control, could disappear."[1] Some also argue that the economic weakness of the Soviet Union made responding to the large increase in defense spending undertaken by the Reagan administration extremely difficult and that trying to do so hastened the collapse of Soviet power (e.g., Gates 1996, 194–96, and 538–40).

---

[1] Quoted in Gaddis (1982, 136). Huntington (1961) also discusses the "New Look."

The fact that resources are limited affects states in many ways. Indeed, the need to mobilize resources more effectively is a significant factor in the development of states themselves. "War made the state, and the state made war," as Tilly (1975, 42; 1990) puts it.[2] This chapter only looks at one of the effects of limited resources—but it is an important one.

Because its resources are limited, a state faces a trade-off when it responds to a threat by increasing its own military capabilities. The more a state devotes to the means of military power, the less it has to devote to satisfying its intrinsically valued ends. Eisenhower described this trade-off clearly when he appealed to the new Soviet leadership for a "reduction of the burden of armaments" and a new political relationship following Stalin's death in the spring of 1953: "Every gun that is made, every warship launched, every rocket fired signifies, in the final sense, a theft from those who hunger and are not fed, those who are cold and are not clothed" (1953, 182). This trade-off has been described variously as a choice between domestic ends and military means, guns and butter, consumption and defense, or wealth and power.

In the stylized version of this choice considered here, each state derives direct benefits solely from the present and future resources it directs toward satisfying its intrinsically valued ends—how much butter it consumes today and in the future. Allocations to the military bring no direct benefits. They may, however, bring important indirect benefits. The more a state devotes to the military sector relative to other states, the stronger it will be and the easier it will be for that state both to defend the resources it already controls and, if it wishes, to conquer additional resources which may subsequently be used to satisfy the victor's intrinsically valued ends. Conversely, the more a state allocates to satisfying its intrinsically valued ends today, the less it can allocate to the military and the weaker it will be tomorrow. Should another state then attack, this military weakness means a higher probability of defeat and, in the event of defeat, fewer resources to devote to intrinsically valued ends in the future.

The states' inability to commit themselves to refraining from using force against each other leads to a commitment problem. As will be seen, the states solve the guns-versus-butter trade-off by devoting some of their resources to intrinsically valued ends and some to the means of military power. These allocations leave both states worse-off than

[2] For a sampling of other discussions of the relation between war and the state, see Brewer (1990), Bean (1973), Downing (1992), Finer (1975), Hale (1985), McNeill (1982), Porter (1994), Tallett (1992), and Tilly (1975).

they would have been if they had been able to commit themselves to abstaining from using military force and, therefore, able to devote all of their resources to satisfying their desired ends.

This chapter models the guns-versus-butter problem as a game between two states that must continually decide how to allocate their limited resources between guns and butter and whether or not to attack each other. The analysis yields three main results. First, it shows how changes in the actors or in the technology of coercion affect the states' military allocations and whether or not they fight. As will be seen, changes that increase a state's payoff to attacking relative to living with the status quo induce both states to allocate more to their military sectors. If, for example, a state becomes more willing to run risks, then its expected payoff to attacking rises and this leads to greater overall military allocations. Similarly, a shift in the offense-defense balance in favor of the offense or a decline in the cost of fighting raises the payoff to attacking relative to living with the status quo and ultimately produces higher military allocations. Allocating more to the military, however, means allocating less to other things. Larger military allocations, therefore, reduce the value the states attach to maintaining the status quo. Internal balancing fails and peace breaks down if at some point the higher payoff to fighting exceeds the reduced value of the status quo.

The second result bears on the question of what to assume about state preferences. This issue has been the subject of much confusion and debate in international relations theory. Assumptions have often been conflated with conclusions, and outcomes have frequently been mistaken for intentions. For example, the notion that states try to maximize their relative power is sometimes treated as an assumption about state preferences and sometimes claimed to be a deduction about state behavior. The greater transparency inherent in the guns-versus-butter model clarifies some of these issues and shows that many "deductions" really do not follow from the assumptions claimed to imply them.

The third result shows how taking a state's resource-allocation decisions explicitly into account can qualify some existing arguments in international relations theory and undermine others. Cooperation theory, for example, generally argues that the more states care about the future, the easier it is to sustain cooperation among them (Axelrod and Keohane 1985, 232; Axelrod 1984; Keohane 1984; Lipson 1984; Oye 1985). The following analysis qualifies this claim by showing that the effects of the shadow of the future depend on the temporal order of costs and benefits. If exploiting others yields a short-run gain followed by a long-run cost—as is often the case when one state fails to live up to a trade agreement—then a longer shadow of the future facilitates cooperation. But if a state exploits others by making a short-run sacrifice to obtain a long-run advantage—for example, when a state forgoes current benefits in order to build up its military capabilities—then a longer shadow of the future makes cooperation more difficult.

Taking states' resource allocation problems into account also works against the standard relative-gains argument. Waltz (1979), Grieco (1988a), Mearsheimer (1994/95), and others argue that states must not only consider the absolute gain a potential international agreement would bring; they must also be concerned about the size of their relative gain, because "one state may use its disproportionate gain to implement a policy intended to damage or destroy the other" (Waltz 1979, 105). These relative-gains concerns in turn make international cooperation extremely difficult and unlikely. The discussion below suggests that the effects of relative-gains concerns have been vastly overstated. Indeed, they generally do not make cooperation more difficult.

The next section describes a simple model of the guns-versus-butter problem, which helps fix ideas and guides the analysis. The model, like any analysis that treats states as unitary actors, must necessarily make some assumptions about state preferences. The third section discusses these assumptions and their relation to the debate in international relations theory about state preferences. In the fourth section, the states' allocations and the conditions needed to ensure stability are derived from the model. The fifth section examines how changes in the technology of coercion and in the states' attitude toward risk and their concern about the future affect the states' military allocations and their ability to maintain peace through internal balancing. A final section investigates the extent to which relative-gains concerns impede cooperation.

Modeling the Guns-versus-Butter Problem

The goal of modeling the guns-versus-butter trade-off is to capture the essence of this problem in a formulation that is both simple enough to be analytically tractable and substantively rich enough to help us think through the strategic logic of the situation. To do this, we need to identify what the essential elements of the problem seem to be so that a model can be built around them. Subsequent analysis may show these elements to be incomplete or incorrect, but a modeling dialogue must start somewhere.

Four elements seem to be crucial to the guns-versus-butter problem. The first is a basic view of power, which underlies all of the issues studied in this book. It is that power is a means and not an end. This view is inherent in many theories of international relations, if sometimes only implicitly so. It is closely associated with Waltz's third image of international politics (1959, 34–36, 187–224) and most explicit in his *Theory of International Politics*, where he assumes "power is a means and not an end" (1979, 126). It is also present in Gilpin's (1981) theory of hegemonic war, where states use military force as the means of imposing a new international order and thereby obtaining a more favorable distribution of benefits. Wolfers (1962), too, sees power as well as influence as the means to a state's foreign policy objectives. Even Morgenthau, who at times seems to assume individuals and states value power as an end in itself, sometimes describes power "as a means to a nation's ends," whether those ends be freedom, security, or prosperity (1967, 25–26).[3] Of course, assuming states see power as a means rather than an end does not imply that states will not be centrally concerned with power and calculate accordingly. Indeed, the strategic environment may force them to do so, and whether or not it does is an issue that will be taken up below.

Second, some assumption must be made about the ends that the states do pursue. The assumption made here is that each state tries to maximize its absolute level of welfare, which depends on both its current consumption and expected future consumption. This assumption will be discussed further below and, as we will see, is compatible with other discussions of state motivations which emphasize that survival is a state's fundamental goal.

The third essential element is implicit in the notion that the guns-versus-butter trade-off arises because a state will be weak tomorrow if it consumes too much today. To capture this situation, the actors must be able to interact over time. If one state consumes a great deal and, consequently, allocates very little to its military sector in the present, the other state must have a chance to decide how to react to this future weakness.

Finally and almost trivially, the states' resources must be limited. Were resources unlimited, then there would be no trade-off and no need to engage in any sort of internal balancing of resources. Allocating

[3] See Waltz (1959, 34–39) for a discussion of Morgenthau's different assumptions about power.

more to the military would not reduce the amount that could be devoted to achieving intrinsically valued ends.

These four elements can be captured in a simple formulation. The interaction begins with one state, say S_1, having to decide how to allocate a fixed amount of resources, say r_1, between military means and desired ends, i.e., between guns and butter. S_1 also has to decide whether or not to attack the other state. If S_1 does not attack, another state, say S_2, begins the second period by deciding how to divide its resources r_2 and whether or not to attack. If S_2 does not attack, then S_1 starts the third period by deciding how to allocate r_1 and whether or not to attack. These alternating allocation decisions continue as long as neither state attacks. If at some point one of the states decides to attack, then the game ends in war.

To simplify the analysis, we will assume that war can end in only one of two possible outcomes. Either S_1 prevails by conquering S_2 and eliminating it as a military power, or S_2 prevails by eliminating S_1. Moreover, the probability that a state prevails is presumed to be a function of the relative sizes of the states' military allocations that exist when the war occurs. In particular, the more a state has allocated to its military sector relative to the other state, the more likely it is to prevail.

Figure 2.1 depicts the sequence of decisions as a game tree. At the start of the game, S_1 must decide how much of r_1 to devote to the military. S_1's allocation can range from zero to r_1, and this set of choices is represented by the arc linking the branches labeled "0" and "r_1." S_1's actual allocation in this period is denoted by $m_1(0)$, where m indicates that this is an allocation to the military, the subscript "1" indicates that it is S_1's allocation, and the number in parentheses notes the time at which the allocation is made. (For notational convenience the first period occurs at time $t = 0$.) Following this allocation decision, S_1 decides whether or not to attack S_2. If S_1 attacks, the game ends. If S_1 does not attack, the next period begins and S_2 must determine how to allocate r_2.

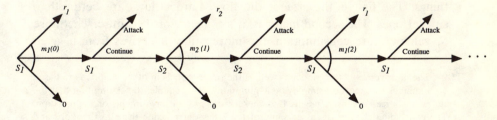

Figure 2.1 The guns-versus-butter game

After making this choice, which is represented by $m_2(1)$, S_2 must decide whether or not to attack S_1. As before, attacking ends the game. If S_2 does not attack, the next period begins with S_1's having to choose a level of military spending $m_1(2)$ and whether or not to attack S_2. The game continues in this way forever or until one of the states attacks.

Thinking of r_1 and r_2 as the capital stocks of the two states may help to make this stylization clearer and more concrete. At the beginning of the first period, S_1 must decide what fraction of its capital stock to devote to producing consumption goods and to military goods and whether or not to attack S_2. If S_1 does not attack, S_2 must decide how to allocate its productive resources and whether or not to attack S_1 in the second period. Resource allocations are sticky in the sense that once S_1 allocates its resources in the first period, they cannot be immediately reallocated in the second period. Rather, S_1's allocation in the first period also fixes its resource allocation in the second period as well. But if S_2 does not attack in the second period, S_1 is free to reallocate its resources in the third period. In this formulation, each state's capital stock remains fixed as long as neither state attacks.[4]

The game tree in figure 2.1 presents all of the possible ways that events can unfold. To begin to form expectations about the way that events actually will unfold, the states' payoffs over the possible outcomes must be specified. Two types of outcomes need to be considered. In the first, the states never fight; in the second, they do.

Suppose that the states never fight. Then each state will have allocated a certain amount of its resources to the military in each period and will have devoted its remaining resources to consumption. Looking across time, these allocation decisions produce a flow of consumption. That is, the amount S_1 consumes in the first period is the difference between its resources and what it devotes to the military in this period, i.e., $r_1 - m_1(0)$. Similarly, S_1 consumes $r_1 - m_1(1)$ in the next period, $r_1 - m_1(2)$ in the next, and so on.

The utility S_1 derives from a consumption flow depends on three things. The first is the size of the flow. Larger flows are better than smaller ones. The second factor is S_1's concern for the future. The more S_1 values future consumption, the more utility it derives from a given

---

[4] The guns-versus-butter model as well as the other models in other chapters are based on a number of important simplifying assumptions. For example, the assumption that the states' resources are fixed means that there is no growth, investment, or depreciation. The concluding chapter discusses some of the effects of relaxing these assumptions and generalizing the models.

flow. Finally, a state's willingness to run risks affects its payoff, and this factor will become relevant when S_1 has to consider the risks of war.

A simple way to represent these three factors formally is to let S_1's utility to a consumption flow be $(r_1 - m_1(0))^{\rho_1} + \delta_1(r_1 - m_1(1))^{\rho_1} + \delta_1^2(r_1 - m_1(2))^{\rho_1} + \delta_1^3(r_1 - m_1(3))^{\rho_1} + \cdots$ where the parameters δ_1 and ρ_1 formalize S_1's concern about the future and its attitude toward risk respectively. (How δ_1 and ρ_1 do this is discussed below.) The first term in this sum is the utility S_1 derives from consuming $r_1 - m_1(0)$ now, i.e., at the beginning of the game when this utility calculation is being made. The second term in the sum is the utility S_1 derives from consuming $r_1 - m_1(1)$ discounted by the fact that this consumption will occur one period in the future. The third term is S_1's utility to consuming $r_1 - m_1(2)$ two periods into the future and so on. This sum can be written more compactly as $\sum_{t=0}^{\infty} \delta_1^t(r_1 - m_1(t))^{\rho_1}$.[5]

The discount factor δ_1 can be used to capture the idea that the more a state discounts the future, the less utility it should derive from a flow of consumption that takes place over time. If, for example, S_1 places no value on future consumption—perhaps because it is extremely impatient—then this preference could be formalized by letting δ_1 equal zero. With $\delta_1 = 0$, the utility S_1 derives from consuming $r_1 - m_1(0)$ in the current period, $r_1 - m_1(1)$ in the next, and so on is just the benefit S_1 obtains from what it consumes in the current period, which is a utility of $(r_1 - m_1(0))^{\rho_1}$. If, by contrast, S_1 values future consumption half as much as it values current consumption, then the discount factor δ_1 would be $\frac{1}{2}$. And, if S_1 is perfectly patient and values future consumption just as much as it does current consumption, then this preference could be represented by setting δ_1 equal to one. In sum, the less S_1 values future consumption relative to present consumption, the smaller S_1's discount factor δ_1 and its utility $\sum_{t=0}^{\infty} \delta_1^t(r_1 - m_1(t))^{\rho_1}$ are.

To see how the parameter ρ_1 summarizes S_1's attitude toward risk, we first need to describe more formally what it means to be risk averse, risk

---

[5] It is often convenient to express sums with the summation sign "$\sum$". To read an expression like $\sum_{t=0}^{n} \delta_1^t(r_1 - m_1(t))^{\rho_1}$ look at the subscript of the summation sign, which is "$t = 0$". The variable on the left of the equals sign is the index of the summation, and the term on the right defines the starting value for this index. The superscript of the summation sign, n, defines the upper limit of the index. Accordingly, $\sum_{t=0}^{n} \delta_1^t(r_1 - m_1(t))^{\rho_1}$ means that we should add the value of $\delta_1^t(r_1 - m_1(t))^{\rho_1}$ starting with the index t equal to 0 to the value of $\delta_1^t(r_1 - m_1(t))^{\rho_1}$ when the index equals 1, and so on until the index t equals n. That is, $\sum_{t=0}^{n} \delta_1^t(r_1 - m_1(t))^{\rho_1} = \delta_1^0(r_1 - m_1(0))^{\rho_1} + \delta_1^1(r_1 - m_1(1))^{\rho_1} + \cdots + \delta_1^n(r_1 - m_1(n))^{\rho_1}$. (If the superscript of $\sum$ is infinity, i.e., ∞, as in the expression for S_1's utility above, then the index t has no upper limit and we just keep adding terms.)

neutral, and risk acceptant. Suppose that an actor can buy a lottery ticket for \$50. The lottery pays \$100 with probability $\frac{1}{2}$, i.e., if the flip of a fair coin comes up heads, and \$0 with probability $\frac{1}{2}$. Note that the price of the ticket is exactly equal to the expected monetary payoff of the lottery: $(\frac{1}{2})(\$100) + (\frac{1}{2})(\$0) = \$50$. Thus, when deciding whether or not to buy the ticket, the actor really faces a choice between having \$50 for sure if he does not buy the ticket and having a risky alternative which has an upside of \$100, a downside of \$0, and an expected monetary payoff of \$50.

If the actor thinks the price of \$50 is too high and is unwilling to pay it, then that actor is said to be *risk averse*. He would rather have \$50 for sure than an uncertain prospect with the same expected payment. If the actor is willing to pay \$50 but no more, then he is *risk neutral*. The maximum price he is willing to pay for the lottery is just equal to the expected payment from the lottery and is not affected by the uncertainty of the actual payment. In other words, the value the actor puts on the lottery depends solely on the expected monetary payoff and is unaffected by the risk inherent in the lottery. If the actor believes that the lottery is a good deal at a price of \$50 and would be willing to pay more, he is *risk acceptant*. If given a choice between \$50 for sure and a lottery with an expected monetary payoff of \$50, a risk-acceptant actor prefers the latter.

Actors, however, are not just risk averse, neutral, or acceptant. There are also gradations of risk aversion and risk acceptance. To see that one actor may be more risk averse than the other, suppose that one actor would be willing to pay \$40 for the lottery ticket but no more, whereas another actor would be willing to pay a maximum of \$45. Both actors are risk averse as neither is willing to pay the expected monetary payoff of \$50 for this gamble. The first actor is, however, more risk averse than the second. She is so put off by the risk inherent in the lottery that she is only willing to pay \$40 for a ticket with an expected monetary payment of \$50, whereas the second actor is willing to pay \$45.

Actors may also be more or less risk acceptant. Suppose another actor is willing to pay \$55 and still another actor is willing to pay \$60. Both of these actors are risk acceptant, as each prefers the risky alternative with an expected monetary payoff of \$50 to having \$50 for sure. But the second actor is more risk acceptant, as she values the upside potential of \$100 so much that she is willing to pay up to \$60 for it whereas the first actor is only willing to pay \$55.

The parameter ρ_1 can be used to capture these ideas mathematically. If S_1 is risk averse, then this attitude toward risk can be formalized by taking ρ_1 to be less than one. If S_1 is risk neutral, then this means that ρ_1 equals one. And, if S_1 is risk acceptant, then $\rho_1 > 1$.[6]

Having described S_1's payoff if the states never fight, we must also specify S_1's payoff if the states do. War is stylized very simply: It can end in only one of two ways. Either S_1 conquers and eliminates S_2 or the opposite happens.[7] Furthermore, the probability that the attacker prevails is solely a function of the offense-defense balance and the amounts that the states are allocating to the military when they go to war. Previous allocations do not affect the likelihood of prevailing.

The probability that the attacker prevails is also assumed to also satisfy three intuitive conditions. First, the larger the attacker's military allocation, the higher the probability of victory, all else held constant. Second, the larger the defender's military allocation, the lower the attacker's probability of victory. Finally, the larger the offensive advantage, the more likely the attacker is to prevail.

A simple expression can be used to capture these ideas. Let m_a and m_d denote the attacker's and the defender's allocations. Then the probability that the attacker prevails when the inventories of forces are at these levels is

$$\frac{\beta m_a}{\beta m_a + m_d}$$

where the offense has the advantage if β is greater than one, the defense has the advantage if β is less than one, and the offense and defense are in balance if β equals one.

This expression clearly satisfies the first two conditions. The larger the attacker's allocation m_a, the more likely it is to prevail. Conversely, the larger the defender's allocation m_d, the less likely the attacker is to prevail.

---

[6] In symbols, let the utility an actor receives from having an amount of money x be $u(x) = x^\rho$. Then the utility an actor attaches to having \$50 for sure is $(50)^\rho$, and the expected utility that actor obtains from a lottery that pays \$0 with probability $\frac{1}{2}$ and \$100 with probability $\frac{1}{2}$ is $\frac{1}{2}(0)^\rho + \frac{1}{2}(100)^\rho = \frac{1}{2}(100)^\rho$. If the actor is risk averse, he prefers having \$50 for sure, which implies $(50)^\rho > \frac{1}{2}(100)^\rho$ or $\rho < 1$. If he is risk neutral, then $(50)^\rho = \frac{1}{2}(100)^\rho$ and $\rho = 1$. And, if he is risk acceptant, then $(50)^\rho < \frac{1}{2}(100)^\rho$ and $\rho > 1$. See Morrow (1994b, 16–49) for a more detailed discussion of formalizing an actor's attitude toward risk.

[7] This simple stylization is used in all of the models in this volume, and chapter 6 discusses some of the limitations of this assumption.

To see that larger offensive advantages also make the attacker more likely to win, we must first describe more precisely what we mean by an offensive advantage. One way to assess the offense-defense balance is to ask "with a given inventory of forces, is it better to attack or to defend" (Jervis 1978, 188). Then, the offense has the advantage if the probability that a state prevails if it attacks is greater than the probability that it prevails if it is attacked *given the existing force levels*. Conversely, the defense has the advantage if the probability that a state prevails if it attacks is less than the probability that it prevails if it is attacked. And, the offense and defense are balanced when the probability of prevailing if a state attacks is the same as it is if it is attacked.

The expression above formalizes this notion of the offense-defense balance. If, for example, there are no offensive or defensive advantages, then $\beta = 1$ and the probability that the attacker prevails is simply the ratio of its military allocation to the total military allocation, i.e., $m_a/(m_a + m_d)$. If, more concretely, S_1's military allocation is twice as large as S_2's when they fight (i.e., $m_1 = 2m_2$) and if S_1 is the attacker, then $m_a = m_1$ and the probability that S_1 prevails is:

$$\frac{m_a}{m_a + m_d} = \frac{m_1}{m_1 + m_2}.$$

Substituting $2m_2$ for m_1 in the previous equation shows that the probability that S_1 prevails if it attacks is $\frac{2}{3}$. If, by contrast, S_1 is attacked, then $m_a = m_2$ and the probability that S_1 prevails is one minus the probability that the attacker S_2 prevails. That is, the probability that S_1 prevails if attacked is

$$1 - \frac{m_a}{m_a + m_d} = 1 - \frac{m_2}{m_2 + m_1}.$$

Substituting $2m_2$ for m_1 again shows that the probability that S_1 prevails if it is attacked is also $\frac{2}{3}$. Thus, the probability that S_1 prevails is the same regardless of whether or not it attacks when $\beta = 1$. There are, therefore, no offensive or defensive advantages in this case.

Now consider the effects of offensive or defensive advantages. Formally, these are akin to "force multipliers," which enhance the effectiveness of the attackers' military capabilities if the offense has the advantage and diminish this effectiveness if the defense has the advantage. Letting β represent this multiplier, then the attacker's effective military allocation is βm_a, which is greater than m_a if the offense has the advantage ($\beta > 1$) and less than m_a if the defense has the advantage ($\beta < 1$).

In turn, the probability that the attacker prevails is the ratio of the attacker's effective military allocation to the total effective allocation.

To illustrate the effects of offensive advantages, suppose $\beta = 1.2$. Then the probability that S_1 prevails if it attacks is $(1.2)m_1/[(1.2)m_1 + m_2]$, which equals .71 when S_1 is allocating twice as much to the military as S_2 (i.e., $m_1 = 2m_2$). By contrast, the probability that S_1 defeats S_2 if S_1 is attacked is $1 - (1.2)m_2/[(1.2)m_2 + m_1]$, which equals .62 when $m_1 = 2m_2$. Thus, the probability of prevailing is larger if S_1 attacks and the offense has the advantage when $\beta = 1.2$.

Suppose, instead, that $\beta = .8$. S_1's probability of prevailing in this case is .62 if it attacks and .71 if it is attacked. Clearly the defense has the advantage here as the probability of prevailing is larger if a state is attacked.[8]

Now that the probability of prevailing has been specified, the expected payoff to fighting can be described. S_1's payoff to attacking at time w is composed of two components: the utility derived from the flow of consumption preceding the war and that due to fighting at w. S_1 consumes $r_1 - m_1(0)$ in the first period, $r_1 - m_1(1)$ in the next, and so on through the period just preceding the war. The utility associated with this consumption stream is $\sum_{t=0}^{w-1} \delta_1^t (r_1 - m_1(t))^{\rho_1}$.

To specify S_1's payoff if it prevails when it attacks at time w, note that war, in effect, transforms the bipolar system into a unipolar system because defeat eliminates the loser as a military power. This transformation deprives military spending of any instrumental value. In the unipolar system, there is no other state to threaten the victor and nothing more for it to conquer. Consequently, the victor can devote all of its resources—including any that it has captured from the defeated state— to satisfying its own ends. Indeed, the elimination of the other state as a potential threat and the reallocation of resources it permits is the payoff to prevailing. Accordingly, S_1 will consume $r_1 - m_1(w)$ during the period in which the war is fought and then reallocate all of the resources it controls after the war to consumption. To express this in symbols, let c represent the cost of fighting measured in terms of resources destroyed. Then S_1 will have $r_1 + r_2 - c$ resources to devote to consumption in period $w + 1$ and thereafter. Thus, S_1's payoff if it prevails is $\delta_1^w (r_1 - m_1(w))^{\rho_1} + \sum_{t=w+1}^{\infty} \delta_1^t (r_1 + r_2 - c)^{\rho_1}$.

[8] The expression $\beta m_a/(\beta m_a + m_d)$ captures the three intuitive conditions described above in a very simple formulation. Appendix 2 shows that the properties of the model discussed below hold for more general formulations. See Hirshleifer (1988) for a discussion of some alternative specifications.

If S_1 loses, it will also consume $r_1 - m_1(w)$ during the period in which the war is fought. Thereafter, S_1 will control nothing and its payoff to this is assumed to be zero. Accordingly, S_1's utility to fighting and losing at time w is just $\delta_1^w(r_1 - m_1(w))^{\rho_1}$.

S_1's expected payoff to attacking at w can finally be specified. It is the payoff to prewar consumption plus the payoff to prevailing weighted by the probability of prevailing plus the payoff to losing weighted by the probability of losing. S_2's payoff is defined analogously (see appendix 2 for this specification).

It will be convenient in analyzing the game below to have an expression for S_1's payoff to attacking S_2 in the current period given that the war is fought with allocations m_1 and m_2. This payoff is the utility S_1 receives from consuming m_1 during the first period when the war is fought plus the payoff to the future consumption it enjoys if it prevails times the probability of prevailing. Letting $A_1(m_1, m_2)$ denote this payoff gives:

$$A_1(m_1, m_2) = (r_1 - m_1)^{\rho_1}$$
$$+ \frac{\beta m_1}{\beta m_1 + m_2} \left[\sum_{t=1}^{\infty} \delta_1^t (r_1 + r_2 - c)^{\rho_1} \right]. \tag{2.1}$$

The first term on the right side of the equality is S_1's utility to consuming $r_1 - m_1$ during the period in which the war is fought, and the second term is S_1's utility to consuming the fruits of victory after the war weighted by the probability that S_1 prevails when it attacks. As can be seen from the previous expression, S_1's payoff to attacking increases if the cost of fighting, c, falls or if the offensive-defense balance shifts toward the offense (i.e., if β increases).[9]

In sum, the model of the guns-versus-butter problem, although very simple, confronts the state with a trade-off between directly desired ends and the means of military power. The more a state consumes today, the weaker it will be tomorrow. This model, like all rational-choice models, has had to make some assumption about the actors' preferences. States, in particular, are assumed to be trying to maximize their expected long-run consumption. The next section relates this assumption to the continuing debate in international relations theory about state preferences.

---

[9] S_2's payoffs are analogous to S_1's and are described in appendix 2.

The Problem of Preferences

International relations theorists have spent an enormous amount of time and effort in recent years debating state preferences.[10] This debate has often treated the question of what to assume about state preferences as if it were an a priori question that could be answered largely by appealing to first principles. This chapter takes a different and more pragmatic approach. It begins with one of several plausible assumptions and then traces its consequences. After we understand these implications, we may want to make different assumptions in a future round of the modeling dialogue and see what they imply. Ultimately, we may conclude after comparing these implications that some assumptions are more useful and insightful than others. But if we are ever to be able to make these comparisons, we have to start somewhere with some assumption about state preferences and see what follows from it. This is the way the modeling enterprise proceeds.

The models in this volume assume that each state tries to maximize its current and expected future consumption. As it happens, this assumption is also compatible with many existing theories of international politics, although it may not initially seem so. Thus, the conclusions derived from the guns-versus-butter model and from the other models described in subsequent chapters can be meaningfully compared to the conclusions claimed to follow from those other theories.

To see that the assumption about state preferences made here is consistent with other theories requires a brief review of what those other theories assume. Two central but somewhat separate disputes are relevant. The first is the absolute-and-relative-gains debate. The second focuses on whether or not states try "to maximize their relative power positions over other states" (Mearsheimer 1994/95, 11).

The absolute-and-relative-gains debate has confounded two issues. The first has been the source of much confusion and wasted effort; the second is important. In *After Hegemony* (1984), Robert Keohane tries to show that neorealism's pessimistic conclusions about the likelihood of international cooperation do not follow from its core assumptions. To this end, he says that he will begin with the same core assump-

---

[10] See, for example, Brooks (1997); Gowa (1986); Greico (1988a, 1988b, 1990, 1993); Greico, Powell, and Snidal (1993); Keohane (1993); Matthews (1996); Moravcsik (1997); Powell (1993, 1994); Schweller (1996); and Snidal (1991).

tions that neorealism does and then demonstrate that international cooperation is more likely than neorealism contends.

> I propose to show, on the basis of their [i.e., realists'] own assumptions, that the characteristic pessimism of Realism does not follow. I seek to demonstrate that Realist assumptions about world politics are consistent with the formation of institutional arrangements, containing rules and principles, which promote cooperation. (67)

Joseph Grieco (1988a, 1988b) challenged this claim. Keohane, according to Grieco, had not started with neorealism's assumptions, and, therefore, his conclusions did not contradict neorealism. In particular, Grieco argued that Keohane had assumed that states were trying to maximize their absolute gains, whereas a key element of neorealism was that states were concerned about relative gains. Grieco cited Waltz (1979, 105), who emphasizes that states must be concerned about their relative gains, and claimed that neorealism

> expects a state's utility function to incorporate *two distinct terms*. It needs to include the state's individual payoff... reflecting the realist view that states are motivated by absolute gains. Yet it must also include a term integrating both the states' individual payoff... and the partner's payoff in such a way that gaps favoring the state add to its utility while, more importantly, gaps favoring the partner detract from it. (Grieco 1988a, 129)

Thus, Keohane's assumptions are actually inconsistent with neorealism, because he assumed a state's utility to be solely a function of its absolute gain and did not include the second term, which Grieco sees as essential.

The first issue in this debate is Grieco's claim that a state's concern for relative gains must be modeled in the state's utility function. If this claim is correct, then the models developed here as well as Keohane's models would be inconsistent with neorealism. While perhaps interesting in their own right, the conclusions derived from the models in this volume would not provide any kind of check on the internal logic of neorealism. Grieco's claim, however, is not correct.

There are at least two different ways to model a state's concern for relative gains. The first, which Grieco pursues, is to formalize this concern as part of the states' preferences or utility functions. In this approach, the extent to which a state is concerned about relative gains is simply assumed when the preferences are specified. The second way of modeling a state's concern for relative gains does not assume it by building it into a state's utility function. Rather, the degree to which a state is concerned about relative gains is derived from a more detailed specification of the strategic arena in which the state finds itself. This second approach explicitly tries to model the ways that a state can "use its disproportionate gain to implement a policy intended to damage or destroy the other" (Waltz 1979, 105) and then studies how this possibility shapes the state's behavior and the extent to which it *induces* a concern for relative gains. In the guns-versus-butter model, for example, S_1 can turn a relative gain for itself into a potential absolute loss for S_2 by allocating this gain to its military and thereby posing a greater military threat to S_2.

The first issue in the absolute-and-relative-gains debate has been a distraction from a second, important issue. *Does* the international environment induce a concern for relative gains, and, if so, how severe are these concerns and to what extent do they impede international cooperation? Modeling a state's relative concerns in its preferences is not a good way to address this second issue, for the severity of these concerns is assumed rather than derived from more basic features of the states' environment. As just noted, the guns-versus-butter game tries to model some of these more basic strategic elements, and the analysis of this game later in this chapter shows that these concerns are not very serious and do not constitute a significant impediment to international cooperation.[11]

The second major dispute in international relations theory is sometimes construed as a debate about state preferences, but it is actually a debate about what, if anything, can be derived from neorealism's core assumptions about the international system. Do states, as many have claimed, "try to maximize their relative power positions" (Mearsheimer 1994/95, 11)? The analysis of the guns-versus-butter model will help resolve this dispute.

The claim that states try to maximize their power can be interpreted in two ways. The first is that power is an end in itself. States or individuals try to enhance their power because they have an innate desire or preference for doing so. The second interpretation is that the strategic incentives that exist in the international environment lead states to try to maximize their power. If states do try to maximize their power, it is because they see this as the most effective means they have of furthering their interests. Maximizing one's power is a goal or preference in the first view and an outcome in the second.

---

[11] See Powell (1994) for a more extensive review of this debate.

The first interpretation is reductive. It ascribes outcomes to motivations and is typically associated with classical realism (Herz 1959, 232; Waltz 1959, 34–36; Wolfers 1962, 81–82; Schweller 1996). Neorealism rejects this interpretation. Power is a "possibly useful means" (Waltz 1979, 129). Rejecting the first interpretation, however, does not imply an acceptance of the second. Indeed, neorealism divides into different schools over the question of whether or not the international system leads states to try to maximize their power.[12]

One school, variously known as aggressive or offensive realism (Labs 1997; Mearsheimer 1994/95, 11; Schweller 1996; J. Snyder 1991, 12; Zakaria 1992), can be traced at least as far back as John Herz's (1950, 1959) early discussion of the security dilemma. In 1950, he argued that states' insecurity drove them "toward acquiring more and more power" (1950, 157).[13] Four decades later, offensive realism asserts "states seek to survive under anarchy by maximizing their power relative to other states" (Mearsheimer 1990, 12). More specifically, the pessimistic view that "daily life is essentially a struggle for power, where each state strives not only to be the most powerful actor in the system but also to ensure that no other state achieves that lofty position . . . can be *derived* from realism's five assumptions about the international system" (Mearsheimer 1994/95, 9–10, emphasis added). These assumptions are that the international system is anarchic; that states possess some offensive military capability; that states cannot be certain that other states will not use their offensive capabilities; that survival is a state's most basic motivation; and that states are instrumentally rational (Mearsheimer 1994/95, 10).

The second school, sometimes known as defensive realism or defensive positionalism (Grieco 1988a, 498–500; Grieco, Powell, and Snidal 1993; Schweller 1996; J. Snyder 1991, 12), also sees power as a means but does not believe that the international system necessarily induces states to try to maximize their power. Rather, states often act like "security seekers" (Glaser 1992, 1994/95, 1997; Schweller 1996, 98–108). This school agrees that states will still be concerned about power and relative gains. But the competitiveness of the international system and the extent to which each

---

[12] It is interesting to note a parallel between these two interpretations of power maximization and of the two issues in the absolute-and-relative-gains debate. Believing states to be attempting to maximize their power or to be concerned about their relative gains, some theories attribute this behavior to state preferences. Other theories see this behavior as an outcome induced by the strategic incentives in the system and states' efforts to achieve their more basic ends—whatever they may be—in this arena.

[13] Butterfield (1950; 1951, 9–36) develops a similar point.

state struggles to increase its relative power varies with other features in the environment, such as the offense-defense balance and the degree to which offensive forces can be distinguished from defensive forces (Glaser 1994/95). In brief, whether or not states try to maximize their relative power depends in part on the underlying technology of coercion.

This exegesis into neorealism underscores two points. The first is that these conflicting claims about power maximization reinforce the need to impose some "accounting standards" on these debates. Either neorealism's five core assumptions imply that the international system will be highly competitive and that states try to maximize their power, or these assumptions do not imply this. And, whether or not they do is important, for it affects our expectations about the likelihood and intensity of arms races, the feasibility of international cooperation, and the prospects for war.[14] Yet, each school believes a different claim to follow *deductively* from neorealism's core assumptions. Modeling these issues will help sort out these and other conflicting claims by making clearer and more transparent what conclusions do and do not follow.

The second point is that the assumption about state preferences made in the guns-versus-butter model is compatible with neorealism's core assumption that states, "at a minimum, seek their own preservation and, at a maximum, drive for world domination" (Waltz 1979, 118). States in the model, like firms trying to maximize their profits, do implicitly seek survival. As Waltz puts it, "to maximize profits tomorrow as well as today, firms first have to survive" (1979, 105). Analogously, in order to maximize their current and expected future consumption, states must survive. Failing to do so brings the lowest possible payoff.

As noted above, this compatibility is important. Whether or not the models developed here are compatible with the assumptions envisioned in neorealism, the models can be evaluated on their own terms by the extent to which they further our understanding of international politics. But if these models are also to provide a check on the internal coherence of other theories of international politics, then the assumptions underlying the models in this volume also need to be compatible with those theories.

A final observation concludes this extended discussion of state preferences. Structural theories of international politics take states to be unitary and often rational, unitary actors. Conceived of in this way, states

---

[14] Glaser (1994/95) offers a very thoughtful effort to trace the implications of these assumptions.

are a theoretical fiction. They do not exist. It is, therefore, slightly odd to debate what to assume about state preferences as if this were an a priori question that could be answered by appealing to first principles. The real issue is whether a particular assumption, along with the model in which it is embedded, is empirically fruitful. Does it lead to interesting, useful, and—at least ultimately—empirically testable insights?

To answer this question, we must be able to tell whether or not a claim actually does follow from the underlying assumptions. Unless we can, debates about preferences become empty, because it is impossible to determine if the implications of one set of assumptions differ from those of another set. Seen in this light, neorealism's inability to determine what does or does not follow from its core assumptions is especially troubling.

The guns-versus-butter model assumes that states try to maximize their absolute gains in a strategic setting in which they face a trade-off between consumption and defense. The rest of this chapter explores what this formulation implies.

The Geometry of Peace, War, and Internal Balancing

This section concentrates on a geometric analysis of the guns-versus-butter model. The next section develops the substantive significance of the geometric results. Figure 2.2 provides a way of visualizing the situation as a first step toward solving the guns-versus-butter game. Each point in the (m_1, m_2)-plane represents a different combination of military allocations. At (a_1, a_2), for example, S_1 is allocating a_1 to the military and, therefore, is consuming $r_1 - a_1$. Similarly, S_2 is devoting a_2 to the military and $r_2 - a_2$ to its internal ends.

Figure 2.2 also illustrates what happens if a state attacks. Suppose that the states are at (a_1, a_2) and it is S_1's move in the guns-versus-butter game. That is, S_1 has the option of altering its military allocation and then deciding whether or not to attack. Given S_2's allocation of a_2, S_1 can move anywhere between 0 and r_1 along the horizontal line through a_2 by reallocating its resources. S_1, for example, could move from (a_1, a_2) to (a_1', a_2) by increasing its military allocation from a_1 to a_1' and then attack. However, allocating a_1' to the military may not be the optimal way to attack S_2. That is, if S_1 were determined to fight S_2, it would want to reallocate its resources in the way that maximizes its expected payoff to attacking S_2 given S_2's allocation of a_2.

More formally, let $a_1^*(a_2)$ denote the value of a_1 that maximizes S_1's payoff to attacking S_2. That is, $a_1^*(a_2)$ maximizes $A_1(m_1, m_2)$ where A_1

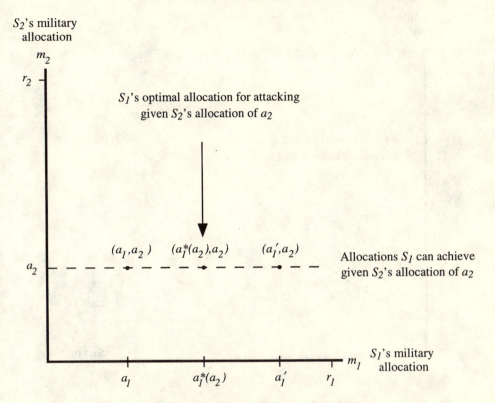

Figure 2.2 The plane of military allocations

is S_1's payoff to attacking S_2 at allocations m_1 and m_2 as defined by expression 2.1. S_1's optimal allocation a_1^* is a function of S_2's allocation because S_1's optimal force level for attacking S_2 depends on S_2's level of forces. If, therefore, S_1 decides to attack, the optimal way to do it is first to allocate $a_1^*(a_2)$ to its military sector and then strike. This gives S_1 an expected payoff of $A_1(a_1^*(a_2), a_2)$.

To solve the game, it will be useful to divide the plane of military allocations into the two regions. A state prefers peace to war in the first and war to peace in the second. As will be shown below, the function $i_1(m_2)$ in figure 2.3 forms the boundary between these regions. At allocations (a_1, a_2) to the left of i_1, S_2 has a relatively large military force, and S_1 prefers remaining there and consuming $r_1 - a_1$ in each period to attacking S_2 at allocation a_2. At allocations to the right of i_1, S_2 has a relatively small military force, which makes it vulnerable, and S_1 prefers attacking. Along i_1, S_1 is indifferent between living with the status quo and attacking.

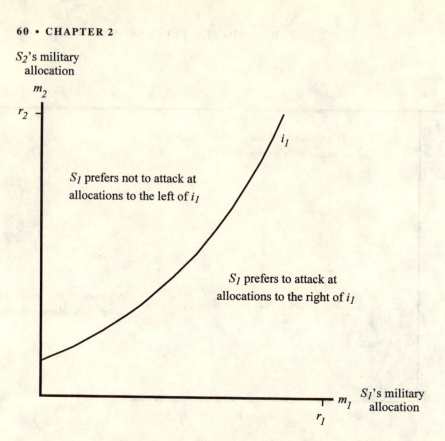

Figure 2.3 S_1's preferences for attacking

To specify these regions and i_1 more precisely, suppose that S_1 could either stay at (a_1, a_2) in figure 2.4 forever or attack S_2. If S_1 remains at this allocation, it would consume $r_1 - a_1$ in each and every period. If, by contrast, S_1 attacks, it would do so in the way that maximizes its expected payoff. S_1, therefore, would allocate $a_1^*(a_2)$ to the military and then attack.

If S_1's military allocation is relatively small—as it is at (a_1, a_2)—then S_1 is consuming most of what it has and the payoff to maintaining the status quo is high. If, moreover, S_2's military allocation is relatively large—as it is at (a_1, a_2)—then S_1's payoff to attacking will be small. In these circumstances, S_1 prefers remaining at (a_1, a_2) to attacking.

Now consider allocations directly to the right of (a_1, a_2) along the dashed line in figure 2.4. S_2's military allocation remains the same at these allocations, and, therefore, S_1's payoff to attacking S_2 remains constant. But as S_1 moves to the right along the dashed line, it devotes more and more of its resources to its military sector and, therefore, consumes

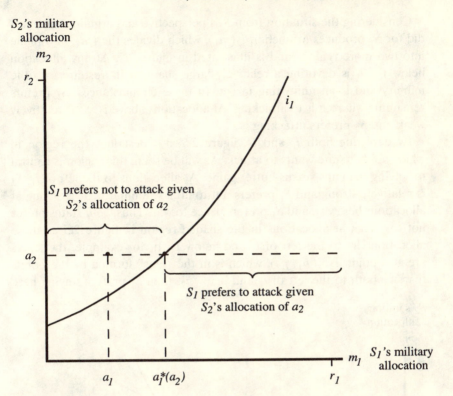

Figure 2.4 Deriving the allocations at which S_1 is indifferent between attacking and not

less and less. Thus, as the allocation moves farther and farther to the right, S_1's payoff to living at that allocation forever declines. If we move sufficiently far to the right, we will come to an allocation at which S_1 is indifferent to remaining at that allocation and attacking. This point is defined to be $i_1(a_2)$. If we move still farther to the right, S_1 will be devoting so much to its military and will be deriving so little benefit from the status quo that it prefers attacking. *In sum, the curve $i_1(m_2)$ is the set of allocations such that S_1 is indifferent between consuming $r_1 - i_1(m_2)$ in each and every period and attacking S_2 given S_2's military allocation is m_2.*[15]

---

[15] Appendix 2 derives the function i_1 formally. Less formally, S_1 is indifferent between remaining at (m_1, m_2) forever if the payoff to doing so equals the payoff to attacking optimally. That is, (m_1, m_2) satisfies $\sum_{t=0}^{\infty} \delta_1^t (r_1 - m_1)^{p_1} = A_1(a_1^*(m_2), m_2)$, and solving this equation for m_1 gives the value of $i_1(m_2)$.

Considering the situation from S_2's perspective and arguing as we just did for S_1 produces a function $i_2(m_1)$, which divides the (m_1, m_2)-plane into two more regions and is illustrated in figure 2.5. At any allocation below i_2, S_1 is devoting a relatively large share of its resources to the military and is an uninviting target. In these circumstances, S_2 prefers remaining where it is to attacking. At allocations above i_2, S_1 is relatively weak and S_2 prefers attacking.

By depicting both i_1 and i_2, figure 2.5 also describes the region in which neither state wants to attack. As will be seen, this region is central to solving the guns-versus-butter game. At allocations to the left of i_1, S_2 is relatively strong and S_1 prefers not to attack. Similarly, S_1 is strong at allocations below i_2, and S_1 prefers peace to war. Thus, *both* states prefer not to attack at allocations in the shaded region in figure 2.5 as these allocations lie to the left of i_1 and below i_2. If, for example, the states are at a point like (p_1, p_2), which is in the "lens" formed by the points that are both to the left of i_1 and below i_2, then S_1 prefers staying here

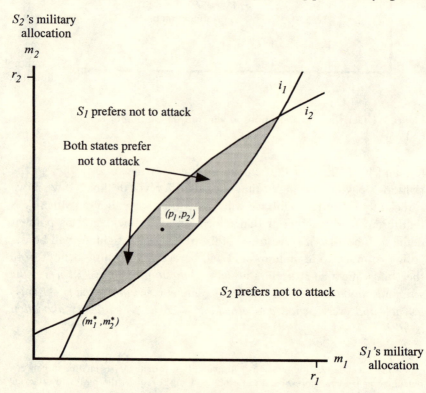

Figure 2.5 S_1's and S_2's preferences for attacking

and consuming $r_1 - p_1$ in each period to attacking S_2 given the latter's allocation of p_2. Similarly, S_2 prefers remaining at (p_1, p_2) and having $r_2 - p_2$ to attacking S_1. The shaded lens formed by the intersection of i_1 and i_2, therefore, defines the set of allocations at which neither state would want to attack if confronted with a choice between attacking and remaining at that allocation.

The curves i_1 and i_2 provide the key to solving the guns-versus-butter game. At the most basic level, we would like to know what the states' optimal allocations are and whether or not the states go to war. When will internal balancing succeed and when will it break down in war? To this end, it will be useful to define a *peaceful equilibrium* as an equilibrium in which no state ever attacks. That is, whenever a state is deciding how to allocate its resources and whether or not to attack in the game, it never opts for attacking in a peaceful equilibrium. The remainder of this section identifies conditions that ensure the existence of a unique, peaceful equilibrium and describes the military allocations associated with it.

In principle, a state might make different allocations at different times in a peaceful equilibrium. But before taking up this more complicated possibility, consider a simpler problem first. What can be said about the existence of a peaceful equilibrium in which each state's military allocation remains constant in each and every period?

Clearly, a constant-allocation peaceful equilibrium cannot exist if i_1 and i_2 do not intersect. To establish this, recall that no player can gain by deviating from its equilibrium strategy. (See appendix 1 for a discussion of equilibria.) If, therefore, a constant-allocation peaceful equilibrium did exist, then both states would have to prefer remaining at that allocation to attacking. But as figure 2.6 shows, there are no allocations that are both to the left of i_1 and below i_2 if these curves do not intersect. Thus, no matter what the allocation is, at least one of the states wants to attack. At, for example, any allocation to the left of i_1, S_2 prefers attacking to remaining at that allocation. Conversely, S_1 wants to attack at any allocation below i_2. The fact that at least one state always prefers attacking precludes the existence of a constant-allocation peaceful equilibrium.

This result can be generalized to the more complicated case in which the states' allocations might vary over time. If i_1 and i_2 do not intersect, then no peaceful equilibrium exists. The basic idea behind this result is that if it is never to be in S_1's self-interest to attack, then the states' allocations must be to the left of i_1 "on average." Similarly, if it is never to be in S_2's self-interest to attack, the states' allocations must

S_2's military
  allocation

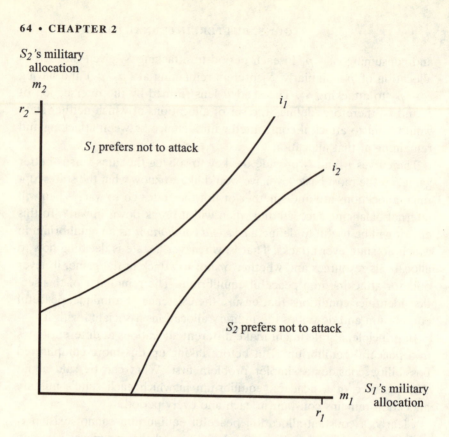

Figure 2.6 The absence of a peaceful equilibrium

be below i_2 "on average." But the allocations cannot be on average both to the left of i_1 and below i_2. Summarizing this:

Proposition 2.1: *Efforts to preserve the peace through internal balancing are doomed to break down in war if the lens formed by the intersection of i_1 and i_2 is empty, i.e., if every allocation is either above i_2 or to the right of i_1. No peaceful equilibria exist in these circumstances.*[16]

This proposition establishes geometric conditions that condemn internal balancing to breaking down in war. The substantive import of these formal requirements will be discussed after we identify the conditions which ensure that a peaceful equilibrium does exist. As we will see, if the lens formed by the intersection of i_1 and i_2 is nonempty, then a peaceful equilibrium exists and internal balancing can maintain the peace. This

---

[16] This proposition is proved formally in appendix 2.

equilibrium is, moreover, unique, and the allocations in it are located at the lower-left tip of the lens illustrated in figure 2.5. This tip will be called (m_1^*, m_2^*).

The first step in demonstrating this claim is to show that the highest payoff a state could possibly attain in any peaceful equilibrium is equal to what it would obtain from being at (m_1^*, m_2^*) in each period. This is clearly so for a constant-allocation equilibrium in which the allocations are the same in each period. Those allocations must lie in the lens formed by the intersection of i_1 and i_2, and each state's military allocation at the lower tip of this lens is less than at any other point in the lens. Thus, each state's consumption at (m_1^*, m_2^*) is higher than at any other point in the lens. Proposition 2.2 shows that this property is true of any peaceful equilibrium whether or not the allocation always remains the same.

Proposition 2.2: *The maximum payoff any state can obtain in a peaceful equilibrium is what that state would obtain if the allocation were at the lower-left tip of the lens formed by the intersection of i_1 and i_2.*

Argument:[17] The basic idea behind this result is the same as that behind proposition 2.1. In order for S_1 to prefer peace to war, allocations must lie to the left of i_1 "on average." If, moreover, S_1 is to do better in a peaceful equilibrium than it does if it stays at (m_1^*, m_2^*) forever, then S_1 on average must also allocate less than m_1^* to the military. That is, the allocations in any peaceful equilibrium must also lie to the left of the dashed line through m_1^* in figure 2.7. Similarly, the allocations in any peaceful equilibrium in which S_2 does better than it does if it is at (m_1^*, m_2^*) must be below both i_2 and the dashed line through m_2^* on average. But as figure 2.7 suggests, no allocations can on average be to the left of i_1 and m_1^* as well as below i_2 and m_2^*. ■

Proposition 2.1 demonstrates that i_1 and i_2 must intersect to form a nonempty lens if there is to be any chance of finding a peaceful equilibrium. Proposition 2.2 shows that the best any state could do in any peaceful equilibrium, if there is one, is what that state would obtain at the lower-left tip of this lens. Proposition 2.3 ensures that a peaceful

---

[17] This and other arguments sketch the intuition and general logic behind the propositions. Formal proofs can be found in the appendixes.

S_2's military
allocation

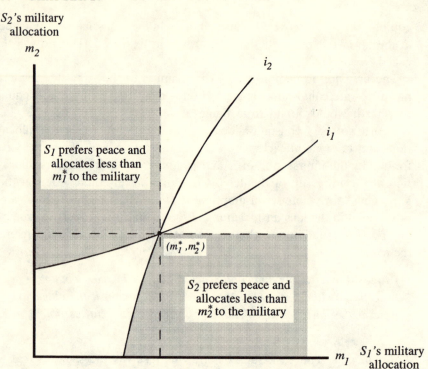

Figure 2.7 The optimal peaceful payoffs

equilibrium yielding these allocations actually does exist. Indeed, there is only one peaceful, perfect equilibrium, and in it S_1 and S_2 devote m_1^* and m_2^* to the means of military power.[18]

> **Proposition 2.3:** *If i_1 and i_2 intersect, then a unique, peaceful, perfect equilibrium of the guns-versus-butter game gives the states their highest possible peaceful payoffs. In this equilibrium, the states' allocations lie at the lower tip of the lens where S_1 and S_2 devote m_1^* and m_2^* to the military in each period. The equilibrium strategies that produce this outcome are:*
>
> *S_1's strategy: S_1's action in any period in which it has to decide what to do depends solely on what S_2 did in the previous period. If S_2's military allocation in the preceding period was less than m_2^*, then S_1*

---

[18] As discussed in chapter 1, an equilibrium is perfect if the threats and promises underlying it are credible. See appendix 1 and Morrow (1994b) for further discussion of perfect equilibria.

exploits S_2's vulnerability by optimally reallocating its resources and attacking S_2. If S_2's allocation in the prior period was at least m_2^*, S_1 devotes m_1^* to its military and does not attack.

S_2*'s strategy: As with* S_1, S_2*'s action in any period in which it has to decide what to do depends solely on what S_1 did in the previous period. If S_1's military allocation in the preceding period was less than m_1^*, then S_2 exploits S_1's vulnerability by optimally reallocating its resources and attacking S_1. If S_1's allocation in the prior period was at least m_1^*, S_2 devotes m_2^* to its military and does not attack.*

Argument: To demonstrate that these strategies constitute an equilibrium, we must show that neither state can gain by deviating from its equilibrium strategy. To see that S_1 cannot gain by reducing its allocation, suppose it did cut its spending below m_1^* to, say, a_1 in figure 2.8. S_1 is now more vulnerable, and S_2 prefers attacking S_1 at a_1 to consuming $r_2 - m_2^*$ in each period. (Recall that S_2 is just

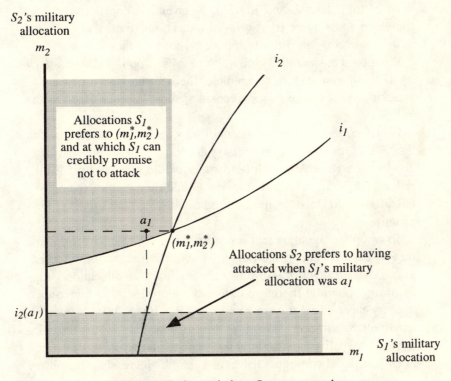

Figure 2.8 Trying to induce S_2 not to attack

indifferent between consuming $r_2 - m_2^*$ and attacking S_1 if S_1's allocation is m_1^*.) If, therefore, S_1 is to gain by cutting its spending below m_1^*, it must do something to induce S_2 not to attack. But, the only thing S_1 can do is promise not to attack S_2 if S_2 cuts its spending and thereby increases its consumption enough to outweigh the gain S_2 would have obtained by attacking S_1. But as we will see, S_1 cannot *credibly* promise to refrain from attacking if S_2 reduces its spending this much. S_2, therefore, attacks S_1 if it cuts its military allocation below m_1^*, and this leaves S_1 worse-off than it would have been had it not cut its forces below m_1^*.

The basic reasoning used in propositions 2.1 and 2.2 can also be employed to show that if S_2 cuts its forces to the point at which it prefers its higher level of consumption to attacking S_1 at a_1, then S_1's promise not to attack S_2 at this lower military allocation is incredible. In order to induce S_2 not to attack, S_1 must agree to a series of allocations that give S_2 at least as much as it could obtain by attacking S_1 at a_1. S_2, moreover, is indifferent between remaining at $(a_1, i_2(a_1))$ forever and attacking S_1 given its allocation of a_1. S_1, therefore, must agree to a series of allocations that lie at or below $i_2(a_1)$ on average in order to induce S_2 not to attack it at a_1.

But now consider the credibility of S_1's promise not to attack S_2. If this promise is to be credible, then S_1 must prefer peace to attacking. That is, the states' allocations must lie on average to the left of i_1.

However, these conditions cannot be satisfied simultaneously, as figure 2.8 indicates. There are no allocations both to the left of i_1 and below $i_2(a_1)$. Although both states would be better-off if they reduced their armaments below the equilibrium levels m_1^* and m_2^*, any attempt to do so would be predicated on inherently incredible promises.

To complete the argument for proposition 2.3, we must also show that S_1 cannot gain by increasing its allocation above m_1^*. According to S_2's strategy, it will not attack unless S_1's allocation drops below m_1^*. It would therefore only make sense for S_1 to increase its military capability if it were going to attack. But S_1 cannot improve its payoff by attacking. Given that S_2 is allocating m_2^* to the military, S_1's payoff to attacking is the same as its payoff to remaining at (m_1^*, m_2^*). S_1, consequently, cannot gain by increasing its military allocation. ∎

In sum, the guns-versus-butter game has a very simple solution. When i_1 and i_2 intersect to form a lens, then the states can achieve their highest possible peaceful payoffs by making the allocations that lie at the lower tip of this lens. Each state is deterred from allocating less than this amount by the fear of making itself vulnerable to attack. Each state is dissuaded from allocating more than this amount by the other's allocation, which makes the other state an uninviting target.

This solution reveals the commitment problem inherent in the guns-versus-butter trade-off. Both states would be better-off if they could commit themselves to refraining from attacking. If, for example, each state could somehow commit itself to abstaining from attacking, then S_1 could reduce its allocation below m_1^* and S_2 could devote less than m_2^* to the military. These reductions would mean more consumption and a higher payoff—if only such commitments were possible.

The simple geometric solution also makes it easy to trace the substantive effects of changes in the states' willingness to run risks, in the length of the shadow of the future, and in the technology of coercion. As will be seen in the next section, these changes shift the i_1 and i_2 curves in particular ways, move the lower tip of the lens, and thereby affect the states' military allocations.

Comparative Statics

Suppose two systems are identical in every way but one. The offensive advantages are, for example, larger in one system than in the other. How does this difference affect the states' military allocations and the existence of a peaceful equilibrium? A comparative-statics analysis answers questions like this by determining how the states' allocations respond to changes in the parameters of the model.

The comparative statics of the guns-versus-butter model turn out to be very simple. *Any change that increases either state's payoff to attacking relative to the status quo leads both states to increase their military allocations. If these changes are sufficiently large, both states have to devote so much to the military and therefore derive so little benefit from maintaining the status quo that internal balancing breaks down in war.*

The relative payoff to attacking may increase for two reasons. The first is a change in the state. If, for example, a state becomes more willing to run risks, then its expected payoff to the gamble inherent in attacking would rise and this would produce greater overall military allocations. The relative payoff to attacking may also increase because of a shift in the technology of coercion. If the offense-defense balance moves toward the offense or if the cost of fighting declines, the payoff to attacking rises and the system sees higher military allocations.

A simple intuition leads from an increase in the relative payoff to attacking to larger military allocations. In a peaceful equilibrium, states must devote enough resources to their military sectors in order to make themselves unattractive targets and thereby deter each other from attacking. However, a change that increases a state's expected payoff to attacking relative to living with the status quo makes the other state a more attractive target. This increased attractiveness must be offset in a peaceful equilibrium, and the only way to do that is through internal balancing and greater military allocations.

Tracing this intuition more formally takes two steps. The first is purely geometric. As is evident from figure 2.9, any change in the model's parameters that moves i_1 in to, say, i_1', or i_2 down to i_2' carries the lower tip of the lens up and to the right. This parametric shift, therefore, leads to higher military allocations as long as a peaceful equilibrium exists. If, however, the shifts are sufficiently large, i_1' and i_2' will no longer intersect and no allocations will lie both to the left of i_1' and below i_2'. No peaceful equilibria exist in this case, and efforts to balance internally break down in war.

The second step is to show that anything that increases S_1's payoff to attacking relative to the status quo shifts i_1 in, and anything that increases S_2's relative payoff to attacking shifts i_2 down. To see this, suppose that S_1 becomes more willing to run risks (i.e., ρ_1 increases). Before the shift, S_1 was just indifferent between the certainty of consuming $r_1 - m_1^*$ by remaining at (m_1^*, m_2^*) and the gamble of attacking S_2. After the shift, S_1 is more willing to run the risk inherent in attacking S_2. Consequently, a more risk-acceptant S_1 prefers war to peace at (m_1^*, m_2^*), and, therefore, this point must lie to the right of the new i_1-curve, which is denoted by i_1' in figure 2.9. (Figure 2.3 shows that if S_1 prefers attacking to remaining at a given allocation, then this allocation lies to the right of the i_1-curve.) Thus, shifts that increase S_1's payoff to attacking relative to maintaining the status quo shift i_1 to the left. Similarly, a change that raises S_2's relative payoff to attacking moves i_2 up.

As the geometry of figure 2.9 makes clear, a shift in *one* state's relative payoff to attacking induces *both* states to make larger military allocations. To see why, consider S_2's initial reaction to the shift in S_1's willingness to run risks. To deter S_1, S_2 must offset S_1's higher payoff to attacking by increasing its military allocation and thereby making

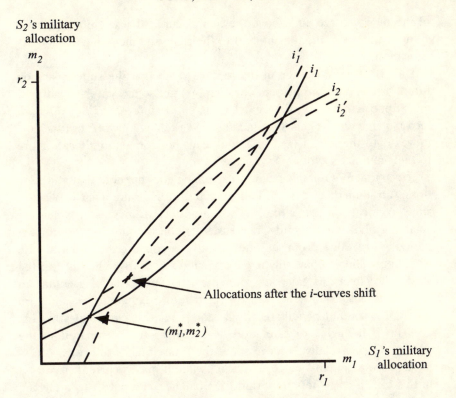

S_2's military
allocation

m_2

r_2 —

i_1'

i_1

i_2

i_2'

Allocations after the *i*-curves shift

(m_1^*, m_2^*)

S_1's military
m_1 allocation

r_1

Figure 2.9 Shifting *i*-curves and higher allocations

itself a less attractive target. If, however, S_2 increases its military allocation above m_2^*, it will be consuming less than $r_2 - m_2^*$, which is what
it consumes at (m_1^*, m_2^*). But S_2 was just indifferent between consuming $r_2 - m_2^*$ in each period and attacking S_1 if it is allocating m_1^* to the
military. Consequently, S_2 will prefer attacking S_1 at m_1^* to remaining at
peace as soon as S_2 increases its allocation above m_2^*. S_1, therefore, must
increase its own armaments above m_1^* in order to deter S_2. Thus, both
states increase their military allocations even though the initial change
only affected one state's willingness to run risks.

The preceding discussion makes it clear that larger offensive advantages (a larger β) or a decline in the cost of fighting (a smaller c) lead to
higher military allocations. Before these changes occur, both states are
indifferent between remaining at the status quo (m_1^*, m_2^*) and attacking.
After the shift, each state's payoff to attacking rises relative to its payoff
to staying at (m_1^*, m_2^*). This implies that (m_1^*, m_2^*) must lie to the right

of the new i_1-curve and above the new i_2-curve. These shifts in i_1 and i_2 move the tip of the lens up and to the right and mean higher military allocations.

The effects of a change in the relative value that the states place on future as compared to present consumption are somewhat more surprising. Suppose that S_1 puts a greater value on the future, i.e., S_1's discount factor δ_1 increases. This shift increases S_1's relative payoff to attacking, moves i_1 to the left of (m_1^*, m_2^*), and leads both states to allocate more to their military sectors.

To see that S_1's relative payoff to attacking goes up, note that attacking brings an immediate cost and an expected future gain. That is, when a state reallocates its resources in order to attack, it increases its military spending and, consequently, decreases its consumption in the current period. This reduced consumption is an immediate cost, which a state would be willing to pay only if the expected gain outweighed it. But the state will collect this gain only after the war. Thus, attacking entails an immediate cost followed by an expected future benefit. This temporal order of costs and benefits is why a state's relative payoff to attacking goes up if it begins to care more about the future compared to the present. Caring relatively more about the future makes future payoffs— in this case a benefit—more significant while it makes current payoffs— in this case a cost—less important. On balance, the payoff to attacking relative to staying at (m_1^*, m_2^*) increases if S_1 cares more about the future, and both states respond by allocating more to the military.

This result is surprising because it runs counter to the thrust of recent work on international cooperation. Cooperation theory generally argues that international cooperation is easier and more likely to obtain if states care more about the future. That is, a longer shadow of the future (i.e., a higher discount factor) facilitates cooperation: "[C]oncern about the future helps promote cooperation" (Axelrod and Keohane 1985, 232; Axelrod 1984; Keohane 1984; Lipson 1984; Oye 1985). However, the opposite holds true in the guns-versus-butter model. What accounts for the difference?

The transparency of the model makes it easier to see the answer. Whether more concern about the future makes cooperation more or less difficult depends on the temporal sequence of costs and benefits. Cooperation theory appeals to an analysis of repeated games (Axelrod 1984; Keohane 1984; Oye 1985) and, especially, the repeated prisoner's dilemma. In a repeated game, actors cooperate to the extent that they forgo opportunities to exploit each other in the short run in order to achieve long-run gains. The states support cooperation and deter exploitation with threats of punishment. Should one actor exploit another and thereby achieve an immediate gain, the other actors will punish it severely enough to make the costs of suffering the future punishment outweigh those gains. Note the pattern of costs and benefits in this sequence. An actor is deterred from an immediate gain by a future cost. If, therefore, this actor begins to be more concerned about the future, future payoffs will loom larger. Since these are costs in this case, caring more about the future reduces the net payoff to exploiting the other states. This sequence implies that the more a state cares about the future, the easier it is to deter exploitation and promote cooperation in a repeated-game framework.

The sequence of costs and benefits is, however, reversed in the guns-versus-butter model. One state exploits another by building up its arms in order to obtain future advantages, as Germany and Japan did during the 1930s. When an immediate cost is followed by a future expected gain, caring more about the future makes this gain seem higher. Deterring an attack becomes more difficult.

Finally, it is important to emphasize that the guns-versus-butter model does not say that a longer shadow of the future always makes cooperation more difficult. Rather, the model reveals a subtlety that has not been appreciated heretofore. The effects of the shadow of the future in specific empirical contexts are likely to be sensitive to the temporal sequence of costs and benefits, and the analysis of those situations should take this into account.[19]

The Struggle for Power and the Concern for Relative Gains

Do the strategic incentives in the international system induce states to maximize their power or to be concerned about their relative gains? The guns-versus-butter model, like many previous analyses (e.g., Wolfers 1962, 81–85; Waltz 1979, 126), makes it clear that states do not try to maximize their power. The model also undermines the standard relative-gains argument. If states really are concerned about relative gains, the

---

[19] Fearon (1998) examines another subtlety that cooperation theory has not appreciated. The longer the shadow of the future, the easier it is to deter deviation once an agreement has been reached. But a longer shadow of the future also makes the agreement more valuable, and this can make obtaining one more difficult.

guns-versus-butter model shows at a minimum that existing arguments really do not provide an adequate explanation of these concerns. But the model also suggests that the importance of any relative-gains concerns that do exist have been vastly overstated and that these concerns generally do not make international cooperation more difficult.

States in the guns-versus-butter model are certainly concerned with their relative power. If a state does not devote enough of its resources to the military, it will be relatively weak and the other state will attack. However, these concerns do not manifest themselves in power maximization.

That the states are not trying to maximize their power in the model is evident in many ways. Most directly, if a state were trying to maximize its power, it would devote all of its resources to the military. Doing so would ensure the highest possible probability of victory should that state attack the other or be attacked by it. But the states do not allocate all of their resources to the means of military power; their allocations are much lower, lying on the lower tip of the lens formed by the intersection of the i-curves.

Another way to see that the states are not trying to maximize their power is to consider one state's reaction to the other state's becoming less threatening. Suppose S_2 becomes less aggressive in the sense that it becomes less willing to run the risks inherent in war. More formally, suppose ρ_2 declines. If S_1 were trying to maximize its power, we would not expect S_1 to reduce its military allocation because S_2 becomes less aggressive. Yet this is precisely what happens. As illustrated in figure 2.10, the decrease in ρ_2 shifts i_2 up, and this moves the lower tip of the lens down and to the left. As a result, both states reduce their military allocations. But the fact that S_1 reduces its military spending in response to a decrease in S_2's aggressiveness seems inconsistent with the claim that it is trying to maximize its power.

If the states are not trying to maximize their power, what are they doing? Tautologically, they are merely living up to the model's assumptions about their goals. The states are attempting to maximize their current and expected future consumption. More substantially, the international system creates a trade-off between current and expected future consumption. The more a state consumes today, the weaker it will be tomorrow and the more likely it is to be defeated if attacked. A state resolves this trade-off by weighing the immediate cost of allocating more to the means of military power against the expected future benefits a greater military allocation brings. More specifically, a state devotes more and more of

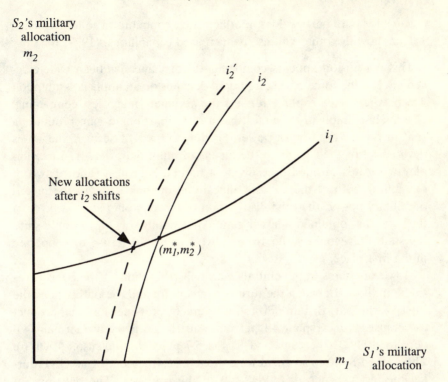

Figure 2.10 The response to a less aggressive adversary

its resources to the military up to the point at which the marginal gain from any further addition when measured in terms of expect future benefits is just offset by the marginal loss of being unable to consume those resources. Military allocations thus reflect a balancing of marginal costs and benefits and not a maximization of power, which is a point Wolfers made long ago (1962, 94).

The concern for relative gains is often said to be a significant impediment to international cooperation. The basic argument is due to Waltz, who maintains that

> when faced with the possibility of cooperating for mutual gain, states that feel insecure must ask how the gain will be divided. They are compelled to ask not "Will both of us gain?" but "Who will gain more?" If an expected gain is to be divided, say, in the ratio of two to one, one state may use its disproportionate gain to implement a policy intended to damage or destroy the other. Even the prospect of large absolute

gains for both parties does not illicit their cooperation so long as each fears how the other will use its increased capabilities. (1979, 105)

This conclusion appears compelling at first and has been widely accepted. But the force of this argument depends on an implicit assumption which, when made explicit, renders the argument much less compelling. The analysis implicitly assumes that a disproportionate gain produces a shift in the distribution of power. Such a shift would occur *if* the states devoted all of their gains to the means of military power. If, for example, two states of equal size divide a mutual gain in a ratio of two to one and *if* both of these states allocate *all* of their gains to the means of military power, then the distribution of power would shift in favor of the state that obtained a larger gain. Anticipating this unfavorable shift, the state that would suffer the relative loss would refuse to cooperate in the first place.

However, states in general allocate only a fraction of their resources to the military. Between the turn of the century and the outbreak of the First World War, Britain devoted 4.1 percent of its net national product to defense, France spent 4.1 percent, Austria 2.6 percent, Germany 4.0 percent, Italy 3.2 percent, and Russia 5.7 percent (Stevenson 1996, 6). The United States also spent an average of 6.4 percent of its GNP during the last two decades (1968–89) of the cold war. The data on Soviet spending is much more problematic and contentious, but the Soviet Union seems to have allocated an average of 13 percent of its GNP to defense.[20]

The fact that states have to decide how to allocate their resources and spend only a fraction of those resources on the military undercuts the standard relative-gains argument and suggests that relative-gains concerns are largely inconsequential. To illustrate the basic logic, suppose S_1 and S_2 devote 10 percent of their resources to the military. Then as a first approximation, S_2 might expect S_1 to allocate 10 percent of what it gains from cooperation to the military. If, therefore, S_1 and S_2 divide the cooperative gains in a ratio of two to one, S_2 could offset S_1's increase in military spending by devoting twice as much of its gain, i.e., 20 percent, to the military. Offsetting S_1's allocation in this way would

---

[20] Estimates of U.S. and Soviet spending are drawn from the *World Military Expenditures and Arms Trade* for various years (1978, 62, 66; 1979, 61, 65; 1980, 66, 71; 1983, 66, 71; 1984, 44, 49; 1985, 81, 85; 1987, 93, 97; 1988, 77, 81; 1990, 65, 69; 1991, 81, 85). For other estimates of Soviet spending and a discussion of various methods of calculating it, see *The Military Balance* (1985, 17–20).

still allow S_2 to consume 80 percent of its cooperative gain. S_2, therefore, would benefit from an agreement that disproportionately benefited S_1. Indeed, the only situation in which S_2 might not benefit is if it had to allocate 100 percent or more of its gain in order to offset S_1's larger military allocation.

This basic reasoning would also seem to extend to a strategic setting in which there was investment and economic growth. (Recall that the guns-versus-butter model excluded the possibility of investment as a way of simplifying the formal analysis.) Suppose S_1 devotes 10 percent of its gain to the means of military power, invests 10 percent in the means of production, which will lead to a larger resource base in the future, and consumes the rest. S_2 can offset this by allocating 20 percent of its gain to the military, investing another 20 percent, and then consuming the remaining 60 percent. This increased consumption makes S_2 better-off with the agreement than without it. (Although this reasoning sounds as though it will carry over to a situation in which there is investment and growth, determining whether it actually does remains a task for a future round of the modeling dialogue.)

Of course, this illustration oversimplifies the situation in at least two important respects. First, if the states do not allocate all of their gains to the military, then cooperation gives them a larger stake in the status quo, which affects the relative attractiveness of attacking. Second, the illustration ignores the interaction between the states' allocation decisions. The model can help trace the effects of these two complications, and it indicates that relative-gains concerns do not make cooperation more difficult.

To formalize this analysis, suppose cooperation would bring a gain that can be divided between S_1 and S_2, and consider the extreme case in which S_1 realizes all of this gain. If relative-gains concerns have any effect at all, we would expect S_2 to be harmed by this lopsided agreement and to block it. But this is not the case. Indeed, even this agreement makes S_2 better-off because of the indirect gain arising from the states' reallocation of resources.[21]

Figure 2.11 depicts these effects. If S_1 receives all of the cooperative gain, then i_1 shifts out to i'_1 and i_2 remains fixed. To see why, note that S_1's payoff to remaining at (m_1^*, m_2^*) increases because it now has a larger stake in the status quo. By contrast, S_1's payoff to attacking is the

---

[21] Morrow (1997) explicitly models the states' decision whether or not to agree to cooperate, and the analysis developed here parallels his.

S_2's military
allocation
m_2

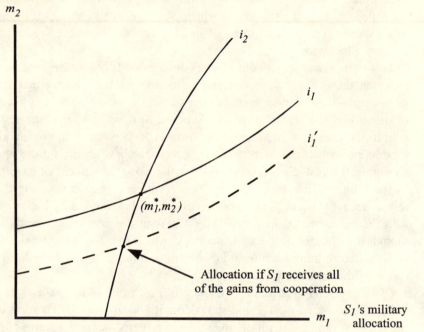

Allocation if S_1 receives all
of the gains from cooperation

m_1 S_1's military
allocation

Figure 2.11 The effects of a relative gain

same as it was. Thus, S_1 strictly prefers being at (m_1^*, m_2^*) to attacking, and, therefore, (m_1^*, m_2^*) must be to the left of i_1'. As for i_2, S_2's payoffs to attacking and to remaining at (m_1^*, m_2^*) are unchanged, because S_1 is receiving all of the direct gains from cooperation.[22] Accordingly, i_2 does not move. Hence, cooperation results in a shift in i_1, which in turn leads both states to lower equilibrium allocations to the military. Because S_2 is now devoting less to the military, its consumption increases and it is better-off even though S_1 is receiving all of the direct gains from cooperation.[23] Interestingly, a model very much focused on military power and threats and grounded in assumptions typically associated

[22] It might seem that S_2's payoff to attacking should rise because it could then incorporate the cooperative gains. If, however, S_2 conquers S_1, S_2 would presumably capture these gains whether or not the states were cooperating before the war. Thus, prior cooperation would not affect S_2's payoff to attacking.

[23] Because a cooperative agreement that gives S_1 a larger stake in the status quo indirectly benefits S_2, it might also seem that an increase in S_1's resources r_1, which also gives S_1 a larger stake in the status quo, would also benefit S_2. If so, then S_2 would prefer to

with neorealism supports the fundamentally liberal conclusion that international trade or, more generally, increased interdependence leads to lower military allocations.[24]

President Nixon's strategy of détente during the 1970s also seems to have reflected these considerations. Détente was supposed

> to involve Soviet interests in ways that would increase their stake in international stability and the status quo. There was no thought that such commercial, technical, and scientific relationships could by themselves prevent confrontations or wars, but at least they would have to be counted in the balance sheet of gains or losses whenever the Soviets were tempted to indulge in international adventurism. (Nixon 1978, 618)

That is, one of the goals of détente was to give the Soviet Union a greater stake in maintaining the peace just as cooperation does in the guns-versus-butter model.

The absence of relative gains in the guns-versus-butter model, like any theoretical deduction, must be interpreted carefully. Just because states do not exhibit relative-gains concerns in the model does not mean that actual states do not care about relative gains. Rather, the model helps us see what follows from what. As discussed in the previous chapter, mathematical models provide a language that helps "to show that certain

---

face a larger rather than a smaller adversary. Such a result would cast doubt on the model. However, S_2 does not prefer a larger adversary.

To see that S_2's payoff generally declines as its adversary becomes larger, note that an increase in r_1 has three effects. Like a cooperative gain, an increase in r_1 raises S_1's payoff to living with the status quo allocations (m_1^*, m_2^*). But unlike a cooperative gain, a larger r_1 also increases each state's payoff to fighting and thereby being able to consume $r_1 + r_2 - c$ if it prevails.

Since S_2's payoff to attacking rises, i_2 shifts down. Numerical analysis also indicates that i_1 shifts out because of the combined effects of S_1's larger payoffs to living with the status quo as well as attacking. Both states' military allocations rise as a result of these shifts, and this leaves S_2 worse-off. However, S_1's military allocation does not rise as much as its resources, and the net effect of an increase in r_1 is an increase S_1's payoff.

[24] Although in keeping with liberalism, this result is not the same as the liberal claim that international trade or economic interdependence makes peace more likely. The focus of the guns-versus-butter model is on military allocations. For reviews of liberalism, see Baldwin (1985, 77–87), Gilpin (1987, 26–31), Keohane (1990), Nye (1988), and Stein (1993). For recent empirical work on the relationship among trade, war, and conflict that shows that trade is generally associated with less war, see Gasiorowski (1986), Gasiorowski and Polachek (1982), Mansfield (1994), Polachek (1978, 1980), and Pollins (1989a, 1989b). Barbieri (1996), by contrast, finds that extensive interdependence increased the likelihood of conflict between 1870 and 1938.

precise assumptions lead to other precise conclusions" (Kreps 1997, 63). The guns-versus-butter model shows in particular that a strategic setting in which "each of the units spends a portion of its effort, not in forwarding its own good, but in providing the means of protecting itself against others" (Waltz 1979, 105) does not by itself imply a concern for relative gains. Other assumptions are needed to sustain this conclusion, although it is not clear what those assumptions are. If states actually are concerned about relative gains, we do not understand why.

Some previous discussions (e.g., Grieco 1988a; Mastanduno 1991; Powell 1991; Grieco, Powell, and Snidal 1993; Keohane 1993; Waltz 1993; Glaser 1994/95; Matthews 1996; Liberman 1996; Morrow 1997) have recognized that the severity of these concerns depends on the states' strategic environment, and some have offered conjectures about which features of the environment may induce these concerns and make them more or less intense. But with one partial exception, none of these conjectures has been established empirically or buttressed with a transparent model.[25] Empirical efforts to see if states actually are concerned with relative gains have generally focused on whether or not states succeeded in cooperating in specific cases, including non-tariff barriers between the United States and European Union (Grieco 1990); fighter aircraft, satellites, and high-definition television (Mastanduno 1991); supercomputers, steel, and arms control (Matthews 1996); and trade between Britain and Germany before the First World War and between the United States and Japan before the Second World War (Liberman 1996). Cooperation sometimes succeeds and sometimes fails in these cases. But these studies generally do not specify how likely cooperation would be to succeed if there were no relative-gains concerns and if the states were simply trying to secure a larger share of the benefits. This failure, as Keohane (1993) observes, makes it impossible to establish the existence, much less assess the significance, of any relative-gains concerns.

If relative-gains concerns are of little or no consequence as the guns-versus-butter model suggests, why do states often fail to cooperate? The next chapter develops one explanation. Although relative-gains considerations may be insignificant, states do have conflicts of interest. The

---

[25] The exception is Morrow (1997), who explicitly models trade and argues that relative-gains concerns do not impede trade for empirically plausible volumes of trade. His analysis is, however, partly based on the guns-versus-butter model and therefore shares some of the limitations of that model.

larger the share of the cooperative gain a state obtains for itself, the less the other state will have. When such conflicts of interest are combined with asymmetric information, bargaining may break down even though there are agreements that both states would have preferred to not reaching an agreement. The next chapter examines states' efforts to respond to threats through bargaining and compromise.

Summarizing this chapter, one of the ways a state can respond to threats in the international system is through balancing internally by reallocating the resources it controls. Because resources are scarce, internal balancing confronts a state with a trade-off between satisfying its intrinsically valued ends and procuring the means of military power. States' efforts to resolve this guns-versus-butter trade-off result in a commitment problem. Both states would be better-off if they could commit themselves to refraining from using military force against each other. Factors that increase either or both states' payoff to attacking relative to the status quo lead to higher military allocations. These larger military allocations mean less consumption and, thus, a lower payoff to remaining at peace. Should the payoff to peace fall too far, internal balancing breaks down in war.

3

Bargaining in the Shadow of Power

Shortly after dawn on December 7, 1941, Japanese forces struck the American naval base at Pearl Harbor. The surprise attack brought the United States into the Second World War, and fears of a "nuclear Pearl Harbor" haunted American thinking about nuclear strategy and vulnerability during the cold war (Freedman 1981; Herken 1985; Kissinger 1957a).[1] But the Japanese attack was not a "bolt out of the blue." Japanese-American relations had been deteriorating since at least 1937 when fighting broke out between China and Japan. Indeed, Tokyo and Washington had been engaged in increasingly tense bargaining over the terms of a settlement in the Far East for more than six months when that bargaining ended in war.[2]

The previous chapter focused on states' efforts to deal with threats through internal balancing. This chapter centers on states' efforts to resolve conflicts of interest and defuse threats to use force through compromise and bargaining. How, in particular, does the shadow of power affect the bargaining between a satisfied state and a dissatisfied state?

Of special interest is the relationship between the likelihood of war and the distribution of power. How does the probability that the bargaining will break down in war vary with the distribution of power between the states? Is war least likely if, as the balance-of-power school argues, power is evenly distributed between the states (Claude 1962; Morgenthau 1967; Mearsheimer 1990; Wolfers 1962; Wright [1942] 1965)? Or, is war least likely if one state preponderates as the preponderance-of-power school claims (Blainey 1973; Organski 1968; Organski and Kugler 1980)?[3]

---

[1] The Japanese attack was formally a surprise in the sense that it preceded a declaration of war. That declaration was being decoded in the Japanese embassy in Washington when the attack occurred (Prange 1981). Blainey (1973, 247), however, observes that going to war without a formal declaration of war has been common since at least 1700.

[2] Barnhart (1987), Borg (1964), Butow (1960, 1961), Dallek (1979), Feis (1950), and Utley (1985) discuss various aspects of Japanese-American relations during the 1930s and the drift to war.

[3] Levy (1989) reviews this debate and Wagner (1994) discusses some of the more general conceptual issues.

The analysis of the bargaining between a satisfied and dissatisfied state would be relatively straightforward were it not for asymmetric information and the problems it creates. If the states had complete information, each would know the other's payoffs. The satisfied state could then infer from this knowledge how much it would have to concede to the dissatisfied state to appease it. The satisfied state would therefore confront a simple, if unpleasant, choice. It could either meet the dissatisfied state's minimal demands or face the certainty of war.

Asymmetric information complicates the bargaining. If the satisfied state is uncertain of the dissatisfied state's payoffs and therefore of its willingness to use force, the satisfied state can no longer be sure that a specific concession will satisfy the dissatisfied state. The satisfied state thus faces a "risk-return" trade-off. The more it offers, the more likely it is to satisfy the other state and thereby avert war. But this higher probability of peace comes at a price. The more the satisfied state concedes, the less it will have if the other accepts.

When confronting this trade-off, a state often finds it optimal *not* to "buy" zero risk by offering enough to be sure of satisfying the other state. States do not act like "security maximizers," if that is taken to mean trying to minimize the probability of being attacked. Rather, a satisfied state generally accepts some risk of war as the price of a more favorable settlement. This risk does not result from miscalculation or misperception. To the contrary, it is a calculated risk.

This chapter uses a game-theoretic model to analyze this trade-off and to examine the relation between the probability of war and the distribution of power. In the model, two states are bargaining about revising the international status quo. The states make offers and counter-offers until they reach a mutually acceptable settlement or until one of them becomes sufficiently pessimistic about the prospects of reaching an agreement that it uses force to try to impose a new international order. The states' equilibrium strategies specify the demands the states make of each other and the circumstances in which they resort to force. These strategies thus make it possible to calculate the probability that the bargaining breaks down in war as a function of the distribution of power between the two states. The shape of this function can then be compared to the relation claimed to exist by the balance-of-power and preponderance-of-power schools.

Two competing factors affect the relation between the probability of breakdown and the distribution of power and make this relation difficult to assess without the aid of a model. First, the weaker a state, the worse it can expect to do in the event of war. This factor suggests that the preponderance-of-power school is correct and that bargaining is less likely to break down if one of the states has a preponderance of power.

To see why, suppose two states, D and S, are bargaining about revising the territorial status quo and that S has just proposed a particular division to D. D would be tempted to use force to impose a settlement rather than accept S's offer only if its expected payoff to using force were at least as large as its payoff to agreeing to the proposal. But the weaker D, the lower its expected payoff to fighting. Indeed, if D is sufficiently weak, its payoff to using force is sure to be less than its payoff to agreeing to S's offer. In this case, D acquiesces to S's demand and is not tempted to use force. Nor would S be tempted to use force, since D is willing to agree to S's demand. This analysis indicates that a preponderance of power makes war less likely and is essentially the reasoning Organski advances for this claim. "A preponderance of power ... increases the chances of peace, for the greatly stronger side need not fight at all to get what it wants, while the weaker side would be plainly foolish to attempt battle for what it wants" (1968, 294).

There is, however, a second, countervailing factor at work. The preceding argument was based on the assumption that S's proposal was fixed. But as S becomes stronger and D becomes weaker, S knows that D is more likely to accept any given proposal. Thus, S will demand more of D as D becomes weaker. D, in turn, may be more likely to resist these larger demands, and war more may become more likely when there is a preponderance of power. By contrast, an even distribution of power would restrain all states' demands and thereby lessen the danger of war. This restraining effect of an even distribution of power underlies the balance-of-power school's analysis of the relation between the probability of war and the distribution of power. As Wolfers argues, "[F]rom the point of view of preserving the peace ... it may be a valid proposition that a balance of power placing restraint on every nation is more advantageous in the long run than the hegemony even of those deemed peace-loving at the time" (1962, 120).

In sum, a shift in the balance of power against D has two competing effects. First, D is more likely to accept any specific demand. But, second, more will be demanded of D than would have been had it been more powerful. The first effect tends to make war less likely, while the second tends to make war more likely. The net result of these two opposing effects on the probability of war is unclear. The preponderance-of-power school generally emphasizes the former factor while minimizing or disregarding the latter, whereas the balance-of-power school emphasizes the latter while minimizing or disregarding the former.[4]

The model makes it possible to take both factors into account, and the results contradict both schools' expectations. The probability of war turns out to be a function of the *disparity* between the status quo distribution of benefits and the distribution of power. *War is least likely when the existing distribution of benefits reflects the underlying distribution of power.* In these circumstances, the division of benefits expected to result from the use of force is approximately the same as the status quo distribution of benefits. The expected gains from using force are therefore too small to outweigh the costs of fighting. Neither state is willing to use force to change the status quo, and the probability of war is zero. When the disparity between the status quo division of benefits and the distribution of power is large, then at least one state is willing to use force to overturn the status quo, and there is a risk of war. As this disparity grows, the probability of war generally increases. Offensive advantages exacerbate the risk. The larger the offensive advantage, the more likely war.

These results seem quite intuitive: as the disparity between the distribution of power and the distribution of benefits grows, the probability of war generally increases. Indeed, this finding echoes Gilpin's (1981) explanation of hegemonic wars. Such wars, he argues, arise because of a decline in the hegemon's power, which leads to a disparity between the distribution of power and the distribution of benefits associated with the existing international order.[5]

Although intuitive, these results contradict the expectations of both the balance-of-power and preponderance-of-power schools. The former expects the probability of war to be smallest when power is evenly distributed, but the probability of war is smallest in the present model when the distribution of power mirrors the status quo distribution of benefits. These claims coincide only in the special case in which the status quo distribution is even. The preponderance-of-power school expects the probability of war to be smallest when the distribution of power is highly skewed and to increase as the distribution of power becomes more even. But the probability of war is largest in the model developed below when the distribution of power is highly skewed.

---

[4] And, of course, there is a third possibility. These factors might just cancel each other out, in which case the probability of war would be independent of the underlying distribution of power, as Fearon (1992) proposes. Wittman (1979) also develops this point.

[5] Gilpin's (1981) analysis of the effects of shifts in the distribution of power will be discussed more fully in chapter 4.

The next section stylizes the bargaining in a simple game. The two subsequent sections then discuss the states' equilibrium strategies when informational problems are absent and when they are present. There follows an analysis of the relation between the probability of war and the distribution of power. The final section examines the effects of changes in the technology of coercion on the likelihood of war.

A Model of Bargaining in the Shadow of Power

The model is designed to highlight four critical aspects of bargaining in the shadow of power. First, it is bargaining, so the states must be able to make offers and counter-offers and, especially, to choose how much to offer in any effort to reach a compromise. This, of course, seems obvious. But it is important to emphasize it, because one common way of simplifying a model is by not allowing the states to determine the size of their offers. In the guns-versus-butter model, for example, the states cannot make any kind of offer. In other models (Bueno de Mesquita and Lalman 1992; Bueno de Mesquita, Morrow, and Zorick 1997; Fearon 1994; Morrow 1989; Powell 1987, 1988, 1989, 1990, 1996), states can decide whether to compromise—typically by backing down— or to escalate. But, if a state chooses to compromise in these models, it cannot decide on the size of the compromise offer it makes. These models, therefore, do not do a very good job of representing the risk-return trade-off in which a state can decide how much to offer and how much risk to run.

The second critical aspect is that the bargaining takes place in the shadow of power. The states must be able to try impose a settlement in the model if they deem that to be in their best interest. Third, the exercise of power is costly. And, finally, the states are uncertain of each other's willingness to impose a settlement.

To model these four features, suppose two states, D and S, are bargaining about revising the international distribution of benefits. More concretely, imagine that two states are negotiating about changing the territorial status quo. Figure 3.1 illustrates the situation. The territory in dispute can be represented by an interval from zero to one which, figuratively speaking, lies between the two states' capitals. The existing status quo is denoted by q where D controls all of the territory to the left of q and S controls all of the territory to the right of q. Proposals in this setting can be thought of as points on the interval between zero and one.

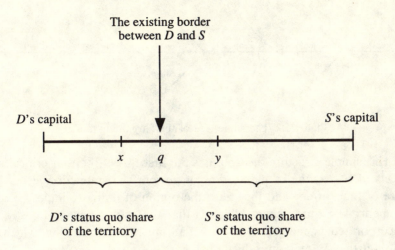

Figure 3.1 Bargaining over territory

If, for example, S proposes x, it is demanding that the status quo be revised in its favor; to wit, that it acquire control of all of the territory to the right of x. If, instead, S proposes y, it would be offering to concede territory to D by withdrawing from q to y. And, an "offer" of q is, in effect, a proposal to maintain the status quo.

Figure 3.2 describes the bargaining game. S begins by making a proposal to D. D can accept this offer; reject it in order to make a counter-offer; or force a settlement by attacking. The game ends if D accepts or attacks. If D rejects, it then proposes a new territorial division which S can now accept, reject, or attack. As before, accepting or attacking ends the game. If S rejects, it again suggests another division and so on. The bargaining continues, possibly forever, with offers alternating back and forth until one of the states agrees to a proposal or becomes sufficiently pessimistic about the prospects of reaching a mutually acceptable resolution that it resorts to force to try to impose a new territorial settlement.[6]

[6] This formulation is an adaptation of Rubinstein's model of voluntary exchange. Rubinstein's (1982) seminal paper analyzes a game in which two actors are trying to divide a pie or, less quaintly, the gains from cooperating. One actor begins by proposing a division of the pie to the other, who can either accept or reject the offer. Acceptance ends the game and the pie is divided as agreed. If the second actor rejects the initial proposal, it makes a counter-offer that the first actor can either accept or reject. Acceptance again ends the game. If the first actor rejects the proposal, it makes a new offer. The actors alternate making offers until they agree on a division. If they never agree, the pie goes undivided and neither player gets anything. The present model simply adds the option of using power to impose a settlement to Rubinstein's basic formulation.

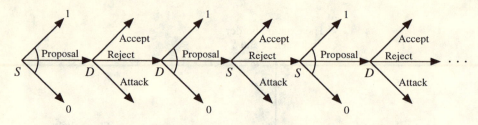

Figure 3.2 The game tree of the bargaining model

This simple structure incorporates the first two of the four critical aspects of bargaining in the shadow of power. The states decide on the size of their offers, and they have the option of trying to impose a settlement. The third aspect, which is that the use of power is costly, is incorporated in the states' payoffs. (Asymmetric information, which is the fourth feature, is introduced below.)

To specify these payoffs, two kinds of outcomes need to be considered. In the first, the states agree to a peaceful division. In the second, they go to war. These outcomes and the payoffs associated with them parallel the payoffs in the guns-versus-butter game. Suppose the states agree to the proposal x in figure 3.1 at time a ("a" for accord). (As before, the first offer is made at time $t = 0$ for notational convenience.) This agreement means that D would have had control over the territory to left of q in each period until time a and control of the territory to the left of x from time a on.

The utility a state derives from an agreement depends on four factors: (i) the amount of territory it controls before and after the agreement; (ii) how long it takes to reach the agreement; (iii) the state's degree of patience; and (iv) its attitude toward risk. In particular, D's payoff to controlling q through time $a - 1$ is $q^{\rho_D} + \delta q^{\rho_D} + \delta^2 q^{\rho_D} + \cdots + \delta^{a-1} q^{\rho_D}$. As in the guns-versus-butter model, the exponent ρ_D reflects D's attitude toward risk and δ is D's discount factor. (To simplify the analysis, the states are assumed to have a common discount factor.) The first term in this sum is the benefit D receives from controlling q in the first period (i.e., at $t = 0$). The second term is the discounted value of controlling q in the second period, and so on. Similarly, D's utility to controlling x from time a on is $\delta^a x^{\rho_D} + \delta^{a+1} x^{\rho_D} + \delta^{a+2} x^{\rho_D} + \cdots$. The first term in this expression is D's discounted payoff to controlling x at time a; the next term is D's discounted payoff to controlling x in the next period; and so on. Combining these two parts, D's payoff to agreeing to x at time a is its payoff to controlling q until time a plus its payoff to having x from time a on. S's payoff to agreeing to x at time a is defined analogously. It is the sum of S's payoff to having control over $1 - q$ until a and $1 - x$ thereafter.[7]

To define the states' payoffs if they fight, suppose they go to war at time w ("w" for war). As in the case of agreement, D controls q until time w and derives the same payoff from this control. To simplify the specification of D's payoff following an attack, war is assumed to end in one of only two ways. As in the guns-versus-butter model, either D is completely victorious, or S is. If D prevails, it takes all of the territory, which gives it a payoff of $(1)^{p_D} = 1$ in each period. Fighting, however, is costly, and the net gain in each period is $1 - d$ where d represents D's cost of fighting. Summing these per-period benefits from time w on gives $\sum_{t=w}^{\infty} \delta^t (1 - d) = \delta^w (1 - d) + \delta^{w+1}(1 - d) + \delta^{w+2}(1 - d) + \cdots$. The first term in this sum is the discounted value of the per-period benefit D obtains during period w; the second term is the discounted benefit D receives during $w + 1$; and so on. If D loses, S captures all of the territory, which leaves D with nothing but the cost of fighting. Thus, the per-period payoff to losing is $-d$ and the total payoff to losing is the sum $\delta^w \cdot (-d) + \delta^{w+1} \cdot (-d) + \delta^{w+2} \cdot (-d) + \cdots$.

To complete the description of D's expected payoff to fighting, the probability that D prevails must be defined. The guns-versus-butter model examined internal balancing and the way the states' resource allocations affected the likelihood that a state would prevail. The present model puts that issue in the background in order to focus on the bargaining between the states. Accordingly, the probability that D prevails is assumed to be constant and denoted by p. This parameter represents the distribution of power between the states. If p is close to one, D is very likely to prevail and has a preponderance of power. If p is close to zero, S is likely to prevail and it has a preponderance of power. At $p = \frac{1}{2}$, both states are equally likely to prevail and there is a balance of power.

Combining these elements, D's payoff to attacking at w is its payoff to controlling q through time $w - 1$ plus its payoff to winning weighted by the probability of prevailing plus the payoff to losing weighted

---

[7] This specification of the states' payoffs supresses or abstracts away from the resource-allocation problem, which was central to the guns-versus-butter trade-off studied in the previous chapter. In the bargaining model, a state's payoff depends on how much territory it controls and not how it allocates the resources that controlling that territory brings. Chapter 6 discusses the possibility of integrating the bargaining problem and the resource-allocation problem.

by the probability of losing. To express this in symbols, let $A_D(w)$ denote D's payoff to fighting at w. Then,

$$A_D(w) = \sum_{t=0}^{w-1} \delta^t q^{\rho_D} + p\left[\sum_{t=w}^{\infty} \delta^t(1-d)\right] + (1-p)\left[\sum_{t=w}^{\infty} -d\delta^t\right] \quad (3.1)$$

The first term in this expression is D's payoff to controlling q through time $w - 1$; the second term is D's payoff to prevailing weighted by the probability that it will prevail; and the last term is its payoff to losing times the probability that it will lose. S's payoff to attacking is defined similarly.

Finally, the formal analysis in appendix 3 assumes that both states are risk neutral or risk averse (i.e., ρ_D and ρ_S are assumed to be less than or equal to one). Precluding the possibility of risk-acceptant states greatly simplifies the characterization of the game's equilibria. But this assumption also seems substantively plausible. Being risk-neutral or risk-averse does not mean that a state is unwilling to take risks. Rather, it means that a state does not derive positive utility or enjoyment from the risk itself. If given a choice between a certain outcome and a risky venture with the same expected outcome, a risk-averse or risk-neutral state would prefer the former whereas a risk-acceptant state would prefer the latter. Although substantively reasonable, assuming the states to be risk neutral or risk averse may nevertheless limit the applicability of the analysis, and this potential limitation should be kept in mind when moving back and forth between the formal and empirical realms in the modeling dialogue. To simplify the algebra in the remainder of this chapter, we will go further and assume that the states are risk neutral (i.e., ρ_D and ρ_S equal one). Assuming risk neutrality does not affect the results but makes it easier to see what is going on.

The model developed so far has complete information. Each state knows the other state's payoffs and, therefore, its willingness to use force. The next section shows that as long as information is complete, bargaining never breaks down regardless of the distribution of power. Incomplete information is a prerequisite to war in this model, as it creates the "risk-return" trade-off.

Bargaining with Complete Information

When there are no informational asymmetries and each state knows the other state's payoffs, there is no risk-return trade-off. A satisfied state, for example, knows exactly how much it has to concede to a dissatisfied state to satisfy it. The choice confronting the satisfied state is clear, if stark. It can meet the dissatisfied state's minimal demands or face the certainty of war. As will be seen, the satisfied state chooses to appease the dissatisfied state and thereby obviate any risk of war when there is complete information.

The first step in analyzing the complete-information bargaining is to describe more precisely what it means for a state to be dissatisfied. A state is *dissatisfied* if it is willing to use force to try to revise the status quo. That is, a state is dissatisfied if its expected payoff to attacking is greater than its payoff to living with the status quo forever. In symbols, D is dissatisfied if its payoff to attacking now, which is $A_1(0)$ in expression 3.1, is greater than its payoff to abiding by the status quo, which is $q + \delta q + \delta^2 q + \delta^3 q + \cdots$. (Recall that the states are presumed to be risk neutral, which implies $\rho_D = 1$ and $q^{\rho_D} = q$.) Simplifying this condition algebraically leads to a much less complicated expression: D is dissatisfied if $p - d > q$.

This expression has a simple interpretation. If D attacks, it either wins or loses all of the territory. D's expected gain to attacking, therefore, is equal to its utility to winning, which is 1 in each period, times the probability that it wins plus its utility to losing, which is 0 in each period, times the probability that it loses. In symbols, D's expected gain on a per-period basis is $1 \cdot p + 0 \cdot (1 - p) = p$. But fighting is also costly, and D pays a total cost equivalent to a per-period cost of d. Consequently, the net per-period expected payoff to attacking is $p - d$. If, however, D did not attack, its utility in that period would have been its status quo payoff of q. Thus, D is dissatisfied if its per-period expected payoff to attacking is greater than its per-period status quo payoff, i.e., $p - d > q$.

Similarly, S's per-period expected payoff to attacking is the utility it receives from winning, which is 1, times the probability that it prevails plus the payoff to defeat, which is 0, times the probability that it loses less the cost of fighting s. In symbols, $1 \cdot (1 - p) + 0 \cdot p - s = 1 - p - s$. S, therefore, is dissatisfied if this payoff is greater than its per-period status quo payoff, i.e., if $1 - p - s > 1 - q$.

Although the particular terms vary, the distinction between satisfied and dissatisfied states is an old one in international relations theory (Schweller 1996, 98). Carr ([1939], 1954) used exactly these terms, whereas Morgenthau ([1948], 1967) distinguished between imperialistic and status-quo powers. Kissinger (1957b) differentiated between revolutionary and status-quo states. And Wolfers (1962) separated revisionist from status-quo states. Despite the different terms, these scholars generally emphasized that whether or not a state is satisfied depends on both the distribution of power and the benefits that state derives from the status quo. The definition of satisfaction employed here simply formalizes this idea. For example, whether D is formally satisfied or not depends on the distribution of power p, D's status quo benefits q, and its cost of fighting. Should the distribution of power change, a once satisfied state may become dissatisfied or vice-versa. (Chapter 4 examines how states cope with shifts in the distribution of power between them.)

Figure 3.3 depicts a situation in which D is dissatisfied and S is satisfied with the status quo, given the underlying distribution of power. The status quo is at q and D initially controls all of the territory to the left of q. However, D's per-period payoff to fighting, which is equivalent to the payoff it would receive from controlling the territory to the left of $p - d$, is larger than its status quo payoff to controlling q. Thus, D prefers fighting and is dissatisfied. By contrast, S is satisfied. Its per-period payoff to fighting is $1 - p - s$. Rewriting this payoff as $1 - (p + s)$ shows that it is

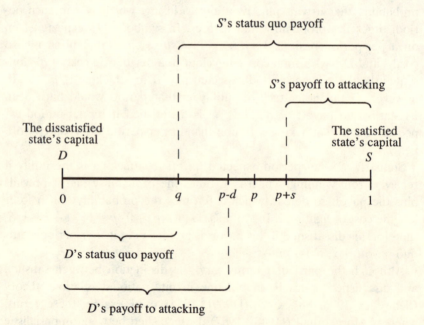

Figure 3.3 The states' satisfaction with the status quo

equal to the payoff to controlling the territory to the right of $p + s$ and is, therefore, less than S's status quo payoff of controlling the territory to the right of q.

Figure 3.3 also shows that at most, only one state at a time can be dissatisfied. Both states cannot be dissatisfied simultaneously. To see this suppose that D is dissatisfied. Then q lies to the left of $p - d$, i.e., $q < p - d$. But $p - d$ lies to the left of $p + s$ because $p - d$ is less than $p + s$. Thus, q lies to the left of $p + s$, which implies that S is satisfied. Less algebraically and more substantively, if both states were dissatisfied, each state's payoff to fighting would be larger than its payoff to living with the status quo. Thus, the sum of their payoffs to fighting would be larger than the sum of their payoffs to living with the status quo. But this cannot be. Because fighting is costly, the sum of the states' payoffs if they fight must be less than the sum of their payoffs if they do not fight.[8]

Because both states cannot be dissatisfied simultaneously, we only need to consider two cases in analyzing the bargaining. Both states are satisfied in the first, and one state is dissatisfied in the second. Even if both states are satisfied, each would still like to revise the territorial status quo in its favor. More territory is better than less. But neither state is willing to use force to do so, because the payoff to living with the status quo is at least as high as the expected payoff to attacking. Nevertheless, a state still might try to secure a favorable revision by threatening to use force. With complete information, however, any such threat will be recognized as an inherently incredible bluff, because each state knows the other's payoffs and, therefore, that it is unwilling to use force. Because these threats are known to be bluffs, they will not be taken seriously and no concessions will be made. When both states are satisfied and there are no informational asymmetries, the status quo remains unchanged and there is no risk of war.

Now suppose that one state, say D, is dissatisfied and consider the decision confronting the satisfied state S. (Since only one state can be dissatisfied, D and S will henceforth be referred to as the dissatisfied and satisfied states, respectively.) The satisfied state S has a simple, if stark, choice. It can refuse to meet the dissatisfied state's minimal demands, go

---

[8] The result that both states cannot be dissatisfied simultaneously depends on the assumption that the states are not risk acceptant. If the states "enjoy" risk or derive utility from it, then the sum of their payoffs to fighting, which includes the enjoyment of running the risk of war, could at least in principle overcome the losses due to the costs of fighting.

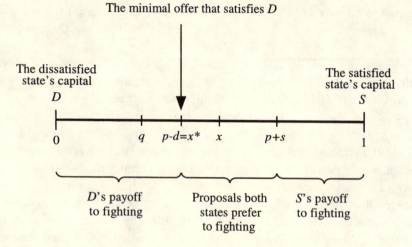

Figure 3.4 Satisfying *D*'s minimal demands

to war, and receive a payoff of $1 - p - s$. Or, the satisfied state can offer its adversary enough to ensure that it no longer finds fighting worthwhile. To do so, *S* has to concede enough territory so that *D* would rather accept this concession than fight. That is, *S* must propose withdrawing from *q* to a new territorial division *x*, which *D* prefers to fighting.

To describe the territorial divisions that meet this condition, recall that the dissatisfied state's payoff to fighting is equivalent to that of controlling all of the territory to the left of $p - d$. If, therefore, *S* is going to offer enough to make fighting unprofitable, *S* must withdraw to at least $p - d$. Hence, *x* must satisfy the condition $x \geq p - d$, and figure 3.4 illustrates the range of proposals that meet this condition. But, the more the satisfied state concedes, the less it will have. Consequently, *S* will not concede more than the minimal amount necessary to ensure that fighting is unprofitable for *D*. Accordingly, the satisfied state will offer to withdraw to $x^* = p - d$ if it decides to appease the dissatisfied state.[9]

Note the proposed agreement x^* is approximately equal to *p* if the cost of fighting *d* is not too large. *Agreements—if they can be had—generally reflect the underlying distribution of power.* This, of course, is an

---

[9] Technically, the dissatisfied state's payoffs to fighting and accepting x^* are equal, so the dissatisfied state is indifferent between these two courses of action. In equilibrium, however, this state accepts x^* (for otherwise the satisfied state could have done better by offering slightly more than x^* instead of offering exactly x^*).

old idea in international relations theory, as E. H. Carr's ([1939], 1954, 102–7) discussion of the Locarno Treaty (1925) illustrates. This treaty guaranteed the existing borders of Belgium, France, and Germany, as well as the demilitarization of the Rhineland, and Carr's analysis of its history is worth quoting at length:

> The history of the Locarno Treaty is a simple and revealing illustration of the workings of power politics. The first proposal for a treaty guaranteeing Germany's western frontier was made by Germany in December 1922, and was emphatically rejected by [France's foreign minister] Poincaré. At this period (it was the eve of the Ruhr invasion), Germany had everything to fear from France; France had nothing to fear from a helpless Germany; and the treaty had no attraction for France. Two years later the position had changed. The Ruhr invasion had brought little profit to France, and had left her perplexed as to the next step. Germany might one day be powerful again. Germany, on the other hand, still feared the military supremacy of France, and hankered after a guarantee. It was the psychological moment when French fear of Germany was about equally balanced by Germany's fear of France; and a treaty which had not been possible two years before and would not have been possible five years later, was now welcome to both....
>
> Ten years after its conclusion, the delicate balance on which it rested had disappeared. France feared Germany more than ever. But Germany no longer feared anything from France. The treaty no longer had any meaning for Germany save as an affirmation of the demilitarisation clause of the Versailles Treaty which she could now hope to overthrow. The only part of the Locarno Treaty which still corresponded to the situation of power politics was the British guarantee to France and Belgium. This was repeated by Great Britain after the rest of the treaty had been denounced by Germany. (1954, 105–6)

In brief, France initially rejected the treaty because it failed to reflect the underlying distribution of power, which favored France at the time. Once circumstances changed and the benefits associated with the treaty reflected the underlying distribution of power, France and Germany agreed to it. Germany then abandoned the treaty when it no longer reflected the underlying distribution of power.

Given the stark choice between fighting and conceding $x^* = p - d$, S will satisfy D's minimal demands if S's payoff to doing so is greater than the payoff to fighting. Figure 3.4 shows this to be the case. S's payoff to fighting is equivalent to its controlling the territory to the right of $p + s$, whereas it will control all of the territory to the right of x^* if it appeases D.[10]

When information is complete, the states do not fight in the model because the payoff to appeasing the dissatisfied state is larger. This result follows from two observations. First, because fighting is costly, there is effectively more to be divided if the states can agree to a peaceful resolution. This additional amount is the "surplus" saved by not fighting and makes a peaceful settlement preferable. Again, Carr captures the idea:

> If the *relations of power* between the leading European powers in 1877 made it inevitable that Bulgaria should be deprived of much of the territory allocated to her by the Treaty of San Stefano, then it was preferable that this result be brought about by discussions round a table in Berlin than by a war with between Great Britain and Austria-Hungry on one side and Russia on the other. (1954, 219, emphasis added)[11]

Second, in order to appease the dissatisfied state, the satisfied state in the model has to concede only enough so that the total territory the dissatisfied state controls is equivalent in value to its payoff to fighting, i.e., $x^* = p - d$. The dissatisfied state accepts this offer because fighting is no longer profitable. Accepting x^*, however, leaves the dissatisfied state no better-off than it would have been had it fought. Accordingly, whatever surplus is saved by not fighting goes to the satisfied state, and the payoff derived from obtaining this surplus is what makes the satisfied state prefer meeting the dissatisfied state's minimal demand.

Summarizing the equilibrium outcome of the bargaining game when it is not plagued by informational problems:

Proposition 3.1: *With complete information, bargaining never breaks down in war, and the states never fight in equilibrium. If both states*

---

[10] More formally, S prefers to meet D's minimal demands if its payoff to doing so is greater than its payoff to fighting, i.e., if $1 - x^* > 1 - p - s$ or, equivalently, if $p + s > x^*$. But x^* equals $p - d$ and can be rewritten as $x^* = p + s - (d + s)$, which is less than $p + s$ if $d + s > 0$. Accordingly, the satisfied state's payoff to appeasing its adversary is larger than its payoff to fighting as long as fighting is costly, i.e., as long as $d + s > 0$.

[11] After its defeat in the Russo-Turkish War, Turkey agreed in the Treaty of San Stefano (1888) to Russia's demands for the creation of a "Big Bulgaria." Britain, however, objected and demanded that Bulgaria be divided along the Balkan mountains. According to A. J. P. Taylor, the important thing for Britain "was to show that Russia did not dominate the Balkans" (1963, 249).

are satisfied, neither can credibly threaten to use force to revise the status quo and the status quo goes unchanged. If one of the states is dissatisfied, the satisfied state offers the dissatisfied state control over an amount equivalent in value to its payoff to fighting. The dissatisfied state accepts this offer, and the status quo is peacefully revised in its favor.

In brief, a satisfied state faces a simple, if unpleasant, choice when there are no informational problems and it is bargaining with a dissatisfied state. The satisfied state can meet the dissatisfied state's minimal demands by offering concessions that make fighting unprofitable for the dissatisfied state. Or, the satisfied state can refuse to appease the dissatisfied state and go to war. Because fighting is costly, the satisfied state prefers to revise the status quo in the dissatisfied state's favor and thereby avert war. The next section examines how informational asymmetries affect this outcome.

Bargaining with Asymmetric Information

With complete information, bargaining in the model never results in war regardless of the distribution of power. The satisfied state always offers the dissatisfied state just enough to appease it. By contrast, bargaining can end in war if there is asymmetric information, because the satisfied state is uncertain of what is needed to appease the dissatisfied state. This uncertainty creates a risk-return trade-off. The more the satisfied state offers, the less likely the dissatisfied state is to attack; but the more the satisfied state offers, the lower its payoff is if the offer is accepted. The satisfied state must therefore balance these two effects when deciding how much to offer, and the result is that the satisfied state often accepts some risk of war. The relation between the likelihood of war the distribution of power is now a live issue.

This section does three things. It formally introduces asymmetric information into the model. The states will no longer be sure of each other's cost of using force. Second, the definition of what it means to be dissatisfied is refined in light of this uncertainty. Finally, the equilibrium of the asymmetric-information bargaining game is described. The states' equilibrium strategies specify what offers the states make, what offers they accept, and the circumstances in which they would resort to force. The next section then uses these strategies to determine the probability that the bargaining breaks down in war as a function of the underlying distribution of power.

To introduce asymmetric information, each state is assumed to be uncertain of the other state's cost of fighting. In particular, the satisfied state is unsure of the dissatisfied state's cost of fighting d. (Information is asymmetric, because the latter is assumed to know its own cost.) Although uncertain of the exact value of d, the satisfied state has beliefs about its adversary's costs. These beliefs will be represented by a probability distribution. Suppose, for example, that the satisfied state S begins the bargaining believing that D's cost cannot be below a certain level, say, $\underline{d}$, and cannot be above some upper limit of, say, $\overline{d}$. That is, S believes that D's cost is bounded between $\underline{d}$ and $\overline{d}$. Suppose, further, that the satisfied state thinks that no particular value in this range is more likely than any other. Then these beliefs can be represented formally by assuming D's cost of fighting follows a uniform probability distribution over the interval $\underline{d}$ to $\overline{d}$. Uniform distributions are especially easy to work with and will be used for the remainder of this chapter. (Appendix 3 shows that the results derived here for uniform distributions also hold for more general distributions.) Similarly, the dissatisfied state is unsure of the satisfied state's cost of fighting s but believes that it is uniformly distributed between $\underline{s}$ and $\overline{s}$.

Although d and s have been described as the states' costs of fighting, these parameters also have a more general interpretation. The lower d, the higher D's payoff to fighting. Accordingly, d can be interpreted more broadly as a measure of the dissatisfied state's willingness to use force or of its resolve. That is, the lower d, the more willing D is to use force and the greater its resolve. Thus, the game may be seen more generally as a model of bargaining between two states that are unsure of each other's willingness to use force.

The introduction of asymmetric information necessitates a more refined definition of what it means to be dissatisfied. From S's perspective, D can be any one of a range of types with costs running from $\underline{d}$ to $\overline{d}$. That is, the satisfied state is unsure of its adversary's type where D's type is its cost of fighting. Similarly, D is uncertain of S's type where S's type is its cost of fighting. *A player-type is dissatisfied if it prefers fighting to the status quo.* So, type d' of D is dissatisfied if $p - d' > q$, and type s' of S is dissatisfied if $1 - p - s' > 1 - q$. A player is potentially dissatisfied if there is some chance that it prefers fighting to the status quo. That is, a state is *potentially dissatisfied* if its toughest type is dissatisfied. Consequently, D is potentially dissatisfied if $p - \underline{d} > q$, and S is potentially dissatisfied if $1 - p - \underline{s} > 1 - q$. As in the complete-information case, at most only one state can be potentially dissatisfied.[12]

Turning to an analysis of the bargaining, the outcome is clear if both states are satisfied. Although each state is uncertain of the other's exact cost of fighting, each is sure that the other's cost is so high that the other state will not fight to overturn the status quo. Thus, neither state can credibly threaten to use force to change the status quo. As in the complete-information case, the status quo goes unchanged if both states are satisfied.

Now suppose that one of the states, say S, is satisfied and that the other, D, is potentially dissatisfied. In the equilibrium of the bargaining game illustrated in figure 3.2, the satisfied state's initial offer maximizes its expected payoff. In order to derive this offer, we first determine the satisfied state's expected payoff to making an arbitrary concession x and then find the offer that maximizes this payoff.[13]

The satisfied state's payoff to offering x depends on how its adversary reacts to it. Lemma 3.1 below shows that the potentially dissatisfied state never rejects an offer in order to make a counter-offer if it is *actually* dissatisfied. D always either accepts the offer on the table or attacks if it is truly dissatisfied, i.e., if $p - d > q$.

D's response to S's offer is still simpler if it is actually satisfied: it accepts any concession that the satisfied state makes. To see why, suppose S offered a concession, i.e., proposed an x greater than the status quo, and that D is actually satisfied. Because D, unbeknownst to S, is actually satisfied, D will certainly not attack as it prefers the status quo to attacking. Accordingly, D will either accept x or make a counter-offer.

Given this choice, D always does better by accepting x. Doing so assures D of x whereas rejecting x in order to make a counter-offer is sure to leave D worse-off. *For if D were to make a counter-offer to x, the satisfied state would infer from this counter-offer that D is satisfied because (by lemma 3.1) D would have either accepted x or attacked if it were truly dissatisfied.* Based on this inference, S would correctly conclude that D is unwilling to use force to overturn the status quo. S, therefore, would be unwilling to make any concessions to D, and the status quo would not be

---

[12] To see that both states cannot be potentially dissatisfied simultaneously, note that if they were then the most resolute types of each, i.e., $\underline{d}$ and $\underline{s}$, would actually have to be dissatisfied. But the argument given above for the complete-information case shows that this is impossible.

[13] Appendix 3 shows that it makes no difference whether the satisfied or dissatisfied state makes the initial offer.

revised. Thus, D would end up with q rather than x and would be worse-off by having made a counter-offer. Because countering a concession is sure to leave D worse-off, it never does.

In sum, the potentially dissatisfied state never counters a concession. It either accepts the concession or attacks. Accordingly, the satisfied state's expected payoff to offering x is its payoff if this offer is rejected times the probability of rejection plus its payoff if this offer is accepted weighted by the probability that the offer is accepted.

To characterize the probability that D rejects x, observe that D would fight rather than accept x if the payoff to fighting is larger. In symbols, D's payoff to fighting is the discounted sum $(p - d) + \delta(p - d) + \delta^2(p - d) + \cdots$, and its payoff to accepting x is $x + \delta x + \delta^2 x + \cdots$. So, D attacks if $p - d > x$ or, equivalently, if $d < p - x$. Thus, the probability that D rejects x is the probability that d is less than $p - x$.

This probability is easy to calculate since d is uniformly distributed between $\underline{d}$ and $\overline{d}$. If, for example, the value of $p - x$ is halfway between $\underline{d}$ and $\overline{d}$, then the probability that d is less than $p - x$ is one-half. If the value of $p - x$ is one-third of the way from $\underline{d}$ to $\overline{d}$, then the probability that d is less than $p - x$ is one-third. And, if $x - p$ is two-thirds of the way to $\overline{d}$, then the probability that d is less than $p - x$ is two-thirds. More generally, the fraction of the way $p - x$ is to from $\underline{d}$ to $\overline{d}$ is the distance from $\underline{d}$ and $p - x$ divided by the distance from $\underline{d}$ and $\overline{d}$. Thus, the probability that D rejects x and attacks is $((p - x) - \underline{d})/(\overline{d} - \underline{d})$. Since D will either accept x or reject it by attacking, the probability that D accepts x is one minus the probability that it rejects x, or $1 - [((p - x) - \underline{d})/(\overline{d} - \underline{d})]$.

The satisfied state's payoff to offering x follows directly from these probabilities. S obtains a per-period payoff of $1 - x$ if its offer is accepted and a per-period payoff of $1 - p - s$ if its offer is rejected and D attacks. Thus, S's expected payoff to offering x is its total payoff if the offer is accepted, which is $\sum_{t=0}^{\infty} \delta^t(1 - x)$, weighted by the probability of acceptance plus the total payoff if the offer is rejected, which is $\sum_{t=0}^{\infty} \delta^t(1 - p - s)$, times the probability of rejection. Letting $U_S(x)$ denote this expected payoff gives:

$$U_S(x) = \left(\sum_{t=0}^{\infty} \delta^t(1 - x) \right) \left[1 - \frac{p - x - \underline{d}}{\overline{d} - \underline{d}} \right]$$

$$+ \left(\sum_{t=0}^{\infty} \delta^t(1 - p - s) \right) \left[\frac{p - x - \underline{d}}{\overline{d} - \underline{d}} \right].$$

Simplifying this expression then leaves:[14]

$$U_S(x) = \left(\frac{1-x}{1-\delta}\right)\left[1 - \frac{p-x-\underline{d}}{\overline{d}-\underline{d}}\right] + \left(\frac{1-p-s}{1-\delta}\right)\left[\frac{p-x-\underline{d}}{\overline{d}-\underline{d}}\right]. \quad (3.2)$$

The expression for $U_S(x)$ embodies the risk-return trade-off confronting the satisfied state. The more it offers, the larger x and the lower its payoff if this offer is accepted, i.e., the smaller $(1-x)/(1-\delta)$ is. But the more the satisfied state offers, the higher the probability that the offer will be accepted, that is, the larger $1-[((p-x)-\underline{d})/(\overline{d}-\underline{d})]$ is.

S's optimal offer balances these opposing factors. More formally, S offers the x that maximizes the payoff $U_S(x)$. This optimal offer is denoted by x^* and can be obtained by differentiating the function $U_S(x)$ with respect to x. This gives:

$$x^* = p + \frac{s - \overline{d}}{2} \quad (3.3)$$

where x^* must be at least as large as q.[15]

As was the case with complete information, agreements, if they can be had, reflect the underlying distribution of power. That is, x^* is close to p if the state's costs s and $\overline{d}$ are not too large or too different. Expression 3.3 also shows that the satisfied state offers more to more powerful adversaries. That is, the larger p, the more S offers (i.e., the larger x^* is). Similarly, the less resolute the satisfied state (i.e., the larger s), the more it offers. Indeed, if the satisfied state is quite irresolute (s is high), it offers enough to be certain of appeasing the dissatisfied state and thereby eliminating any danger of war. If the satisfied state is more resolute, it makes some concessions and runs some risk of war.

Summarizing the results about bargaining when one of the states is potentially dissatisfied and there are informational asymmetries:

Proposition 3.2: *In equilibrium, the potentially dissatisfied state never rejects an offer in order to make a counter-offer. Accordingly, when the*

---

[14] The key to simplifying this expression is the fact that if a is a positive number less than one and k is any number, then the sum $\sum_{t=0}^{\infty} a^t k = k/(1-a)$. Accordingly, S's payoff to fighting, $\sum_{t=0}^{\infty} \delta^t(1-p-s)$, can be be written more simply as $(1-p-s)/(1-\delta)$ by letting $a = \delta$ and $k = 1-p-s$. Similarly S's payoff if x is accepted can also be written more compactly as $\sum_{t=0}^{\infty} \delta^t(1-x) = (1-x)/(1-\delta)$ by letting $a = \delta$ and $k = 1-x$.

[15] Strictly speaking, the analysis of S's optimal offer has assumed that S was making a concession, i.e., that $x > q$. It is tedious to show and left to appendix 3 to do, but x^* is also the optimal offer when S can make demands as well as proposals, i.e., when x can be greater than, less than, or equal to q.

satisfied state makes the initial offer in the game, its payoff to offering x is given by $U_S(x)$ in expression 3.2, and the satisfied state proposes $x^* = p + (s - \bar{d})/2$, which maximizes $U_S(x)$. If D prefers fighting to accepting x^*, i.e., if D's cost of fighting d is less than $p - x^*$, then D rejects x^* and attacks. Otherwise, D accepts x^*. Thus, the probability of war is the probability that the potentially dissatisfied state's cost of fighting is less than $p - x^*$.

The forgoing discussion has been based on the assumption that a potentially dissatisfied state never rejects an offer in order to make a counter-offer if it is *actually* dissatisfied. The remainder of this section justifies this claim. Alas, the justification turns much more on some properties of games and not on substantive insights about bargaining, so readers less interested in the formalities of games may want to skip the rest of this section.

Lemma 3.1: *The potentially dissatisfied state never rejects an offer in order to make a counter-offer.*

Argument: The demonstration proceeds by contradiction. We will assume that the claim does not hold and show that this assumption subsequently leads to a contradiction.

If the claim does not hold, then there is an equilibrium in which S makes a proposal, say z, and some player-type of D that is actually dissatisfied, say d_z, counters this offer. Let r be the toughest or most resolute type to counter z. That is, of all the types of D that counter z, r is the one with the smallest cost. Therefore r is also dissatisfied because its cost of fighting is at most d_z, and d_z is assumed to be dissatisfied. Figure 3.5 represents the situation. S has offered z at some time c, which r has rejected in order to counter.

Note that when making this counter-offer, r could have attacked instead and thereby obtained a payoff of $A_D(c)$, which is defined in expression 3.1. As will be shown momentarily, this payoff is larger than what r receives by countering z. Thus, r has a positive incentive to deviate from its purported equilibrium strategy of countering z. This is a contradiction, as no player can have an incentive to deviate from its equilibrium strategy, and this contradiction establishes the claim made in the lemma.

To see that r's payoff to attacking is larger than its payoff to countering, observe that if it counters z, then the game can subsequently end in one of only two ways. Either the states fight at some future

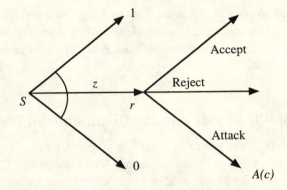

Figure 3.5 The consequences of countering an offer

date, or they reach a peaceful settlement. Consider the first possibility in which the states eventually fight at, say, a later date of f.
Clearly fighting later means living with the status quo longer. But
r's per-period payoff to fighting is greater than its per-period payoff
to living with the status quo, i.e., $p - r > q$, because r is actually dissatisfied. Consequently, r prefers fighting sooner by not countering
z at time c rather than countering z and fighting later. In symbols,
$A_D(c) > A_D(f)$ since $f > c$ and $p - r > q$.

Suppose now that r's countering z leads to a peaceful resolution. Keeping in mind that r is the most resolute type that makes a
counter-offer, consider what concession the satisfied state might be
willing to make. In the equilibrium of a game, each actor knows
what the other actors' strategies are and plays optimally against
those strategies. If, therefore, the dissatisfied state counters z, the
satisfied state, knowing the other state's strategy, infers that r is the
most resolute type it might now be facing. Based on this inference,
the satisfied state would never concede more than the minimum
amount needed to appease the most resolute type it might be facing,
namely r. In symbols, S would never offer more than $x_{max} = p - r$,
which is r's per-period payoff to fighting.

This means that if r counters z and the bargaining eventually
ends peacefully at the later time a, the most that r could hope to
attain is control over an amount of territory x_{max} at a where x_{max} is
equal in value to its payoff to fighting. Thus, r's payoff to agreeing
to x_{max} at a is equal to its payoff to living with the status quo until
a and then fighting. But we have just seen that r prefers the payoff
to fighting earlier rather than later. Hence, r prefers fighting when

z is offered to countering it even if the bargaining ultimately ends peacefully. Because r prefers attacking to countering z no matter how the game might subsequently end, r would never counter z in equilibrium. ■

The Probability of War and the Distribution of Power

When one state is unsure of another's willingness to use force, it faces a trade-off. The more it offers, the more likely the concession is to be accepted and the lower the risk of war. But offering more also means having less if the proposal is accepted. The previous section showed that the satisfied state balances these competing pressures by offering x^* and that the probability of war equals the probability that the dissatisfied state counters this offer by attacking. This section studies how the probability of war varies with changes in the distribution of power and compares these results with the expectations of the balance-of-power and preponderance-of-power schools. It also suggests one possible explanation for the equivocal results of statistical efforts to determine the relation between the likelihood of war and the distribution of power.

As will be seen, the results derived from the model contradict the claims made by both the balance-of-power and preponderance-of-power schools. But, there is an important qualification. Some arguments about the relation between the risk of war and the distribution of power emphasize states' alignment decisions and the number of coalitions that could form to block any state's bid for hegemony. For example, the larger the number of states and the more even the distribution of power, the larger the number of potential blocking coalitions and the less likely war (Levy 1989, 231–32; Mansfield 1994, 17–18; Wright [1942], 1965, 755). The formal analysis of these arguments clearly requires a model with more than two states and is, therefore, beyond the scope of this chapter. Elements of these arguments will be examined in chapter 5 where we investigate states' alignment decisions.

It is, however, important to emphasize that although some arguments about the relation between the distribution of power and the probability of war presuppose the existence of more than two states, other arguments do not. Wright, for example, explicitly considers the situation in which there are only two states. In this case, balance-of-power theory expects that "there would be great instability unless they [i.e., the two states] were very nearly equal in power or their frontiers were widely separated or difficult to pass" (755). Similarly, Mearsheimer considers the case of two Great Powers and claims that a balance of power makes war less likely: "Power can be more or less equally distributed among the major powers of both bipolar and multipolar systems. *Both* are more peaceful when equality is greatest among the poles" (1990, 18, emphasis added). In sum, the conflicting claims of the balance-of-power and preponderance-of-power schools apply to systems in which there are only two states, as well as to systems with more than two states.

The probability of war depends on one's perspective. From the point of view of a state that knows what it is going to offer, the probability of war is the chance that the dissatisfied state rejects the offer by attacking. But from the perspective of an outside observer who is trying to determine the relation between the probability of war and the distribution of power, the risk of war derives from two sources. The first is the size of the concession that the satisfied state will actually make. As expression 3.3 shows, the lower the satisfied state's cost s, the smaller the offer. But an outside observer, like the dissatisfied state, is unsure of s and therefore unsure of what will be offered.[16] The second source of uncertainty is, of course, the dissatisfied state's cost, which determines whether or not a specific offer will be accepted. Thus, the probability of war when examined from the perspective of an outside observer depends on both the likelihood that any particular offer will be made and on the chances that this offer will be countered with an attack.

When these two sources are taken into account, the probability of war in the model turns out to be a simple function of the *disparity* between the distribution of power and the status quo distribution of territory, which can be measured by the absolute value of the difference between the distributions of power and benefits, $|p - q|$. If this disparity is small, the distribution of benefits mirrors the distribution of power. Both states are satisfied, as neither can expect to gain from the use of force, and there is no risk of war. As this disparity grows, one state eventually becomes dissatisfied. At that point, the other state confronts the risk-return trade-off, and there is some danger of war. Indeed, as the disparity between the distributions of power and benefits grows still larger, the risk of war generally increases until it flattens out at some maximal level.

---

[16] If there were some way for an outside observer to determine a state's cost or resolve, then it also seems reasonable to assume that that state's adversary could also make this determination by looking at the same indicators the outside observer did. But if this were the case, then the informational problems would disappear.

Figure 3.6a plots the relation between the probability of war and the distribution of power if the dissatisfied state's status quo share of territory is $\frac{1}{3}$; i.e., if $q = \frac{1}{3}$.[17] This distribution of benefits reflects the underlying distribution of power when p also equals one-third. In these circumstances, there is no disparity between the distributions of power and benefits, i.e., $|p - q| = 0$, and both states are satisfied. Thus the probability of war is zero at $p = \frac{1}{3}$ in figure 3.6a. Indeed, the probability of war remains zero as long as p and q are approximately equal and the disparity is correspondingly small.[18] As p diverges still farther from $\frac{1}{3}$, the disparity grows and eventually the most resolute type of one of the states becomes dissatisfied. At this point, the other state begins to face a risk-return trade-off, and there is some chance of war. As the disparity grows still more, more types become dissatisfied, and the risk of war rises.

Figures 3.6b and 3.6c graph the relation between the probability of war and the distribution of power when the dissatisfied state's status quo share is $\frac{1}{2}$ and $\frac{2}{3}$. The probability of war in these figures exhibits the same overall pattern as that in figure 3.6a. When the distribution of benefits mirrors the underlying distribution of power as it does at $p = \frac{1}{3}$ in figure 3.6a, $p = \frac{1}{2}$ in figure 3.6b, and $p = \frac{2}{3}$ in figure 3.6c, the probability of war is zero because both states are satisfied. As p begins to diverge from q, the probability of war begins to grow.

These results clearly contradict the expectations of both the balance-of-power and the preponderance-of-power schools. As illustrated in figure 3.7a, the preponderance-of-power school expects the probability of war to be smallest when one of the states is predominant (that is, when p is large or small) and to increase as the distribution of power becomes more even (that is, as p approaches $\frac{1}{2}$). But in the case analyzed here, the probability of war is smallest at $p = q$ and generally largest when one of the states is preponderant.

Figure 3.7b illustrates the balance-of-power school's expectations. The probability of war is smallest when there is a roughly even distribution of power (p is approximately $\frac{1}{2}$) and increases as the distribution of power becomes skewed. These expectations correspond to the formal results derived here only in the special circumstance in which the status quo

---

[17] The graphs in figure 3.6 are based on the assumption that the states' costs s and d are uniformly distributed between .05 and .95.

[18] D is satisfied if $p - \underline{d} \leq q$ or, equivalently, if $p - q \leq \underline{d}$. S is satisfied if $1 - p - \underline{s} \leq 1 - q$ or $q - p \leq \underline{s}$. Consequently, both states will be satisfied if the disparity $|p - q|$ is less than or equal to the smaller of $\underline{d}$ and $\underline{s}$.

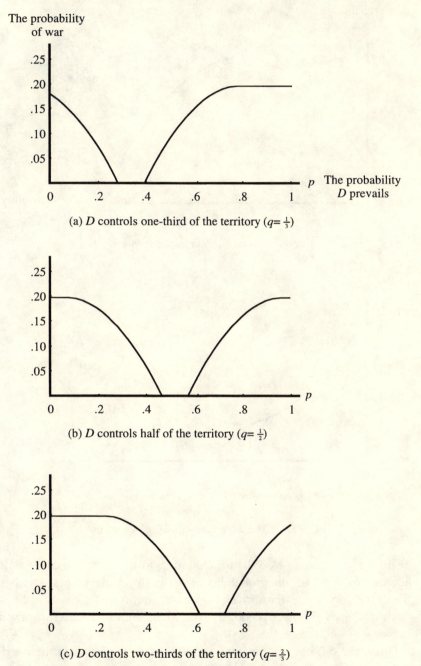

(a) *D* controls one-third of the territory ($q=\frac{1}{3}$)

(b) *D* controls half of the territory ($q=\frac{1}{2}$)

(c) *D* controls two-thirds of the territory ($q=\frac{2}{3}$)

Figure 3.6 The probability of war and the distribution of power

The probability
    of war

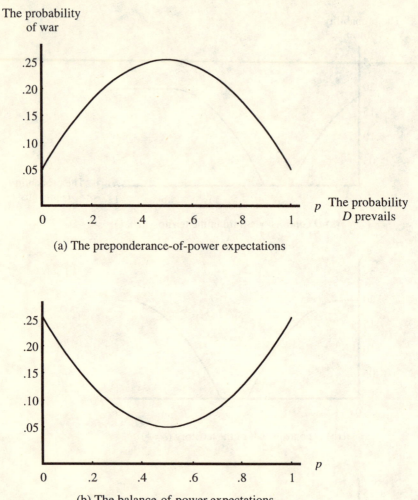

(a) The preponderance-of-power expectations

(b) The balance-of-power expectations

Figure 3.7 The expectations of the two schools

division is even ($q = \frac{1}{2}$). When the status quo division is uneven, as in figures 3.6a and 3.6c, the probability of war in the model is smallest when the distribution of power mirrors the uneven status quo division and not, as the balance-of-power school asserts, when the distribution of power is even.

Given the different predictions about the relation between the distribution of power and the likelihood of war, it is natural to try to evaluate the conflicting claims empirically. Unfortunately, numerous statistical efforts to estimate this relation have failed to produce clear results.[19] Siverson and Tennefoss (1984) find an even distribution of power to be more peaceful. Ferris (1973) also concludes that an even distribution of power is weakly associated with a lower risk of war. By contrast, Kim (1991, 1992), Moul (1988), and Weede (1976) determine that a preponderance of power is more peaceful. Singer, Bremer, and Stuckey (1972) find evidence for both claims, depending on the historical period. An even distribution of power is more peace prone in the nineteenth century but less so in the twentieth century. Mansfield (1992, 1994) uncovers evidence of a nonlinear, quadratic relationship in which the probability of war is smallest when there is both an even distribution of power and a preponderance of power. The greatest instability occurs somewhere between a preponderance and a balance of power. Finally, Maoz (1983) and Bueno de Mesquita and Lalman (1988) find no significant relation between stability and the distribution of power.

These studies vary in terms of the way they operationalize and measure the variables and in terms of what independent variables they include in the analysis. Some studies also focus on dyadic interactions between two states whereas others consider the concentration of power in the system as a whole. However, these differences do not seem sufficient to account for the conflicting statistical results. Three other possibilities seem more likely. First, even if there is a consistent relation between the probability of war and the distribution of power, its overall effect may be so small that it does not appear in the data because it is overwhelmed by other factors endemic to the tumult of international politics. The effect is, statistically speaking, lost in the "noise."

A second possibility for dyadic studies is that the historical data is too badly contaminated by third-party effects. Because many of the balance-of-power and preponderance-of-power arguments as well as the bargaining model focus on the interaction of two states, the ideal data for evaluating the competing empirical claims would be a set of isolated dyads. History, alas, has not been kind enough to provide this kind of experience. Small states interact in the shadow of larger states, and Great Powers, by definition, must be concerned about what other Great Powers are doing. This suggests that the historical data that we do have may be heavily influenced by these third-party effects and, therefore, may not

[19] See Bueno de Mesquita and Lalman (1988), Geller and Singer (1998), and Levy (1989) for more extensive reviews of this work. Wagner (1994) provides a thoughtful discussion of some of the conceptual issues involved.

be very useful in evaluating these claims. Indeed, Kim (1991, 1992), Kim and Morrow (1992), and Moul (1988) find that war between two states is more likely if there is an even distribution of power between them when the strength of their allies is taken into account. But there is no significant relation between the risk of war and the distribution of power between states if we compare the relative strength of these two states by themselves.

A third reason for the mixed statistical results may be that important systematic factors have been omitted from the statistical analysis, and this omission may have led to biased and unstable estimates. Indeed, the analysis of the bargaining model points toward two such factors. In addition to the distribution of power, the probability of war in the game also depends on the status quo distribution of benefits and, as will be shown below, the technology of coercion. Thus, any attempt to assess the relation between the probability of war and the distribution of power should control for these factors. Failing to do so will lead to biased estimates if these factors are correlated with the distribution of power, which seems especially likely to be the case for the distribution of benefits.[20] But empirical efforts to estimate this relation have generally not controlled for these factors, and this omission may partially account for the equivocal empirical results.[21]

The Technology of Coercion and the Risk of War

How do changes in the technology of coercion affect the relationship between the risk of war and the distribution of power? Consider the

[20] See King, Keohane, and Verba (1994) for a discussion of this bias.

[21] Unfortunately, it is much easier to see that we need to control for the status quo distribution and the technology of coercion than it is to see how to do it. Although it is very easy to specify what we mean by offensive advantages in a simple model and then use this specification to discipline the logic of our arguments about the effects of these advantages, it has proven very difficult to operationalize this concept empirically. Levy (1984), Fearon (1995a), Glaser and Kaufmann (1998), and Van Evera (1998) discuss some of these difficulties.

It is also very difficult to measure the utility states attach to the status quo. Bueno de Mesquita and Lalman's (1992) measure of this utility may offer a start in this direction, but their current formulation is inadequate. If the states are risk neutral as assumed above, then Bueno de Mesquita and Lalman's measure reduces to assuming that the status quo distribution is always equal to $\frac{1}{2}$. (To obtain $q = \frac{1}{2}$, assume that state A is risk neutral by taking $r_A = 1$ in equation A1.3 in Bueno de Mesquita and Lalman [1992, 294].) Controlling for the status quo, however, requires the status quo to be treated as a variable across cases, and it is unclear how to do this with their measure as it is currently formulated.

effects of an increase in the cost of fighting. One tends to think intuitively that more costly outcomes are less likely, and this turns out to be the case. An increase in the cost of fighting does reduce the likelihood of war. But this simple intuition masks the complicated interaction of three competing pressures that have to be weighed to reach this "intuitively obvious" conclusion.

First, as war becomes more costly, the potentially dissatisfied state becomes more likely to accept a given offer. This tends to make war less likely. The second factor, however, points in the opposite direction. Knowing that the other state is more likely to accept a given concession, the satisfied state is inclined to concede less. This makes war more likely. Finally, the satisfied state's inclination to offer less is tempered by the fact that fighting is also more costly for it. This would seem to make fighting less likely. A model is needed to weigh the net effect of these opposing pressures.

Suppose the cost of fighting increases by c. The effect of this in the model is that every player-type's cost rises by c. If, for example, the satisfied state's cost of fighting was s, it is now $s + c$. Similarly, the cost of war for each type of the potentially dissatisfied state goes up from d to $d + c$.

Figure 3.8 depicts the effects of an increase in the cost of fighting given that $q = \frac{1}{2}$. The higher the cost of fighting, the larger the disparity must be between the distributions of power and benefits before one of the states becomes potentially dissatisfied. Accordingly, the region of complete stability around the point at which these distributions mirror each other (i.e., where $p = q$) is wider when fighting is more costly. As the disparity rises, eventually one state does become dissatisfied and the risk of war begins to rise. Nevertheless, a higher cost of fighting reduces the danger from what it would have been were war less costly.

A shift in the offense-defense balance also creates opposing pressures. Suppose the balance shifts in favor of the offense. By increasing the payoff to attacking, this shift makes a potentially dissatisfied state less likely to accept any specific offer, and war becomes more likely. But, the satisfied state, knowing this, will generally propose more favorable settlements and thereby make war less likely. The model shows that on balance a shift in favor of the offense makes war more likely.

We can introduce the offense-defense balance into the model by thinking of the probability of prevailing as being composed of two parts. The first reflects the overall distribution of power, and the second represents the offense-defense balance. Let the probability that the dissatisfied state

The probability
of war

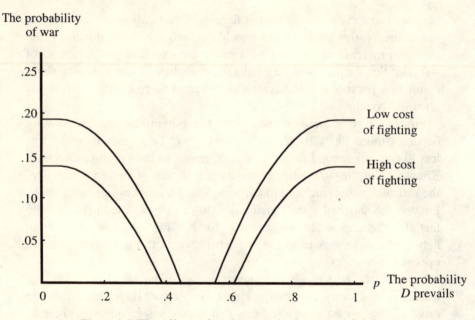

Figure 3.8 The effects of an increase in the cost of fighting

would prevail if it attacks be $p + f$ and the probability that it would prevail if it is attacked be $p - f$. As before, p measures D's overall strength.
The larger p, the more likely D is to prevail whether it attacks or is attacked. The parameter f measures the size of the offensive advantage.
The larger this advantage, the larger the difference between D's probability of prevailing if it attacks and if it is attacked. More formally, this
difference is $p + f - (p - f) = 2f$. If the offense has the advantage,
it is better to attack than be attacked and $f > 0$. If the defense has the
advantage, it is better to wait and $f < 0$. And, there are no offensive advantages if the probability of prevailing if a state attacks is the same as
if it is attacked and $f = 0$.

When the offense-defense balance is incorporated in the model, the
satisfied state's optimal offer is:

$$x^* = p + f + \frac{s - \bar{d}}{2}.$$

This expression formalizes the effect of an offensive advantage on S's
offer. The larger the offensive advantage f, the larger x^* and the more
the satisfied state offers. Figure 3.9 traces the effects of a shift in favor of
the offense on the probability of war. The region of stability around the

The probability
   of war

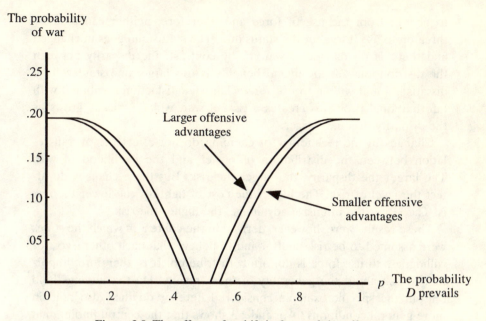

Figure 3.9 The effects of a shift in favor of the offense

point where the distribution of power mirrors the distribution of benefits
becomes narrower when the offensive advantage increases. Outside this
narrower region, the risk of war is higher if there are larger offensive
advantages.

Conclusion

When states are bargaining about revising the international status quo,
informational problems can create risk-return trade-offs. The more a
state offers another, the greater the prospects of satisfying that state's
minimal demands and thereby averting war. But the more a state concedes, the less it will have if its concession is accepted. In balancing
these factors, states often accept some risk of war. This is a calculated
risk. Miscalculation and psychological biases may exacerbate the risk.
But eliminating them would not eliminate the trade-off and the risk inherent in it.

   If the states agree to revise the status quo without war, the agreement
generally reflects the underlying distribution of power. A corollary to
this is that war is least likely when the distribution of benefits mirrors
the distribution of power. In these circumstances, neither state expects

to benefit from the use of force and, therefore, neither can credibly threaten to use it to alter the status quo. The status quo goes unchanged and there is no danger of war. If, by contrast, the disparity between the distributions of power and benefits is too large, one state will be dissatisfied and willing to use force. This dissatisfaction combined with informational problems creates a risk of war, which typically grows as the disparity becomes larger.

Changes in the technology of coercion do not affect the overall relation between the distribution of power and the likelihood of war. The larger the disparity, the larger the risk. But these changes do affect the level of risk. The higher the cost of fighting, the lower the risk is. The larger the offensive advantage, the higher the risk.

These results were, however, derived in the context in which the states were assumed to be risk neutral and to believe that each other's cost or willingness to use force is uniformly distributed. It is, therefore, important to ask about the generality of these results. Do the findings hold only in the specific example considered here or do they also hold in more general conditions? Appendix 3 shows that the central finding that the probability of war is at a minimum when the distribution of power mirrors the status quo distribution is quite robust. It obtains as long as the states are risk neutral or risk averse, regardless of the particular shapes of the states' utility functions or of the particular shapes of the probability distributions representing their beliefs. By contrast, the relation between the likelihood of war and disparity between the distributions of power and benefits appears to be less robust and is discussed further in chapter 6 (pp. 208–9).

Finally, the model analyzed in this chapter poses a question it cannot help answer. The analysis highlights the importance of disparities between the distributions of power and benefits. But where do these disparities come from? If a shift in the distribution of power is creating a disparity, why does the declining state allow it to grow? Why does this state not launch a preventive war to stop the other state before it becomes too strong? The present formulation cannot address these issues because the distribution of power p is assumed to be constant throughout the interaction. The next chapter examines how states cope with a shift in the distribution of power.

4

Bargaining in the Shadow
of Shifting Power

The previous chapter emphasized the importance of the relation between the distributions of power and benefits. Peace is most likely to
prevail if the distribution of benefits reflects the underlying distribution
of power. But the distribution of power rarely remains fixed in international politics. Great Powers rise and fall.[1]

Uneven rates of economic growth and development eventually manifest themselves in changes in the distribution of power, and these shifts
may lead to disparities between the distributions of power and benefits.
A state once weak but now strong may become dissatisfied with the existing international order. As a result, that state may demand that the
status quo be revised in its favor. Should these demands go unmet, the
rising state may resort to force to try to impose a new, more favorable
international order.

Shifts in the distribution of power have long been seen as a significant source of stress in the international system and an important cause
of war. The rise of Athenian power led to conflict with Sparta and, in
Thucydides' view, to the Peloponnesian War. The growth of German industrial might at the end of the nineteenth century and the friction it
created underlay the First World War. Paul Kennedy summarizes the
dilemma:

> Even if there had not existed those domestic tensions which pushed
> the German establishment towards external adventures before 1914
> and simultaneously increased the fears of influential Britons about
> national decline, the problem of Germany's "proper" place in Europe
> and the world would have been an immensely troublesome one, simply
> because its industrial growth would have brought with it quasi-political
> influence over its smaller neighbors. (1980, 470)[2]

---

[1] Kennedy (1987) provides a historical overview of the shifting distribution of economic
and military power among the Great Powers and its effects on international conflict.
Kindleberger (1996) surveys some of the sources of economic primacy and decline.

[2] Howard (1984, 19) reaches similar conclusions.

China's rapid economic growth at the end of the twentieth century has also begun to raise similar concerns (Betts 1993/94; Brzezinski 1997; Goldstein 1997/98; Huntington 1996; Nye 1998; Roy 1994).

Uneven rates of economic growth also form the basis of Gilpin's (1981) explanation of hegemonic wars, which are those fought to determine which state will dominate the international system. He reasons that as

> its relative power increases, a rising state attempts to change the rules governing the international system, the division of spheres of influence, and, most important of all, the international distribution of territory. In response, the dominant power counters this challenge through changes in its policies that attempt to restore equilibrium in the system. The historical record reveals that if it fails in this attempt, the disequilibrium will be resolved by war. (187)

Similarly, the power-transition school argues that uneven rates of socioeconomic and political development may lead to disparities between the distributions of power and benefits (Organski 1968; Organski and Kugler 1980; Kugler and Lemke 1996). When it does, the rising state may become dissatisfied, and it is this "general dissatisfaction with its position in the system, and the desire to redraft the rules by which relations among nations work, that move a country to begin a major war" (Organski and Kugler 1980, 23).[3]

How do states cope with the threats arising from a shift in the distribution of power between them? This chapter analyzes this issue by making a simple modification to the bargaining model developed in the last chapter. In that formulation, the distribution of power between the states, which was represented by the parameter p, remained constant throughout the states' interaction. In the game specified in this chapter, p varies over time. At the outset, the distributions of power and benefits initially favor one of the states. Then the distribution of power begins to shift in favor of the other state. This shift, if not redressed, eventually creates a disparity between the rising state's power and the benefits it derives from the international order.

Informational problems played a key role in the previous chapter and are critical here as well. If information were complete, the declining state would know how much it would have to concede to the rising state in

---

[3] For related arguments, see Doran and Parsons (1980), Kennedy (1987), Modelski (1987), and Thompson (1988).

order to satisfy the latter's minimal demands which, of course, will be growing over time as it becomes more powerful. Thus, the declining state would face a simple, if stark, choice, which is the dynamic analogue of the decision that the satisfied state confronted in the previous chapter. The declining state can either appease the rising state by conceding more and more or go to war.

Asymmetric information creates a now familiar risk-return trade-off. Unsure of the rising state's willingness to use force, the declining state is uncertain of what it has to concede to appease the rising state and thereby avert or at least postpone war. The more this state offers, the less likely the rising state is to attack now. But conceding more implies having less if the proposal is accepted. It also means letting the decline continue and having to fight on less favorable terms in the event of future conflict.

As will be seen, the declining state resolves this trade-off by making a series of concessions to the rising state. This solution to the risk-return trade-off usually entails some risk of war. That is, these concessions are large enough to satisfy the rising state's minimal demands if that state is relatively unwilling to use force. In these circumstances, the status quo is revised in favor of the rising state, and the shift in power passes without war. The shift in power between Britain and the United States during the nineteenth century illustrates this pattern. If, by contrast, the rising state is relatively willing to use force, the declining state's concessions are too small to appease the rising state. In this case, the states' efforts to deal with a shift in the distribution of power between them break down in war. And, the more willing the rising state is to use force, the sooner war comes.

While investigating the general problem of bargaining in the shadow of shifting power, this chapter also examines two more specific questions. The power-transition school, like the preponderance-of-power school, claims that an even distribution of power is most likely to break down in war. Consequently, the most dangerous time during a shift in the distribution of power occurs at a transition when the rising state catches up with the declining state and the two states are roughly equal in power. The first question is whether a shift in the distribution of power is most likely to end in war when there is an even distribution of territory. The power-transition school also expects that more rapid shifts in the distribution of power are more likely to end in war (Organski and Kugler 1980, 21; Levy 1987, 97–98), and the second issue is whether or not this is the case.

The following analysis shows that contrary to the claims of the power-transition school, there is nothing special about power transitions. They are not the most dangerous phase of a shift in the distribution of power. Nor are faster shifts in the distribution of power more dangerous than slower shifts. Slow shifts and fast shifts are just as likely to end in war. However, changes in the technology of coercion that make fighting more costly do make shifts in power less likely to break down in war. These formal results find general support in the data.

The next section of this chapter modifies the bargaining model developed in the previous chapter to allow for a changing distribution of power. The third and fourth sections derive the states' equilibrium strategies when there is complete and incomplete information. These strategies are then used to examine the relative danger of war during power transitions and whether faster shifts in power are more dangerous.

A Model of Bargaining in the Shadow of Shifting Power

A shift in the distribution of power presents a complicated strategic problem to the states trying to contend with it. To illustrate the complexities, suppose a declining state, D, and a rising state, R, are bargaining about revising the territorial status quo. At the outset, the distributions of power and benefits favor the declining state. Both states are, however, satisfied because the distribution of benefits mirrors the distribution of power and, therefore, neither expects to gain from using force to overturn the status quo.

Figure 4.1 summarizes this situation. At time $t = 0$ when the interaction begins, the status quo distribution of benefits q_0 mirrors the initial distribution of power $\underline{p}$, i.e., $q_0 = \underline{p}$. (The lower bar on "p" indicates that the distribution of power starts at this low level and increases from there.) The rising state R initially controls all of the territory to the left of the status quo q_0. Paralleling the analysis in the previous chapter, the rising state's expected payoff to attacking is equivalent to its payoff to controlling an amount of territory equal to its probability of prevailing less its cost of fighting. In symbols, R's payoff to striking is $\underline{p} - r$ where r denotes the rising state's cost of fighting. Clearly, the rising state prefers the status quo to fighting *given the existing distribution of power $\underline{p}$ and therefore is satisfied at this distribution of power.* The declining state is also satisfied as its expected

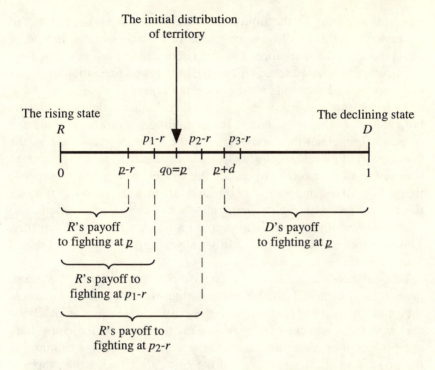

Figure 4.1 The distribution of territory and the shifting distribution of power

payoff to fighting is equivalent to its payoff to controlling the territory to the right of $\underline{p} + d$ where d is its cost of fighting.

All of this begins to change if the distribution of power starts to shift in the rising state's favor. Suppose that the rising state's probability of prevailing increases from $\underline{p}$ to p_1, then to p_2, and finally on to p_3. As depicted in figure 4.1, the shift to p_1 makes the rising state more powerful. Nevertheless, the expected payoff to fighting $p_1 - r$ is still less than the status quo payoff q_0, and therefore the rising state is still unwilling to use force. But this changes once the distribution of power shifts to p_2. The rising state is now dissatisfied and willing to use force to overturn the status quo because the expected payoff to fighting, $p_2 - r$, exceeds the status quo q_0.

What should the declining state do now that it is facing a dissatisfied state which will only become stronger over time? Should it appease the rising state or launch a preventive war against it? The former averts a war at least temporarily but also means having to deal with a still more powerful adversary in the future. Attacking makes war a certainty but at least the fighting will be done on more favorable terms. Indeed, if attacking is better than appeasing the rising state at p_2, would it have been better to have attacked still earlier when the distribution of power was $\underline{p}$ or p_1 and the rising state was even weaker?

To investigate these decisions, we modify the game developed in the last chapter. In that formulation, the distribution of power, p, remained constant throughout the interaction. In the game described below, the distribution of power initially favors one of the states and then begins to shift in favor of the other. To specify this model more precisely, suppose that the initial distributions of power and territory are $\underline{p}$ and q_0 and that the game starts with the declining state's having to decide whether to launch a preventive attack or to propose a new distribution of territory. This proposal can be represented formally as a point x_0 in the interval from zero to one in figure 4.1.

The game ends if the declining state attacks. If the declining state proposes a new territorial division instead, then the rising state can accept this offer, reject it and continue with the existing status quo, or attack the declining state. Attacking, as always, ends the game. If the rising state accepts the offer, then this becomes the new territorial status quo and the first round of the game ends. If the rising state rejects the proposal, the status quo remains unchanged and the round ends.

In the second round, the states face the same set of choices they did in the first round. However, the distribution of power has now shifted in the rising state's favor in that the probability that the rising state prevails in the event of war has increased from $\underline{p}$ to p_1. As in the first round, the declining state can either end the game by attacking or it can propose a distribution of benefits x_1. If D does make a proposal, the rising state can respond by attacking, accepting the offer, or rejecting it and continuing with the present division of territory. If the rising state does not attack, the game moves to the third round and continues in this way as long as neither of the states attacks.

Figure 4.2 depicts the situation at time t. The declining state can attack or make a proposal, which is denoted by x_t. The rising state must then decide to attack, accept the offer, or reject it. If neither state attacks, play moves on to the next round.[4]

---

[4] This sequence of moves is simpler than that in the bargaining model studied in the previous chapter. Only the declining state can make proposals in the present formulation, whereas both states could make offers in the previous model. This assumption is made for purely technical reasons. Allowing both states to makes offers when the distribution of power is changing complicates the analysis.

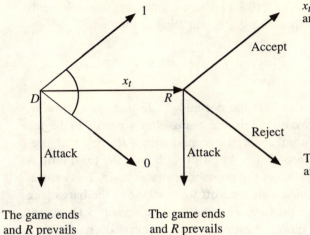

Figure 4.2 A round in the bargaining game

To complete the model, the states' payoffs and the way that the distribution of power shifts over time must be described. The specification of the states' payoffs directly parallels that of the previous chapter. Suppose the states never fight and let q_0 be the distribution of territory that exists at the outset of the game at time 0; let q_1 be the distribution at time 1; let q_2 be the distribution at time 2; and so on. Then the rising state's utility to controlling q_0 for the initial period is $q_0^{\rho_R}$ where the exponent ρ_R reflects that rising state's attitude toward risk. Similarly, the rising state's discounted value to having q_1 during period one is $\delta q_1^{\rho_R}$, where the discount factor δ summarizes a state's concern about future payoffs. (In order to simplify matters, the states are assumed to have a common discount factor and to be risk neutral or averse, i.e., $\rho_R \leq 1$.) Thus, the rising state's payoff to having $q_0, q_1, q_2, \ldots$ is $q_0^{\rho_R} + \delta q_1^{\rho_R} + \delta^2 q_2^{\rho_R} + \cdots$.

Now consider the rising state's payoff if the states go to war at time w. Until that time, the rising state controls the territory $q_0, q_1, q_2, \ldots, q_{w-1}$, which provides a utility of $\sum_{t=0}^{w-1} \delta^t q_t^{\rho_R} = q_0^{\rho_R} + \delta q_1^{\rho_R} + \cdots + \delta^{w-1} q_{w-1}^{\rho_R}$. As in the previous chapters, prevailing brings control of all of the territory. Thus, the rising state's per-period payoff if it prevails is the utility it derives from having all of the territory less its cost of fighting. Summing these per-period benefits from time w on gives $\delta^w(1 - r) + \delta^{w+1}(1 - r) + \delta^{w+2}(1 - r) + \cdots$. If, by contrast, the rising state loses, it reaps nothing but the cost of fighting and its payoff is

$\delta^w(0-r) + \delta^{w+1}(0-r) + \delta^{w+2}(0-r) + \cdots$. Combining these elements gives the rising state's expected payoff to fighting at time w:

$$A_R(w) = \sum_{t=0}^{w-1} \delta^t q^{P_R} + p_w \left[\sum_{t=w}^{\infty} \delta^t(1-r) \right] + (1-p_w) \sum_{t=w}^{\infty} -r\delta^t \qquad (4.1)$$

where p_w is the probability that the declining state prevails at time w. The first term in expression 4.1 is the rising state's payoff to having $q_0, q_1, q_2, \ldots, q_{w-1}$ before the war; the second term is R's payoff to prevailing weighted by the probability that it prevails; and the third term is its payoff to losing weighted by the probability that it loses. This expression mirrors the dissatisfied state's payoff to attacking in the bargaining game formulated in the previous chapter (see expression 3.1), except that the distribution of power in expression 4.1 can vary over time.

The final step in specifying the model is describing more precisely how the distribution of power changes over time. The substantive problem we want to examine is how states cope with shifts in the distribution of power between them. To this end, we assume that the rising state's probability of prevailing starts out small and then increases until it levels off at some higher level. Figure 4.3 represents the simplest formulation.

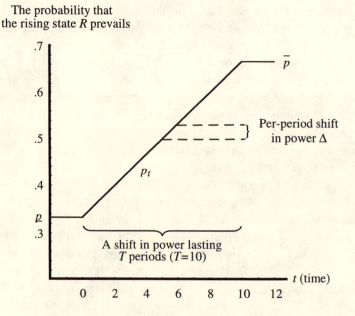

Figure 4.3 A shift in the distribution of power

The distribution of power is initially at $\underline{p}$, rises by a fixed amount Δ in each of the next T periods, and then levels out at some higher value $\overline{p}$.

More precisely, the probability that the rising state prevails at time t is $p_t = \underline{p} + t\Delta$ for $t \leq T$ and $p_t = \overline{p} = \underline{p} + T\Delta$ for $t \geq T$. Thus, the overall change in the distribution of power is the difference $\overline{p} - \underline{p}$ and the rate at which this shift occurs is $\Delta = (\overline{p} - \underline{p})/T$. Finally, if the initial distribution of power favors the declining state, i.e., if $\underline{p} < \frac{1}{2}$, and if the ultimate distribution of power favors the rising state, i.e., if $\overline{p} > \frac{1}{2}$, then the shift in the distribution will also have taken the states through a transition at which point they are both roughly equal in power.

In this formulation, the distribution of power is assumed to shift for reasons which are exogenous to or outside of the analysis. These shifts may, for example, be due to uneven rates of long-run economic growth not formalized in the model. Although this formulation seems consistent with many discussions of shifts in power (e.g., Doran and Parsons 1980; Gilpin 1981; Kennedy 1987; Kugler and Lemke 1996; Organski 1968; and Organski and Kugler 1980), it does preclude the interesting case in which a state's current power depends on the resources that it has acquired or given away in the past. Fearon (1996) considers this situation, and his findings will be compared below with the results derived from the present formulation.

Shifting Power and Complete Information

The dynamic effects of a shift in the distribution of power are simple if there is complete information. Because the states know each other's payoffs, the declining state can infer from this knowledge how much it has to concede to the rising state at each point during a shift in power in order to satisfy the rising state's minimal demands. The declining state thus faces a clear choice in each period. It can either grant the requisite concessions and avert war for that period, or it can refuse these demands and fight.

As will be seen, the declining state prefers appeasement to war if it has a large stake in the initial distribution of benefits and if the distribution of power does not shift too rapidly. As E. H. Carr once observed, "'Yielding to threats of force' is a normal part of the process of peaceful change" ([1939] 1954, 218). If, by contrast, the declining state has a small stake in the status quo or if the distribution is expected to change quickly, the declining state prefers to fight and attacks in the early phase of the shift in power. Regardless of the decision, there is no risk-return trade-off with complete information.

To derive these results, we have to determine what the declining state would have to concede at any point during the shift in power in order to satisfy the rising state's minimal demands and thereby ensure that it does not attack. There are two cases to consider. The first centers on what the declining state has to offer while the distribution of power is changing (i.e., at times before T). The second focuses on what the declining state would have to offer once the distribution of power levels off at $\overline{p}$.

Taking up the first case, suppose the declining state offers x_t at time $t < T$. If the rising state rejects this proposal and attacks, its expected future payoff is $(p_t - r) + \delta(p_t - r) + \delta^2(p_t - r) + \cdots$. The first term in this sum is the rising state's per-period expected payoff to fighting at time t; the second term is the discounted value of receiving this per-period payoff at time $t + 1$; and so on.

If, by contrast, the rising state were to accept x_t, then this state could always attack in the next period when it would be stronger. This option brings the rising state an expected payoff of $(x_t)^{\rho_R} + \delta(p_t + \Delta - r) + \delta^2(p_t + \Delta - r) + \cdots$. The first term in this sum is the rising state's utility to having x_t in period t. The second term is the rising state's discounted expected per-period payoff to fighting in the next period when the distribution of power will have shifted from p_t to $p_t + \Delta$. And, the third and subsequent terms are discounted values of the per-period payoff of having fought at time $t + 1$ when the distribution of power was $p_t + \Delta$.

Thus, the declining state can avoid war in the current period by offering the rising state enough to make the payoff to accepting the current offer and delaying an attack for at least one period as large as the payoff to attacking in the current period. In symbols, the declining state can induce its adversary to postpone an attack by proposing an x_t that satisfies $(x_t)^{\rho_R} + \delta(p_t + \Delta - r) + \delta^2(p_t + \Delta - r) + \cdots \geq (p_t - r) + \delta(p_t - r) + \delta^2(p_t - r) + \cdots$. Simplifying this condition, the rising state prefers accepting an offer and delaying an attack as long as this offer is at least as large as x_t^* where[5]

$$x_t^* = \left(p_t - r - \frac{\delta\Delta}{1-\delta}\right)^{1/\rho_R}.$$

(4.2)

---

[5] To simplify the previous inequality, rewrite the infinite sums using the properties described in footnote 14, chapter 3, and then solve for x_t.

In sum, the rising state prefers accepting a proposal and postponing an attack if the declining state offers at least x_t^*. Indeed, proposition 4.1 shows the rising state would attack if offered anything less than this amount. Thus, x_t^* is the smallest concession that induces the rising state to refrain from attacking. If, therefore, the declining state offers x_t^*, the rising state accepts and the new territorial status quo becomes $q_t = x_t^*$.

But the declining state can then do the same thing in the next period. That is, it can induce the rising state to delay attacking in that period by offering it x_{t+1}^*. The rising state accepts this offer and the new territorial status quo becomes $q_{t+1} = x_{t+1}^*$. And, in period $t+2$, the declining state offers x_{t+2}^*, and so on. Thus, the declining state can induce the rising state not to attack while the distribution of power is still shifting by offering $x_t^*, x_{t+1}^*, x_{t+2}^*, \ldots, x_{T-1}^*$.

What the declining state has to offer to appease the rising state changes once the distribution of power levels off at p_T. Because the distribution is now constant, the rising state no longer has any incentive to wait to become stronger. The states are therefore in the situation analyzed in the previous chapter. That analysis implies that if the declining state wants to appease the rising state, then it must offer the rising state control over an amount of territory equivalent in value to its expected payoff to attacking. That is, the declining state's offer at time T when the distribution of power levels off must satisfy $(x_T^*)^{\rho_R} = p_T - r$ where $(x_T^*)^{\rho_R}$ is the rising state's per-period utility to controlling x_T^* and $p_T - r$ is its per-period payoff to fighting. Solving for x_T^* gives $x_T^* = (p_T - r)^{1/\rho_R}$. As before, the rising state accepts this offer in equilibrium, and the distribution of territory moves to $q_T = (p_T - r)^{1/\rho_R}$. At this point the distribution of territory stops changing and remains at q_T. Both states are satisfied with this distribution given the new distribution of power p_T.

Figure 4.4 illustrates the effects of a shift in the distribution of power. At the outset, the distributions of power and territory favor the declining state. In particular, the rising state controls $\frac{1}{4}$ of the territory ($q_0 = \frac{1}{4}$), the declining state controls $\frac{3}{4}$ of the territory, and the declining state is twice as strong as the rising state ($p = \frac{1}{3}$).[6] The distribution of power then shifts over ten periods to $\overline{p} = \frac{2}{3}$, where the rising state is twice as powerful. The curve p_t in figure 4.4a plots the distribution of power, and q_t graphs the total territory the rising state controls at time t. Figure 4.4b

---

[6] At $\underline{p} = \frac{1}{3}$, the probability that the declining state prevails is $1 - \underline{p}$ or $\frac{2}{3}$ and, therefore, twice as large as the probability that the rising state prevails.

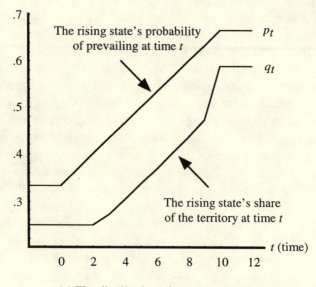

(a) The distribution of power and territory.

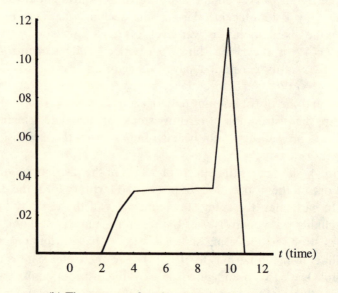

(b) The amount of territory conceded in each period.

Figure 4.4 The dynamics of a complete-information shift

shows how much additional territory the declining state concedes in each period. Although the distribution of power begins to shift at $t = 1$, it takes a few periods for the rising state to become powerful enough to be willing to use force to change the status quo. During this interval, the declining state does not make any concessions, and the initial distribution of territory remains unchanged place. However, once the rising state can credibly threaten to use force, the declining state makes a series of concessions that leave the rising state in control of ever more territory. When the shift in power ends and the distribution of power levels off at $\overline{p} = \frac{2}{3}$, the declining state makes one last, large concession in order to deprive the rising state of any incentive to attack at $\overline{p}$. Thereafter, the distributions of power and territory remain constant.

To describe the pattern of concessions more precisely, observe that if the rising state is in control of x_t^* at time t, it will not attack. But during the initial phase of the shift in power the rising state already controls more territory than this. That is, the rising state has no incentive to attack because $q_0 > x_t^*$ during the first few periods during the shift in power. The declining state, therefore, makes no concessions. Eventually, however, the distribution of power shifts sufficiently far in the rising state's favor that it is willing to attack unless it obtains some concessions At this point, the amount of territory that the rising state must control in order to be induced not to attack, x_t^*, is greater than its status quo share, q_0, and the declining state offers x_t^*. After the initial phase, the declining state grants the rising state an additional amount of territory roughly equal to the amount by which the distribution of power shifts in each period, Δ. Then, the declining state makes one last, larger concession of $\Delta/(1 - \delta)$ once the distribution of power levels off in period T.[7]

The reason for this "spike" in the declining state's concessions at T is that as long as the distribution of power is moving in the rising state's favor, then the rising state will be more powerful in the next period. This gives the rising state an incentive to put off attacking and wait until the next period when it will be stronger. This added incentive to wait in turn reduces what the declining state has to offer the rising state in

[7] More precisely, the additional amount of territory a declining state grants in period t is the difference between what it offers in that period, x_t^*, and what it offered (and what was accepted) in previous period, namely x_{t-1}^*. If we assume that the declining state is risk neutral ($\rho_R = 1$) for the moment in order to simplify the algebra, then expression 4.2 shows that $x_t^* - x_{t-1}^* = \Delta$ as long as the distribution of power is still shifting, i.e., as long as $t < T$. Once the distribution of power levels off at T, the declining state makes a final, larger incremental concession of $x_T^* - x_{T-1}^* = \Delta/(1 - \delta)$ and then makes no further concessions.

order to make the payoff to not attacking at least as large as the payoff to attacking. But this incentive to wait disappears when the distribution of power stops changing at time T. The declining state must therefore make a larger concession to compensate for this missing incentive, and this results in the spike at T.[8]

Summarizing the analysis, if the declining state decides to satisfy the rising state's minimal demands, it would not have to do anything for the first few periods of the shift in power. After this first phase, the declining state would have to make a series of concessions $x_t^*, x_{t+1}^*, \ldots, x_T^*$, which the rising state would accept. Thus, the simple choice facing the declining state at any time t is to decide whether to attack or to offer x_t^* and move on to the next period.

Proposition 4.1 below shows that *if the initial distribution of benefits favors the declining state and if the distribution of power does not shift too rapidly, then the declining state prefers making these concessions.* Thus, the complete-information shift in power passes without war and the distribution of benefits is revised in the rising state's favor. If, by contrast, the distribution of power shifts very rapidly or if the declining state has little or no stake in the initial distribution of benefits, then the declining state prefers fighting a preventive war to conceding x_t^* and the states face a commitment problem.

To see why the declining state's decision depends on the speed of the shift, observe that if the declining state attacks at the outset, its expected payoff to attacking is equivalent to controlling all of the territory to the right of $\underline{p} + d$ in figure 4.5. That is, the declining state can "lock in" a payoff equal to controlling the territory to the right of $\underline{p} + d$ by fighting at $\underline{p}$. The declining state, therefore, will attack and the shift in power will end in war unless making the concessions x_t^* as the distribution of power shifts to $\overline{p}$ will give the declining state an expected payoff of at least as much as it would derive from controlling the territory to the right of $\underline{p} + d$. Similarly, the rising state can "lock in" a payoff equal to controlling the territory to the left of $\overline{p} - r$ *by attacking once the distribution of power has shifted to* $\overline{p}$. Accordingly, the rising state will attack once the distribution of power has shifted to $\overline{p}$ unless it controls an amount of territory equal to $\overline{p} - r$.

---

[8]This spike can be seen, therefore, as an artifact of the simplifying assumption that the distribution of power shifts by a constant amount in each period, namely Δ, and then abruptly stops at T. If the distribution of power shifted more smoothly and slowly leveled out at $\overline{p}$, then this spike would also be smoothed out.

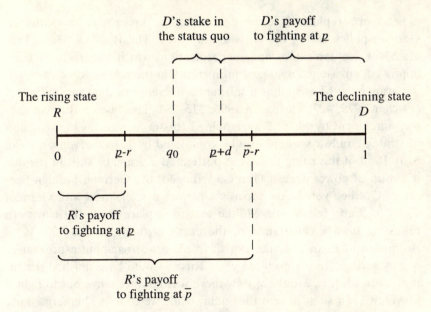

Figure 4.5 The effects of complete-information shift in the distribution of power

If the shift in the distribution of power is large enough, then $p + d$ lies to the left of $\overline{p} - r$ and the sum of these territorial "lock-ins" exceeds the total amount of territory there is to be divided. This implies that the declining state cannot control the territory to the right of $p + d$ at the same time as the rising state controls an amount of territory at least as large as $\overline{p} - r$. But if the shift from $\underline{p}$ to $\overline{p}$ happens very quickly or, in the limit, instantaneously, both states would have to do just that if both were to prefer a peaceful shift to fighting. This is impossible and the shift in power triggers a war.

A rapid shift in the distribution of power thus creates a commitment problem, which results in a preventive war. Both states would be better-off if the rising state could commit itself to refraining from exploiting its future strength to overturn the initial status quo. More specifically, suppose the declining state locks in an expected payoff equal to controlling the territory to the right of $\underline{p} + d$ by attacking before the distribution of power begins to shift against it. This attack also locks in an expected payoff for the rising state equal to controlling the territory to the left of $\underline{p} - r$. Clearly, both states would have been better-off if they could have committed themselves to not using force to alter the status quo q_0.[9]

[9] See Fearon (1993) for a discussion of this kind of commitment problem.

Fears of a rapid shift in the distribution of power may have affected German policy during the crisis of July 1914. The Russian "Great Program" of reorganization and modernization, which had recently been approved, envisioned a 40 percent increase in the size of Russia's standing army by 1917 as well as a substantial increase in the army's artillery (Fischer 1975, 427; Stevenson 1996, 315–28). The Franco-Russian railway agreement by which France helped Russia finance the construction of strategic railways would also be completed by 1918 (Stevenson 1996, 326). If all of this came to pass, it portended a dramatic shift in the distribution of power against Germany. Indeed, the German Foreign Secretary Gottlieb von Jagow records a private conversation with German Chief of Staff Helmut von Moltke that took place while the two were returning from a celebration of the czar's birthday on May 20, 1914. According to Jagow, Moltke explained his concerns about a preventive war by saying: "In two to three years Russia would have finished rearming.... In his [i.e., Moltke's] view there was no alternative but to fight a preventive war so as to beat the enemy while we could still emerge fairly well from the struggle. The Chief of Staff therefore put it to me that our policy should be geared to bringing about an early war."[10]

The United States also discussed a preventive war against the Soviet Union before it developed a large nuclear arsenal. In April 1947, George Kennan, who was then about to become the first director of the State Department's Policy Planning Staff, discussed the possibility of preventive war against the Soviet Union as a last resort during an address to the U.S. Air War College (Gaddis 1982, 49). Indeed, Bernard Brodie, one of the founders of nuclear deterrence theory, wrote in a 1953 paper for the RAND corporation that a policy of preventive war was "the prevailing philosophy at the Air War College" during the postwar years (Trachtenberg 1991, 106). Preventive war was also one four options listed in NSC-68, the extensive national security review undertaken in conjunction with Truman's decision to proceed with the hydrogen bomb in 1950 (Trachtenberg 1991, 107–15; Wells 1979). In 1953, Eisenhower wrote to Secretary of State John Foster Dulles that the United States

would have to be constantly ready, on an instantaneous basis, to inflict greater loss on the enemy than he could reasonably hope to inflict on us. This would be a deterrent—but if the cost to maintain this relative

---

[10] Quoted in Fischer (1975, 401). For other discussions of German fears and thinking about preventive war, see Geiss (1976), J. Snyder (1984a, 1984b), and Van Evera (1984).

position should have to continue indefinitely, the cost would either drive us to war—or into some form of dictatorial government. In such circumstances, we would be forced to consider whether or not our duty to future generations did not require us to *initiate* war at the most propitious moment that we could designate.[11]

A commitment problem also arises if the shift from $\underline{p}$ to $\overline{p}$ happens more slowly but the declining state has little or no stake in the initial status quo. To establish this, we must first specify more precisely what it means for the declining state to have a small stake in the status quo. If both states are satisfied at the initial distribution of power $\underline{p}$, then the status quo division of benefits, q_0, must lie between $\underline{p} - r$ and $\underline{p} + d$ in figure 4.5. Thus, the larger q_0 and the closer it is to $\underline{p} + d$, the smaller the declining state's share or stake in the initial territorial distribution.

To illustrate the effects of the declining state's having little or no stake in the initial distribution of territory, consider the extreme case in which the declining state has no stake in the status quo because its payoff to attacking at $\underline{p}$ is equal to its payoff to living with the status quo, i.e., $(1 - q_0)^{p_D} = 1 - \underline{p} - d$. Because it has no stake in the status quo, the declining state is sure to do better by fighting a preventive war at $\underline{p}$ than by waiting and thereby letting the distribution of power begin to shift against it.

To see that the declining state prefers fighting, observe that the declining state can lock in a payoff equivalent to preserving the status quo q_0 forever by attacking at $\underline{p}$. If, however, the declining state waits and allows the distribution of power to shift against it, then it will ultimately have to fight when it is weaker or it will have to make some concessions to the rising state. In either case, the declining state will be worse-off than it would have been had it locked in a payoff equivalent to maintaining the status quo q_0. Thus, the declining state prefers attacking preventively at $\underline{p}$ before the distribution of power shifts against it, and the ensuing preventive war leaves the states worse off than they would have been had they been able to commit themselves to abstaining from the use of force.[12]

---

[11] Quoted in Gaddis (1982, 149). Eisenhower, however, publicly rejected the idea of a preventive war at a press conference a few months later (Gaddis 1982, 149). Also see Trachtenberg (1991, 132–46).

[12] More precisely, fighting does make the rising state strictly worse-off. But the declining state is indifferent between fighting and preserving q_0 if it has *no* stake in the status quo. If, by contrast, the declining state has a small stake in the status quo, it still prefers attacking preventively and both states are strictly worse-off.

Finally, suppose that the initial distribution of benefits favors the declining state and that the shift occurs more slowly. In this case, the declining state prefers paying the price of gradually making a series of concessions x_t^* *in the future* to paying the *immediate* cost of fighting now. The status quo is revised in favor of the rising state, and the shift in power passes without war. Proposition 4.1 summarizes these results:

Proposition 4.1: *Suppose that the initial distribution of benefits favors the declining state and that the distribution of power shifts slowly. (In particular, the amount by which the distribution of power shifts in a single period is less than the total per-period cost of fighting, i.e., $\Delta <$ $d + r$.) Then the complete-information shift in the distribution of power passes without war. The declining state offers the rising state just enough in each period to ensure that the rising state has no incentive to attack, and the rising state accepts these concessions. In symbols, the declining state offers x_t^* in the t-th period where x_t^* is given by $(x_t^*)^{\rho_R} = p_t - r -$ $\delta\Delta/(1 - \delta)$ while the distribution of power is shifting (i.e., for $t < T$) and $(x_t^*)^{\rho_R} = \overline{p} - r$ once the distribution of power stops shifting and levels out (i.e., for $t \geq T$).*

Appendix 4 sketches the proof of this claim, and two final comments conclude the discussion of the complete-information case. First, commitment problems can arise in the strategic setting studied here because the distribution of power is assumed to shift for reasons exogenous to the analysis. These shifts may, for example, be due to uneven rates of long-run economic growth not formalized in the model. This contrasts with a situation in which the distribution of power changes because of the resources that are transferred when one state makes a concession to another. Fearon (1996), for example, examines the case in which the rising state's power in the current period depends on the concessions it has received in previous periods. The more the rising state has acquired in the past, the more powerful it will be today. In principle, we might expect a commitment problem to arise in this situation because each concession to the rising state makes it stronger and thereby necessitates another concession, which makes the rising state still stronger, and so on. Given the choice between attacking now or conceding ever more to the rising state, we might anticipate that the declining state would prefer to attack. This would leave both states worse-off than they would have been had the rising state been able to commit itself to abstaining from exploiting its ever-growing strength. Fearon, however, shows that this situation often does not produce a commitment problem.

Rather, the declining state makes small concessions to the rising state, which produce a very gradual increase in its power.

Second, the remainder of this chapter assumes that the declining state prefers making concessions to launching a preventive war. That is, we will ensure that proposition 4.2 holds by assuming that the per-period shift in the distribution of power is less than the per-period cost of fighting ($\Delta < d + r$) and that the initial distribution of benefits favors the declining state. Two considerations motivate this assumption. First, it brings the informational problems inherent in a shift in power to the fore by pushing commitment issues into the background. Second, assuming otherwise would appear to posit rates of change in the distribution of power or costs of fighting that seem empirically implausible given that the substantive focus here is on long-run shifts due to differential rates of economic growth and development.[13]

Shifting Power and Asymmetric Information

Asymmetric information creates a now familiar risk-return trade-off. If the declining state is unsure of the rising state's willingness to use force, it does not know how much it has to offer to meet the rising state's minimal demands. It only knows that the more it offers, the more likely it is to satisfy its adversary's demands and the less likely war becomes. But larger offers also mean having less if they are accepted.

The declining state resolves this trade-off by making a series of concessions during the shift in power. These concessions satisfy the rising state if that state is relatively irresolute and unwilling to use force. In this case, the status quo is continually revised in the rising state's favor and the shift in power passes without war. By contrast, the declining state's concessions do not satisfy the rising state if that state is relatively resolute. In these circumstances, the rising state attacks, and the shift in power ends in war. Indeed, the more resolute the rising state, the earlier the fighting starts.

---

[13] Over the period 1816–1990 the *maximum* annual change in the distribution of power between any two Great Powers that were not at war in that year is 6.8 percent when military capabilities are calculated on the basis of Correlates of War data. (This maximal change occurred between Great Britain and Russia between 1925 and 1926.) Of the almost two thousand Great-Power, non-warring dyads, only 14 or .73 percent had an annual change in the distribution of power greater than 5 percent. If we take these calculated annual changes as proxies for the per-period shift in the distribution of power Δ, then plausible assumptions about the total per-period cost of fighting $r + d$ would suggest that $\Delta < d + r$.

This account implies that if we were to examine a number of historical cases, we should expect to see that shifts in the distribution of power sometimes lead to war but not always. Of those cases that do end in war, the model indicates that those wars occur at all stages of the shift. Some wars occur before the distribution has shifted very far. Other wars occur at or near a transition when the distribution of power is roughly even. (We examine below whether war is most likely to occur around a transition as the power-transition school argues.) And still other wars occur after the distribution of power has shifted substantially in favor of the rising state.

To study the risk-return trade-off facing the declining state, asymmetric information must be added to the model. In the bargaining game analyzed in the previous chapter, both states were unsure of the other's resolve. This two-sided uncertainty complicates the analysis immensely, and, to avoid these complexities, we assume in the present formulation that only the declining state is unsure of the rising state's willingness to use force. Although uncertain of the rising state's cost of fighting, r, the declining state has beliefs about it. In particular, the declining state believes that the rising state's cost is at least as large as some lower limit of, say, $\underline{r}$ and no more than some upper bound of, say, $\bar{r}$. Moreover, no particular value in this range is any more likely than any other. In other words, the declining state believes that r is uniformly distributed over the interval $[\underline{r}, \bar{r}]$.[14]

Although the declining state is uncertain of the rising state's willingness to use force, it takes several periods for the risk-return trade-off to develop. Because of the added incentive that a shifting distribution of power gives the rising state to wait, that state is unwilling to use force to overturn the status quo in the early phase of the shift, and the declining state does not make any concessions. However, after a few periods, the rising state becomes willing to use force if it is very resolute, i.e., if its cost is close to $\underline{r}$. At that point (which will be called time s), the declining state begins to face a risk-return trade-off, which it resolves by making a series of concessions $x_s^*, x_{s+1}^*, \ldots, x_T^*$.

How the rising state responds to these concessions depends on its willingness to fight. As will be seen, the declining state's concessions create a series of "cut-points" $\tilde{r}_s, \tilde{r}_{s+1}, \ldots, \tilde{r}_T$ between $\underline{r}$ and $\bar{r}$ such that the rising state is just indifferent between accepting x_t^* and attacking if its cost is $\tilde{r}_t$. (The tilde over "r_t" represents indifference.) If, therefore,

---

[14] Appendix 4 shows that the following analysis also holds for more general distributions.

the rising state's actual cost r is greater than $\tilde{r}_{t-1}$ but less than $\tilde{r}_t$, the rising state accepts offers $x_s^*, x_{s+1}^*, \ldots, x_{t-1}^*$ and attacks at time t when offered x_t^*. These cut-points are illustrated in figure 4.6.

To see that the rising state responds to these offers in this way, consider how the rising state reacts if it is very resolute, i.e., if its cost is close to $\underline{r}$. Even if very resolute, the rising state is initially unwilling to use force to overturn the status quo q_0. The benefits of waiting and thereby becoming stronger outweigh the costs of living with the status quo a little longer. But eventually, the rising state becomes just strong enough that it is willing to use force to change the status quo if its cost of fighting r is very low (i.e., if r is close to $\underline{r}$).

At this time (s), the declining state faces a risk-return trade-off which it generally resolves by making an offer that is likely but not certain to appease the rising state. That is, the declining state usually does not offer enough to satisfy the toughest type of rising state it might be facing. Consequently, the rising state prefers rejecting x_s^* and attacking if its actual cost is close to $\underline{r}$ and prefers accepting x_s^* if its cost is actually high and close to $\bar{r}$. Thus, there is some intermediate value, which will be called $\tilde{r}_s$, such that the rising state is indifferent between attacking and accepting x_s^* if its cost is $\tilde{r}_s$. Hence, the rising state attacks in period s and the shift in power ends in war at that time if the rising state's cost is less than $\tilde{r}_s$. If, by contrast, the rising state's cost is greater than $\tilde{r}_s$, it accepts x_s^*, the status quo shifts from q_0 to $q_s = x_s^*$, and the bargaining continues on to the next round. These decisions are depicted in figure 4.6.

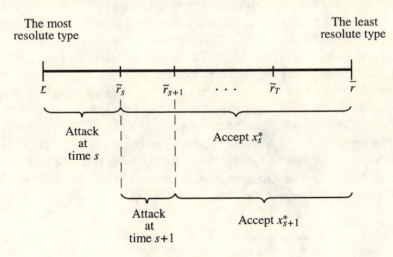

Figure 4.6 The cut-points

Two opposing factors influence the declining state's offer in this next round. First, the declining state updates its beliefs about the rising state's willingness to use force in light of its acceptance of x^*_s and concludes that the rising state is less willing to use force than it initially believed. In particular, the declining state infers from the rising state's acceptance of its previous offer that the rising state's cost is at least $\tilde{r}_s$, whereas it initially believed that this cost might be as low as $\underline{r}$.[15] But the rising state is also stronger in this period than it was in the previous period, and this means that the rising state will now be willing to use force to overturn q_s if its cost of fighting is close to $\tilde{r}_s$. The declining state thus faces a new risk-return trade-off, which it resolves by making another concession x^*_{s+1}.

As in the previous round, this offer generally will not be enough to be sure of satisfying the rising state. That is, x^*_{s+1} is not enough to satisfy the rising state if its cost of fighting is low (i.e., if r is close to $\tilde{r}_s$). But the offer x^*_{s+1} is enough to satisfy the rising state if its cost of fighting is high and close to $\bar{r}$. Thus, there is an intermediate cost, which will be called $\tilde{r}_{s+1}$, such that the rising state is indifferent between attacking and accepting x^*_{s+1} if its cost is $\tilde{r}_{s+1}$. The rising state, therefore, accepts x^*_s in period s and then attacks in period $s + 1$ when offered x^*_{s+1} if its cost is between $\tilde{r}_s$ and $\tilde{r}_{s+1}$. If, by contrast, the rising state's cost is greater than $\tilde{r}_{s+1}$, it accepts x^*_{s+1}, the status quo moves to $q_{s+1} = x^*_{s+1}$, and the bargaining continues into the next round. These groups are also illustrated in figure 4.6.

This pattern continues as long as the distribution of power continues to shift. In each round, the declining state revises its beliefs about the rising state's willingness to use force and then makes another offer that generally satisfies some but not all of the types it might be facing. More precisely, these offers create a series of cut-points $\tilde{r}_s, \tilde{r}_{s+1}, \ldots, \tilde{r}_T$ such that if the rising state's actual cost is between $\tilde{r}_{t-1}$ and $\tilde{r}_t$, then the rising state accepts the declining state's concessions until offered x^*_t at time t when, finding this offer insufficient, it attacks.

Figures 4.7, 4.8, and 4.9 depict a shift in power in which the initial distributions of benefits and power favor the declining state. In particular, the declining state controls three-quarters of the territory at the outset and is twice as strong as the rising state (i.e., $q_0 = .25$ and $\underline{p} = \frac{1}{3}$). The

---

[15] In equilibrium, each player-type knows the strategy of every other player-type. Thus, the declining state knows which types would accept x^*_s and which would reject it. What that state does not know is its adversary's actual cost.

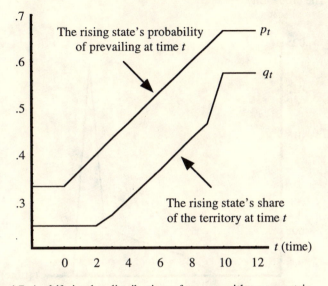

Figure 4.7 A shift in the distribution of power with asymmetric information

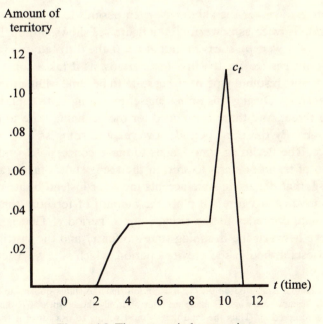

Figure 4.8 The per-period concessions

The probability
of war

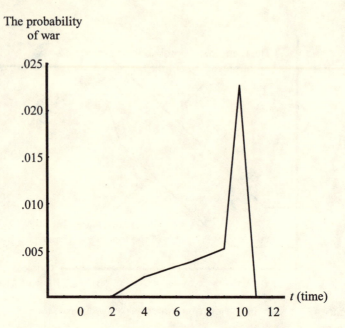

Figure 4.9 The per-period probability of war

distribution of power then shifts over ten periods to $\overline{p} = 2/3$ where the rising state is twice as powerful.[16] As figure 4.7 shows, although the distribution of power, p_t, starts to shift at $t = 0$, the distribution of territory, q_t, does not change for the first few periods, as it takes some time for even the most resolute type of rising state to become willing to use force to overturn q_0. During this initial phase, the rising state cannot make a credible threat, and there is no need for the declining state to offer any concessions. By the third period, however, the rising state is willing to use force. The declining state begins to make concessions, and the distribution of territory starts to shift in the rising state's favor (assuming, of course, that the rising state accepts the offer instead of attacking).

The curve c_t in figure 4.8 plots the amount of territory that the declining state concedes to the rising state in period t. That is, c_t is the difference between the declining state's offer x_t^* and the distribution of territory established in the previous period, which is q_{t-1}. After the ini-

---

[16] The example is also based on the assumption that the status quo q_0 arose at some time in the distant past when D made an offer and only those types of R that prefer q_0 to fighting accepted q_0. Thus the type that is most willing to use force at the outset of the shift in power, $\underline{r}$, is just indifferent between living with the status quo q_0 forever and fighting at the initial distribution of power $\underline{p}$. In symbols, $(q_0)^{p_R} = \underline{p} - \underline{r}$.

tial phase, the declining state makes roughly equal concessions until the distribution of power stops shifting at $T = 10$. At this point, the rising state no longer has any incentive to wait to be stronger in the next period. Recognizing this, the declining state makes one last, larger concession. War ensues if the rising state rejects this offer. If it accepts, the status quo becomes $q_T = x_T^*$. The declining state also infers from this acceptance that the rising state prefers x_T^* to fighting and therefore makes no further concessions. The distribution of territory stabilizes.

Finally, figure 4.9 shows how the probability of war varies throughout the shift in power. It is zero in the initial phase when the rising state is unwilling to use force and the declining state makes no concessions. Then the probability of war slowly increases during the shift. When the distribution of power stops shifting, the rising state loses any incentive to wait to be stronger in the next period and this makes the risk-return trade-off facing the declining state more acute. The declining state in turn resolves this more severe trade-off by both making a larger concession (see figure 4.8) and accepting a larger risk than in previous periods.

Proposition 4.2 formally defines the offers $x_s^*, x_{s+1}^*, \ldots, x_T^*$ and the cut-points $\tilde{r}_s, \tilde{r}_{s+1}, \ldots, \tilde{r}_T$. These concessions balance the marginal gain to offering slightly more against the marginal cost of doing so, and the cut-points describe how the rising state responds to these offers given its actual cost of fighting. To wit, the rising state accepts offers $x_s^*, x_{s+1}^*, \ldots, x_{t-1}^*$ and fights at time t when it is offered x_t^* if its actual cost of fighting is between $\tilde{r}_{t-1}$ and $\tilde{r}_t$. Readers less interested in the formal specification of these offers and cut-points may want to skip the rest of this section.

Proposition 4.2: *In equilibrium, the declining state does not make any concessions until the calculated value of x_t^* exceeds the initial status quo q_0. Once x_t^* is greater than q_0, the declining state offers x_t^* in period t. If the rising state's cost of fighting is between $\tilde{r}_{t-1}$ and $\tilde{r}_t$, it accepts $x_s^*, x_{s+1}^*, \ldots, x_{t-1}^*$ and fights when offered x_t^*. Consequently, the probability of war in period t is the probability that the risings state's cost of fighting is actually between $\tilde{r}_{t-1}$ and $\tilde{r}_t$.*
The offer x_t^* solves:

$$[(1 - x_t^*)^{\rho_D} - (1 - \pi_t - d)]\frac{\partial(\pi_t - (x_t^*)^{\rho_R})}{\partial x_t^*}$$
$$= \frac{\partial(1 - x_t^*)^{\rho_D}}{\partial x_t^*}[\bar{r} - (\pi_t - (x_t^*)^{\rho_R})]$$

$$(4.3)$$

where $\pi_t = p_t - \delta\Delta/(1 - \delta)$ during the shift (i.e., for $t < T$) and $\pi_t = \bar{p}$ after the distribution of power levels off (i.e., at $t \geq T$) and $\tilde{r}_t$ is given by $\tilde{r}_t = \pi_t - (x_t^*)^{\rho_R}$.

Expression 4.3 has a straightforward interpretation. If we think of π_t rather than p_t as the probability that the rising state prevails at time t after "adjusting" for the fact that the distribution of power is changing, then this equation formalizes the declining state's equating of the marginal gain expected from offering slightly more to the expected marginal cost of doing so. To wit, the left side of expression 4.3 is the marginal gain to offering slightly more than x_t^* and the right side is the marginal cost of doing so.

To verify this interpretation of expression 4.3, consider the declining state's expected gain to offering $x_t + \varepsilon$ instead of x_t in period t where ε is small. This expected gain is just the net benefit to settling on $x_t + \varepsilon$ instead of fighting weighted by the probability that the rising state accepts $x_t + \varepsilon$ but would have fought if offered x_t. This net benefit to a peaceful settlement is the difference between D's payoff to having $1 - (x_t + \varepsilon)$ and fighting, which is $(1 - (x_t + \varepsilon))^{\rho_D} - (1 - \pi_t - d)$ where $1 - \pi_t$ is the adjusted probability that the declining state prevails. To specify the probability that the rising state accepts $x_t + \varepsilon$ but would reject x_t, let $\tilde{r}_t(x_t)$ be the type of rising state that is indifferent between accepting x_t and fighting given the adjusted distribution of power π_t. That is, the rising state's payoff to fighting equals its payoff to having x_t if its cost of fighting is $\tilde{r}_t(x_t)$. In symbols, $\tilde{r}_t(x_t)$ satisfies $\pi_t - \tilde{r}_t(x_t) = (x_t)^{\rho_R}$. Then the set of types that would reject x_t but accept $x_t + \varepsilon$ are those types with a cost of fighting between $\tilde{r}_t(x_t + \varepsilon)$ and $\tilde{r}_t(x_t)$, as illustrated in figure 4.10. Hence, the probability that the rising state would reject x_t but accept $x_t + \varepsilon$ is the probability that r is between $\tilde{r}_t(x_t + \varepsilon)$ and $\tilde{r}_t(x_t)$ given that r is uniformly distributed between $\tilde{r}_{t-1}$ and $\bar{r}$. This is $(\tilde{r}_t(x_t) - \tilde{r}_t(x_t + \varepsilon))/(\bar{r} - \tilde{r}_{t-1})$. Consequently, the expected gain to offering slightly more than x_t is $[(1 - (x_t + \varepsilon))^{\rho_D} - (1 - \pi_t - d)](\tilde{r}_t(x_t) - \tilde{r}_t(x_t + \varepsilon))/(\bar{r} - \tilde{r}_{t-1})$.

The expected cost of offering $x_t + \varepsilon$ instead of x_t is the net loss due to settling on $x_t + \varepsilon$ rather than x_t weighted by the probability that the rising state would have agreed to x_t and did not need to be offered $x_t + \varepsilon$. D's net loss to having $1 - (x_t + \varepsilon)$ instead of $1 - x_t$ is $(1 - x_t)^{\rho_D} - (1 - (x_t + \varepsilon))^{\rho_D}$. The rising state would also have accepted x_t if its cost is at least $\tilde{r}_t(x)$, so the probability that R would have accepted x_t is $(\bar{r} - \tilde{r}_t(x_t))/(\bar{r} - \tilde{r}_{t-1})$. Thus, the expected cost to offering slightly more than x_t is $[(1 - x_t)^{\rho_D} - (1 - (x_t + \varepsilon))^{\rho_D}](\bar{r} - \tilde{r}_t(x_t))/(\bar{r} - \tilde{r}_{t-1})$.

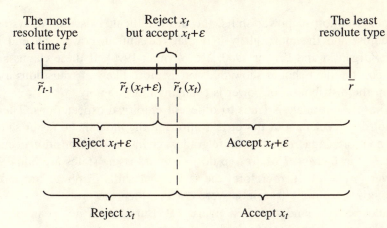

Figure 4.10 The marginal effects of offering slightly more

Expression 4.3 then follows by equating the expected gain to the expected cost; substituting $\pi_t - (x_t)^{\rho_R}$ for $\tilde{r}_t(x_t)$; multiplying both sides by $\bar{r} - \tilde{r}_{t-1}$; dividing both sides by ε; letting ε go the zero in the limit; and recalling that the derivative $\partial f(x_t)/\partial x_t$ is the limit of $(f(x_t + \varepsilon) - f(x_t))/\varepsilon$ as ε approaches zero.

Thus by satisfying expression 4.3, x_t^* equates the expected marginal benefit to conceding slightly more to the expected marginal cost of doing so given an effective distribution of power π_t. Of course, $\pi_t = p_t - \delta\Delta/(1 - \delta)$ is not really the probability that the declining state prevails. But it is interesting to find that the dynamic problem of a shift in power reduces to the static problem examined in the previous chapter when the distribution of power is "adjusted" down from p_t to π_t to reflect the fact that the distribution of power is shifting in favor of the rising state. This shift creates incentives for the rising state not to attack or, in other words, to behave as if it were less powerful.

Power Transitions, Faster Shifts, and Some Empirics

What does the model imply about the effects of shifts in the distribution of power on the risk of war? What empirical patterns should we expect to see if we look at the data? The power-transition school argues that the most dangerous phase during a shift in the distribution of power occurs at a power transition where the declining and rising states are roughly equal in power (Organski 1968; Organski and Kugler 1980, 18–28; Levy 1987, 97–98). This school also asserts that the more rapidly the distribution of power shifts, the more difficult it is for the system to adjust and the more likely it is that the shift in power will end in war (Organski and Kugler 1980, 21; Wayman 1996). If these claims are correct, the data should show that war is more likely at transitions and when the distribution of power is changing more rapidly.

The present analysis leads to different empirical expectations. There is nothing special about power transitions in the model, and faster shifts are no more dangerous than more gradual changes. The transition occurs at $t = 5$ in figure 4.7 where the declining and rising states are equal in power ($p_5 = \frac{1}{2}$). If, therefore, the claim that shifts in power are most dangerous around a transition were correct, then the probability of war should peak around $t = 5$ in figure 4.9. But it does not peak there. Rather, the probability of war rises throughout the shift in power.

The reasoning underlying the declining state's equilibrium strategy also suggests that there is nothing special about an even distribution of power and no reason to expect the probability of war to peak there. As we have seen, the declining state's optimal offer in any period balances the marginal gain to reducing the risk of war by conceding slightly more against the marginal cost to having a slightly less favorable allocation if the offer is accepted. The value of $p_t = \frac{1}{2}$ would seem to play no special role in these marginal calculations. Rather, the salient issues would seem to be the states' marginal values of consumption and the way that small changes in the size of a concession affect the probability of acceptance.

The model also undercuts the claim that faster shifts in power are more dangerous, and it brings to the fore an important distinction that has not been fully appreciated in previous analyses. Consider figure 4.11, which depicts two shifts in power. Both shifts begin at $\underline{p}$ and end at $\overline{p}$, but one shift, p'_t, occurs more rapidly than the other. This figure suggests that the effects of a shift in the distribution of power on the risk of war can be decomposed into two components, a *static effect* and a *dynamic effect*.

The former arises from the fact that however fast the shifts occurs, the distribution of power changes from $\underline{p}$ to $\overline{p}$. As will be seen, this change in and of itself may affect the likelihood of war. But, the static effect depends on where the shift starts and stops, not on how fast it takes place. Accordingly, the static effect on the risk of war is identical in p'_t and p_t.

The dynamic effect measures how the speed at which the shift takes place affects the chances of war. If, for example, faster changes are more

The probability that
the rising state R prevails

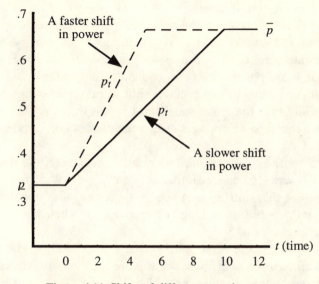

Figure 4.11 Shifts of different speeds

dangerous, then p'_t would be more likely to end in war than p_t, and the dynamic effect would be larger in p'_t. If, by contrast, faster shifts are no more dangerous than slower shifts, then p'_t and p_t will be equally likely to end in war, and there would be no dynamic effect.

The model shows that the dynamic effect is zero. More rapid shifts in power are not more dangerous.[17] A shift in power may make war more likely than it would have been had the distribution of power not changed. But the increase is due solely to the static effect.

To see that the dynamic effects are zero, consider the two shifts in the distribution of power illustrated in figure 4.11. Both begin at $\underline{p}$ and end at $\overline{p}$, but one shift is faster than the other. The distribution of power shifts at a rate Δ and reaches $\overline{p}$ at time T in the slower shift, whereas the distribution of power changes at a faster rate Δ' (i.e., $\Delta' > \Delta$) and reaches $\overline{p}$ at an earlier time T' in the second.

To determine the probabilities that these shifts end in war, recall that the declining state makes a series of offers $x^*_s, x^*_{s+1}, \ldots, x^*_T$, which gen-

---

[17] This, of course, is based on the assumption that this faster shift still satisfies the condition that the per-period change in power is less than the total per-period cost of fighting, i.e., $\Delta < \underline{r} + d$.

erate a series of cut-points $\tilde{r}_s, \tilde{r}_{s+1}, \ldots, \tilde{r}_T$. If the rising state's cost of fighting is between $\tilde{r}_{t-1}$ and $\tilde{r}_t$, the rising state accepts these concessions until it is offered x_t^* at time t, at which point it rejects that offer and attacks. This implies that the rising state ultimately finds an offer unacceptable and attacks if its cost of fighting is less than $\tilde{r}_T$, whereas the rising state accepts every concession and the shift in power passes without war if the rising state's cost of fighting is greater than $\tilde{r}_T$. Thus, the overall probability that the slower shift in power ends in war is just the probability that the rising state's cost is less than $\tilde{r}_T$, i.e., that it would prefer fighting to accepting x_T^* when the distribution of power levels out at $\overline{p}$.

Now consider the second, faster shift. Once again the declining state makes a series of concessions, say $y_{s'}^*, y_{s'+1}^*, \ldots, y_{T'}^*$. The overall probability that this shift ends in war is, therefore, the probability that the rising state prefers attacking to accepting $y_{T'}^*$ when the distribution of power levels out at $\overline{p}$.

It follows that these two shifts will be equally likely to end in war if the offers made when each levels out at $\overline{p}$ are the same. In symbols, $x_T^* = y_{T'}^*$. This would imply that the probability that the rising state finds x_T^* or a previous offer insufficient and attacks is the same as the probability that it finds $y_{T'}^*$ or a previous offer inadequate and attacks.

Proposition 4.2 formally shows that the offers x_T^* and $y_{T'}^*$ are identical.[18] To see why these offers are the same in a less formal and more intuitive way, consider the situations facing the declining state when the slower shift levels out at time T and when the faster shift levels out at T'. These situations are similar in many ways. In both, the declining state has to resolve a risk-return trade-off by making one last offer given that the distribution of power is $\overline{p}$ and will remain constant at that level.

The only real difference between these situations is that the declining state's beliefs about the toughest types it might be facing may differ. In the slower shift, the declining state believes that it is facing only those types that would have accepted the previous offer x_{T-1}^*. That is, the declining state believes that the rising state's cost is at least as large as $\tilde{r}_{T-1}$ where $\tilde{r}_{T-1}$ is the type that is indifferent between accepting

---

[18] To establish this equality, note, first, that x_T^* solves expression 4.3 at the end of the shift when $t = T$ and $\pi_T = \overline{p}$ and, second, that the speed of the shift Δ does not appear in this equation once T and $\overline{p}$ are substituted for t and π_T. Similarly, $y_{T'}^*$ solves expression 4.3 at the end of the faster shift when $t = T'$ and $\pi_{T'} = \overline{p}$, and this equation is identical to the one defining x_T^*. Thus, x_T^* equals $y_{T'}^*$.

x^*_{T-1} and attacking. Thus, the toughest type the declining state might be facing when the slower shift ends is $\tilde{r}_{T-1}$.

At the end of the faster shift, by contrast, the declining state believes that it is facing only those types that would have accepted the previous offer $y^*_{T'-1}$. In other words, the declining state believes that its adversary's cost is at least $\tilde{r}'_{T'-1}$. Hence, the toughest type that the declining state might be facing is $\tilde{r}'_{T'-1}$.

It turns out that this difference in beliefs has no effect on the declining state's optimal offer. This offer balances the marginal gain of offering slightly more against the marginal cost of doing so, and these toughest types have no effect on these marginal calculations. The marginal gain has to do with "marginal" types that would reject one offer but accept a slightly more favorable offer. But both $\tilde{r}_{T-1}$ and $\tilde{r}'_{T'-1}$ are far from the margin and therefore do not affect this calculation. Similarly, the marginal cost of offering slightly more is the net loss to having slightly less weighted by the probability that the slightly smaller offer would have been accepted. But this probability depends on the types that accept the offer and not on types like $\tilde{r}_{T-1}$ and $\tilde{r}'_{T'-1}$ that reject it.

In sum, the only difference between the situations facing the declining state at the end of the two shifts is that the declining state may have different beliefs about the most resolute types it might be facing. But these extreme types have no effect on the declining state's offer. Thus, the declining state makes the same offer at the end of both shifts, and the overall probability that the rising state will be appeased by the declining state's offer is the same. Faster shifts are no more likely to break down in war than slower shifts.

If the speed of the shift does not affect the risk of war, what does it do? During a shift in power the declining state's concessions effectively "screen" the rising state according to its willingness to use force. If the rising state's cost is actually between, say, $\tilde{r}_{t-1}$ and $\tilde{r}_t$, it is screened out at time t; i.e., it attacks at t. The speed of the shift in power affects the size and timing of the declining state's concessions and, therefore, the rate at which the declining state screens the rising state. The faster the distribution of power shifts, the faster the declining state screens the rising state and the larger the risk of war in a particular period. But because the distribution of power is shifting more quickly, this screening occurs over fewer periods. The net effect of screening more quickly over fewer periods is that the probability of war remains.

Although the speed of the shift does not affect the probability of war, the cost of fighting does. The higher the cost, the less likely a shift is to end in war. This result follows directly from the analysis in this chapter and the last. As just shown, the likelihood that a shift in power breaks down in war is the same as the probability that the rising state rejects the declining state's offer when the distribution of power is $\bar{p}$. But the previous chapter showed that this probability decreases as the cost of fighting increases. Thus, shifts in power are less likely to end in war if fighting is more costly.

This account of the way that states cope with a shift in the distribution of power suggests at least three broad empirical patterns. First, some shifts in the distribution of power should pass without war. Second, war should occur at various distributions of power in those cases in which war does occur. There should not be any clustering around an even distribution of power as the power-transition school suggests. Third, faster shifts should not make war more likely.

The data generally support these expectations. If, for example, we operationalize a shift in power as a Great-Power dyad in which the distribution of power changes by at least 5 percent in the twenty years preceding a war or over the intervals 1816–35, 1836–55, 1856–75, 1876–95, 1896–1914, 1920–39, 1946–65, 1966–75, then 23 out of 70 shifts or one-third, end in war. Houweling and Siccama (1988) also find that 8 out of 17 transitions among the most powerful states in the system ended in war. Kim (1989, 1991) and Kim and Morrow (1992) also find that war is neither more nor less likely when the distribution of power is even. This is in keeping with Wayman's (1996) finding that it is a shift in the distribution of power and not a power transition per se that makes war more likely. Finally, Kim (1989, 1991) and Kim and Morrow (1992) also find no relation between the speed of the shift in power and the likelihood of war.[19]

---

[19] Although the expectations derived from the model do find support in the data, this should not be pushed very hard. Efforts to evaluate the effects of shifts in the distribution of power or the power-transition argument must identify cases that did not end in war as well as those that did. Many studies do this by following Organski and Kugler (1980), who decompose the post-1815 period into a number of intervals and then look at the dyads in those intervals. But this procedures suffers from at least three weaknesses.

First, it includes too much in the sample. The power-transition argument as well as the model developed here focus on cases in which the distribution of power is expected to change. This means that dyads in which the distribution of power remains constant or, more accurately, is expected to remain constant should be excluded. Accordingly, dyads in which the distribution of power shifts by less than 5 percent are excluded in the sample above.

Second, a still more basic weakness that imposes overwhelming demands on the data is that a case is a shift in power and not an interval of time. So, for example, the shift in

Conclusion

This chapter and the last have focused on bargaining and compromise as a means of dealing with threats. These threats arise because of disparities between the distributions of power and benefits. When such disparities exist, a state may be willing to use force to try to overturn the existing international order and distribution of benefits associated with that order. The previous chapter assumed that the distribution of power between the states remained constant. This chapter examined how states cope with shifts in the distribution of power.

If there were no informational problems, the declining state would know how much it has to concede to the rising state to satisfy its minimal demands, and its choice would be simple. It could either grant these concessions or face the certainty of war. When confronted with this decision, the declining state generally prefers to satisfy the rising state's minimal demands if the distribution of power is not changing too rapidly and if the distribution of benefits initially favors the declining state. In these circumstances, the distribution of benefits adjusts to reflect the changing distribution of power, and the shift in power passes without war.

Asymmetric information and shifting power create the dynamic analogue of the risk-return trade-off studied in the previous chapter. The more the declining state offers, the more likely the rising state is to accept the offer; but the more the declining state offers, the less it will have if its offer is accepted. The declining state resolves this trade-off by

---

the distribution of power between Britain and Germany following the Franco-Prussian War should probably be seen as one shift in power which ultimately ended in war in 1914 and not as two or possibly three twenty-year cases (1856–1875, 1876–95, 1896–1914) in which only the latter ended in war.

Thinking of the Anglo-German dyad as a single independent case illustrates the third weakness. This procedure ignores strategic interaction with other states and decomposes wars that involve more than two belligerents into dyadic wars assumed to be independent of each other. Unless we do this, there are not enough cases to analyze statistically, but the assumption is obviously troubling.

In light of these difficulties, it is not surprising that statistical efforts to study the relation between the likelihood of war and the distribution of power during a shift in power have led to conflicting findings. For example, Kim (1989, 1991) and Kim and Morrow (1992) do not find any relation between the distribution of power and the likelihood of war when they measure the distribution of power in terms of the internal capabilities of the states in a given dyad. (This is the result reported above.) But they do find a relation when they adjust each state's capabilities by incorporating the capabilities of their respective allies. For surveys of this work, see Kugler and Lemke (1996) and Geller and Singer (1998).

making a series of concessions that "screen" the rising state according to its resolve. If the rising state is relatively unwilling to use force, these concessions satisfy its minimal demands, and the shift in power passes peacefully. If the rising state is more willing to use force, these concessions are not enough, and the shift ends in war. And, the more resolute the rising state, the earlier it attacks.

5

Alignment Decisions in the Shadow of Power

When one state threatens another, a third state has at least three options. It can align with the threatened state, align with the state making the threat, or try to avoid taking part in the conflict by waiting. All three behaviors are common and have a long history in international politics.

In May 1667, France began the War of Devolution by invading the Spanish Netherlands. Within a few months, England and the Dutch Republic had ended the war between them and joined with Sweden in the Triple Alliance to mediate a settlement between France and Spain and to use force against France to impose one if necessary. But, when the Dutch War began four years later, England and Sweden had switched sides by allying with France. Indeed, England was the first to declare war (McKay and Scott 1983, 20–36; Stoye 1969, 259–95).

In the spring of 1741, France, Bavaria, Prussia, and Spain bandwagoned together against a weakened Austria in the War of the Austrian Succession. Count Belle-Isle, who was, in effect, the French foreign minister, was trying to "create a coalition to break up Austria: the Southern Netherlands should go to France, Silesia to Prussia, Bohemia to Bavaria, and the Italian lands to Savoy and the Spanish princes." Britain, realizing that "Austria's existence was at stake and that her destruction would raise the power of France and her German allies to a level which would threaten Hanover and ultimately Britain herself" (McKay and Scott 1983, 165–66), then balanced by allying with Austria (Anderson 1995; Browning 1993; Thomson 1957).

A decade and a half later, the growing conflict between Britain and France in the New World triggered a "Diplomatic Revolution" on the Continent. A now stronger Austria allied with Russia to partition Prussia, and France subsequently joined in when Prussia preemptively attacked after the initial Austro-Russian attack had been delayed. Meanwhile Britain balanced with Prussia to keep French forces on the Continent and to protect Hanover (Horn 1957; McKay and Scott 1983, 181–96; Robson 1957).

States bandwagoned with stronger states, balanced against them, and tried to remain neutral throughout the French Revolutionary and Napoleonic Wars as well. Britain, for example, initially tried to remain neutral and then balanced against France from 1793 onward. Prussia fought against France in the First Coalition, let others do the fighting during the War of the Second Coalition, and subsequently fought with and against France until Napoleon's final defeat at Waterloo. Surveying this period, the diplomatic historian Paul Schroeder concludes that "every major power in Europe except Great Britain—Prussia, Austria, Russia, Spain—bandwagoned as France's active ally for a considerable period" (1994a, 121). Indeed, Austria's decision following Napoleon's disastrous invasion of Russia to join the Fourth Coalition with Britain, Prussia, and Russia can be seen as an effort to shape the final settlement by bandwagoning against France.[1]

Bandwagoning, balancing, and waiting were also common throughout the nineteenth and twentieth centuries. Britain and France allied against Russia in the Crimean War and were eventually supported by Austria while Prussia remained neutral. In 1866, France stood aside when Austria and Prussia went to war, and Austria reciprocated four years later by standing aside when France and Prussia went to war. In 1894, Republican France and Czarist Russia aligned against Germany, and Britain and France moved closer together after the turn of the century in the Entente Cordiale. After war broke out in 1914, the United States waited until 1917 before it entered the war. The United States also remained neutral in the Second World War until attacked by Japan. And Stalin, after trying to ally with Britain and France to oppose Hitler, joined with him in the partition of Poland.

Previous chapters examined how a state responds to threats through reallocating its internal resources or through bargaining and compromise. This chapter considers a state's efforts to deal with threats by aligning with other states and drawing on their resources. What factors affect a state's alignment decisions?

Is there a strong relation between the distribution of power and the choices states make, and, if so, can we explain this relation theoretically? Do states generally balance against the most powerful or most threatening state? Or do states bandwagon by aligning with the most

---

[1] For discussions of balancing, bandwagoning, and remaining neutral during this period, see Gulick (1955), Rosecrance and Lo (1996), Schroeder (1994a, 1994b), and Schweller (1994).

powerful or most threatening state? Or does a state's behavior vary depending on the circumstances facing it?

And, how does the technology of coercion affect states' alignment decisions? Suppose there are "increasing returns to scale in the aggregation of military capabilities" in the sense that the effective military capability of two aligned states fighting together is greater than the sum of the states' individual capabilities. Does this kind of increasing returns to scale make bandwagoning or balancing more likely?

This chapter probes these questions by extending the two-actor bargaining model developed in chapter 3 to a three-actor setting. The alignment game developed below investigates the relation between the distribution of power and states' alignment decisions in the simplest possible formal setting. Even more than in the previous chapters, the present analysis is exploratory and tentative, and is, at most, an early step in a modeling dialogue. As such, it advances our understanding in three ways.

First, specifying the model helps frame the problem and identify critical issues that any analysis—whether formal or not—would have to address. Second, even if states generally do balance as a matter of empirical fact (and this factual claim is contentious as elaborated below), several current arguments explaining why they do are inadequate. The model shows that the link these arguments make from assumptions to purported conclusions is at best incomplete. The analysis in this chapter thus illustrates Krugman's observation that "model-building, especially in its early stages, involves the evolution of ignorance as well as knowledge." (1995, 79). Third, the model suggests that the circumstances that produce balancing behavior are much more restrictive than has been previously appreciated.

Whether a state balances, bandwagons, or waits depends very much on the underlying technology of coercion and, especially, the extent to which there are increasing returns to scale in the aggregation of military capabilities. If these returns are small, i.e., if the effective military capability of two aligned states fighting together is about the same as the sum of the states' individual capabilities, then states generally prefer waiting to balancing or bandwagoning. That is, states tend to "pass the buck" (Christensen and Snyder 1990) to other states by letting them bear the cost of fighting when the returns to scale are slight.

Larger returns to scale undermine the strategy of waiting. The more that military forces cumulate, the more the distribution of power shifts against a state if it stands aside while others fight. This adverse shift makes waiting more costly relative to aligning and induces a state to join the conflict. This can be seen as a form of "chain-ganging" (Christensen and Snyder 1990) in which one state's attack on another compels a third state to enter the fray in order to prevent an adverse shift in the distribution of power.

A state faces a trade-off when deciding how to enter the conflict. A state makes itself relatively more powerful with respect to its coalition partner if it balances by aligning with the weaker of the two other states. This more powerful position reduces its vulnerability to its coalition partner and subsequently enhances that state's ability to secure its interests *if the coalition prevails*. This consideration would seem to make balancing more likely. But there is an opposing factor at work. A state maximizes its chances of being part of a winning coalition if it bandwagons by aligning with the stronger of the two other states. This consideration would seem to make bandwagoning more likely. The model developed in this chapter takes both of these opposing factors into account, and the latter consideration generally outweighs the former. States usually bandwagon if there are large returns to scale. Balancing does occur, however, if there are large returns to scale *and if* the attacker is much more willing to use force than the other states are.

The next section briefly surveys some of the existing work on the relation between alignment decisions and the distribution of power. The third section describes the model which, to keep the analysis manageably simple, focuses only on the case of complete information. As will be seen, a number of assumptions have to be made in order to specify the model and define the states' payoffs. The fourth section examines the payoffs to balancing, bandwagoning, and waiting to ensure that the combined effect of the individually plausible assumptions underlying these payoffs is also reasonable. There follows an analysis of a state's alignment decisions when the states are equally resolute. The sixth section then traces the feedback effects that this decision has on the would-be attacker's decision about whether and whom to strike. The final section reexamines the states' decisions when the attacker is more willing to use force than the other two states.

Balancing versus Bandwagoning

What is the relationship between a state's alignment decisions and the distribution of power among the states? Balance-of-power theory offers one answer to this question: When deciding on which coalition to join, a state generally chooses to align with the weaker of two coalitions. The combined effect of the states' individual decisions in turn produces a balance or roughly even distribution of power between the two coalitions.

The notion that rulers or states balance has a long history. David Hume ([1752]/1898) finds the idea in the writings of Thucydides and Xenophon and in the politics of ancient Greece. It was also present in Italy during the Renaissance: "In the 1440s there began to form in certain Italian minds a conception of Italy as a system of stable states, coexisting by virtue of an unstable equilibrium which was the function of statesmen to preserve" (Mattingly 1955, 71).[2] And, reflecting the then new Newtonian ideas of mechanics and equilibrium, "[T]he conception of a natural balance between states of unequal capabilities provided the foundation for early eighteenth-century theories of international relations. This idea is clearly present in the balance-of-power theories of the period" (Knutsen 1997, 121).[3]

Efforts to explain states' alignment decisions theoretically by explicitly deriving them from clear assumptions about states' ends and the strategic environment in which states pursue their ends are more recent. Indeed, constructing just such an explanation has been one of the major objectives of realist and, later, structural realist theories. As Waltz observes, "If there is any distinctively political theory of international politics, balance-of-power theory is it. And yet one cannot find a statement of the theory that is generally accepted" (1979, 117).

After making this observation, Waltz goes on to provide one of the clearest statements of the theoretical problem and attempts to solve it (116–28).[4] For him, balance-of-power theory "is a theory about the results produced by the uncoordinated actions of states" (122). The theory begins with "assumptions about the interests and motives of states" (122) and about the strategic setting in which those states pursue their interests. Based on those assumptions, the theory then makes predictions about the outcomes that emerge from the states' interaction in this environment.

---

[2] For a skeptical view of the existence of a coherent conception of balancing before the middle of the seventeenth century, see Butterfield (1966, 139).

[3] See Haas (1953), Hinsley (1963), and Knutsen (1997) for historical overviews of balance-of-power theories and thinking.

[4] For earlier realist efforts to construct a balance-of-power theory, see Gulick (1955), Kaplan (1957), and Morgenthau (1967). Haas (1953), still earlier, takes an important initial step by helping to clear the theoretical ground by systematically describing the different ways that the term "balance of power" had been used.

Waltz's formulation of balance-of-power theory is very spare. Indeed, he argues that two assumptions are sufficient to explain the tendencies of balances of power to form. The first pertains to the motives of the units. The states are assumed to be "unitary actors who, at a minimum, seek their own preservation and, at a maximum, drive for universal domination" and which "try in more or less sensible ways to use the means available in order to achieve the ends in view" (1979, 118). The second assumption characterizes the environment in which the states seek their ends. It is that the system is anarchic, i.e., there is "no superior agent to come to the aid of states that may be weakening or to deny to any of them the use of whatever instruments they think will serve their purposes" (118). According to Waltz, these two assumptions lead to the "recurrent formation of balances of power" (119). "Balance-of-power politics prevail whenever two, and only two requirements are met: that the order be anarchic and that it be populated by units wishing to survive" (121).

Believing that balances of power "often fail to form," Stephen Walt offers what he calls "balance-of-threat theory" as a refinement of balance-of-power theory (1988, 279–82; 1987). States respond to imbalances of power in balance-of-power theory, and balancing and bandwagoning are defined in terms of power. To wit, a state balances if it joins the weaker of two coalitions and bandwagons if it aligns with the stronger coalition. Walt, however, argues that states respond to threats rather than capabilities alone, and he redefines balancing and bandwagoning accordingly. A state balances if it joins the less threatening coalition and bandwagons if it aligns with the more threatening coalition in an effort "to appease it or profit from its victory" (1988, 278). Based on a study of alliances in the Middle East from 1955 to 1979, Walt (1987) then concludes that states generally balance against threats.[5]

The claim that states tend to balance has been criticized recently on two scores. The central thrust of Randall Schweller's criticism is that balance-of-threat theory focuses only on

cases in which the goal of alignment is security, and so systematically excludes alliances driven by profit. Yet, as Walt himself claims, one of the primary motivations for bandwagoning is to share in the spoils of victory. When profit rather than security drives alliance choices,

---

[5] Walt (1988) subsequently examines the cases of Iran, Turkey, India, and Pakistan during the cold war and claims that these cases also support the hypothesis that states balance against threats.

there is no reason to expect that states will be threatened or cajoled to climb aboard the bandwagon; they do so willingly.... Thus we will not observe cases of bandwagoning for profit by examining alliances as a response to threats. We must look instead at alliance choices made in the expectation of gain. (1994, 79)

Schweller in effect believes that Walt's cases suffer from a selection bias (King, Keohane, and Verba 1994). That is, Walt's sample of cases is biased toward finding balancing to be more common than bandwagoning. This bias arises because Walt focuses on a set of cases in which the states deciding how to align are under direct threat rather than focusing on a broader and more representative set of cases in which the aligning states might bandwagon in order to share in the spoils of victory. Based on this analysis and a brief review the Italian Wars of 1494–1517, the French bid for hegemony in 1667–79, and the Napoleonic Wars, Schweller concludes that bandwagoning is more prevalent than Walt believes (1994, 93).[6]

Paul Schroeder's criticism centers on balance-of-power theory. He asks whether the theory "is adequate and useful as an explanatory framework for the history of international politics in general, over the whole Westphalian era from 1648 to 1945" (1994a, 110). Based on his reading of history, he concludes that balance-of-power theory fails in this task (1994a, 1994b). The theory "is incorrect in its claims for the repetitiveness of strategy and the prevalence of balancing in international politics" (1994a, 120). Indeed, numerous historical examples "make a *prima facia* case" against these claims (1994a, 120). Overall, Schroeder sees "bandwagoning as historically more common than balancing" (1994a, 117).

This brief review of the conflicting theoretical and empirical claims about the relative prevalence of balancing and bandwagoning suggests that the answer to the question of whether states generally balance or bandwagon is that it depends on the circumstances in which they find themselves. For if this decision did not depend on circumstances and if there were a strong tendency to act in one way or the other, then this pattern should have been readily apparent in the historical record. We would have several large-scale statistical and comparative case studies demonstrating this tendency.

But suggesting that a state's alignment depends on circumstances is to beg the most important question. On what circumstances does it depend and does this decision vary systematically with changes in these

---

[6] See Labs (1992), Kaufman (1992), and Walt (1992) for additional critiques of Walt's analysis and his response.

circumstances? The model developed in the next section takes a step toward answering this question by examining the effects of the distribution of power and the technology of coercion on a state's alignment decisions. Ideally, the analysis will give us a clearer and sharper idea of what patterns we should expect to see in the historical data and experience.

A Model of Alignment

The specification of a model is guided by the questions it is intended to help answer. Three questions are of primary concern here. What is the relation between the distribution of power and a state's alignment decision? How does this decision affect whether or not a dissatisfied state actually attacks and, if so, which state it attacks? And, how do changes in the technology of coercion affect these choices?[7]

In order to address these issues, the model needs to include at least three features. First, one state must have the option of deciding whether or not to attack, and, if it does decide to strike, it must also be able to select which state or states will be attacked. Second, if there is an attack, then the state that is *not* attacked must have the choice of bandwagoning with the attacker, balancing by aligning against the attacker, or waiting.[8] Third, the states' payoffs to these different choices should depend on the distribution of power among the states and on the technology of coercion. A fourth feature would also be desirable. It would be nice if the model grew naturally out of the models considered in previous chapters. Such a connection would bring both technical and substantive benefits.

---

[7] Other game-theoretic efforts to study the relation between the distribution of power and states' alignment decisions include Wagner (1986), who renewed interest in the problem, and Niou and Ordeshook (1990, 1991). Kaplan, Burns, and Quandt (1960) provide an early game-theoretic discussion of this problem.

A major difference between the model developed below and Niou and Ordeshook's is the technology of coercion. They assume what might be called a "voting" technology in which a state is *certain* to prevail over another even if the former is only slightly larger than than the latter, i.e., if the former has slightly more than 50 percent of the resources. Thus a larger state is always dissatisfied with a smaller state. By contrast, the present model assumes that a state that has only slightly more military resources or capabilities than another state is also only slightly more likely to prevail in the event of war.

[8] Unless otherwise noted, the term "bandwagoning" is used throughout the rest of this chapter to mean aligning with the attacking state and "balancing" is used to mean aligning with the attacked state. This usage is more akin to the way the these terms are used in the balance-of-threat analysis than in the balance-of-power argument. This usage is, however, purely a matter of convenience, and we will discuss below whether or not states generally bandwagon or balance and, if so, whether it is against power or threats.

Technically, it might be possible to use the solutions to the previous models to help solve the model of alignment decisions. Substantively, the more closely related the alignment model is to previous models, the easier it is to see the effects of moving from the two-actor setting in those models to the multiple-actor setting of the alignment model.

These features can be captured most simply in a three-actor, two-stage game. Let these three states be called A, S_1, and S_2, and suppose that, as in past models, there is an initial distribution of power among these states as well as an initial distribution of benefits. The distribution of power is discussed at length below. For now, let the probability that state j defeats state k if these two states fight each other and the third state stays out of the conflict be denoted by p_k^j. (The key to this notation, which is employed throughout this chapter, is that $p_{\text{subscript}}^{\text{superscript}}$ denotes the probability that the state or coalition in the superscript defeats the state or coalition in the subscript.) As in previous models, war always eliminates one of the states, so the probability that k defeats j is just $p_j^k = 1 - p_k^j$. Then the initial distribution of power can be described in terms of three probabilities: the probability that the potential attacker, A, would defeat S_1 if they fought in isolation; the probability that the potential attacker would defeat S_2 if they fought in isolation; and the probability that S_1 would defeat S_2 if they fought in isolation. These three probabilities are denoted by p_1^A, p_2^A, and p_2^1.

The distribution of benefits may be thought of as the amount of territory each state initially controls. If, for example, the states initially control the same amount of territory, then the distribution is $\frac{1}{3}$ for the first state, $\frac{1}{3}$ for the second, and $\frac{1}{3}$ for the third where, by assumption, the total amount of territory is one. More generally, the initial distribution of territory can be represented by q_A, q_1, and q_2 which are, respectively, the amount of territory A, S_1, and S_2 control and where $q_A + q_1 + q_2 = 1$.

The first stage of the game models the states' alignment decisions and whether or not one of the states attacks given the initial distributions of power and benefits. If there is no attack in this stage, the game ends peacefully. If there is an attack, then at least one of the states is eliminated as was the case in previous models. This elimination transforms the three-actor game into a two-actor game and begins the second stage. This two-actor, second stage is modeled like the two-actor bargaining game studied in chapter 3.

Figure 5.1 illustrates the sequence of moves in the first stage. The game begins at the open dot where the potential attacker, A, must

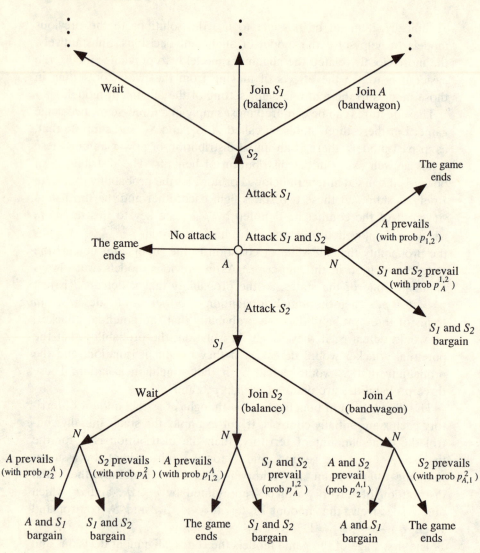

Figure 5.1 The alignment game

choose from four alternatives. It can decide not to attack anyone, in which case the game ends. Or, A can attack S_1 alone, S_2 alone, or attack both S_1 and S_2 at once. If A attacks both states, then either A prevails and eliminates its adversaries, in which case the game ends because there is only one state left, or the coalition of S_1 and S_2 eliminates A and the second bargaining stage begins.

If A attacks only one of the other two states, then the state that has not been attacked must decide what to do. For example, suppose that A attacks S_2. Then S_1 can wait by letting A and S_2 fight it out by themselves; S_1 can balance by aligning with S_2 to oppose the attack; or S_1 can bandwagon by joining with A in the attack.

If S_1 waits, then A prevails and eliminates S_2 with probability p_2^A, and S_2 prevails with probability $p_A^2 = 1 - p_2^A$. In the game tree, this uncertain outcome is represented by a random move made by a player called N (for "Nature"), which plays the branch "A prevails" with probability p_2^A and the branch "S_2 prevails" with probability p_A^2. If A does prevail, then the first stage ends in the elimination of S_2 and the second stage begins with A and S_1 bargaining with each other. If, by contrast, S_2 prevails, then A is eliminated and the second stage begins with S_1 and S_2 facing each other.

If S_1 bandwagons with A, then either the coalition of A and S_1 prevails by eliminating S_2, or S_2 prevails by eliminating A and S_1. If the coalition prevails—which it does with probability $p_2^{A,1}$ where, recall, $p_{\text{subscript}}^{\text{superscript}}$ denotes the probability that the state or coalition in the superscript defeats the state or coalition in the subscript—then the second round begins with A and S_1 confronting each other. If, by contrast, S_2 prevails, the game ends with S_2 in control of all of the territory.

Finally, if S_1 balances by joining S_2, then the coalition of S_1 and S_2 prevails with probability $p_A^{1,2}$. In that event, S_1 and S_2 go on to the second stage. If, however, A prevails, then the game ends and there is no second round as A controls all of the territory and faces no other states.

The second stage begins once one of the states has been eliminated, and what happens in this stage is completely analogous to the complete-information version of the bargaining game studied in chapter 3. The elimination of one of the states in the first stage results in a new distribution of power and a new distribution of benefits between the two remaining states, and these two states bargain about revising this distribution of benefits during the second stage. In particular, one of the states can propose a new territorial division, which the other state can accept, counter with another proposal, or reject in order to impose a new distribution. If the second state accepts, the territory is divided as agreed and the game ends. If the second state attacks, then one or the other of the states is eliminated and the game ends. If the second state makes a counter-offer, then the first state can accept, attack, or make a counter-proposal and so on as in the model described in chapter 3. (The second stage of the alignment game is defined formally in appendix 5.)

Four points should be made about this tree. First, states decide what to do in the first stage based on their expectations about how these decisions will ultimately affect the outcome of the second stage. If, for example, a state believes that it will have to make significant concessions during the bargaining round if it waits while others fight in the first round, then this state is less likely to wait and more likely to align with one of the other states. The bargaining round, therefore, has an important effect on the states' alignment decisions even though it comes after these decisions have been made.

The second observation is that the bargaining stage is closely related to the principle of compensation according to which a victim's territory is divided so "as not to change decisively the strength of any victor in relation to his partners" (Mattingly 1955, 141). Mattingly argues that this principle played an important role in Renaissance diplomacy: "In the arrangements for cutting up the Milanese between France and Venice, or Naples between France and Spain, or the Venetian territories among the allies of the League of Cambrai, the principle was more or less consciously observed (141)." Similarly, Morgenthau (1967, 173) observes that the Treaty of Utrecht (1713), which ended the War of Spanish Succession, divided Spain's possessions between Austria and France so as to conserve the balance of power. The principle was also at work at the Congress of Vienna at the end of the Napoleonic Wars (Gulick 1955) and most dramatically in the partitions of Poland in 1772, 1793, and 1795:

> Since territorial acquisitions at the expense of Poland by any one of the interested nations—Austria, Prussia, and Russia—to the exclusion of the others would have upset the balance of power, the three nations agreed to divide Polish territory in such a way that the distribution of power among themselves would be approximately the same after the partitions as it had been before. (Morgenthau 1967, 173)

Something like this happens in the bargaining stage of the model. As shown in chapter 3, the bargaining results in a distribution of benefits that mirrors the underlying distribution of power. Thus, the victim's territory is divided between the victors in proportion to the distribution of power between the victors. But this division does not reflect a principle in the model, it reflects the underlying distribution of power.

The third point to be made about the game tree is that the model focuses on intra-war alignment decisions. S_1, for example, decides to wait, balance, or bandwagon only after A has decided to attack. This focus is, however, broader than it might first seem. If, for example, S_1 and

S_2 had previously formed an alliance (something not explicitly modeled), then S_1's first-stage decision could be seen as a choice between honoring an alliance or reneging on it.

The analysis of intra-war alignment decisions is, moreover, a prerequisite to analyzing prewar alignment decisions. Just as the states' expectations about the bargaining stage affect the alignment decisions they make in the first stage of the game, the states' expectations about what others will actually do in the event of war affects their peacetime alignment decisions. As noted at the beginning of the chapter, the game is an early step in the modeling enterprise.

The fourth observation about the tree is that the current analysis focuses on alignment decisions and not specifically on alliances, which are usually defined as "a subset of alignments—those that arise from or are formalized by an explicit agreement, usually in the form of a treaty" (G. Synder 1997, 8). The model does not explicitly address the important question of why states sign "scraps of paper" (G. Snyder 1997, 9). How and to what extent formal alliances can create credible commitments is discussed briefly and informally below.[9]

Now consider the state's payoffs. Three kinds of assumptions have to be made in order to specify the payoffs. These assumptions will be discussed informally first and then more formally at the end of this section.

The first assumption pertains to the basic goals of the states. As in the models discussed in chapters 3 and 4, each state derives benefits from the amount of territory it controls. Each state therefore tries to maximize the total amount of territory under its control.

The second kind of assumption describes the cost of fighting. A state's cost of fighting is assumed to reflect two factors: that state's general willingness to use force and the size of its adversary. In particular, the more resolute a state or the smaller its adversary, the lower that state's cost to fighting that adversary. Suppose, for example, that the potential attacker A fights S_1 in isolation, then A's cost is taken to be $c_A \cdot q_1$ where c_A represents A's marginal cost to fighting and q_1 is the size of its opponent S_1. This expression formalizes the idea that the more resolute the potential attacker (i.e., the smaller c_A) or the smaller an adversary's size (i.e., the smaller q_1), then the lower A's cost to fighting.[10]

[9] Other informal discussions of the issue are Stein (1990, 151–69) and G. Snyder (1997, 9–11). Fearon (1994), Morrow (1994a), and Smith (1998) model these issues formally.

[10] Allowing the cost of fighting to depend on the size of the adversary provides a richer formulation than that considered in the bargaining models in chapters 3 and 4. The effects of including this richer but also more complicated formulation in those models is discussed in chapter 6.

To specify the costs of fighting in and against a coalition, suppose that the potential attacker fights the coalition of S_1 and S_2. Then, A's cost is taken to be $c_A(q_1 + q_2)$ where the sum $q_1 + q_2$ is the combined size of A's adversary. If, instead, A and S_2 fight in a coalition against S_1, then A's cost is assumed to depend on its willingness to fight, the size of the third state S_1, and on the distribution of power between the members of the coalition. In particular, A's cost of fighting with S_2 against S_1 is $p_2^A \cdot c_A \cdot q_1$. This expression is just the cost A would bear if it alone fought S_1, namely $c_A \cdot q_1$, weighted by the distribution of power between A and S_2. This cost increases as A becomes more powerful relative to its coalition partner (p_2^A increases) and presumably bears a larger share of the fighting; decreases as A becomes more willing to use force (a lower c_A); and increases with the size of the third state q_1.

Finally, the third type of assumption needed to specify the states' payoffs describes the ways that various alignments affect the distribution of power. Indeed, three questions about the distribution of power must be answered in order to complete the specification:

(i) If two states align, what is the distribution of power between the coalition and a the third state?
(ii) If two states fight together in a coalition and are victorious, what happens to the distributions of power and benefits between them as a result of the fighting?
(iii) If one state waits while two others fight, what will be the resulting distributions of power and benefits between the victor and the state that waited?

The answer to the first question affects a state's payoff to bandwagoning and balancing by specifying the probabilities that it will be on the winning side if it aligns with the stronger or weaker state. The answer to the second question also helps determine a state's payoff to bandwagoning and balancing by describing the distributions of power and benefits that will exist between the coalition partners at the end of the first round of the game if their coalition prevails. These distributions thus determine which state, if either, will be dissatisfied at the outset of the second-stage bargaining and which state will have to make concessions to its former coalition partner. Finally, the answer to the third question essentially defines the payoff to waiting by characterizing the distributions of power and benefits that obtain if a state waits.

Although the accounting mechanism of the model forces these three questions to the surface, it is hard to believe than any systematic analysis of the relation between states' alignment decisions and the distribution of power—whether formal or not—could successfully avoid these issues. As just noted, the answers to these questions describe how the states' decisions affect the distribution of power and, ultimately, the states' pay-offs. The model does not make these questions important; it only makes them explicit and compels us to address them. Unfortunately, we do not have well-established empirical or theoretical answers to these questions, and this is an important task for furture work. We will proceed here by making analytically simple and, we hope, substantively fruitful assumptions.[11]

The first question really asks to what extent do military forces "add up"? How, that is, does forming a coalition affect the probability that the coalition will prevail? The basic idea behind the formulation used here begins by assuming that each state has a latent military capability at the outset of the game. Then the likelihood that one state prevails against another if they fight in isolation is the ratio of that state's military capability to that of its adversary. If, for example, one state's capability is twice that of another, then the odds that the former would prevail are two-to-one. Thus, the states' underlying military capabilities determine the initial distribution of power p_1^A, p_2^A, and p_2^1.[12]

Generalizing this idea, the likelihood that a coalition of two states defeats a third state is the ratio of the coalition's capability to that of the third state. The coalition's capability in turn depends on the individual capabilities of the member states and on the technology of coercion, which describes the degree to which military capabilities "add up." If, for example, there are *increasing returns to scale in the aggregation of military capabilities*, then a coalition's capability is larger than the sum of the individual capabilities of the members of the coalition. If there are

[11] As observed in chapter 1, one of the benefits of a modeling dialogue is that it helps make critical issues and assumptions explicit so that they can be more readily discussed and subjected to empirical and theoretical scrutiny.

[12] This way of specifying a state's power is typically used in quantitative work in international relations based on the Correlates of War data (see Singer and Small 1972; Small and Singer 1982) where a state's relative capability is generally taken to be a weighed average of its shares of total and urban population, military personnel and spending, and energy consumption along with iron and steel production. Accordingly, the use of relative capabilities as a measure for power in the present model not only provides a simple and consistent way of describing the effects of alignment decisions on the probability of prevailing, but it also makes it easier to relate the results derived from the model to empirical work. For a cautionary study that compares perceptions of Russian power before the First World War with estimates based on Correlates of War data, see Wohlforth (1987).

constant returns to scale, a coalition's capability is just equal to the sum of the members' capabilities. And if there are *decreasing returns to scale*, a coalition's capability is less than the sum of the members' capabilities. As will be seen, whether there are increasing, decreasing, or constant returns to scale has an important effect on states' alignment decisions. The parameter g is used to represent the degree to which military forces cumulate. As will be shown below, if there are decreasing, constant, or increasing returns to scale, then g is less than, equal to, or greater than one.

The answer to question (ii) above defines what the distributions of power and benefits are between the victors immediately after the defeat of the third state. These distributions specify the conditions under which the bargaining in the second stage takes place and makes it possible for a state to determine what its payoff would be if it survives into the second round. As we saw in chapter 3, if the distribution of power between the victors mirrors the distribution of benefits between them, then both states are satisfied and there are no further changes in the territorial status quo. If, by contrast, the distribution of benefits following the elimination of the third state does not reflect the distribution of power, then one of the victors is dissatisfied. In these circumstances, the satisfied state meets the dissatisfied state's minimal demands during the complete-information bargaining by conceding just enough territory to the dissatisfied state to make the dissatisfied state indifferent between attacking and accepting the concession.

A very simple assumption defines the initial distributions of power and benefits between the members of a winning coalition. The fighting involved in defeating and eliminating the third state is assumed to leave each of the victors in possession of an amount of the defeated state's territory proportional to the distribution of power between the victors. If, for example, one member of a coalition is twice as strong as the other, then the fighting ends with the former in control of twice as much of the defeated state's territory. It is important to emphasize that this is the distribution of territory resulting *directly* from the fighting, and it is subject to revision during the second stage of bargaining. Indeed, that is what the victors bargain about.

The distribution of power between the members of a coalition following the defeat of a third state is taken to be the same as it was before the war. That is, forming a coalition and fighting together effectively "freezes" the distribution of power between the members of the coalition. If, therefore, one member of a coalition is twice as strong as the other member when the coalition forms, then the former will also be twice as strong as the latter if the coalition fights and prevails.

Finally, suppose that one state attacks another and the third state stands aside while the other two fight. Because it waited, the third state is sure to survive into the bargaining stage. The answer to question (iii) defines the distributions of power and benefits that exist between the third state and the victor at the outset of the bargaining between them.

Suppose more concretely that A attacks S_2 and S_1 waits. The distribution of benefits between S_1 and the victor of the struggle between A and S_2 seems straightforward. By waiting and letting A and S_2 fight it out alone, S_1 neither gains nor loses any territory. Thus, S_1 controls q_1, and the victor controls $q_A + q_2$. What to assume about the distribution of power is, however, less clear. Once the victor has consolidated both A's and S_2's military capabilities, should we assume it to be stronger, weaker, or equal in strength to a coalition composed of A and S_2? To keep things as simple as possible, we assume that the victor in a fight between A and S_2 is equal in strength to the coalition formed between A and S_2. (The consequences of relaxing this assumption are discussed below.)

The remainder of this section describes the preceding assumptions about probabilities and payoffs in more detail and formalizes some of the payoffs. (Appendix 5 characterizes all of the payoffs.) Readers less interested in these details and formalities may want to skip the remainder of this section.

As a first step, it will be helpful to conceive of each state in terms of the territory it controls and its military capability. The territorial distribution is represented by q_A, q_1, and q_2, and the states' capabilities are denoted by k_A, k_1, and k_2. These capabilities define the probabilities that a state or coalition prevails. Suppose that two states, say A and S_1, fight in isolation. Then the probability that A prevails is the ratio of its capability to the total of A's and S_1's capabilities. That is, the probability that A prevails, p_1^A, is $k_A/(k_A + k_1)$.

Now suppose that the potential attacker and S_1 form a coalition and fight S_2. The probability that the coalition prevails, $p_2^{A,1}$, is the ratio between the coalition's military capability, which is $g(k_A + k_1)$, and the total capability of the coalition's and S_2's capabilities. This gives

$$p_2^{A,1} = \frac{g(k_A + k_1)}{g(k_A + k_1) + k_2}$$

where the parameter g measures the extent to which military forces "add up."[13] There are constant returns to scale if $g = 1$, because the coalition's capability is equal to the sum of the states' individual capabilities, i.e., $g(k_A + k_1) = k_A + k_1$. There are increasing returns to scale if $g > 1$, because the coalition's capability is greater than the sum of the states' individual capabilities. And there are decreasing returns if $g < 1$, because the coalition's capability is less than the sum of the members' separate capabilities.

To illustrate the way that the states' payoffs are specified, it is useful to consider some specific paths through the game tree in figure 5.1. Suppose A attacks S_2 and that S_1 then bandwagons by aligning with A and joining in the attack. The specification of S_2's payoff is straightforward because it fights alone and the game ends if it prevails. Accordingly, S_2's payoff to fighting the coalition is its payoff if it prevails times the probability of prevailing plus its payoff if it is defeated weighted by the probability of losing. Prevailing brings S_2 control over all of the territory and a payoff of one less the cost of fighting $c_2(q_A + q_1)$ where, recall, c_2 reflects S_2's willingness to fight and $q_A + q_1$ is the size of its adversary. In symbols, S_2's payoff to prevailing is just $(1 - c_2(q_A + q_1))$. Defeat, however, means that S_2 loses control over all of its territory and pays the cost of fighting. Thus, S_2's expected payoff to fighting the coalition of A and S_1 is $p^2_{A,1}(1 - c_2(q_A + q_1)) + (1 - p^2_{A,1})(0 - c_2(q_A + q_1))$, which reduces to $p^2_{A,1} - c_2(q_A + q_1)$ where $p^2_{A,1}$ is the probability that S_2 prevails over the coalition of A and S_1.

A's and S_1's payoffs depend on the probability that their coalition prevails and on whether the distribution of territory following the elimination of S_2 subsequently changes during the bargaining between A and S_1. If the coalition prevails, then the distribution of power following the conflict is assumed to be the same as it was before the defeat of S_2. Accordingly, the distribution of power at the start of the bargaining stage is the probability that A would defeat S_1 or p_1^A. As for the distribution of benefits between A and S_1 at the start of bargaining phase, each of the victors obtains a share of the defeated state's territory proportional to the distribution of power between them. The attacker A receives $p_1^A q_2$ of S_2's territory, and S_1 obtains $(1 - p_1^A)q_2$.

What happens during the bargaining between A and S_1 depends on the distributions of power and benefits between them. Recall that a state

---

[13] This is just one of many possible formulations. For a discussion of some of the alternatives, see Hirshleifer (1988).

is dissatisfied if its expected payoff to fighting is greater than its payoff to living with the territory it controls. Both states, moreover, cannot be dissatisfied. As shown in chapter 3, at least one of the states has to be satisfied.

If both states are satisfied, i.e., if the distribution of power following the defeat of S_2 roughly mirrors the distribution of benefits, then neither A nor S_1 can credibly threaten to use force to revise the territorial status quo. The bargaining phase therefore ends with A controlling an amount of territory equal to its original share of the territory, q_A, plus what A captures from S_2, which is $p_1^A q_2$. Similarly, the game ends with S_1 in control of $q_1 + (1 - p_1^A)q_2$.

If, by contrast, one of the states, say A, is dissatisfied, then S_1 concedes just enough territory during the bargaining stage to make A indifferent between accepting the concession or attacking. As in chapter 3, A's payoff to attacking equals its probability of prevailing, p_1^A, less its cost of fighting S_1, $c_A(q_1 + (1 - p_1^A)q_2)$. Accordingly, the bargaining ends with A in control of an amount of territory equal to $p_1^A - c_A(q_1 + (1 - p_1^A)q_2)$ and S_1 in control of the remainder.

To illustrate the combined effects of the first and second stages, suppose that A attacks S_2, S_1 subsequently aligns with A, and A and S_1 would be satisfied with each other if their coalition prevails. Then A's payoff to attacking is the payoff A would receive during the bargaining phase weighted by the probability that the coalition prevails plus A's payoff to losing (which is zero minus its share of the cost of fighting S_2) weighted by the probability that the coalition is defeated. In symbols, A's payoff is $p_2^{A,1}(q_A + p_1^A q_2 - c_A p_1^A q_2) + (1 - p_2^{A,1})(0 - c_A p_1^A q_2)$, which simplifies to $p_2^{A,1}(q_A + p_1^A q_2) - c_A p_1^A q_2$. The first term of this simpler expression is just the amount of territory A controls if the coalition prevails weighted by the probability that the coalition prevails. The second term is A's share of the cost of fighting S_2.

Now suppose that A would be dissatisfied with S_1 after their coalition prevails. Then A's payoff to attacking S_2 if S_1 subsequently aligns with A is its bargaining-stage payoff weighted by the probability of surviving the first stage less the cost of fighting. In symbols, this is $p_2^{A,1}[p_1^A - c_A(q_1 + (1 - p_1^A)q_2)] - c_A p_1^A q_2$.[14]

---

[14] In order to simplify the analysis, these payoffs focus on the territory A obtains during the bargaining phase and disregard the territory A controls during the first phase. In effect, then, these payoffs ignore the role of discounting.

The Payoffs to Balancing, Bandwagoning, and Waiting

As the previous section made clear, many crucial assumptions have to be made in order to specify the states' payoffs to balancing, bandwagoning, and waiting. There are, moreover, several plausible alternatives for each of these assumptions, and, unfortunately, the existing theoretical and empirical work in international relations provides little or no guidance in choosing among these possibilities. The choices described here were made with an eye toward both substantive richness and analytic simplicity. Seen in this light, each assumption seems plausible when considered individually. But the payoffs to balancing, bandwagoning, and waiting combine these individual assumptions in different ways, and this poses a question. Do these combinations also seem plausible? This section examines the gross behavior of these payoffs to ensure that it, too, seems reasonable. Once this has been done, the next section will compare these payoffs to each other in order to determine how the states align.

We will use a simple comparative-static analysis to study the behavior of the individual payoffs and, later, the states' alignment decisions. This analysis begins at the point at which the distributions of power and benefits mirror each other. Then it traces the effects of an increase in the potential attacker's military capability while the other two states' military capabilities remain constant. This change increases the potential attacker's strength relative to each of the other states while leaving the relative strength between the other two states unchanged.

To specify the comparative-static analysis more precisely, we first need to identify the starting point of the analysis, i.e., the distribution of power that mirrors a particular territorial distribution. Recall that the distribution of territory is q_A, q_1, and q_2 where the potential attacker controls q_A, S_1 controls q_1, and S_2 controls q_2 with $q_A + q_1 + q_2 = 1$. Then, just as in the model examined in chapter 3, the distribution of power between two states, say A and S_1, mirrors the distribution of benefits between them if the probability that A defeats S_1 equals A's share of the total territory that these states control. That is, the distributions of power and benefits between A and S_1 mirror each other if $p_1^A = q_A/(q_A + q_1)$. Similarly, the distribution of power between A and S_2 and between S_1 and S_2 is the same as the distribution of benefits between them if $p_2^A = q_A/(q_A + q_2)$ and $p_2^1 = q_1/(q_1 + q_2)$. Thus we can find the distribution of power that mirrors any initial distribution of territory, and this is where the comparative-static analysis starts.

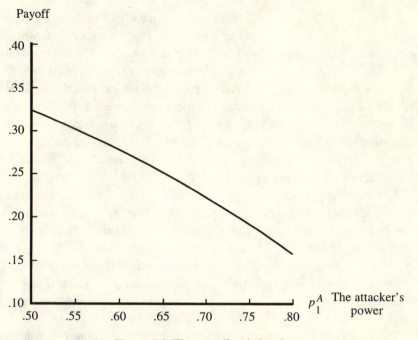

Figure 5.2 The payoff to balancing

As the potential attacker's military capability grows, it becomes relatively more powerful, and the probability that it would prevail over S_1 in a bilateral contest rises. In symbols, p_1^A increases as A's capabilities grow. Similarly, the probability that A would prevail over S_2, p_2^A, also increases. However, the distribution of power between S_1 and S_2, p_2^1, remains constant because there has been no change in these states' capabilities.

Figure 5.2 illustrates the effects of an increase in A's capabilities on the payoff to balancing given that each state initially controls an equal share of the territory ($q_A = q_1 = q_2 = \frac{1}{3}$). More specifically, the figure plots S_1's payoff to aligning with S_2 given that A has attacked S_2.[15] Intuitively, we would expect the payoff to balancing against a stronger attacker to be less than the payoff to balancing against a weaker attacker, and this is precisely what the figure shows. Starting at $p_1^A = \frac{1}{2}$ where the distribution of power mirrors the distribution of benefits, i.e., where

[15] S_1's and S_2's payoffs to balancing are the same because these states are identical in size, power, and willingness to use force. Thus, figure 5.2 also depicts S_2's payoff to balancing with S_1 against A if A attacks S_1.

$p_1^A = q_A/(q_A + q_1) = (\frac{1}{3})/(\frac{1}{3} + \frac{1}{3}) = \frac{1}{2}$, the payoff to balancing steadily declines as A's military capability grows and p_1^A increases. (It will be convenient to represent the changes in the potential attacker's military capabilities implicitly by plotting p_1^A along the horizontal axis.)

The effects of changes in the cost of fighting and of the degree to which military forces cumulate are depicted in figure 5.3. If S_1 balances by fighting with S_2 against A, then S_1 is certain to pay the cost of fighting. Accordingly, an increase in the cost of fighting should decrease the payoff to balancing, and this turns out to be the case. Figure 5.3a shows the effect of an increase in the cost.

The extent to which two states' military forces cumulate when they align with each other affects the probability that S_1 and S_2 will defeat the attacker. The more that these states' forces cumulate, the higher the probability of defeating A and the larger S_1's payoff to aligning with S_2. Figure 5.3b illustrates this in the case in which there are decreasing returns to scale $(g < 1)$, constant returns to scale $(g = 1)$, and increasing returns to scale $(g > 1)$. As expected, the payoff to balancing increases in g.

The payoff to waiting is somewhat more complicated because it incorporates several factors. Suppose A attacks S_2 and S_1 waits. Waiting ensures that S_1 makes it into the bargaining stage of the game. Therefore, S_1's payoff to waiting is determined by the outcome of the bargaining that takes place between S_1 and the victor in the conflict between A and S_2. As shown in chapter 3, this outcome depends in turn on whether the victor is satisfied or dissatisfied with S_1.

Consider first the case in which the victor is satisfied with S_1. That is, the victor is unwilling to use force against S_1 given the distributions of power and benefits that exist between the victor and S_1 at the beginning of the bargaining. Because the victor is unwilling to use force, S_1 does not have to make any concessions to appease its adversary and, therefore, maintains control over all of its territory. Thus, S_1's payoff to waiting in these circumstances is its payoff to controlling its original share of the territory.

If, by contrast, the victor is dissatisfied with S_1, then S_1 has to concede some of its territory to its adversary. And, the more powerful its adversary, the more that S_1 has to surrender. (Recall that S_1 must give its adversary control over an amount of territory equal in value to its adversary's payoff to fighting, and, therefore, the more powerful the adversary, the more S_1 must concede.)

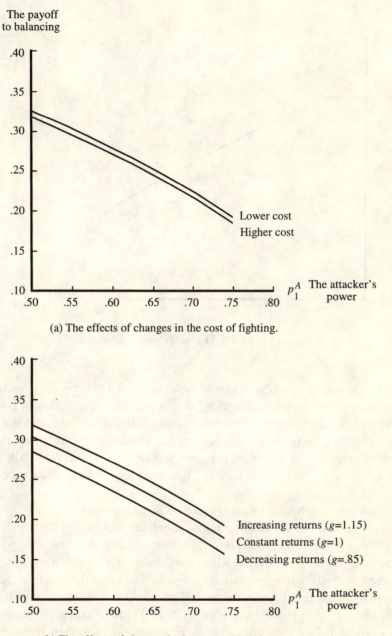

The payoff
to balancing

.40

.35

.30

.25

.20 Lower cost
     Higher cost

.15

.10
   .50   .55   .60   .65   .70   .75   .80 p_1^A The attacker's
                                                      power

(a) The effects of changes in the cost of fighting.

.40

.35

.30

.25

.20 Increasing returns (g=1.15)
     Constant returns (g=1)

.15 Decreasing returns (g=.85)

.10
   .50   .55   .60   .65   .70   .75   .80 p_1^A The attacker's
                                                      power

(b) The effects of changes in the returns to scale.

Figure 5.3 The effects of changes in the technology of coercion on the payoff to balancing

Payoff

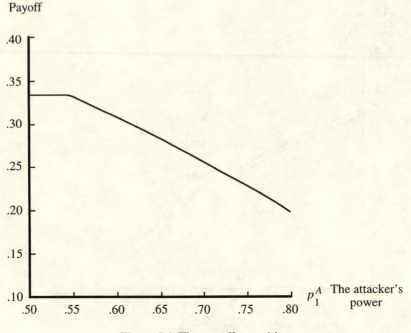

Figure 5.4 The payoff to waiting

The shape of S_1's payoff to waiting in figure 5.4 reflects these factors. As before, the graph begins at $p_1^A = \frac{1}{2}$ where the distribution of power mirrors the distribution of benefits. Then, as the potential attacker's capabilities begin to grow, p_1^A becomes a little larger than $\frac{1}{2}$. In these circumstances, the victor of the contest between A and S_2 is still satisfied with S_1, and, consequently, S_1 retains all of its territory and its payoff is $\frac{1}{3}$.

The reason why the victor is satisfied is that its military capability depends on two key factors: the initial capabilities of A and S_2, which the victor combines after defeating its adversary, and the extent to which these capabilities cumulate when combined. If the potential attacker is only a little stronger than it would be if the initial distribution of power among the three states exactly mirrored the distribution of benefits (i.e., if p_1^A is not too much larger than $\frac{1}{2}$) and if military capabilities do not cumulate too much (i.e., if g is not too big), then the victor's power grows in roughly the same proportion as its territory does when it incorporates the defeated state's military capabilities *and* its territory. This implies that the distribution of power between the victor and S_1

is approximately the same as the distribution of benefits between them. In these circumstances, the victor is satisfied and S_1 does not have to make any concessions.

If, by contrast, the attacker's military capabilities are relatively large so that p_1^A is large in comparison to A's territorial share of $\frac{1}{3}$, then when the victor in the war between A and S_2 combines both states' military capabilities, its power will be proportionately larger than its territory. In these circumstances, the victor is dissatisfied with S_1 at the beginning of the bargaining stage, and S_1 has to appease its adversary. This leaves S_1 with a payoff of less than $\frac{1}{3}$. Indeed, the stronger A, the stronger the victor of the struggle between A and S_2 is after combining the states' capabilities, and the more S_1 has to concede during the subsequent bargaining. Accordingly, S_1's payoff to waiting declines as p_1^A increases as figure 5.4 shows.[16]

A change in the technology of coercion, which increases the extent to which military forces cumulate, makes the victor in the fight between A and S_2 stronger in the bargaining with S_1. This has two effects on S_1's payoff to waiting. First, it shrinks the range over which S_1 can stand aside without then having to make concessions to the victor during the bargaining stage. That is, if military capabilities cumulate more (a higher g), the victor becomes dissatisfied with S_1 when A's military capabilities are smaller and p_1^A is lower. Accordingly, S_1's payoff to waiting begins to decline earlier, as it has to make concessions to satisfy its adversary at lower values of p_1^A. Second, if S_1 already had to make a concession to appease a dissatisfied victor, then S_1 would have to make an even larger concession if there were larger returns to scale. Thus, larger returns to scale reduce S_1's payoff to waiting. These effects are depicted in figure 5.5.

---

[16] These complications did not arise when calculating the payoff to balancing because the attacker's strength affects the chances that the balancing coalition of S_1 and S_2 prevails, but it does not affect whether or not there is a dissatisfied state in the bargaining round. Indeed, S_1 and S_2 are always satisfied with each other if their coalition prevails. Thus, S_1's payoff to balancing against A continually decreases as A becomes stronger.

The fact that S_1 and S_2 remain satisfied with each other regardless of A's strength follows from three assumptions. First, the initial distribution of power between these states mirrors the distribution of benefits between them ($p_2^1 = \frac{1}{2}$, $q_1 = q_2 = \frac{1}{2}$), and, therefore, these two states are initially satisfied with each other. Second, the distribution of power between S_1 and S_2 is unaffected by the defeat of A, and, third, the fighting that defeats A results in an initial division of A's territory between S_1 and S_2, which is proportional to the distribution of power between them. Consequently, the distributions of power and benefits between S_1 and S_2 mirror each other at the beginning of the bargaining stage.

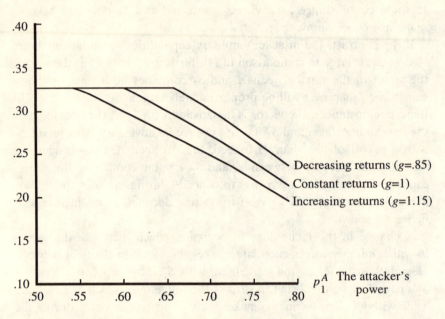

Payoff

Figure 5.5 Returns to scale and the payoff to waiting

Finally, consider S_1's payoff to bandwagoning with A by joining in the attack on S_2. Here, S_1's payoff depends on what happens in the bargaining stage that takes place if the coalition of A and S_1 defeats S_2. If A is satisfied with S_1 following the elimination of S_2, then S_1 keeps all of its own territory plus the share of territory it takes from S_2. If, by contrast, A is dissatisfied with S_1, then S_1 has to appease A during the bargaining stage by conceding some territory. And, the stronger A, the more S_1 concedes and the lower is its payoff to bandwagoning.

These features are reflected in figure 5.6. As in the past, the distribution of power among the three states mirrors the distribution of benefits at $p_1^A = \frac{1}{2}$, given that each state initially controls one-third of the territory. If the potential attacker is only a little more powerful than this, then A would be satisfied with S_1 following the defeat of S_2. The reason is that because A and S_1 incorporate S_2's territory in proportion to the distribution of power between them, the distributions of power and territory at the start of the bargaining stage will roughly mirror each other if p_1^A is not too much larger than $\frac{1}{2}$.

As long as A would be satisfied with S_1 following the defeat of S_2 (i.e., as long as p_1^A is not too much larger than $\frac{1}{2}$), we might expect S_1 to

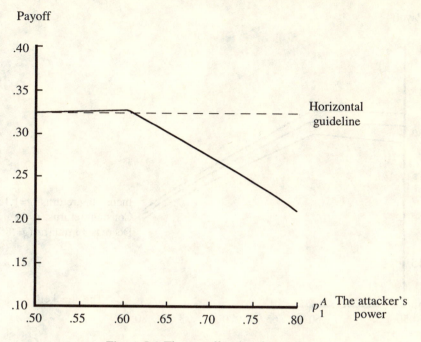

Figure 5.6 The payoff to bandwagoning

benefit from having a stronger coalition partner, and this is illustrated in figure 5.6. S_1's payoff to bandwagoning with A increases as A becomes stronger and p_1^A increases as long as p_1^A is not too much larger than $\frac{1}{2}$. (The horizontal guideline makes this easier to see.)

But this changes once the attacker is so strong that it would be dissatisfied with S_1 following S_2's elimination. S_1 no longer benefits from having a stronger coalition partner. Indeed, the stronger A is, the more S_1 has to concede and the lower its payoff. Accordingly, S_1's payoff to bandwagoning eventually begins to decline as p_1^A continues to rise.[17]

The effect of a change in the technology of coercion that increases the extent to which military capabilities cumulate makes the coalition of A and S_1 stronger. This in turn raises the coalition's probability of prevailing, but it does not affect the distributions of power and benefits

---

[17] Even when S_1 is not facing a dissatisfied coalition partner, an increase in its partner's strength has two opposing effects. It makes the coalition more likely to win, but it also reduces S_1's share of the spoils because these are divided according to the distribution of power between the states in the coalition. In the present formulation, the first effect dominates the latter, and S_1 benefits from having a stronger coalition partner.

Payoff

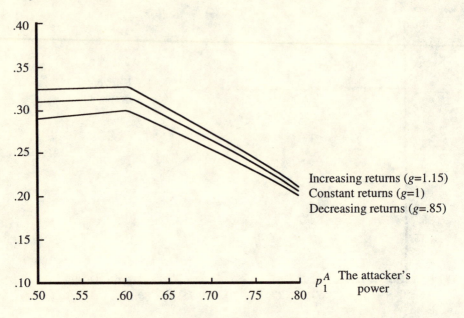

Figure 5.7 Returns to scale and the payoff to bandwagoning

between the coalition partners. Thus, the payoff to bandwagoning rises as the returns to scale increase as is shown in figure 5.7.

In sum, an increase in A's military capabilities may affect another state's payoffs to balancing, bandwagoning, and waiting through two channels. First, it may affect the likelihood that a state survives the first stage of the game and makes it into the bargaining round. Second, an increase in A's capabilities may also affect the distributions of power and benefits that exist between the two surviving states at the beginning of the bargaining. These distributions subsequently determine whether or not the territorial status quo changes during the bargaining. As we have seen, the first factor largely determines the payoff to balancing, both factors shape the payoff to bandwagoning, and the second factor decides the payoff to waiting.

The Alignment Decision

States do not balance, bandwagon, or wait because they attach intrinsic value to any of these behaviors. States align for instrumental reasons. Balancing, bandwagoning, and waiting are means through which a state tries to obtain more basic ends. The questions to ask therefore are: What kinds of alignment decisions do the strategic incentives in the international system induce? Are there dominant patterns of state behavior? Do these incentives generally lead to balancing, and, if so, do states usually align against the most powerful state as Waltz (1979) and others argue or against the most threatening state as Walt (1987, 1988) claims? Or is bandwagoning more prevalent than balancing as Schroeder (1994a) believes? And, how do changes in the technology of coercion affect these decisions?

This section examines the states' alignment decisions in the model when the states are all equally willing to use force, i.e., when the states' marginal costs c_A, c_1, c_2 are the same. (This assumption will be relaxed below.) Balancing behavior is largely absent in these circumstances; states wait or bandwagon.

Whether a state waits or aligns with another depends on the extent to which there are increasing returns to scale in the aggregation of military capabilities. If capabilities do not cumulate very much, a state is more likely to "pass the buck" (Christensen and Snyder 1990) by letting others bear the burden and pay the cost of fighting. If, by contrast, there are larger returns to scale, then a state suffers a large adverse shift in the distribution of power if it waits while others fight. Worse, the victor's power grows disproportionately large compared to the additional territory it acquires from the defeated state. Thus, the victor will be dissatisfied with the state that waited, and the latter will have to make a large concession to appease the victor. This large concession makes waiting very costly if there are large returns to scale, and a state will join the fray by either balancing or bandwagoning to prevent the distribution of power from shifting against it. In this sense, the states are chain-ganged (Christensen and Snyder 1990) together.

A state faces a different trade-off when choosing between balancing and bandwagoning. *By aligning with the weaker of two other states, a third state makes itself more powerful with respect to its coalition partner than it would have been had it aligned with the stronger of the two other states.* Because of this more favorable distribution of power, a state is less vulnerable to being exploited by its coalition partner and better able to further its interests should the coalition prevail. More formally, a state will be more powerful in the bargaining stage of the model if it aligns with the weaker of the two other states and, consequently, will obtain a "better deal" from its coalition partner than it would have received from aligning with the stronger state. This consideration makes balancing more attractive than bandwagoning.

But the accounting mechanism of the model shows that there is an opposing factor at work. The advantages of the more favorable distribution of power created by aligning with the weaker of two possible coalition partners will only be realized if the coalition prevails. As Waltz puts it, "Secondary states, if they are free to choose, flock to the weaker side; for it is the stronger side that threatens them. On the weaker side, they are both more appreciated and safer, *provided, of course, that the coalition they join achieves enough defensive or deterrent strength to dissuade adversaries from attacking*" (1979, 127, emphasis added). But states are rarely sure of defeating or deterring another state and usually can only affect the chances of doing so. *A state is less likely to be part of a winning coalition if it aligns with the weaker side and more likely to be part of a winning coalition if it aligns with the stronger side*. This consideration makes bandwagoning more appealing.

Thus, the states face a complicated trade-off when deciding between balancing and bandwagoning. Balancing entails a lower probability of being part of a winning coalition but being relatively more powerful if the coalition prevails. Bandwagoning entails a higher probability of being part of a winning coalition but being relatively weaker if the coalition prevails. The latter usually outweighs the former in the model, and states generally bandwagon if there are large returns to scale.

To examine the alignment decisions in more detail, consider first the situation in which the states, in addition to being equally resolute, are all the same size and there are moderately large increasing returns to scale. In symbols, $q_A = q_1 = q_2 = \frac{1}{3}$ and $g = 1.15$. Suppose further that A attacks S_2. Then figure 5.8 plots S_1's payoffs to waiting, balancing against A by aligning with S_2, and bandwagoning with A by joining in the attack on S_2.[18]

The graph begins where the distribution of power among the three states exactly mirrors the distribution of benefits, i.e., at $p_1^A = q_A/(q_A + q_1) = \frac{1}{2}$. At this point, S_1's payoff to balancing equals its payoff to bandwagoning because A and S_2 are equal in size and power. Thus, it makes no difference to S_1 whether it aligns with S_2 to fight A or with A to fight S_2. However, S_1 has to bear the cost of fighting if it balances or bandwagons. If, by contrast, S_1 waits, it avoids these costs. Furthermore,

---

[18] These are also S_2's payoffs if A attacks S_1 because S_1 and S_2 are identical in size, power, and willingness to use force.

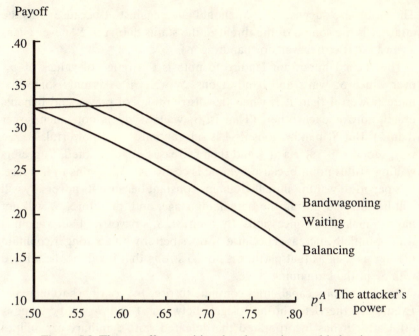

Figure 5.8 The payoffs to waiting, bandwagoning, and balancing

S_1 will not have to make any concessions during the bargaining because the distributions of power and benefits mirror each other. These factors make the payoff to waiting higher than the payoffs to bandwagoning or balancing. Consequently, S_1 prefers not to fight—even if aligned with another state—when the distribution of power reflects the distribution of benefits and fighting is costly. As was the case in the two-actor model in chapter 3, states are generally unwilling to use force to overturn the status quo when the distribution of benefits mirrors the distribution of power.[19]

Two aspects of figure 5.8 are especially noteworthy. First, S_1 never balances regardless of how strong A is. This contradicts the expectations of both the balance-of-power and balance-of-threat analyses. The former argues that S_1 should align against A because A is the stronger power.[20]

---

[19] This unwillingness depends in a multipolar setting on the extent to which military capabilities cumulate. If there are very large returns to scale, then the expected payoff to fighting as a member of a coalition may outweigh the costs even if the distributions of power and benefits among the states are identical.

[20] If $p_1^A > \frac{1}{2}$, then the probability that A will defeat S_2 is greater than $\frac{1}{2}$ since $p_1^A = p_2^A$, and therefore A is more powerful than S_2.

The latter also suggests that S_1 should align against A because A as the attacker is the source of the threat to the status quo. Yet, S_1 never aligns against A. It either waits or bandwagons.

The second important feature to note is the range of values of p_1^A over which S_1 waits and bandwagons. S_1 waits if A is only somewhat more powerful than it is when the distributions of power and benefits exactly mirror each other. (That is, S_1 waits if p_1^A is not much larger than $\frac{1}{2}$). But S_1 bandwagons if A is substantially more powerful. To see why, suppose p_1^A starts at $\frac{1}{2}$ and then increases. As just noted, S_1 prefers waiting at this point because fighting is costly. As p_1^A begins to increase, S_1's payoff to waiting initially remains constant because its adversary will still be satisfied during the bargaining stage, and, therefore, S_1 will not have to make any concessions. By contrast, S_1's payoff to bandwagoning with A initially increases because S_1 does better with a stronger coalition partner as long as that partner is not so strong that it will be dissatisfied with S_1 in the bargaining stage.

As A's military capabilities continue to rise, p_1^A continues to increase. Eventually, the victor in the struggle between A and S_2 will be so powerful after it has incorporated the defeated state's military capabilities that the victorious state will be dissatisfied with S_1 when the bargaining begins. If S_1 waits in these circumstances, it will have to appease its adversary during the bargaining; and the stronger the adversary, the more S_1 will have to concede. Accordingly, S_1's payoff to waiting begins to decline and continues to do so as p_1^A increases. At some point, waiting means such a large adverse shift in the distribution of power against S_1 that the cost of appeasing S_1's adversary during the subsequent bargaining becomes larger than S_1's cost to fighting in a coalition with A. At that point, S_1 switches from waiting to bandwagoning to forestall this adverse shift in the distribution of power.

We can think of this switch as a change from what Christensen and Snyder (1990) call buck-passing to chain-ganging. States pass the buck when they let others bear the costs of fighting and are chain-ganged together when no state can sit out a conflict because doing so would allow the distribution of power to shift too far against it. And, as we have just seen, S_1 changes from waiting to bandwagoning to avoid just such a shift.[21]

---

[21] Christensen and Snyder (1990) discuss buck-passing and chain-ganging solely in the context of the internal dynamics of alliances, whereas these terms are used here to refer to states' alignment decisions.

How do changes in the technology of coercion affect when S_1 switches from waiting to bandwagoning? Roughly, the more military capabilities cumulate, the more states tend to be chain-ganged together and the earlier they begin to bandwagon. To see this, observe that the larger the returns to scale, the more quickly S_1 faces a dissatisfied adversary if it waits and the more quickly its payoff to waiting begins to decline. If, by contrast, S_1 bandwagons, then larger returns to scale make the coalition of A and S_1 stronger and, thereby, increase S_1's payoff. The combined effect of these changes is that S_1 switches from waiting to bandwagoning sooner (i.e., at a lower p_1^A) as figure 5.9 indicates.

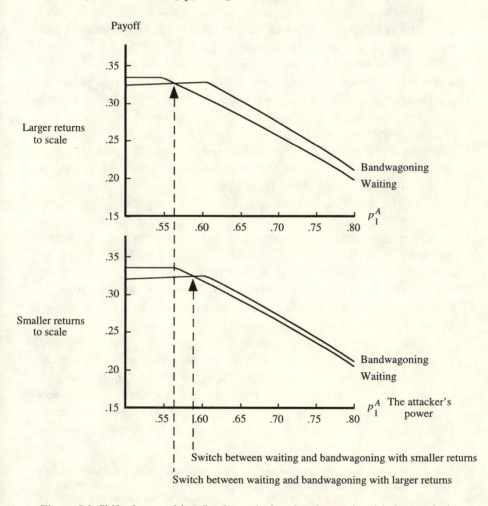

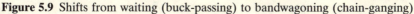

Figure 5.9 Shifts from waiting (buck-passing) to bandwagoning (chain-ganging)

This section concludes with a discussion of two variants of the model. The preceding analysis has assumed that it does not matter how resources are combined. If one state conquers another, the victor is neither more nor less powerful than the coalition composed of these two states would have been. To relax this assumption, suppose that coalitions are relatively less efficient at combining resources. This change has no effect on a state's payoff to waiting but does lower the payoffs to balancing and bandwagoning. To wit, if a state waits while others fight, then no coalitions ever form and the fact that they would be less efficient if they had does not affect the payoff to standing aside. If, by contrast, a state bandwagons or balances, the coalition is less likely to prevail because it is relatively less efficient. This reduces the payoff to aligning and increases the range over which states wait.

The second variant examines the states' alignment decisions when the states differ in size. Suppose, for example, that S_1 is larger than the potential attacker and that S_2 is smaller. More concretely, assume that S_1 is, say, one-third larger than the potential attacker and S_2 is one-third smaller. In symbols, $q_A = \frac{1}{3}$, $q_1 = \frac{4}{9}$, and $q_2 = \frac{2}{9}$.

Figure 5.10 plots S_1's and S_2's payoffs starting from the point at which the distribution of power mirrors the distribution of benefits, i.e., $p_1^A = q_A/(q_A + q_1) = \frac{3}{7} \approx .43$. As in the past, the states prefer waiting to aligning. But the payoffs to balancing and bandwagoning are now different because the states are different sizes. In particular, the larger state S_1 prefers bandwagoning to balancing whereas the smaller state S_2 prefers balancing at $p_1^A \approx .43$. Or, put another way, if a state has to align with another state rather than wait, it prefers to align with the larger and, therefore, more powerful state. To wit, S_1 joins with A when choosing between A and the smaller S_2, and S_2 aligns with S_1 when choosing between A and the larger S_1.[22]

Increases in A's military capabilities have the same general effect on a state's alignment decision regardless of the state's size. As long as A is not too powerful, i.e., as long as p_1^A is not too large, the cost of appeasing a dissatisfied adversary during the bargaining phase is less than the cost of fighting, and the state waits. Once A becomes sufficiently powerful, waiting entails accepting too adverse a shift in the distribution

[22] Appendix 5 shows that if the distribution of power mirrors the distribution of benefits, then the conclusion that the payoff to aligning with the larger state is greater than the payoff to aligning with the smaller state holds in general and not just for the particular values of $q_A = \frac{1}{3}$, $q_1 = \frac{4}{9}$, and $q_2 = \frac{2}{9}$.

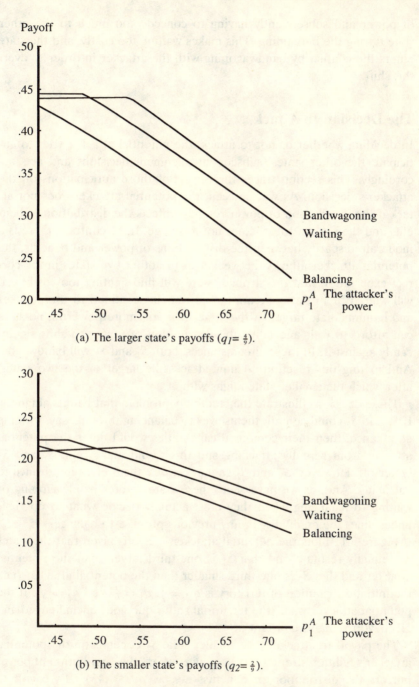

(a) The larger state's payoffs ($q_1 = \frac{4}{9}$).

(b) The smaller state's payoffs ($q_2 = \frac{2}{9}$).

Figure 5.10 The payoffs of differently sized states

of power and subsequently having to concede too much to the other state during the bargaining. This makes waiting too costly, and the state enters the conflict by bandwagoning with the attacker in order to avert this shift.

The Decision to Attack

In deciding whether or not to attack, the potential attacker tries to anticipate the other states' subsequent alignment decisions and acts accordingly. This section traces the effects of those anticipations on the attacker's decision. As will be seen, the potential attacker does not attack if the distribution of power roughly reflects the distribution of benefits and the returns to scale are not too large. If, by contrast, there is a moderate disparity between the distributions of power and benefits, the potential attacker attacks the weaker of the other two states in the correct expectation that the stronger state will find fighting too costly and will wait. War in these circumstances remains confined to the attacker and its immediate target. If the attacker is still more powerful, no state can afford to wait and allow the distribution of power to shift significantly against it. In these circumstances, both S_1 and S_2 will bandwagon. Anticipating this reaction, A now attacks the larger of the two states, after which the smaller state aligns with A.

These decisions illustrate the credibility problem that haunts alliances. If S_1 and S_2 could commit themselves to balancing through, say, forming an alliance, then their combined capabilities would deter the potential attacker from actually attacking and this would make both S_1 and S_2 better-off. However, S_1 and S_2 cannot *commit* themselves in advance to balancing. And, as we have seen, these states prefer bandwagoning or waiting to balancing when they must actually decide what to do. This undermines the credibility of any previous promise to balance.

Figure 5.11 plots the potential attacker's payoffs given that the states are equally resolute and that S_1 is one-third larger than the potential attacker and that S_2 is one-third smaller than the potential attacker (i.e., the initial distribution of territory is $q_A = \frac{1}{3}$, $q_1 = \frac{4}{9}$, and $q_2 = \frac{2}{9}$). If the potential attacker waits, the territorial status quo goes unchallenged and A's payoff remains constant at $\frac{1}{3}$.

The payoff to attacking the smaller state S_2 depends on the potential attacker's military strength. At the outset where the distribution of power mirrors the distribution of benefits (i.e., at $p_1^A \approx .43$), A's payoff to striking S_2 is less than its payoff to waiting. This follows because the

Payoff

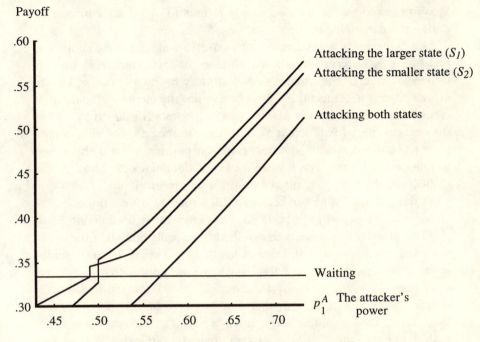

Figure 5.11 The potential attacker's payoffs

conflict between A and S_2 remains completely isolated and unaffected by S_1's presence. That is, S_1 waits while A and S_2 fight (see figure 5.10a) and then does not have to offer any concessions in the subsequent bargaining because the victor of the struggle between A and S_2 is satisfied with S_1. Since the conflict between A and S_2 remains isolated, then the analysis of the bilateral bargaining game in chapter 3 shows that A is satisfied with S_2 and therefore prefers not to attack S_2 as long as fighting is costly and the distribution of benefits between A and S_2 reflects the distribution of power between them.

As the potential attacker's capabilities start to rise, p_1^A begins to increase and A's payoff to attacking S_2 also grows. This higher payoff results solely from the fact that A is stronger and therefore more likely to defeat S_2 in a war that still remains isolated. To see that S_1's presence continues to have no effect, observe from figure 5.10a that S_1 still prefers to wait and does not have to make any concessions during the bargaining phase until $p_1^A \approx .48$ (which is where S_1's payoff to waiting begins to decline because it starts making concessions). Consequently,

S_1 continues to wait and subsequently refuses to make any concessions during the bargaining as long as $p_1^A < .48$.

As p_1^A increases a little more, A's payoff to attacking S_2 jumps up, and figure 5.10a explains why. S_1 switches at this point from waiting to bandwagoning. This change in S_1's strategy has two opposing effects on A's payoffs to attacking S_2. First, it significantly increases the military capabilities brought to bear against S_2, which boosts A's payoff by raising the chances that A will defeat S_2. But, second, the spoils of victory now have to be divided with A's new coalition partner S_1, and this tends to reduce A's payoff. The former, however, dominates the latter in the model, and the net effect on A's payoff is an upward jump.

As the potential attacker becomes still stronger, p_1^A continues to increase and A's payoff to attacking S_2 rises moderately until about $p_1^A \approx .53$. This gradual rise is solely due to the higher probability that the coalition of A and S_1 prevails. If it does, then there will be no further changes in the status quo during the bargaining stage as neither A nor S_1 will be dissatisfied. However, once p_1^A exceeds .53, A will be dissatisfied with S_1 if their coalition defeats S_2. S_1 therefore begins to have to make concessions during the bargaining stage, and S_1's payoff to bandwagoning starts to decline (see figure 5.10a). A's overall payoff to attacking S_2 therefore rises more rapidly.

The potential attacker's payoff to striking the larger state S_1 resembles its payoff to fighting the smaller state S_2. At the outset where the distributions of power and benefits are identical (i.e., at $p_1^A \approx .43$), A's payoff to attacking S_1 is less than its payoff to waiting as shown in figure 5.11. As long as A is not too powerful, S_2 waits (see figure 5.10b) and A's payoff to attacking S_1 rises as A becomes stronger and p_1^A increases. This changes at about $p_1^A \approx .50$, where waiting becomes too costly for S_2 and it enters the fray by aligning with A. At this point, A's payoff to attacking S_1 jumps up and thereafter rises as p_1^A increases.

Finally, figure 5.11 also depicts A's payoff to attacking both S_1 and S_2 at once. The simplifications made in the model imply that this payoff equals A's payoff to attacking one of the other states given that the third state subsequently balances. Increases in the attacker's capabilities then simply raise the probability that A would prevail over the de facto coalition of S_1 and S_2, and A's payoff rises smoothly in p_1^A.

Now consider what these payoffs imply about the potential attacker's decision. A prefers to wait and the status quo goes unchallenged when the distribution of power approximates the distribution of benefits. This result parallels that derived from the bargaining model in chapter 3.

As the potential attacker becomes more powerful, waiting remains optimal until $p_1^A \approx .49$. At that point, A begins to prefer attacking the smaller state S_2 in the correct expectation that S_1 will join in the attack. A continues to prefer attacking the smaller state S_2 until A is so powerful that S_2 could no longer afford to stand aside if A attacked S_1. Once the potential attacker becomes this strong, it attacks S_1 and thereby drags S_2 into the conflict on A's side.

Three important points about balancing emerge from this discussion of the potential attacker's decision. First, balancing is generally absent in the model when the states are equally resolute. States typically do not align against the most powerful state or against the most threatening state. But, second, there is a rough sense in which a balance of power might be said to occur: if A attacks, then for all but a small range of p_1^A, it attacks the larger of S_1 and S_2. This suggests that the two most powerful states, namely A and S_1, will usually be on opposite sides, and, in this loose way, balances of power might be said to form even though the states themselves do not balance by opposing the strongest or most threatening state.

Finally, note that if S_1 and S_2 could commit themselves to balancing through, say, an alliance, then both would be better-off as long as A is not too powerful. To see this, observe that A's payoff to fighting both S_1 and S_2 is less than its payoff to waiting as long as p_1^A is less than .57 or so (see figure 5.11). Consequently, A would not attack the alliance of S_1 and S_2 as long as p_1^A is less than .57 and *the alliance is credible*. The original status quo, therefore, would remain unchanged, and S_1 and S_2 would be better-off. However, the states cannot commit themselves to balancing, and the credibility of any promise to do so is undone by the fact that if a state ever had to follow through on its promise, it would do better by bandwagoning instead of balancing. A therefore attacks (as long as p_1^A is at least .49).

This reasoning suggests that states at times would like to be able to create a "commitment device." That is, they would like to find ways of making it costly for them to renege on their promises to support each other. Such steps make an alliance more than a scrap of paper; they raise the cost of waiting or bandwagoning. This in turn makes balancing more likely and the promise to do so more credible. Indeed, creating a structure that made it costly for the United States not to support Western Europe in the event of a Soviet invasion was one of the guiding principles behind the North Atlantic Treaty Organization (NATO). The remark generally attributed to Lord Ismay, NATO's first secretary general, aptly captures this concern (as well as two others): the purpose of NATO is "to keep the Russians out, the Americans in, and the Germans down."[23]

Alignment Decisions with Asymmetric Resolve

Until now the analysis has focused on the symmetric case in which all of the states were assumed to be equally resolute. This is the simplest case and the one most in keeping with a "billiard-ball" approach to international relations theory in which states are presumed to be identical. But as we have seen, balancing is generally absent in the model if states are equally resolute, and this seems to conflict with the historical record. Whether or not balancing is historically more prevalent than bandwagoning, states do balance at times.

This conflict between the formal implications of the model and historical experience suggests that the circumstances that give rise to balancing are more restricted than has previously been appreciated. The model shows, for example, that the absence of a central authority in a strategic setting in which states can use power against each other does not in and of itself induce balancing: There is no central authority in the model and the states can use power to further their ends, yet balancing is absent. The model therefore provides a counter-example to the claim that anarchy implies a strong tendency to balance.[24] This counter-example in turn indicates that our existing understanding of the circumstances that produce balancing is at best incomplete.

But, the conflict between the alignment game and historical experience can do more than show us that we "know" less than we thought we did when we impose the accounting standards of a formal model. This "evolution of ignorance" (Krugman 1995, 79) may also motivate us to take the next step in the modeling dialogue. In particular, it may prompt us to ask, what might account for balancing that is not currently in the model?

The previous discussion of bargaining points to a possible answer. Actions generally reveal information about an actor. More conciliatory offers, for example, suggest a state is less willing to use force, whereas

---

[23] If alliances are costly to break, then states can use them as a costly signal of their resolve to support each other. Fearon (1994), Morrow (1994), Nalebuff (1991), and Smith (1998) develop this costly signaling perspective formally.

[24] For an example of the claim that anarchy induces balancing, see Waltz (1979, 114–28, especially 121).

an attack demonstrates a higher level of resolve. Germany's calculations on the eve of the First World War illustrate the point.

Germany believed that if Russia mobilized first and therefore appeared to be the aggressor, then Britain would remain neutral and not align with Russia against Germany. Consequently, German Chancellor Bethmann Hollweg delayed Germany's general mobilization even in the face of a partial Russia mobilization in the hope that this delay would force Russia to be the first to order a general mobilization. According to the minutes of a meeting with the chief of the general staff on the eve of war, German Chancellor Theobald von Bethmann Hollweg argued:

> We must wait for this [i.e., Russia's general mobilization] because otherwise we shall not have public opinion on our side either here or in England. The second was desirable because in the Chancellor's opinion *England* could not stand by Russia if Russia unleashed the furies of general war by attacking Austria and so assumed responsibility for the great mess.[25]

In other words, whether Germany or Russia attacked first would reveal information about their aggressiveness and this revelation would affect Britain's alignment decision.[26]

This section draws on the idea that an attack may indicate that the attacker is more willing to use force (i.e., has a lower marginal cost) than the other states. In particular, the section examines how states align when the attacker is much more willing to use force than the other states. Do bandwagoning and waiting continue to be the predominant behaviors, or does the aggressiveness of the attacker induce states to begin to balance by aligning against the attacker?

We might expect intuitively that balancing is more likely if the potential attacker is more willing to use force than the other states and if there are large returns to scale. The latter condition means that a state suffers a large adverse shift in the distribution of power if it waits. This makes waiting very costly and induces states to align. But, as we have seen, this

---

[25] Quoted in Fischer (1975, 494). Still hoping that Britian might remain neutral, Germany subsequently fabricated French border violations in order to justify Germany's invasion of Belgium. In the end, of course, all of these international efforts failed as Britain entered the war against Germany. But the attempt to paint Russia as the aggressor was more successful domestically in that Bethmann Hollweg did secure the support of the Social Democrats in the Parliament (Fischer 1975, 470–515). See Fischer (1988) and Levy (1990/91, 163–70) for further discussions of Germany's beliefs about British neutrality.

[26] And, of course, believing that Britain would be influenced by who mobilized first, Germany tried to use this strategically to manipulate British behavior.

decision to align generally leads to bandwagoning rather than balancing if all of the states are equally willing to use force.

But the terms of the trade-off between balancing and bandwagoning change if the attacker is more willing to use force than the other two states. If a state bandwagons with an attacker that is more willing to use force, then the bandwagoning state has to make larger concessions to the attacker during the bargaining stage. This lowers the payoff to bandwagoning and makes balancing more likely.

To trace this intuition more formally, suppose the potential attacker is more willing to use force than the other states (i.e., c_A is smaller than c_1 and c_2) and consider the effects of this change on the states' payoffs. The expected payoff to waiting decreases, because waiting implies having to make larger concessions during the bargaining stage if the attacker prevails during the first stage. The payoff to bandwagoning also declines for the same reason. If the attacker is more aggressive, the bandwagoning state has to offer more during the bargaining phase.

By contrast, the payoff to balancing remains the same even if the attacker is more willing to use force. Regardless of the attacker's cost, the balancing coalition either eliminates the attacker or is eliminated by it. If the coalition prevails, the attacker's cost does not affect the states' payoffs because the attacker's cost has no effect on the subsequent bargaining between the coalition partners. And, of course, the attacker's cost does not have any effect on the states' payoffs if they are eliminated. Thus, the net effect of the attacker's being more willing to use force reduces the payoffs to waiting and bandwagoning while leaving the payoff to balancing unchanged. This makes balancing more likely.

In brief, the payoffs to waiting and bandwagoning decline relative to balancing when the attacker is more aggressive than the other states. Figure 5.12 illustrates these effects when there are large returns to scale (say $g = 1.25$) and all of the states are equal in size.[27] At $p_1^A = \frac{1}{2}$, the distribution of benefits mirrors the distribution of power, and S_1's payoffs to balancing and bandwagoning are equal because A and S_2 are equivalent coalition partners (i.e., A and S_2 are the same size, equally powerful, and S_1 would not have to make a concession to either A or S_2 during any subsequent bargaining). The payoffs to bandwagoning and balancing are also greater than the payoff to waiting because the returns to scale are large. Larger returns to scale mean that if S_1 waits, the vic-

---

[27] In the numerical illustrations, S_1's and S_2's costs are assumed to be $c_1 = c_2 = .15$ as before, but $c_A = .005$.

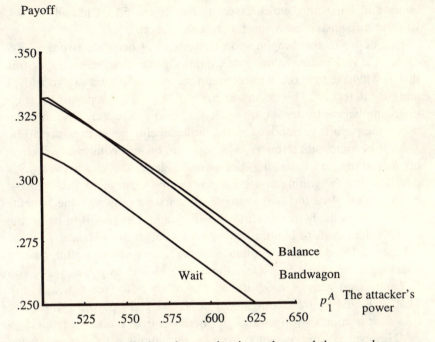

Figure 5.12 The payoff when the attacker is resolute and there are large returns to scale

tor in the conflict between A and S_2 will be stronger and this implies that S_1 will have to make larger concessions during the bargaining phase. Waiting, therefore, entails accepting a large, adverse shift in the distribution of power, and to forestall this possibility, S_1 would enter the fray by either balancing or bandwagoning.[28]

As the potential attacker's capabilities begin to grow, A becomes more powerful and p_1^A increases. This increase reduces S_1's payoffs to balancing against A. S_1's payoff to waiting also goes down as A becomes stronger, because S_1 will have to concede more during the bargaining phase. By contrast, S_1's payoff to bandwagoning by aligning with A initially increases because S_1 benefits from having a stronger but still satisfied ally. Thus, the difference between the payoffs to bandwag-

---

[28] This contrasts with the situation depicted in figure 5.8 where the returns to scale are smaller. In that situation, S_1 did not have to make any concessions if it waited at $p_1^A = \frac{1}{2}$, and the payoff to waiting was greater than the payoff to bandwagoning or balancing. S_1, however, still prefers peace to war in figure 5.12. Athough its payoffs to balancing and bandwagoning are greater than its payoff to waiting, the former are smaller than S_1's status quo payoff of $\frac{1}{3}$.

oning and balancing, which is plotted in figure 5.13a, initially grows. In these circumstances, S_1 prefers to bandwagon.

This desire to bandwagon soon changes as A becomes stronger. Because A is very willing to use force, it quickly becomes sufficiently strong that S_1 will have to make some concessions to A if S_1 bandwagons with A and they defeat S_2. This occurs at $p_1^A \approx .504$ where S_1's payoff to bandwagoning begins to decline in figure 5.12 and where the difference between the payoffs to bandwagoning and balancing peaks in figure 5.13a.

As A becomes still stronger, S_1's payoff to bandwagoning, like its payoff to waiting and balancing, decreases. Indeed, the gap between S_1's payoff to bandwagoning and balancing narrows. At $p_1^A \approx .54$, the cost of appeasing A in the bargaining stage starts to outweigh the benefits of being more likely to prevail in the first stage. The payoff to balancing exceeds the payoff to bandwagoning, and S_1 begins to balance.

Figure 5.13b depicts the potential attacker's payoffs to waiting and to attacking either S_1 or S_2.[29] Over the range $p_1^A = .5$ to $p_1^A \approx .54$, S_1 and S_2 bandwagon with A if A attacks the other state (see figure 5.13a). That is, S_1 and S_2 are chain-ganged to A. Thus, A's payoff to attacking rises as it becomes stronger and p_1^A increases over the range from .5 to .54. However, S_1 and S_2 switch from bandwagoning with A to balancing against it at $p_1^A \approx .54$, and A's payoff to attacking drops. Indeed, A's payoff to attacking drops below its payoff to waiting over the range .54 to .56 and A is deterred from attacking. Balancing over this range preserves the peace. However, once A becomes sufficiently powerful ($p_1^A > .56$), its payoff to fighting the coalition of S_1 and S_2 exceeds the payoff to waiting and A attacks.

In sum, balancing seems to take place in a limited set of circumstances. If there are large returns to scale in the cumulation of military capabilities, then waiting implies accepting a large, adverse shift in the distribution of power and this makes it too costly to do. If the attacker is also much more willing to use force than the other states, then bandwagoning with the attacker means having to make large concessions to the attacker during any subsequent bargaining. This makes bandwagoning very costly, too, and the combination of large returns to scale and a very resolute attacker lead to balancing.

Pushing this idea beyond the present model, a state faces a difficult inference problem when it sees one state attack another. Does the at-

---

[29] A's payoffs to attacking S_1 or S_2 are equal because S_1 and S_2 are identical in size and territory and make the same alignment decisions.

The difference
between payoffs

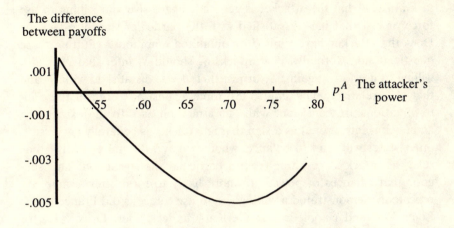

(a) The payoff to bandwagoning less the payoff to balancing.

Payoff

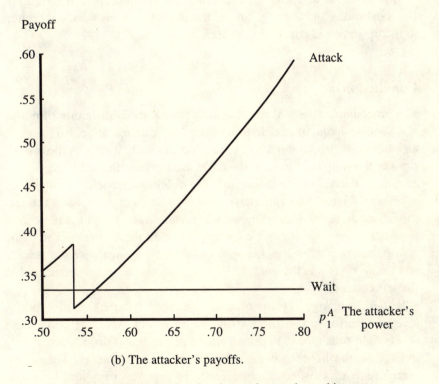

(b) The attacker's payoffs.

Figure 5.13 Balancing, bandwagoning, and attacking

tack indicate that the attacker is generally aggressive and willing to use force or just that it is dissatisfied with the particular state it attacked? Does the attacker have limited or unlimited ambitions? (Putting these questions more formally, if A attacks S_2 should S_1 infer that A is also willing to use force against S_1 or just that A was dissatisfied with S_2 and that A is relatively unwilling to use force against S_1? Both of these interpretations are consistent with A's attack on S_2.) To the extent that an attack is interpreted as a sign that an attacker is generally aggressive, other states will tend to balance, whereas they will tend to wait if they read the attack as resulting from a particular dissatisfaction. This suggests that balances of power are more likely to form after a state has repeatedly demonstrated a willingness to use force, as did France under Louis XIV and Napoleon and Germany under Hitler. Louis XIV, for example, frustrated other states' attempts to stand aside or bandwagon "because France would not let their efforts succeed; they resisted [by balancing] because France kept on attacking them" (Schroeder 1994a, 135). Resistance to Hitler also solidified after he occupied the rump of Czechoslovakia and thereby demonstrated that his aims were not limited to incorporating Germans in the Reich.

Conclusion

The preceding analysis of the relation between the distribution of power and states' alignment decisions is exploratory and tentative. It is at most an early effort in the modeling enterprise. As such, it studies these decisions in the simplest formal setting. Yet even in this simple setting, states' alignment decisions reflect a complex and delicate trade-off of opposing influences. Figure 5.14 summarizes some of these decisions and the factors affecting them. Generally speaking, states tend to wait if the extent to which military capabilities cumulate is low. In these circumstances, the distribution of power does not shift significantly against a state if it waits and doing so avoids the cost of fighting. This situation is represented in the left column.

If there are large returns to scale (the right column), waiting brings a large adverse shift in the distribution of power. Standing aside while others fight thus means that the victor's power grows disproportionately more than the benefits it gains by defeating its adversary. The victor, therefore, is dissatisfied after defeating its first adversary and has to be appeased by the state that waited. The prospect of having to grant these

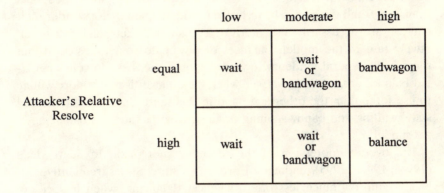

Figure 5.14 The alignment decision

large concessions makes waiting very costly and induces a state to join the fray by aligning with one of the other states.

Whether a state balances or bandwagons when it enters the conflict depends on how it resolves a trade-off. Balancing with the weaker state offers a lower probability of prevailing but a more favorable distribution of power if the coalition prevails. Bandwagoning, by contrast, offers a higher probability of prevailing but a less favorable distribution of power. The latter dominates the former if the states are equally resolute (the upper-right cell), and the states bandwagon. But, the former dominates the latter and states balance if the attacker is much more willing to use force than the other states, as in the lower-right cell (see figures 5.12 and 5.13 for an example).

If there are moderate returns to scale (the middle column), the states generally bandwagon or wait depending on the interaction of the size of the returns to scale and the attacker's willingness to use force. The less military capabilities cumulate, the less the distribution of power shifts against a state if it waits and the larger the benefit of avoiding the cost of fighting. A state is more likely to wait in these circumstances. However, the more willing the attacker is to use force compared to the other states, the more likely it is to be dissatisfied during the bargaining stage even if there has only been a relatively small shift of power. This makes waiting costly and bandwagoning more likely.

These results are consistent with some of the claims made about the relation between the distribution of power and states' alignment decisions and are inconsistent with others. By themselves, anarchy and the desire to survive do not produce a general tendency for states to balance against the most powerful state. The strategic environment in the model is anarchic, and the states, by trying to maximize the territory under their control, are necessarily also motivated to survive. Yet balancing is relatively rare in the model. Balances of power do sometimes form, but there is no general tendency toward this outcome. Nor do states generally balance against threats. Even when the attacker is much more willing to use force than the other state and in this sense the most threatening state, waiting and bandwagoning occur at least as much as balancing in the model.

The overall impression of the results is more akin to Schroeder's (1994a, 1994b, 1995) reading of European history. States frequently wait, bandwagon, or, much less often, balance. Balancing, when it does occur, is usually a response to a state—like France under Louis XIV or Napoleon, or Germany under Hitler—that has shown itself to be much more willing to use force than other states.

6

Conclusion

States do interact in a Hobbesian state of nature in which there is no superior authority to prevent one state from using the means of power to its own advantage and to the possible disadvantage of others. But this characterization of the states' strategic environment is too broad to be very useful. The strategic arena in which states interact can be described more narrowly and more productively in terms of the commitment issues, informational problems, and the underlying technology of coercion. These strategic features define the trade-offs states confront, and the previous chapters used a series of game-theoretic models to examine how states resolve those trade-offs.

This chapter does three things. First, it briefly reviews the results of this examination and compares the findings to existing arguments. The chapter then considers some of the models' limitations and offers a few conjectures about what will happen when some of these restrictive assumptions are relaxed in future rounds of the modeling dialogue. The chapter concludes with a discussion of the relation between international relations theory and political science more generally. International relations theory has often used the assumption of anarchy as a kind of analytic wall to set it off and separate it from the from the rest of political science. Exactly the opposite perspective emerges from the preceding chapters. Viewing the strategic environment confronting states in terms of commitment issues, informational problems, and the technology of coercion serves as a bridge to other areas in political science.

Some New and Old Results

One of the ways that a state can respond to a threat is by reallocating resources it already controls. However, internal balancing entails a trade-off. The more a state allocates toward satisfying current wants, the less it can devote to the means of military power and the weaker it will be in the future.

The key to resolving this guns-versus-butter trade-off turns out to be the expected payoff to attacking. If the payoff to attacking increases relative to that of living with the status quo—perhaps because of changes in the technology of coercion such as a decrease in the cost of fighting or a larger offensive advantage or because of changes in the actors themselves such as an increase in the states' willingness to run risks or in their relative patience—then a state will try to offset its adversary's higher payoff to fighting by building up its own military strength. Thus, changes that increase the payoff to attacking relative to living with the status quo lead to larger military allocations.

Allocating more to the military, however, reduces a state's payoff to living with the status quo. Internal balancing preserves the peace as long as the payoff to living with the status quo exceeds the cost of fighting. But the status quo may become quite unattractive relative to the gamble of war if a state's military allocations become too large, and peace may break down.

The guns-versus-butter model shows that many existing arguments do not go through when states' resource-allocation decisions are taken into account. This stylized international system does not induce states to try to maximize their power. Nor does it induce a concern for relative gains. The standard relative-gains argument holds that a self-help system in which "each of the units spends a portion of its effort, not in forwarding its own good, but in protecting itself from others" compels states to be concerned about their relative gains (Waltz 1979, 105). But, the states in the guns-versus-butter model must provide for their own protection. Indeed, the need to do so creates the trade-off that defines the strategic problem underlying internal balancing. Nevertheless, there are no relative-gains concerns to obstruct cooperation.

The basic reason why these concerns are absent seems likely to be quite robust: Once a state's ability to reallocate resources is taken into account, a state that suffers an absolute gain but relative loss in a cooperative agreement may be able to compensate for this by allocating relatively more of its gain to the means of power. If a state still has something leftover after reallocating its resources and offsetting its relative loss, then that state will prefer the agreement to not having one *if those are the only two alternatives.*

The choice, however, is rarely between one specific agreement and no agreement, as there are generally many ways to divide the gains from cooperation. This, in turn, makes it very difficult to test relative-gains arguments empirically because states may bargain very hard to obtain a larger share. Cooperation may still be very difficult to achieve but not because of relative-gains concerns.

A state can also respond to a threat through bargaining and compromise. The bargaining model in chapter 3 assumed that the distribution of power remained constant throughout the negotiations. The danger that bargaining will break down in war in this model derives from two sources. First, there must be a sufficiently large disparity between the distribution of power and the distribution of benefits such that one state might be willing to use force to overturn the status quo. This disparity creates a credible threat to the status quo.

The second source is an informational problem. The satisfied state, for example, may be uncertain of the dissatisfied state's willingness to use force and therefore of how much it has to offer to the dissatisfied state to be sure of appeasing it. This informational asymmetry creates a risk-return trade-off. The more a state offers, the more likely it is to satisfy its adversary but the less it will have if its offer is accepted. A state typically resolves this trade-off by accepting some risk of war by not offering enough to be sure of appeasing the most resolute adversary it might be facing.

Once we see bargaining in this way, it is clear that the key to stability is not a particular distribution of power but the relation between the distributions of power and benefits. If the distribution of benefits mirrors the distribution of power, no state can credibly threaten to use force to change the status quo and the risk of war is smallest. If, however, there is a sufficiently large disparity between the distributions of power and benefits, the status quo may be threatened regardless of what the underlying distribution of power is.

These results contradict the claims of both the preponderance-of-power and balance-of-power schools. The former argues that war is least likely when there is a preponderance of power, whereas the latter asserts that war is least likely when there is an even distribution. As we saw, these schools reach these conflicting conclusions in part because they emphasize opposite factors. The preponderance-of-power school underscores the fact that the weaker a state, the lower its payoff to fighting and the less likely it is to reject a given offer in favor of war. By contrast, the balance-of-power school, recognizing that a stronger state may be tempted to demand more, stresses the restraining effects that an even distribution of power has on all of the states' demands. Both of these influences are intuitively reasonable. But they point in opposite directions, and, lacking the accounting mechanism of a model, neither school takes both of them into account very well.

The bargaining model in chapter 4 focuses on how states cope with shifts in the distribution of power. When states are bargaining in the shadow of shifting power, the declining state makes a series of concessions which are enough to satisfy the rising state if that state is relatively reluctant to use force. In these circumstances, the status quo is slowly revised in the rising state's favor and the shift in power passes without war. If, however, the rising state is more resolute, the declining state's offers are not enough and the shift breaks down in war. Indeed, the declining state's concessions effectively "screen out" the rising state according to its willingness to fight. The more resolute the rising state, the earlier it fights.

Viewing shifts in power from this screening perspective explains much about states' efforts to cope with these shifts, and it casts doubt on some of the claims that have been made about the effects of these shifts. As just noted, it is clear why some shifts end in war and others do not. This perspective also tends to undermine the power-transition school's assertion that the most dangerous phase of a shift in power occurs at a power transition where the two states are equally powerful. In deciding how much to offer, the declining state balances the marginal gain of offering slightly more and thereby securing a slightly lower chance of war against the marginal cost of having slightly less if its offer is accepted. An even distribution of power seems to play no special role in these marginal calculations, and a transition does not appear to be the most dangerous period during a shift in power.

Nor do faster shifts seem to be more dangerous than slower ones if the kinds of shifts we have in mind are long-run changes brought about by differential rates of economic growth and development. The speed of the shift does affect the rate at which the declining state screens out the rising state. But the overall probability that the declining state's offers are rejected and that the shift ends in war is the same.

A third way that a state can respond to threats is by trying to draw on others' resources. Ironically, a very simple model of this response paints a very complicated picture of states' alignment decisions. In so doing, the analysis contradicts existing claims that states generally balance against power or threats or, for that matter, that they generally do any one thing. Rather, the states' alignment decisions seem to be quite conditional and to depend on the technology of coercion and the states' relative resolve.

Whether a state waits while others fight or joins the conflict depends on a trade-off between avoiding the immediate cost of fighting and ultimately having to contend with an adverse shift in the distribution of power. If, for example, fighting is costly and military capabilities do not cumulate very much, then a state does not have to fear a large adverse shift in the distribution of power if it stands aside while others fight. In these circumstances, that state is likely to prefer waiting to aligning. If, by contrast, there are larger returns to scale, waiting entails a larger adverse shift. This makes waiting costly because the state that waits while others fight eventually faces a powerful, dissatisfied adversary that will have to be appeased. States, therefore, generally do not wait if there are large returns to scale.

Whether a state balances or bandwagons when it decides to join the conflict depends on how it resolves another trade-off. By aligning with the stronger of the two other states, a third state benefits by maximizing the chances that it will be on the winning side. This consideration makes bandwagoning with the more powerful state more appealing. But there is a countervailing factor at work. Aligning with a more powerful coalition partner means that a state will be more vulnerable to that partner if the coalition prevails. This is the cost of aligning with a stronger state and makes balancing with the weaker state more attractive. When both of these opposing factors are taken into account, the former consideration generally outweighs the latter in the models analyzed here, and states usually bandwagon. Balancing does occur, however, if there are large returns to scale and if the attacker is much more resolute than the other states.

But these alignment results seem fragile. Different formal specifications seem likely to produce different decisions, and this may make us skeptical about any claims that states generally balance or bandwagon. These may not be very useful analytic concepts.

Limitations, Qualifications, and Extensions

The models studied in the preceding chapters are at best templates which provide a framework for analysis and a point of departure. As such, the models make a number of strong and restrictive assumptions that simplify the problem and highlight some of the basic mechanisms at work and some of the fundamental trade-offs that the states face. But these restrictions also limit and qualify the conclusions derived from the models. A natural next step in the modeling enterprise is therefore to try to relax some of these restrictions. This section tries to anticipate some of that future work by discussing some of the models' limitations and by offering a few conjectures about what will be found when these are relaxed.

There are three parts to this discussion. The first focuses on some simplifications that are common to all of the models: that states are rational, unitary actors and that war is modeled as a costly lottery which always results in the elimination of one of the billigerents. The second part examines some of the limitations and possible extensions of the individual models. The last part considers some of the likely consequences of combining different ways of responding to threats in a single formulation. The previous chapters discussed the three responses to threat separately. The states in the guns-versus-butter model cannot bargain or align with a third state. The states in the bargaining models cannot reallocate their resources or align with a third state. And the states in the alignment model cannot reallocate their resources or bargain during the first stage of the game. But what would happen if, for example, a state could respond to a threat by bargaining and reallocating its resources?

Some Shared Assumptions and Limitations

As noted in chapter 1, the preceding models abstract away from the complexities of domestic politics by taking states to be rational, unitary actors. This assumption, of course, does not imply that domestic politics is unimportant. Rather, it reflects the belief that we can learn some interesting things by treating states in this limited way and that what we learn may help us see how to relax this assumption in productive ways.

One way that rational-unitary-actor models do help is that they provide a baseline of what to expect. When outcomes deviate from these baseline expectations, i.e., when a model that assumes states to be rational unitary actors gets things wrong, it is natural to ask if this failure is because of this assumption. If this seems likely, then one can try to relax this assumption in the context of a model that has been tailored to this issue.

A second way that unitary-actor models may help is by identifying things that would be most interesting to "endogenize" or "problematize" in subsequent rounds of the modeling dialogue. For example, much of the existing formal work in international relations as well as the bargaining models developed here highlight the role of asymmetric information as an important cause of war (Fearon 1995b). But these models generally take the existence of asymmetric information as given and focus on tracing its consequences. These models make no effort to explain the origins of these asymmetries or how they might be mediated by domestic institutions. This suggests that an important task for future work is to "endogenize" these asymmetries by explaining where they come from. Indeed, Schultz (1996) has taken up this task in his efforts to account for the absence of war among democratic states. He breaks the unitary-actor assumption in order to investigate how democratic institutions affect the informational asymmetries that exist between different kinds of states.[1]

Another assumption that all of the models share is that they formalize war as a costly lottery between two sides in which one of them is sure to be eliminated. There are no costly stalemates in this formulation. Nor are there any strategic decisions to make during the conflict. There are no decisions about when and where to fight and no logistic and resource-allocation problems to solve.[2] Intra-war bargaining, bluffing, or demonstrations of resolve are also absent as Wagner (1997) emphasizes. If two sides go to war in the models, certain outcomes happen with certain probabilities.

Abstracting away from any strategic interaction that follows the start of a war is, of course, a tremendous simplification. The strategic problems facing states during a conflict may be extremely complex, as even the most cursory glance at the history of international relations shows, and Great Powers are usually not eliminated even after suffering a major defeat, as the fates of France after 1815, Germany after 1914 and 1945, and Japan after 1945 show.

The obvious advantage of this simplification is that it facilitates the formal analysis of the games. The equally obvious disadvantage is that it leaves open the question of how incorporating some aspects of the intra-war strategic dynamics or the possibility of fighting to a stalemate would affect the outcomes derived from the present formulations. Exploring this question is an important task for future rounds of the modeling enterprise.

Unfortunately, efforts to examine the strategic interaction of states during a conflict may quickly run into the problem that the modeling efforts in chapter 5 encountered. The accounting mechanism inherent in formalization showed that very critical assumptions had to be made about the technology of coercion for which there is scant theoretical or empirical support—e.g., the way that military capabilities combine if two states form a coalition or if one state defeats another. Formalizing the states' strategic environment during a conflict may require equally

---

[1] See Downs and Rocke (1994, 1995) and Bueno de Mesquita et al. (1997, 1998) for other interesting efforts to break the unitary-actor assumption.

[2] Van Creveld (1977) discusses wartime logistics.

204 • CHAPTER 6

critical assumptions for which there is little empirical support. This lack
of support underscores the need for a modeling dialogue between the
theoretic and empirical realms about these issues. But even with a better
dialogue, striking an insightful balance between analytic simplicity and
empirical relevance seems likely to prove to be a hard problem in the
art of modeling.[3]

Limitations, Qualifications, and Extensions of the Individual Models

States' inability to commit themselves to refraining from using force
against each other creates an intertemporal trade-off. The more resources a state allocates to meeting its immediate wants, the weaker
it will be in the future and the less able it will be to achieve its future
wants. The guns-versus-butter model tries to capture the essence of this
trade-off in a very simple formal setting. To this end, the model makes
two kinds of simplifying assumptions which limit the present analysis and
provide a point of departure for subsequent work.

Because the fundamental problem is an intertemporal trade-off, time
must be in the model. There must be a present and a future. The first
kind of simplifying assumption affects the way that time enters the formalization. Recall that the states in the model can either "consume" or
allocate resources to the military. There is no capital sector and no economic growth. The states cannot invest today in order to be able to have
more of both guns and butter tomorrow. Nor can the states stockpile
arms. Furthermore, a state, when deciding what to do, can allocate as
much of its resources to the military as it wants regardless of what it has
done in the past. Previous allocations do not constrain future choices.

The effect of all of these assumptions is that time enters the model
in a very simple way. A state faces essentially the same problem each
time it has to decide how to allocate its resources. The only thing that
is relevant to a state's allocation decision is the other state's *current*
allocation. Neither that state's past allocations nor a state's own past
allocations have any direct effect on a state's current decision. Having
time enter in this very simple way makes the formal analysis much easier.

This simplification also leads to a surprising result—at least it initially
surprised this author. One might have thought that the intertemporal

---

[3] Smith (1997) provides an interesting start in this direction by using an actual war to
motivate his stylization of the technology of coercion.

trade-off in the guns-versus-butter model would have been enough to produce arms races. After all, this model, although very simple, is in some ways an elaboration of other models that do produce arms races.[4] But proposition 2.3 shows that this is not the case. There are no arms races in the model.

To see why there are no arms races, suppose that state 1 had allocated more to the military than its equilibrium level m_1^*. If state 2 responds by increasing its armaments, then this would set off an arms race. But, state 2 does not react to this higher level of spending by increasing its own allocation above its equilibrium level m_2^* in the guns-versus-butter model. There is no need. Recall that state 2 allocates m_2^* to the military because this is just sufficient to deter state 1 from optimally reallocating its resources and attacking state 2. But because of the very simple way that time enters this analysis, the optimal allocation state 1 would make to the military if it intended to attack does not depend on its past armament decisions. Thus, m_2^* is sufficient to deter state 1 regardless of state 1's previous allocations, and state 2 need not increase its allocation in response to an allocation above m_1^*.

The absence of arms races provides an example of how models can inform us even when they get things wrong. The missing arms races show that the initial expectation that the existence of an intertemporal trade-off would be enough to produce arms races was incorrect. Something more is needed. And, the model suggests what some of these additional factors might be. Suppose, for example, that we relax the assumption that the amount a state can allocate to the military is unaffected by past allocations. To keep things simple, the maximum a state can allocate to defense might be a fixed percentage above the amount that it allocated in the previous period. This "stickiness," which might represent capacity constraints that limit production, seems likely to produce arms races.

Future work might also relax the way that time enters the game in order to focus on economic growth rather than arms races. What is the relation among guns, butter, and economic growth? Are, for example, richer states more or less likely to engage in arms competition

---

[4] See, for example, Richardson's (1960) classic analysis as well as Gillespie, Zinnes, and Tahim (1977); Gillespie et al. (1977); and Simaan and Cruz (1975). These models are basically reduced forms in that they do not explicitly model the decision to attack. Rather, a state is assumed to suffer a direct loss of utility if another state increases its armaments. The guns-versus-butter model, by contrast, explicitly represents this decision and in this sense at least would seem to be a generalization of them. (See Sandler and Hartley [1995] for a survey of arms-race models.)

than other states? To explore this issue, one might allow the states to divide their resources among three alternatives—consumption, defense, and investment—and assume further that investing more today gives a state more resources tomorrow.

The guns-versus-butter model also simplifies the state's strategic setting by pushing informational issues into the background in order to bring the commitment problem and the intertemporal trade-off it creates to the fore. This was achieved by assuming that the states have complete information. A future step in the modeling enterprise might relax this by assuming instead that one of the states, say state 1, is uncertain of state 2's willingness to run risks and use force.

In such a formulation, state 1 would seem to face a now familiar risk-return trade-off. The more it allocates to the military, the more likely it is to dissuade state 2 from attacking but the less it will have to consume. Drawing on the analysis of the trade-off that the declining state faced in the shifting-power bargaining model, we might speculate that state 1 will resolve the trade-off in the guns-versus-butter model by making a relatively large military allocation at the outset. This allocation will be enough to dissuade state 2 unless that state is very willing to use force. If so, then state 2 will attack and there will be war. If state 2 is less willing to use force, it will not attack and this decision leads state 1 to revise its initial beliefs about state 2's willingness to use force. In light of these updated beliefs, state 1 may reduce its armaments. Over time we should expect to see states' military allocations gradually decline (unless, of course, state 2 attacks). This conjecture means that if we look at actual states in a long-term relationship in which there is an initial upheaval—a revolution or a coup perhaps—followed by a period of domestic stability, then we should find that states' arms expenditures gradually fall toward the complete-information levels characterized in chapter 2.[5]

Turning to the limitations of the bargaining models, chapter 3 investigates the effect of the shadow of power on bargaining when the distribution of power remains constant throughout the interaction. A key finding is that the probability of breakdown is smallest when the distributions of power and benefits mirror each other. As long as fighting is

---

[5] Walt (1996) makes a related argument about why revolutions make war more likely.

A still more interesting but more complicated way to introduce asymmetric information is to suppose that there is some chance that a new regime will come to power in each period or that crises arise periodically and that the states are uncertain of each other's willingness to fight over the issue. These possibilities mean that a state's "type" can change from time to time, and this makes the other state's inference problem even more difficult.

costly, the states are risk neutral or risk averse, and any first-strike advantages are small, then neither bargainer can credibly threaten to impose a costly settlement when the existing distribution of benefits reflects the distribution of power.

The model made several simplifying assumptions. It assumed, for example, that the cost of fighting is always the same regardless of an adversary's size and that the states agree on the distribution of power but are unsure of each other's resolve. Both of these limitations could be relaxed. We might suppose, for example, that it is more costly to fight a larger adversary, as is the case in the alignment models. Or, the states might have private information about their military capabilities and therefore disagree about the distribution of power between them.[6]

Allowing the cost of fighting to depend on an adversary's size seems unlikely to affect the central result that breakdown is least likely if the distribution of power mirrors the distribution of benefits. When this condition holds, both states are satisfied and neither can credibly threaten to use force to change the status quo. If, however, one of the states is dissatisfied because of a disparity between the distributions of power and benefits, then the fact that the cost of fighting depends on an adversary's size seems likely to affect the bargaining. The satisfied state will have to make a concession or fight. But a concession will lower the dissatisfied state's cost of fighting and thereby make it more willing to fight in the future. An adversary's appetite will grow with the eating, as it were. The satisfied state will therefore have to make yet another concession and so on.[7]

These concessions lead to a simple outcome, at least in the complete-information case. Drawing on the notation from chapter 3, suppose that the dissatisfied state initially controls an amount of territory q_0, p is the probability that the dissatisfied state prevails, and its cost of fighting is $d(1 - q_0)$, where d is now its marginal cost of fighting and $1 - q_0$ is the size of the other state. Because this state is dissatisfied, its payoff to attacking exceeds its payoff to living with the status quo, which

---

[6] Morrow (1989) and Bueno de Mesquita, Morrow, and Zorick (1997) take a step in this direction. They study a model in which the states have private information about their capabilities but can decide only whether to escalate or not. The states cannot bargain by offering concessions to each other. Schweizer (1989) does allow for bargaining and his model will be discussed below.

[7] There is a close parallel between a model in which the cost of fighting depends on an adversary's size and Fearon's (1996) analysis of a situation in which a concession today makes a state more powerful tomorrow. In both formulations, obtaining a concession increases a state's payoff to fighting and thereby enhances its bargaining power.

means $p - d(1 - q_0) > q_0$.[8] The satisfied state, therefore, must either fight or make a concession. As in chapter 3, the satisfied state prefers the latter.

But rather than making one single concession, the satisfied state now makes a series of them. It initially offers a territorial concession x_1, which is just large enough to make the dissatisfied state indifferent between attacking now at cost $d(1 - q_0)$ or accepting x_1 and then attacking in the next period at the lower cost $d(1 - x_1)$. But before the dissatisfied state attacks, the satisfied state makes another concession $x_2 > x_1$, which is just enough to induce the dissatisfied state to wait and so on.

The concessions $x_1, x_2, x_3, \ldots$ slowly converge to x^*, where x^* is the smallest amount of territory the dissatisfied state will accept on a long-term basis.[9] Comparing this series of concessions with the single concession the satisfied state would make if the cost of fighting did not depend on an adversary's size, the satisfied state initially offers less than it would if size were not a factor but eventually has to concede more. In sum, letting the cost of fighting depend on an adversary's size affects the pattern of concessions but not the general result that the status quo is stable if it reflects the underlying distribution of power.

Relaxing the assumption that the states agree on the distribution of power p also seems unlikely to affect the central finding that war is least likely when the distributions of power and benefits mirror each other. But what happens to the probability of war as these distributions diverge and a disparity develops is less clear. Wagner (1994, 597–99), for example, argues that if states lack information about other states' military capabilities, then this informational asymmetry is less significant if there is a preponderance of power. Because the informational asymmetries are less significant, a satisfied state is more likely to meet the dissatisfied state's minimal demands and the probability of war is smaller.

Combining these two considerations suggests that the probability of war does not invariably increase as the disparity grows, as is the case in figure 3.6. Rather, the probability of war may initially increase as the distribution of power begins to diverge from the distribution of benefits. But as this disparity grows larger, it becomes less significant. The probability of war consequently peaks and then begins to decline. As

---

[8] The states are assumed to be risk neutral to simplify the illustration.

[9] The dissatisfied state prefers living with x on a long-term basis to fighting if the payoff to the former is as large as its payoff to attacking at cost $d(1 - x)$, i.e., if $x \geq p - d(1 - x)$. The smallest allocation satisfying this condition is $x^* = (p - d)/(1 - d)$.

it happens, Mansfield (1994) finds some statistical evidence supporting the idea that the probability of war follows this pattern.[10]

The bargaining model in chapter 4 makes strong assumptions about the shift in the distribution of power. It assumes, for example, that the distribution of power moves in a very simple and predictable way. To wit, the distribution of power changes by the same known amount in each period and does so for a known number of periods.

This stark assumption could be relaxed in at least two ways. First and most simply, the distribution of power might gradually level off rather than stop abruptly. The effects of this seem straightforward. The abrupt stop in the model in chapter 4 instantly eliminates the rising state's incentive to postpone attacking until it is stronger, and this makes the risk-return trade-off facing the declining state much more acute during the period in which the distribution of power stops changing. As we saw, the declining state resolves this more acute trade-off by both conceding more territory and accepting a larger risk, and these appear as "spikes" in figures 4.8 and 4.9. These spikes should disappear if the distribution of power levels off gradually rather than stops suddenly. As the distribution of power slowly flattens out, the additional amount that the declining state concedes in each period will slowly decline.

A more interesting way to relax the formulation in chapter 4 would be to assume that the states are uncertain about how much the distribution of power will actually shift. One simple way to introduce some uncertainty would be to suppose that there is always some chance that the distribution of power will stop shifting and remain where it is. The implications of this uncertainty are less clear, but it seems likely that the possibility that the distribution of power might stop shifting reduces the rising state's incentive to delay an attack as the rising state is no longer certain of being stronger in the next period. To offset this lower incentive, the declining state may have to make a larger concession and to accept more risk than it would if the distribution of power were certain to continue shifting.

The shifting-power bargaining model also assumes that the distribution of power changes for reasons exogenous to the model. In particular, the concessions one state makes to another do not affect the distribu-

---

[10] The statistical model Mansfield estimates is not strictly comparable to the formal model developed here. He focuses on major power interactions in which there are generally more than two states, and he uses the concentration of power to measure the distribution of power.

tion between them. Rather, the shift is due to other factors such as the differential rates of long-run economic growth, which Gilpin (1981) emphasizes, or to uneven rates of political development, which Organski (1968) and Organski and Kugler (1980) underscore.

But what if concessions do affect the distribution of power as, for example, they may have done during the Munich crisis?[11] Fearon (1996) provides some answers. He studies a game in which two states are bargaining about revising the territorial status quo and in which a state's power depends on the amount of territory it controls. Thus, conceding territory to an adversary makes that state stronger and may lead to further demands.

Fearon observes that this situation may create a commitment problem. A state might be willing to satisfy an adversary's demands *if* that adversary could commit itself to refraining from exploiting its stronger position and making any further demands. But if an adversary cannot deny itself this option, then a state might prefer to fight a preventive war rather than make these concessions and subsequently find itself in a weaker position. If so, then the inability to make commitments results in war.

Fearon shows that this commitment problem generally does not arise. States do not go to war if there are no informational problems and if small territorial concessions do not produce discrete shifts in the distribution of power.[12] It turns out that the satisfied state can concede just enough to appease the other state and that the satisfied state prefers granting these concessions to fighting even though each concession makes its adversary stronger in the next period and therefore leads to another concession. If the defense dominates the offense, these concessions ultimately produce states that are approximately the same size, whereas offense dominance leads to a situation in which the dissatisfied state grows ever larger and the satisfied state grows ever smaller.

---

[11] Whether Britain was weaker vis-à-vis Germany in 1939 than in 1938 is a matter of some historical dispute. As German pressure mounted on Czechoslovakia, some British officials, especially those representing the military, argued that Britain's relative military position would be better in a few months (Howard 1972, 123). By contrast, Murray (1984) and T. Taylor (1979, 984–89) contend that a careful analysis of the politico-military situation at the time would have shown that Britain and France in combination with the Czech forces would have been stronger compared to Germany in 1938 than they were in 1939 when they stood firm against Germany over Poland.

[12] That is, the distribution of power must be a continuous function of the distribution of territory. Fearon points out that geographic features like rivers or mountain ranges that provide natural barriers may make this assumption problematic.

Fearon's (1995b, 1996) analysis and chapter 4's finding that complete-information shifts in the distribution of power typically do not end in war suggest that shifts in the distribution of power are not in themselves a cause of war. These results focus attention instead on the existence of a "lumpy" or discontinuous relationship between the concessions that states make and the shifts in the distribution of power they produce; on the effects of informational problems chapter 4 examines; and, possibly, on the kind of commitment problem present in the guns-versus-butter model. (This latter possibility is discussed below.)

The model used in chapter 5 to study the relationship between the distribution of power and state's alignment decisions has many limitations. The model is at best a first cut at this problem. At most, it provides a template that helps us organize our thinking, identify critical assumptions, and explore some basic issues. Because the model is so spare, it could be extended or refined in many different ways. Three are sketched here.

One extension would allow the states to bargain during the first stage before any one attacks. It is not at all clear what to expect from such a model. For example, we might at first suspect that allowing the three states to bargain before an attack would lead to a peaceful settlement, as it did in the two-state bargaining in chapter 3. Such a result would be in keeping with the flavor of much of the formal work on bargaining in international relations and economics. Bargainers in this analysis generally avoid costly and inefficient outcomes like fighting if there is complete information. But this is not always the case, especially if an agreement between two bargainers can adversely affect a third, as seems likely in international politics. (See Jehiel and Moldovanu [1995] for just such a model.)[13]

A second extension would focus on prewar alliance and alignment decisions and would allow states to do something to overcome the credibility problem that haunts these decisions. As we saw in chapter 5, the two satisfied states sometimes have an incentive to ally with each other before the dissatisfied state attacks either of them. Such an alliance, if credible, would deter an attack and thereby make both of the satisfied states better-off. However, these alliances are generally incredible in the

[13] Niou and Ordeshook (1990, 1991) study the multilateral bargaining that takes place between states prior to any fighting. But as noted in chapter 5, they assume a "voting" technology in which a state is *certain* to prevail over another even if the former is only slightly larger, and this assumption makes it difficult to compare their results with those derived above.

model, because the dissatisfied state knows that if it attacks one of the other states, then the third state would rather wait or bandwagon than balance with its alliance partner. This preference, in turn, undermines the credibility of any alliance between the two satisfied states.

Alliances in this formulation lack credibility in part because it does not cost anything to break them. Alliances are tantamount to "cheap talk." However, states sometimes take steps when forming an alliance that make it costly for them to renege on their promises in the event of war. These costs enhance an alliance's credibility and help states signal their determination to stand together.

Fearon (1994), Morrow (1994a), and Smith (1995, 1998) study prewar alliance formation when there is a cost to reneging. However, they do not treat the underlying distribution of power in any detail. The present analysis, by contrast, disregards the costs of breaking an alliance and focuses instead on the effects that the distribution of power has on alignment decisions. Combining these two elements is an interesting future task for the modeling enterprise.

This richer formulation would let the states decide how "deep" they want to make an agreement by deciding how much to invest in it and therefore how costly it will be to break in the event of war. Britain, for example, was willing to engage in some coordinated military planning with France as part of the Entente Cordiale but was unwilling to commit itself to fighting with France (S. Williamson 1969). These arrangements created some costs if Britain and France failed to cooperate in the event of war, as is clear in the plea for support that the French ambassador made to the British foreign secretary after Austria and Russia had mobilized. As a result of the coordinated planning, he implored, France "had concentrated her fleet in the Mediterranean and had left her northern and western coasts exposed."[14] A model that allowed states to decide how much it would cost to renege on an agreement might help explain the varying degrees of institutionalization that we see in different alliances and alignments.[15]

---

[14] Quoted in S. Williamson (1969, 352).

[15] This decision, of course, is limited by the existing technology of coercion. If, for example, fighting is largely done by mercenaries, then it may be difficult to make agreements that are costly to break even if states want to do so. The technology of coercion may, therefore, help explain why alliances are more or less "rigid" in different periods. See Downs, Rocke, and Barsoom (1996) for discussion of the relationship between institutional depth and compliance with arms control agreements. Lake (1999) offers a different approach to the institutionalization of security arrangements.

A third extension of the alignment model would introduce asymmetric information. If states are uncertain about other states' overall aggressiveness and their willingness to use force, then an attack may act as a signal that convinces other states of the attacker's aggressiveness and thereby induces these states to balance. Chapter 5 explored this issue in a very preliminary way by showing that states may balance if the attacker is *known* to be much more willing to use force than the other states. That is, there is a type of attacker against which states do balance. An asymmetric information model would help us understand the process through which states become convinced that they are facing this type.[16] Indeed, Britain and France ultimately stood firm against Hitler only after repeated acts of aggression.

Combining the Three Responses to Threat

The preceding chapters considered the three responses to threats in isolation. The guns-versus-butter model precludes bargaining or aligning with other states. The bargaining models do not allow the states to make a resource-allocation decision or to bargain. And, the alignment model excludes the options of reallocating resources or of bargaining before the outbreak of war. These restrictions make it possible to examine each of the three responses in a simpler setting, but this setting makes it impossible to study how these responses interact.[17]

A natural next step in the modeling enterprise would be to allow the states to respond to a threat in more than one way. Two examples foreshadow the potential importance of this extension. These examples indicate that taking the resource-allocation problem explicitly into account may recast some existing arguments and conclusions.

The first example came up in chapter 2. The standard relative-gains argument claims that states have to be concerned about relative gains because one state could use a "disproportionate gain to implement a policy intended to damage or destroy" another state (Waltz 1979, 105). But, this argument seems to assume that a disproportionate gain translates

---

[16] One of the complications the discussion in chapter 5 ignores is that war may also signal that the defender is also more willing to use force. Otherwise, the defender would have made a larger concession as in the bargaining model in chapter 3, and there would have been no war.

[17] Doyle (1997, 166), Morgenthau (1967, 172–80), Morrow (1993), Most and Starr (1984), Most and Siverson (1987), and Sorokin (1994) discuss various aspects of this interaction.

directly into a favorable shift in the distribution of power. This assumption is problematic, however, if states can reallocate their resources. As long as a state can completely offset a relative loss and still have some of its absolute gain leftover, then that state should prefer this outcome to one in which it gains nothing. Resource reallocation seems to undermine the standard relative-gains argument.

The second example addresses a dubious feature of the bargaining models. Bargaining generally does not break down in the games in chapters 3 and 4 if there are no informational problems. If the states know each other's payoffs, then a satisfied state can infer from these payoffs how much it has to offer to appease a dissatisfied state. And as we saw, a satisfied state prefers making these concessions to fighting as long as fighting is costly, the states are risk averse or risk neutral, and the distribution of power, if it is shifting, is not doing so too rapidly.

The reasoning underlying the absence of war is straightforward (see pp. 95–96 above). There is more to be divided if the states avoid fighting because fighting is costly. But the dissatisfied state's payoff is the same whether or not it fights. (Recall that the satisfied state concedes just enough to the dissatisfied state to make it indifferent between attacking and accepting the offer.) The satisfied state, therefore, gets to keep the "surplus" saved by not fighting if it appeases the dissatisfied state. And the prospect of obtaining this surplus is what makes the satisfied state prefer making concessions to fighting.

The fact that bargaining does not break down in war if there is complete information highlights the role of informational problems. But the absence of war when the states know each other's payoffs also seems likely to be an instance in the modeling dialogue where a model gets important things wrong. War, for example, did not come in 1939 because Britain and France would have been willing to satisfy Hitler's ultimate demands *if only they had known what these demands were but offered too little because of informational problems.* Rather, Hitler's occupation of the rump state of Czechoslovakia a few months after the Munich crisis convinced Britain and France that they would rather fight than satisfy Hitler's demands.

When a model gets important things wrong, a natural next step in the modeling enterprise is to look at the assumptions that drive the formally correct but substantively incorrect result. Three assumptions are primarily responsible for the absence of war when there is full information in the bargaining models in chapters 3 and 4 as well as in most of the existing formal work in international relations.[18] First, these formulations assume that the states are risk averse or risk neutral. They also assume that the issue in dispute is not an all-or-nothing affair. In particular, the set of intermediate outcomes is sufficiently large that the satisfied state can actually offer something that meets the dissatisfied state's minimal demands and yet leaves the satisfied state with some of the surplus saved by not fighting. Fearon (1995a, 338–39) discusses these restrictive assumptions and suggests that risk acceptance or the lack of intermediate outcomes are not empirically important causes of war.

The third assumption is of more interest here because it illuminates the potential importance of combining different ways that states can respond to threats in a single formulation. It is costly to fight in the bargaining models, but it does not cost anything to maintain a new territorial division once it has been established. Thus, there are more benefits to be divided if the states can avoid fighting, and this is the "surplus" the satisfied state gets to keep by appeasing the dissatisfied state.

This third assumption, however, contrasts with the guns-versus-butter model. In that formulation, a state must devote a significant share of its resources to the means of military power in order to deter an attack, and this makes preserving any territorial division costly. If, in particular, the costs of preserving the status quo are very high—perhaps because an adversary is relatively willing to use force—then internal balancing may break down in war even though there is complete information. States fight in the guns-versus-butter model because the cost of fighting a *known* adversary is less than the cost of living with that state and of constantly trying to ward off an attack at a time and place of its choosing. (See proposition 2.1 and figure 2.6.)

But to what extent does this fighting reflect the fact that a state can only respond to a threat in a single way in this model? What would happen if a state could bargain in a model as well as reallocate its resources? The answer is a matter of speculation at this stage in the modeling en-

---

[18] It may seem odd to assume that there are no fundamental differences over which states would fight and that war results from uncertainty. But some versions of neorealism also seem to make this assumption—albeit implicitly. As Glaser (1992, 1997) and Schweller (1996) have recently emphasized, neorealism typically assumes that states are security seekers. As such, these states would not fight unless their security was threatened, and there is no reason to feel threatened *if all states are known to be security seekers*. War, therefore, results not from a deep conflict of interest but from the states' uncertainty about the motivations of other states. This is the essence of Herz's early discussion of the security dilemma: "[I]t is his uncertainty and anxiety as to his neighbor's intentions that places man in this basic dilemma" (1959, 232).

terprise. But it seems likely that war could still arise with complete information. The cost of deterring an adversary may sometimes be too high as in the guns-versus-butter model.

Indeed, the fact that a state can both bargain and reallocate its resources seems likely to affect its willingness to bargain. Suppose a satisfied state faces a dissatisfied adversary. If the satisfied state makes a concession, this increases the dissatisfied state's resource base, and this may make the dissatisfied state more willing to fight. If so, then the effects of making a concession when there is bargaining in the guns-versus-butter model parallel the effects of making a concession when the cost of fighting depends on an adversary's size or when the distribution of power depends on the distribution of territory as in Fearon (1996). One concession leads to another and then another and then another. But if a state can choose which way it will respond to a threat, it does not have to appease an adversary by making concessions to it. A satisfied state can increase its military allocation instead. A larger military allocation, like a concession, is costly, but, unlike a concession, it does not make an adversary stronger and thereby trigger a series of future concessions. This may make internal balancing more attractive and make the distribution of territory more stable than the bargaining models suggest.

As this extended discussion of the limitations and qualifications makes clear, the models developed in the previous chapters are very spare and can be extended in many directions. Future work will no doubt qualify some of the conclusions derived from these models just as they qualify many existing claims in international relations theory. Indeed, one of the measures of the success of the models studied here is the degree to which they help provide the foundation for this future work. This is the way that the modeling enterprise moves forward.

International Relations Theory and Political Science

International relations theory has often treated the assumption of anarchy as a kind of analytic wall dividing it from the rest of political science. Anarchy, defined as the lack of an overarching supranational authority, "is the characteristic that distinguishes international politics from ordinary politics" for Wight (1979, 102), and it is the key structural difference between international and national politics for Waltz (1979, 102–04). Indeed, Robert Art and Robert Jervis begin their introductory text by defining the domain of international politics: "Unlike domestic politics, international politics takes place in an arena that has no central governing authority.... This—the absence of a supreme power—is what is meant by the anarchic environment of international politics (1992, 1)." The idea here seems to be that the strategic problems actors encounter in the anarchic environment of international politics are fundamentally different than those typically encountered by actors in nonanarchic settings.

The previous chapters suggest exactly the opposite. Viewing the strategic environment confronting states in terms of commitment issues, informational problems, and the technology of coercion serves as a bridge to other areas in political science. The strategic problems confronting actors in the anarchy of international politics often have close parallels in these other areas. Three examples illustrate the point.

First, there is a surprising parallel between the bargaining that occurs in the anarchy of international politics and in the presumably hierarchical realm of courts, adjudication, and enforcement. The strategic situation facing potential litigants "bargaining in the shadow of the law" (Cooter, Marks, and Mnookin 1982) and that facing states bargaining in the shadow of military power are strikingly similar at least to a first approximation.[19] The actors in each setting can resort to some form of power to impose a settlement. In the former, the parties can appeal to the courts to render a verdict and enforce a settlement. In the latter, the states can appeal to force to impose a settlement. But the exercise of power is costly in both environments, and this gives each actor an incentive to try to reach a mutually agreeable resolution and thereby avoid these costs. More specifically, the potential litigants can make offers and counter-offers until they agree or until one of them becomes sufficiently pessimistic about the prospects of reaching an agreement that that party takes the matter to court. Litigation, like the use of military power, is costly. Moreover, each party is unsure of the other's willingness to go to court, perhaps because each is uncertain of the other's cost of litigation or of the strength of its case. In this setting the parties face a now familiar risk-return trade-off. "The optimal bargaining strategy of a litigant balances a larger share of the stakes against the higher probability of a trial" (Cooter, Marks, and Mnookin 1982, 226).

These similar strategic settings have led theorists to ask similar substantive questions and propose similar answers. Central questions in the work on legal disputes are: Why do cases go to court? Why does bargaining sometimes break down in costly litigation and result in a court-

---

[19] See Cooter and Rubinfeld (1989) for a review of work on legal disputes.

imposed settlement? Is there, as Priest and Klein (1984) ask, a relationship between the chances that a dispute will go to court and the strength of the case? Are, for example, clear-cut cases in which the court is very likely to find in favor of one of the parties more likely to go to court than a case in which the ultimate verdict is much less clear? These questions have direct analogues in international relations theory. Why do disputes between states sometimes end in war and costly fighting? What is the relationship between the risk of war and the distribution of power? Is war more likely if there is a preponderance of power and the victor seems assured or if there is an even distribution of power and the victor is less certain?

These parallel questions have also produced parallel answers. One explanation for why cases go to trial is that the parties disagree about the expected outcome. At least one of the litigants is too optimistic about its prospects of prevailing or about the size of its award (Cooter, Marks, and Mnookin 1982; Gould 1973; Landes 1971; Schweizer 1989). For example, Priest and Klein (1984) argue that excessive optimism is less likely in clear-cut cases. Thus, the probability of litigation is smallest when one party has a preponderance of legal power on its side. And, this argument has a direct analogue in international relations theory. Blainey (1973) claims that a primary cause of war is that states are uncertain of the distribution of power between them and of the likely verdict of fighting: "Wars usually begin when fighting nations *disagree* on their relative strength" (122). Moreover, such disagreements are less likely when one state preponderates. Consequently, a preponderance of power is more peaceful.[20]

In addition to these substantive parallels, the formal work on legal bargaining often has analogous interpretations in international relations. At the most general level, asymmetric information is now seen as an important source of the litigants' failure to settle a dispute out of court (Cooter and Rubinfeld 1989, 1080), just as it is now seen as an important cause of war. At a more detailed level, Schweizer (1989) studies a model in which the defendant and the plaintiff are unsure of the strength of each other's case and thus of their chances of prevailing if the case goes to court. If this model were reinterpreted by taking the defendant and the plaintiff to be the satisfied and dissatisfied state, respectively, and if the probability of winning in court were taken to be the probability of

---

[20] Both arguments also fail to take into account the possibility that more will be demanded of a weaker actor and that this tends to make agreement less likely.

winning a war, then this game would be one of the best models we have of bargaining in international relations when the states are uncertain of the distribution of power existing between them.[21]

These parallels breach the analytic wall built on the concept of anarchy by undermining its importance as a distinctive feature of international politics. What realm could be less anarchic than one in which the courts can impose and enforce a settlement? Yet, the strategic problem facing litigants in this presumably hierarchical realm is akin to that facing states in the anarchic realm of international politics.

The second example linking international relations theory to political science centers on the states' inability to make binding agreements with each other. This feature hardly distinguishes international politics from other political settings. The inability of actors to make binding commitments characterizes many domains in both politics and economics. In American politics, for example, no Congress can bind another. Nor can individual politicians appeal to the courts to enforce a "log-roll" if someone does not follow through on his or her part of an agreement. Indeed, just as Keohane (1984) sees international institutions as a way of helping states achieve cooperative gains in an environment in which they cannot make binding commitments, Shepsle and Weingast (1987), Weingast and Marshall (1988), and Cox and McCubbins (1993) explain the institutional structure of Congress and parties as resulting at least in part from an effort to solve commitment problems.[22]

In institutionally weak states, civil violence may result from the inability of a majority group to commit itself to abstaining from exploiting minority groups (Fearon 1993; Walter 1997). The basic logic is similar to the preventive war logic in international relations. Even if an initial settlement would ensure minority rights, such an agreement may let the majority group consolidate its power over time—especially if the settlement entails the disarmament of the minority group. As the majority group becomes stronger vis-à-vis the minority group, it may become dissatisfied with the original agreement and use its greater strength to renegotiate a new one. Foreseeing all of this, the minority group may prefer the preventive use of force.

---

[21] For other game-theoretic work on legal bargaining, see Kennan and Wilson (1993), Nalebuff (1987), Reinganum and Wilde (1986), and Spier (1992).

[22] Shepsle and Weingast (1995) survey this work, as well as a second line of research which sees the institutional structure of Congress as a way of overcoming informational problems (e.g., Gilligan and Krehbiel 1989 and Krehbiel 1991).

In economics, actors often may not be able to commit themselves because they cannot write complete, enforceable contracts. Contracts may be incomplete because the actors cannot foresee all possible contingencies or because unambiguously specifying what to do in each of these contingencies would make the contract too complex and unwieldy. Indeed, complete contracts may be unenforceable if the courts cannot independently verify the occurrence of a relevant contingency. The assumption of incomplete contracts underlies much recent work in economics and organization theory, including transaction-cost economics, the theory of the firm, and regulation.[23] In sum, many domains are effectively anarchic when we look at them closely, and much work is being done in trying to work out their strategic logic.

The third and final illustration brings this book full circle by returning us to the Hobbesian state of nature. For Hobbes, the Leviathan or sovereign offers an escape from the state of war (1991, 117–21). By using its overwhelming power to keep its subjects in awe, a sovereign can end the state of war existing among its subjects by protecting them from each other. Once these subjects are freed from having to devote their own energies and resources to providing for their own security, they can devote themselves to more productive activities. For absent "a common power to keep them all in awe ... there is no place for industry; because the fruit thereof is uncertain" (Hobbes 1991, 88–89). In other words, the sovereign—if it follows the precepts of natural law—allows its subjects to reallocate their resources away from appropriative behavior and to pursue "all the other contentments of life" (1991, 231).

But suppose the sovereign does not follow the precepts of natural law, which it was under no obligation to do in Hobbes's view. What if the Hobbesian Leviathan takes bribes?[24] Or, less colorfully, suppose we

[23] See, for example, Grossman and Hart (1986), Laffont and Tirole (1993), Salanie (1997), Tirole (1988), and O. Williamson (1985).

[24] In Hobbes's view, the sovereign was not obligated to his subjects to refrain from taking bribes or, more generally, to establish secure property rights and a system of good laws which, among other things, would let its subjects enjoy the fruits of their industry. The sovereign's failure to provide these things did not give the subjects a just cause for resisting their sovereign as long as it continued to protect them from returning to a state of war of all against all (1991, 117–29, 145–54). Nevertheless, the sovereign was obligated to God to follow the precepts of natural law, and this implied that the soverign should provide these things to the extent possible (Hobbes 1991, 231–44). As Ryan puts it, "It is easy to feel that as long as nobody talked about their 'rights,' a Hobbesian state would be indistinguishable from a liberal constitutional regime.... But if the sovereign breaches it [i.e., the dictates of natural law], we are not to resist but to reflect that it is the sovereign whom God will call into account, not ourselves" (1996, 237).

look at domestic politics from a rent-seeking perspective. In this view, domestic actors can often engage in two kinds of activities. They can pursue productive endeavors which, loosely speaking, increase the size of the social "pie," or they can engage in rent-seeking or appropriative behavior in which they try to acquire a larger share of a smaller pie. (The pie is smaller because rent-seeking itself is costly and because it may lead to economic distortions and still larger social costs.) These activities include trying to secure favorable legislation, regulation, tariffs, quotas, subsidies, patents, and licenses as well as extra-legal activities like bribery, robbery, intimidation and coercion.[25] Domestic actors in this account must decide how to allocate their resources between production and appropriation where the payoff to the latter depends in part on how much other actors devote to that activity. This strategic problem resonates with the one that states face in the guns-versus-butter model. In that situation, a state has to decide how to divide its resources between spending on the means of military power and meeting its direct ends where the indirect benefits of the former also depend on how much others allocate to the means of power.

The three preceding examples suggest that commitment issues, informational asymmetries, the technology of coercion, and the strategic problems inherent in them provide an analytic bridge connecting international relations theory with other areas of political science and economics. The models studied in the previous chapters were motivated by the three ways that states can respond to threats and some old questions these responses raise: How do states resolve the guns-versus-butter trade-off? What is the relation between the distribution of power and the likelihood of war? How do states cope with shifts in the distribution of power between them? Do states tend to balance? But, the basic issues and trade-offs underlying these models are much more general and transcend this particular motivation. How actors interact in the shadow of power is crucial to much of politics.

---

[25] The term "rent-seeking" sometimes carries the connotation that rents only exist because governments create them (and therefore the ideal solution to them would be to eliminate or reduce governments) and that agents only pursue these rents through legal means. The term "appropriation" is broader and includes both legal and extra-legal activities (Hirshleifer 1988, 202) an actor may or may not pursue depending on circumstances. Garfinkel and Skaperdas (1996) and Hirshleifer (1995) survey recent work in economics on conflict and appropriation. Mueller (1989) summarizes some of the work on rent-seeking, and Eggertson (1990) puts this work in the broader context of a theory of property rights. Neary (1997) compares models of rent-seeking and economic conflict.

However, this emphasis on the similarity between international relations theory and other areas of political science does not mean that there are no significant differences between them. The models developed here bring some important similarities and parallels to the fore. But the models are very spare and at best offer a template which clarifies some basic issues and provides a foundation for future work. That work may eventually reveal fundamental differences between the strategic problems that arise in international politics and those that arise in other political arenas. If so, then appreciating both the similarities as well as the more subtle genuine differences will deepen our understanding of international politics and politics more generally.

APPENDIXES

Appendix 1

Game Trees, Strategies, and Equilibria

Chapters 2–5 use a series of game-theoretic models to analyze three ways that states can respond to threats and to help clarify the complicated interactions underlying these responses. That discussion presumes that the reader has a passing familiarity with game trees, strategies, and equilibria, and this appendix provides a brief review of these concepts.[1]

A *game tree* is a stylized representation of an interaction among a group of actors. A tree describes four key aspects of this interaction: (i) the order in which the actors make decisions, i.e., who moves first, second, third, and so on; (ii) what options or alternatives each actor has to choose from when making a decision; (iii) what each actor knows when making a decision about the other actors' past decisions; and (iv) what the actors' preferences are over the various ways that the interaction could unfold, i.e., how the actors rank the possible outcomes of their interaction.

An example helps to make these features more concrete. Suppose a buyer and a seller are bargaining about the price of a used book. To simplify matters, assume that the buyer can only make one take-it-or-leave-it offer which the seller can then either accept or reject. If the seller accepts, the sale takes place at the agreed price. If the seller rejects the offer, the interaction between these two actors ends and there is no sale. Suppose further that the buyer has only five ten-dollar bills with him and that the seller does not have any change. These simplifications mean that the buyer has only six options: he can decide not to make any offer at all or he can offer to pay $10, $20, $30, $40, or $50. Suppose further that the book is worth more to the buyer than the seller (otherwise there would be nothing to bargain about). In particular, the book is worth

[1] Morrow (1994b) provides a more comprehensive development of these topics.

$45 to the buyer and $25 to the seller. Finally, the buyer and seller are assumed to know each other's payoffs.[2]

The tree in figure A1.1 represents this interaction. The tree begins with the buyer, *B*, having to decide what to do. By assumption, *B* can decide not to make an offer or can offer $10, $20, $30, $40, or $50. Each of these alternatives is represented by a different branch in the tree.[3] If the buyer does make an offer, the seller must decide whether to accept it or reject it, and each of these options also corresponds to a different branch in the tree.

A tree summarizes all of the possible ways that events could unfold. In this particular case, there are eleven possibilities: the buyer could decide not to make an offer; or the buyer could make one of five possible offers to which the seller could react in one of two possible ways. Each of the ways that events could unfold traces a different path through the tree. If, for example, the buyer offered $40 and the seller accepted this offer, this sequence of decisions would trace out a path through the tree along the branch labeled "$40" followed by the branch labeled "accept."

The players are assumed to have preferences over the different ways that events could unfold, and these preferences are represented by payoffs at the end of each path. If, for example, the seller accepts an offer of $40, then the buyer's payoff is $55 (the $50 the buyer started with less the $40 he paid for the book plus the value of the book which is $45), and the seller's payoff is the price she receives for the book, namely $40. Accordingly, the pair of payoffs $55 and $40 appear at the end of the path "$40" followed by "accept." If, by contrast, the seller rejected this offer, the buyer would have his original $50 and the seller would still have the book, which is worth $25 to her. In this case, the payoffs of $50 and $25 are at the end of the path "$40" followed by "reject." Similarly, the buyer's payoff if the seller accepts an offer of $30 is $65 ($50 − $30 + $45), and the seller's payoff is $30.

A game tree describes the arena in which a group of actors interacts. Loosely speaking, an actor's *strategy* describes one of the many possible ways that an actor could interact with the other actors in this arena.

---

[2] This assumption simplifies the discussion of the players' interaction and is relaxed in the chapters above where the effects of the states' uncertainty about each other's payoffs are studied.

[3] Restricting the number of alternatives the buyer has simplifies the tree for expository purposes. In a more realistic setting, the buyer might be able to offer any price between one cent and fifty dollars. In this case it would take five thousand branches to represent each of the buyer's options explicitly, and the tree would be very cumbersome.

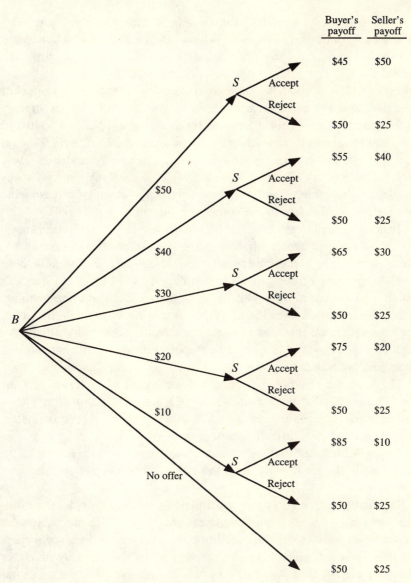

	Buyer's payoff	Seller's payoff
	$45	$50
	$50	$25
	$55	$40
	$50	$25
	$65	$30
	$50	$25
	$75	$20
	$50	$25
	$85	$10
	$50	$25
	$50	$25

Figure A1.1 A game tree for a buyer-seller interaction

More precisely, a player's strategy specifies what that player would do in any contingency. One can, therefore, think of a player's strategy as a set of contingent statements which stipulate the action that that player would take in each and every place in a game tree (i.e., in each and every contingency) where it could have a decision to make.

More concretely, a strategy for the seller in the game in figure A1.1 is a set of contingent statements which describe how the seller would respond to each of the five possible offers it might receive. In particular, one of the seller's strategies is to accept offers of $40 or $50 and to reject offers of $10, $20, and $30. Another strategy for her is to accept offers of $30, $40, and $50 and to reject $10 and $20. And, still another strategy is for the seller to accept offers which are multiples of 20, i.e., $20 and $40, and to reject offers which are not multiples of 20, i.e., $10, $30, and $50. (As this last example illustrates, a player's strategy describes a way that that player *could* play the game and not necessarily a sensible way of playing the game. Whether or not a particular strategy is reasonable will be discussed below in the context of the game's equilibria.)

Turning to the buyer's strategy, he really faces only one "contingency," which is having to decide what, if anything, to offer at the outset of the game. Accordingly, the buyer's strategy simply describes what it does at the beginning of the game. One strategy is, therefore, to offer $20; another strategy is to offer $40; and still another is not to offer anything.

A game tree describes the ways that events *could* unfold. An actor's strategies describe the ways that an actor *could* interact with others. An equilibrium of a game is a prediction about how the actors *actually* will react and how events *actually* will unfold.

The games in chapters 2 through 5 are analyzed in terms of their perfect equilibria. A *perfect equilibrium* of a game is a set of strategies— one for each player in the game—which satisfy two general requirements. These requirements formally define what it means for a set of strategies to be "sensible," and strategies that satisfy these two criteria are taken to be plausible predictions about how the actors will behave and how events will unfold.

The first requirement is that each player's strategy must be a reasonable response to what the other players are doing. More precisely, a set of strategies satisfies this first condition if no player can increase its payoff by switching from its predicted strategy to another strategy *given that the other players are following their predicted strategies*. If a set of strategies meets this requirement, then no player can benefit by deviating from its predicted strategy, and the set of predicted strategies is, in this sense, self-reinforcing.

Focusing on strategies that satisfy this requirement in effect forces the analyst to look at his or her prediction about the strategies the players will follow from the perspective of each and every player and to make sure that the strategy the analyst is predicting each actor will follow is in that actor's best interest given that the other actors follow their predicted strategies. The motivation behind this requirement is that if a set of strategies did not satisfy this criterion, then at least one actor would have an incentive to behave other than in the predicted way and this would undercut the prediction. A set of strategies that satisfies this first requirement is called a *Nash* equilibrium of the game.

The following strategies are a Nash equilibrium of the buyer-seller game in figure A1.1. The seller accepts any price higher than the value she attaches to keeping the book. More formally, the book is worth $25 to *S*, so she accepts offers of $30, $40, or $50 and rejects offers of $10 or $20. The buyer's strategy is to offer the lowest price that the seller will accept, namely, $30.

To verify that these two strategies satisfy the first requirement and therefore are a Nash equilibrium of the game, consider the buyer's strategy first. His payoff to offering $30 is $65 *given the seller's strategy of accepting offers of $30 or more.* Can the buyer obtain a better payoff than $65 by switching to another strategy by making a different offer? The answer is no. If the buyer offers more, the seller would accept, but the buyer's payoff would be less than $65 because he would have paid a higher price. If the buyer offers a price less than $30, the seller would reject this offer and the buyer's payoff would be the $50 he has in his pocket. Thus, the buyer is maximizing his payoff by offering $30 and therefore has no incentive to switch to a different strategy.

Now consider the seller's strategy of accepting any offer of $30 or more. Can she do better by adopting a different strategy *given the buyer's strategy of offering* $30? The answer again is no. The payoff to following her strategy of accepting any offer of $30 or more is $30. Suppose, however, that the seller switched to any other strategy in which she would reject an offer of $30, e.g., the seller would only accept offers of $40 or more. This strategy would lead the seller to reject the buyer's offer of $30, and the seller's payoff would drop to $25, which is the value she places on retaining the book. Suppose, instead, that she switched to any other strategy in which she would accept an offer of $30, e.g., accepting any offer of $20 or more. Following strategies of this type give her a payoff of $30, which is the same payoff she receives from following her original strategy of accepting offers of $30 or more. Thus, *given the buyer's strategy of offering* $30, the seller cannot increase her payoff by deviating from her strategy of accepting any offer of $30 or more.

In sum, if the buyer's strategy is to offer $30 and the seller's strategy is to accept $30 or more, then neither player can gain by deviating from his or her strategy given that the other player is playing according to his or her strategy. These strategies are therefore self-reinforcing and constitute a Nash equilibrium of the game.

A set of strategies satisfies the first requirement of being a perfect equilibrium if no player can benefit by deviating from its strategy *given that the other players play according to their strategies*. But a set of strategies can satisfy this condition and yet still not seem like a reasonable prediction about how the actors will actually play the game. The reason for this failure is that a set of Nash equilibrium strategies begs an important prior question: Is it reasonable in the first place for a player to believe that the other players will follow their strategies? Often it is not reasonable, and the set of strategies, although they meet the first requirement, fail to provide a plausible prediction about how the game will be played and how events will actually unfold.

A second, simple example illustrates these points. Suppose that the seller's strategy is to accept offers of only $40 or more. That is, the seller threatens to reject any offer of $30 or less. Faced with this threat, the buyer's strategy is to offer $40. These strategies satisfy the first requirement and are a Nash equilibrium of the game. To see that this is so, consider the buyer's strategy first. His payoff to offering $40 is $55 (the original $50 less the price paid for the book plus the value of the book). *If* the seller follows her strategy, the buyer cannot increase his payoff by switching to another strategy by offering something else. Offering less than $40 *given the seller's strategy* results in no sale and a payoff of $50 for the buyer. Offering more than $40 does produce a sale, but at a higher price and this too leaves the buyer worse-off. Thus, the buyer cannot benefit by deviating from his strategy of offering $40.

Now consider the seller's strategy of threatening to reject any offer less than $40. The seller cannot increase her payoff by switching strategies *given the buyer's strategy of offering* $40. The payoff to following her strategy of only accepting offers of $40 or more is $40. If, however, the seller switched to any other strategy in which she would reject an offer of $40, then there would be no sale and the seller's payoff would be that of retaining the book, or $25. If, by contrast, the seller switched to another strategy in which she accepted an offer of $40, then her payoff to that strategy would be $40. The seller, therefore, cannot increase her payoff by deviating from her strategy of accepting any offer of $40 or more *given the buyer's strategy of offering* $40. Thus, these two strategies satisfy the first requirement and thereby constitute a Nash equilibrium of the game.

As just shown, the buyer maximizes his payoff by offering $40 *if* he believes the seller's threat to reject any offer less than that. But is it reasonable for him to believe this threat in the first place? The following argument suggests that it is not reasonable because the threat is inherently incredible. Suppose that the buyer presented the seller with a fait accompli by offering $30 rather than $40. Although the seller would have preferred to have received an offer of $40, the choice now confronting her is to accept the offer and obtain a payoff of $30 or to reject the offer, retain the book, and obtain a payoff of $25. Given our assumption that actors try to do the best they can in the situations they face, the seller would accept the offer of $30. Based on this reasoning, the buyer concludes that the seller's threat to reject an offer of $30 is incredible and will not believe that the seller will play according to her strategy.[4]

The second requirement that a perfect equilibrium imposes on a set of strategies is that the threats and promises implicit in each player's predicted strategy must be credible. That is, the contingent statements that define an actor's strategy must specify that that actor always takes the action which is in its best interest. In terms of a game tree, this second condition requires each player to act in a way that maximizes its payoff at every place in the tree it has to make a decision.

The second example described above fails to meet this second criterion, whereas the first example does and, indeed, is the only set of strategies that does. Thus, the only strategies that satisfy these two conditions are: the seller accepts any offer of $30 or more and the buyer offers $30. These strategies, therefore, constitute the unique perfect equilibrium of the game in figure A1.1.

To see that the second example does not satisfy this requirement, observe that the seller's strategy of rejecting any offer less than $40 means that there is a place in the game tree where the seller is not acting in her own best interest. To wit, the seller's strategy has her rejecting an offer of $30, which leaves her with $25 rather than the $30 that she could have had by accepting the offer.

---

[4]One might wonder if the seller would still prefer to reject an offer of $30 in order to maintain a reputation for being a "tough" bargainer, which would help her obtain higher payoffs in future bargaining. Such reputational considerations may be important in some substantive situations and not in others. But these substantive considerations are not at issue in the take-it-or-leave-it-offer game, and we would need a different model if we wanted to study them. After the seller reacts to the buyer's offer in the game in figure A1.1, there is no further interaction. Thus, reputational considerations do not affect the seller's decision in the game.

To see that the first example is the only combination of strategies that satisfies the second condition, note that if the seller is always going to act in her own best interest given the offer that confronts her, then she must accept any offer of $30 or more, because rejecting it would leave her with the lower payoff of $25. Furthermore, she must reject offers of $20 or $10, because the payoff to keeping the book is higher. And given that the seller will react in this way, the buyer's optimal offer is $30, which is the lowest price he can offer and that the seller will accept. But these are just the strategies that were considered in the first example above, so these strategies are the unique perfect equilibrium of the bargaining game.

To summarize, analyzing a game by finding its perfect equilibria imposes two intuitive requirements on our predictions about the actors' strategies. First, the prediction must make sense when viewed from the perspective of each and every player. That is, no actor can benefit from deviating from its predicted strategy given that the other actors are playing according to their predicted strategies. Second, the threats and promises inherent in the contingent statements that define each player's predicted strategy must be credible. For if a player's predicted strategy were based on incredible threats or promises, then the other players would not believe that that player actually would follow its predicted strategy.

Appendix 2

The Formalities of the Guns-versus-Butter Model

This appendix presents the formal analysis of the guns-versus-butter model. The first section defines the states' strategies and payoffs. The second proves the propositions discussed in chapter 2, and the last analyzes the comparative statics of the model.

Strategies and Payoffs

In the game, state S_1 has to decide how to allocate its resources and whether or not to attack in rounds $t = 0, 2, 4, \ldots$, and S_2 has to make the same decisions in rounds $t = 1, 3, 5, \ldots$ Because the game starts with S_1's making the first decision at time $t = 0$, S_2's initial allocation $m_2(0)$ is an exogenously given parameter of the game.

To specify the states' strategies, let $h(t)$ be the history of both states' allocations through period $t - 1$: $h(t) = \{m_1(j), m_2(j)\}_{j=0}^{t-1}$ where $m_1(j) \in [0, r_1]$ and $m_2(j) \in [0, r_2]$. Assume further that $H(t)$ is the set of all possible histories $h(t)$. If t is even, then S_1 has to decide what to do. A behavioral strategy for S_1 at time t is therefore a function $\sigma_1(t)$, which specifies what S_1 allocates to the military and whether or not it attacks following any possible history $h(t)$. That is, $\sigma_1(t) : H(t) \to [0, r_1] \times \{A, \sim A\}$ where "A" and "$\sim A$" stand for "attack," and "not attack," respectively. A pure strategy for S_1 is an infinite sequence $\{\sigma_1(2j)\}_{j=0}^{\infty}$ which specifies what S_1 does in any period in which it has to make a decision.

If the states never attack, then their allocation decisions generate an infinite stream of consumption. S_1's payoff is simply $\sum_{t=0}^{\infty} \delta_1^t (r_1 - m_1(t))^{\rho_1}$. (By assumption, S_1's allocation in any even t also locks in that allocation for period $t + 1$. This implies $m_1(t) = m_1(t + 1)$ for $t = 0, 2, 4, \ldots$)

In order to generalize the specification of the states' payoffs to attacking, which were discussed in chapter 2, let $\pi(m_a, m_d, \beta)$ represent the probability that the attacker prevails given that the attack takes place when the attacker is allocating m_a to the military, the defender is allocating m_d, and the offense-defense balance is β. (Chapter 2 assumed that $\pi(m_a, m_d, \beta) = \beta m_a/(\beta m_a + m_d)$.) Suppose further that π is increasing in the attacker's allocation m_a but with a nonincreasing marginal effect ($\partial\pi/\partial m_a > 0$ and $\partial^2\pi/\partial m_a^2 \leq 0$); π is decreasing in m_d with a nonincreasing marginal effect; and π is increasing in β. Then, S_1's payoff to attacking at time w (where w is even) is:

$$\sum_{t=0}^{w-1} \delta_1^t(r_1 - m_1(t))^{\rho_1} + (1 - \pi(m_1(w), m_2(w), \beta))[\delta_1^w(r_1 - m_1(w))^{\rho_1}]$$

$$+ \pi(m_1(w), m_2(w), \beta)\left[\delta_1^w(r_1 - m_1(w))^{\rho_1} + \sum_{t=w+1}^{\infty} \delta_1^t(r_1 + r_2 - c_1)^{\rho_1}\right]$$

The first term is S_1's payoff to its prewar consumption. The second term is S_1's payoff if it is defeated weighted by the probability that S_1 loses, and the third term is S_1's payoff to prevailing weighted by the probability of victory. S_2's strategies and payoffs are defined analogously.

Proofs

Before proving the propositions it will be useful to introduce some notation and definitions. Let $P_1(m_1)$ denote S_1's payoff to allocating m_1 to the military and therefore consuming $r_1 - m_1$ in every period. Consequently, $P_1(m_1) = \sum_{t=0}^{\infty} \delta^t(r_1 - m_1)^{\rho_1} = (r_1 - m_1)^{\rho_1}/(1 - \delta)$. S_1's payoff to attacking at (m_1, m_2) is $A_1(m_1, m_2) = (r_1 - m_1)^{\rho_1} + \pi(m_1, m_2, \beta)\sum_{t=1}^{\infty}\delta_1^t(r_1 + r_2 - c_1)^{\rho_1} = (r_1 - m_1)^{\rho_1} + \pi(m_1, m_2, \beta)[(r_1 + r_2 - c)^{\rho_1}/(1 - \delta)]$. This expression simply generalizes expression 2.1 by letting π represent the probability that the attacker prevails. If S_1 is at (m_1, m_2) and decides to attack, it will reallocate its resources so as to maximize its payoff to attacking. With this in mind, let $a_1^*(m_1) \in [0, r_1]$ maximize $A_1(m_1, m_2)$ and take $A_1^*(m_2) = A_1(a_1^*(m_2), m_2)$. Then S_1 allocates $a_1^*(m_1)$ to the military if it decides to attack.

S_1 weakly prefers remaining at an allocation (m_1, m_2) to reallocating its resources and attacking whenever $P_1(m_1) \geq A_1^*(m_2)$. The set of all of these allocations is $\mathcal{P}_1 = \{(m_1, m_2) : P_1(m_1) \geq A_1^*(m_2)\}$. By definition, S_1 is indifferent between staying at $(i_1(m_2), m_2)$ and attacking. That is, $i_1(m_2)$ solves $P_1(i_1(m_2), (m_2)) = A_1(m_2)$ if a solution exists. $P_2(m_2)$, $A_2^*(m_1)$, $\mathcal{P}_2$, and $i_2(m_1)$ are defined analogously.

Two definitions will also be helpful. Suppose that S_2 has disarmed, i.e., $m_2 = 0$. If S_1 were to reallocate its resources and attack, then it would obtain $A_1^*(0)$. Similarly, S_2 prevails and receives a payoff of $A_2^*(0)$ if it attacks a disarmed S_1. The states are said to have a *conflict of interest* if they prefer attacking a disarmed adversary to living with it. In symbols, $A_1^*(0) > P_1(0)$ and $A_2^*(0) > P_2(0)$.

This condition implies that the origin is not in the lens formed by the intersection of i_1 and i_2: $(0,0) \notin \mathcal{P}_1 \cap \mathcal{P}_2$. If this allocation were in the lens, then neither state would attack the other state under any circumstances, and this does not seem to be an analytically interesting case. Accordingly, the states will be assumed to have a conflict of interest.

Because a conflict of interest exists, S_2 always has to devote some of its resources to the military if it is to deter S_1. In particular, let $\underline{m}_2$ denote the amount that S_2 has to spend on the military that makes S_1 indifferent between consuming r_1 in each period and attacking. That is, $\underline{m}_2$ solves $A_1^*(\underline{m}_2) = P_1(0)$, which means $i_1(\underline{m}_2) = 0$. Similarly, let $\underline{m}_1$ be the value of m_1 at which $i_2(m_1) = 0$.

Finally, define a *peaceful equilibrium* to be an equilibrium in which the states attack with probability zero along the equilibrium path. (States can attack in subgames off the equilibrium path in a peaceful equilibrium.)

Proof of Proposition 2.1

The proof that there is no peaceful equilibrium if the lens formed by i_1 and i_2 is empty, i.e., if $\mathcal{P}_1 \cap \mathcal{P}_2 = \emptyset$, proceeds by contradiction. Assume that a peaceful equilibrium does exist and that $\mathcal{P}_1 \cap \mathcal{P}_2 = \emptyset$. This leads to a contradiction.

The first step in deriving this contradiction is to describe two useful properties of i_1 and i_2. Because these curves do not intersect, $i_1^{-1}(m_1)$ lies above $i_2(m_1)$ and $i_2^{-1}(m_2)$ lies above $i_1(m_2)$, i.e., $i_1^{-1}(m_1) > i_2(m_1)$ and $i_2^{-1}(m_2) > i_1(m_2)$. To show the former, recall that $\underline{m}_1$ is defined so that $i_2(\underline{m}_1) = 0$. Furthermore, $i_1^{-1}(m_1)$ is increasing in m_1 and $i_1^{-1}(0) = \underline{m}_2$. This means $i_1^{-1}(\underline{m}_1) > i_1^{-1}(0) = \underline{m}_2 > 0 = i_2(\underline{m}_1)$. Thus $i_1^{-1}(m_1)$ lies above $i_2(m_1)$ at $\underline{m}_1$. But then the continuity of i_1^{-1} and i_2 and the assumption that $\mathcal{P}_1$ do not intersect $\mathcal{P}_2$ ensures that i_1^{-1} is always above i_2.

The second property is that either $i_1(r_2) < r_1$ or $i_2(r_1) < r_2$. Otherwise, $\mathcal{P}_1$ and $\mathcal{P}_2$ would intersect at (r_1, r_2). Without loss of generality, take $i_1(r_2)$ to be less than r_1.

Now let (σ_1^*, σ_2^*) be a peaceful Nash equilibrium. S_1 is certain to have to respond to an allocation in the interval $[\underline{m}_2, r_2]$. This interval is bounded below by $\underline{m}_2$, because S_2 can never allocate less than $\underline{m}_2$ to the military in any peaceful equilibrium. To see why, note that the best that S_1 could possibly do in a peaceful equilibrium is to devote all of its resources to its domestic ends and thereby consume r_1. This would give it a payoff of $P_1(0)$. But if S_1 optimally attacks S_2 at an $m_2 < \underline{m_2}$, it receives $A_1^*(m_2)$, which is greater than $P_1(0)$ because $m_2 < \underline{m_2}$. Thus, S_1 would have an incentive to deviate from any peaceful equilibrium strategy if S_2 ever allocates less than $\underline{m_2}$ to its military sector. But no actor can benefit by deviating in an equilibrium, so it must be that S_2 always allocates at least $\underline{m_2}$ to the military along the equilibrium path in a peaceful equilibrium.

If S_1 optimally attacks at any $m_2 \in [\underline{m_2}, r_2]$, then it follows from the definition of i_1 that S_1 would receive a payoff of $P_1(i_1(m_2))$. But $P_1(i_1(m_2))$ is decreasing in m_2, so S_1 must obtain at least $P_1(i_1(r_2))$ by attacking. Thus S_1 must attain at least $P_1(i_1(r_2))$ in a peaceful equilibrium for otherwise it would prefer to attack.

The only way that S_1 can obtain this payoff is if there is a positive probability that S_1 will play an allocation less than or equal to $i_1(r_2)$. Then S_1's allocation is also bounded below in a peaceful equilibrium by $\underline{m_1}$ for the same reason that S_2's allocation was bounded below by $\underline{m_2}$. Thus, S_1 must play some $m_1 \in [\underline{m_1}, i_1(r_2)]$ with positive probability.

The payoff S_2 receives by attacking S_1 at any $m_1 \in [\underline{m_1}, i_1(r_2)]$ is bounded below by $P_2(i_2(i_1(r_2)))$. To deter S_2 from attacking in a peaceful equilibrium, S_2 must obtain at least this lower bound, which is possible only if S_2's allocation lies in the interval $[\underline{m_2}, i_2(i_1(r_2))]$ with positive probability. The upper bound of this interval is less than r_2, because $i_1^{-1}(m_1)$ lies above $i_2(m_1)$.

But for any $m_2 \in [\underline{m_2}, i_2(i_1(r_2))]$, S_1 will attain at least $P_1(i_1(i_2(i_1(r_2))))$ by attacking. Thus, S_1 must obtain at least this amount by not attacking, which implies that it must play some point in the interval $[\underline{m_1}, i_1(i_2(i_1(r_2)))]$ with positive probability. The upper bound of this interval is strictly less than $i_1(r_2)$, because $i_2^{-1}(m_2)$ lies above $i_1(m_2)$ and therefore $i_1(i_2(i_1(r_2))) < i_2^{-1}(i_2(i_1(r_2))) = i_1(r_2)$.

Once again, S_2 can attain at least $P_2(i_2(i_1(i_2(i_1(r_2)))))$ by attacking S_1 in the interval $[\underline{m_1}, i_1(i_2(i_1(r_2)))]$. To achieve this much in a peaceful equilibrium, S_2 must play some allocation in the interval $[\underline{m_2}, i_2(i_1(i_2(i_1(r_2))))]$ with some probability. The upper bound of this interval also satisfies $i_2(i_1(i_2(i_1(r_2)))) < i_2(i_1(r_2)) < r_2$.

Continuing in this way generates the well-defined, strictly decreasing sequence $I_1 = \{i_1(r_2), i_1(i_2(i_1(r_2))), i_1(i_2(i_1(i_2(i_1(r_2))))), \ldots\}$ which is bounded below by $\underline{m_1}$. I_1, therefore, converges to some $m_1^* \geq \underline{m_1} > 0$. Now form the new sequence I_2 by applying i_2 to each element in I_1. Because each element of I_1 is at least as large as $\underline{m}_1$, I_2 is well defined. The continuity of i_2 then ensures that the new sequence converges to some $m_2^* = i_2(m_1^*)$.

But this leads to a contradiction, for it implies that i_1 and i_2 intersect at (m_1^*, m_2^*). To derive this implication, it suffices to show that $m_1^* = i_1(m_2^*)$. But except for the first element, I_2 is derived from I_1 by applying i_1 to each element of I_2. The continuity of i_1 then gives $m_1^* = i_1(m_2^*)$. Thus, i_1 and i_2 intersect at (m_1^*, m_2^*), and this contradiction establishes the proposition.

Proof of Proposition 2.2

To show that the maximum a state can obtain in a peaceful Nash equilibrium is given by the lower tip of the lens formed by the intersection of $\mathscr{P}_1$ and $\mathscr{P}_2$, this intersection must first be described more formally. If $\mathscr{P}_1$ and $\mathscr{P}_2$ intersect, so must $i_1(m_2)$ and $i_2(m_1)$. Define the lower tip of the lens (m_1^*, m_2^*) to be the smallest m_1 at which $i_1(m_2)$ and $i_2(m_1)$ intersect. That is, $m_1^* = \min\{m_1 : i_1(i_2(m_1)) = m_1\}$ and $m_2^* = i_2(m_1^*)$. (The set of m_1 such that $i_1(i_2(m_1)) = m_1$ is closed and bounded, so a minimum is sure to exist.)

To establish that the combination of payoffs at (m_1^*, m_2^*) Pareto dominates any pair of peaceful payoffs (except possibly itself), assume that one state, say S_1, could do better than $P_1(m_1^*)$ in some peaceful equilibrium (σ_1^*, σ_2^*). To do strictly better, there must be some positive probability that S_1's allocation will lie in $[\underline{m}_1, u_1]$ for a $u_1 < m_1^*$. Consequently, S_2 must be able to achieve at least $P_2(i_2(u_1))$ by not attacking, since this is a lower bound on what could be attained by attacking.

By construction $\mathscr{P}_1$ and $\mathscr{P}_2$ do not intersection and $i_1^{-1}(m_1)$ lies above $i_2(m_1)$ in the set $[\underline{m}_1, m_1^*) \times [\underline{m}_2, m_2^*)$. Accordingly, the argument used in the proof of proposition 2.1 can be repeated to obtain the contraction that i_1 and i_2 must intersect in this region. This contradiction establishes proposition 2.2.

Proof of Proposition 2.3

Before stating and proving proposition 2.3 formally, one further condition must be specified. Suppose that S_1 believes that war is inevitable at the lower tip of the lens at (m_1^*, m_2^*), i.e., that S_2 is going to attack regardless of what S_1 does. Conceivably, S_1 might prefer cutting its forces and standing on the defensive rather than attacking. Waiting, however, gives S_2 the opportunity to reallocate its resources optimally and then attack, and it seems more likely that S_1 would do worse by conceding this reallocation advantage to S_2 even if the offense-defense balance favors the defense.

In what follows, we will assume that if a state believes war is inevitable at (m_1^*, m_2^*), its payoff to attacking is higher than its payoff to cutting its forces and letting its adversary attack. For S_1, this assumption means:

$$A_1(m_2^*) > (r_1 - m_1)^{\rho_1} + [1 - \pi(a_2^*(m_1), m_1, \beta)] \frac{\delta_1(r_1 + r_2 - c)^{\rho_1}}{1 - \delta_1} \quad (A2.1)$$

for any $m_1 \leq m_1^*$. (Note that the factor in the brackets is the probability that S_1 prevails given that S_2 is the attacker and strikes after allocating $a_2^*(m_1)$ to its military sector.) The analogous condition is presumed to hold for S_2.

Proposition 2.3 formally claims that if the previous condition holds, then there exists a unique, pure-strategy, peaceful, Markov-perfect equilibrium that yields the peaceful Pareto dominant payoffs $P_1(m_1^*) = (r_1 - m_1^*)^{\rho_1}/(1 - \delta)$ and $P_2(m_2^*) = (r_2 - m_2^*)^{\rho_2}/(1 - \delta)$. (See Fudenberg and Tirole 1991, 501–13, for a discussion of Markov-perfect equilibria.) This equilibrium is given by:

$$R_1(m_2) = \begin{cases} (m_1^*, \sim A) & \text{if } m_2 \geq m_2^* \\ (a_1^*(m_2), A) & \text{if } m_2 < m_2^* \end{cases}$$

$$R_2(m_1) = \begin{cases} (m_2^*, \sim A) & \text{if } m_1 \geq m_1^* \\ (a_2^*(m_1), A) & \text{if } m_1 < m_1^* \end{cases}$$

where $R_1(m_2)$ and $R_2(m_1)$ are the Markov reaction functions for S_1 and S_2, respectively.

In order to establish this claim, note each state's action depends only on the other state's current allocation. Each state's reaction function therefore satisfies the Markov property. These allocations also produce a peaceful equilibrium as long as S_2's initial exogenous allocation is at least m_2^*. Therefore, it will suffice to show that (R_1, R_2) constitutes a subgame perfect equilibrium and that it is the unique, peaceful, Markov-perfect equilibrium supporting the payoffs $P_1(m_1^*)$ and $P_2(m_2^*)$.

Subgame perfection can be established by showing that neither player can improve its payoff by deviating from its reaction function in one period and then conforming to it thereafter. (See Fudenberg and Tirole

1991, 110) for a proof of this claim in multistage games with finite actions. Their argument applies equally well to the current game in which there is a continuum of actions.) Without loss of generality, consider any subgame beginning with S_1's having to decide what to do.

Consider first any subgame in which S_2's allocation m_2' is at least as large as m_2^*. Following R_1 brings S_1 a payoff of $P_1(m_1^*)$ given that S_2 is following R_2. S_1 cannot improve its payoff by attacking in this period. The best that S_1 can do by attacking is $A_1^*(m_2')$, which is bounded above by $A_1^*(m_2^*)$ because A_1^* is decreasing in m_2. But $A_1^*(m_2^*) = P_1(m_1^*)$, so $A_1^*(m_2') \leq P_1(m_1^*)$.

Nor can S_1 improve its payoff by allocating $m_1 \neq m_1^*$ and not attacking. If S_1 allocates $m_1' > m_1^*$ to the military, its payoff is $(r_1 - m_1')^{\rho_1} + \delta_1/(1 - \delta_1)P_1(m_1^*) < P_1(m_1^*)$. If, by contrast, S_1 allocates less than m_1^* to the military and does not attack, S_2 will attack and expression A2.1 ensures that S_1's payoff to this outcome is less than $A_1(m_2^*)$. But $A_1(m_2^*) = P_1(m_1^*)$, so S_1 does worse by allocating less than m_1^* to the military and not attacking. Thus, S_1 cannot improve its payoff with a single-period deviation in any subgame in which S_2's allocation is at least m_2^*.

Now consider a subgame in which S_2's allocation is less than m_2^* and S_1 must decide what to do. Following R_1 by optimally attacking S_2 brings $A_1^*(m_2')$ to S_1, which is greater than $P_1(m_1^*)$ because $P_1(m_1^*) = A_1^*(m_2^*)$ and A_1^* is decreasing in m_2. If S_1 deviates to some $m_1' \geq m_1^*$ without attacking and then conforms to R_1 thereafter, then S_1 receives $(r_1 - m_1')^{\rho_1} + \delta_1/(1 - \delta_1)P_1(m_1^*)$. But this payoff is less than $P_1(m_1^*)$ and therefore less than $A_1^*(m_2')$. Thus, S_1 has no incentive to deviate in this way.

If S_1 deviates to some $m_1' < m_1^*$ without attacking and then conforms to R_1 thereafter, expression A2.1 shows that S_1's payoff is less than $A_1(m_2^*)$. But $A_1(m_2^*) = P_1(m_1^*)$, so S_1 has no incentive to deviate in this way. In sum, no player has any incentive to deviate from its reaction function in a single period and conform to it thereafter. This establishes that (R_1, R_2) is subgame perfect.

It remains to be shown that (R_1, R_2) is the only peaceful, Markov-perfect equilibrium that supports the Pareto-dominating payoffs $P_1(m_1^*)$ and $P_2(m_2^*)$. Let (R_1', R_2') be any peaceful, Markov-perfect equilibrium that supports these payoffs. It suffices to show $R_1 = R_1'$ and $R_2 = R_2'$.

The first step is to demonstrate that S_1 is certain to attack at all $m_2 < m_2^*$. Suppose that there is some positive probability that S_1 does *not* attack at some $m_2' < m_2^*$. The equilibrium payoff to refraining from attacking must be at least as large as the payoff to attacking. That is, there must be some m_1' such that S_1's payoff to allocating m_1' and abstaining from attacking is at least $A_1^*(m_2')$. But, $A_1^*(m_2') > P_1(m_1^*)$, so the payoff to playing m_1' is greater than $P_1(m_1^*)$. This, however, immediately leads to a contradiction; for S_1 can now do better than its purported equilibrium payoff of $P_1(m_1^*)$ by simply playing m_1' at the outset of the game. Thus, $R_1(m_2) = R_1'(m_2)$ for $m_2 < m_2^*$, and a similar argument gives $R_2(m_1) = R_2'(m_1)$ for $m_1 < m_1^*$.

Now suppose that S_1 attacks with some positive probability at m_2^* according to $R_1'(m_2)$. Then S_2 must always allocate $m_2 > m_2^*$ in $(R_1'(m_2), R_2'(m_1))$ because this equilibrium is peaceful. But these allocations give S_2 a payoff strictly less than $P_2(m_2^*)$, which is a contradiction. Hence, S_1 does not attack at m_2^* in $R_1'(m_2)$. Similarly, S_2 does not attack at m_2^* in $R_2'(m_1)$.

Finally, consider S_1's reaction to some $m_2 \geq m_2^*$. S_1 never attacks in these circumstances and always allocates at least m_1^* to the military. As just shown, S_1 does not attack at m_2^*. To see that S_1 does not reallocate its resources and attack if S_2's allocation is larger than m_2^*, note that S_1's payoff to such an attack would be less than $A_1(m_2^*)$ since A_1 is decreasing in m_2. But $A_1(m_2^*) = P_1(m_1^*)$, so attacking at any $m_2 > m_2^*$ brings S_1 a lower payoff than it could have had by simply continuing to allocate m_1^* to the military. Finally, S_1 never responds to $m_2 \geq m_2^*$ by allocating less than m_1^* to the military and not attacking; observe that doing so would result in S_2's optimally allocating its resources and then attacking. But expression A2.1 ensures that S_1's payoff to this outcome is less than $P_1(m_1^*)$. Thus, S_1 never attacks or allocates less than m_1^* if $m_2 \geq m_2^*$. Similarly, S_2 never attacks or allocates less than m_2^* if $m_1 \geq m_1^*$.

Since neither state attacks as long as $(m_1, m_2) \in [m_1^*, r_1] \times [m_2^*, r_2]$ and neither moves out of this rectangle, the equilibrium path of any subgame beginning in this rectangle must remain there. But then S_1 can achieve $P_1(m_1^*)$, which it must do in (R_1', R_2'), only if S_1 always allocates m_1^*. That is, $R_1'(m_2)$ must be $(m_1^*, \sim A)$ for $m_2 \geq m_2^*$. A similar argument holds for S_2. This leaves $R_1 = R_1'$ and $R_2 = R_2'$.

Comparative Statics

Three comparative-static claims will be demonstrated here. First, an increase in the states' discount factors leads to higher military allocations. Second, military allocations also increase if one of the states becomes more willing to run risks. And, third, an increase in the value of the status quo to one of the states induces both states to reduce their military allocations.

As noted in chapter 2, the effects of changes in the values of the model's parameters can generally be analyzed in terms of their effects on i_1 and i_2. For example, anything that shifts i_1 to the left or shifts i_2 down moves the intersection of i_1 and i_2 up and to the right and thereby leads to higher military and lower consumption allocations. The intersection moves in this way because i_1 and i_2 are increasing in m_2 and m_1, respectively, and i_2 cuts i_1 from below at (m_1^*, m_2^*).

These considerations make it easy to see that the states increase their armaments if one of the states' discount factors increases and if a state would increase its armaments if it decides to attack at (m_1^*, m_2^*), i.e., if $a_1^*(m_2^*) > m_1^*$ and $a_2^*(m_1^*) > m_2^*$. To establish this claim, consider any point (m_1, m_2) on $i_1(m_2)$, i.e., (m_1, m_2) satisfies $A_1^*(m_2, \delta_1) = P_1(m_1, \delta_1)$. Then it suffices to show that S_1 strictly prefers to fight at (m_1, m_2) if δ_1 increases slightly to δ_1'. That is, $A_1^*(m_2, \delta_1') > P_1(m_1, \delta_1')$ for $\delta_1' > \delta_1$. Because $A_1^*(m_2, \delta_1') = A_1(a_1^*(m_2, \delta_1'), m_2, \delta_1') \geq A_1(a_1^*(m_2, \delta_1), m_2, \delta_1')$, the inequality $A_1^*(m_2, \delta_1') > P_1(m_1, \delta_1')$ is sure to hold if $A_1(a_1^*(m_2, \delta_1), m_2, \delta_1') - P_1(m_1, \delta_1') > 0$. But,

$$A_1(a_1^*(m_2, \delta_1), m_2, \delta_1') - P_1(m_1, \delta_1')$$
$$= (r_1 - a_1^*(m_2, \delta_1))^{\rho_1} - (r_1 - m_1)^{\rho_1}$$
$$+ \frac{\delta_1'}{1 - \delta_1'} \left[\pi(a_1^*(m_2, \delta_1), m_2, \beta)(r_1 + r_2 - c)^{\rho_1} - (r_1 - m_1)^{\rho_1} \right]$$

By assumption, S_1 would increase its armaments if it were to attack at (m_1^*, m_2^*), i.e., $a_1^*(m_2^*, \delta_1) > m_1^*$. This means that the difference between the first two terms on the right side of the last inequality is negative at (m_1^*, m_2^*). Thus, the factor multiplying $\delta_1'/(1 - \delta_1')$ must be positive, because the entire expression is zero if evaluated at $\delta_1' = \delta_1$. The positive coefficient implies that the entire expression on the right side of the inequality is positive for $\delta_1' > \delta_1$, and this establishes the result.

The second claim is that an increase in ρ_1 or ρ_2 leads to higher military allocations. To show this, we demonstrate that $i_1(m_2, \rho_1)$ is decreasing in ρ_1. To this end, let $\rho_1' > \rho_1$. Then it is sufficient to establish that $A_1^*(m_2, \rho_1') > P_1(i_1(m_2, \rho_1), \rho_1')$, for that inequality and the relation $A_1^*(m_2, \rho_1') = P_1(i_1(m_2, \rho_1'), \rho_1')$ give $i_1(m_2, \rho_1') < i_1(m_2, \rho_1)$.

Because $A_1(a_1^*(m_2, \rho_1), m_2, \rho_1') \leq A_1^*(m_2, \rho_1')$, showing that $P_1(i_1(m_2, \rho_1), \rho_1') < A_1(a_1^*(m_2, \rho_1), m_2, \rho_1')$ establishes the claim. This last inequality is equivalent to

$$\frac{(r_1 - i_1(m_2, \rho_1))^{\rho_1'}}{1 - \delta_1} < (r_1 - a_1^*(m_2, \rho_1))^{\rho_1'}$$

$$+ \pi(a_1^*(m_2, \rho_1), m_2, \beta)\frac{\delta_1(r_1 + r_2 - c)^{\rho_1'}}{1 - \delta_1}.$$

Multiplying through by $1 - \delta_1$ and raising to the power of ρ_1/ρ_1' give

$$(r_1 - i_1(m_2, \rho_1))^{\rho_1} < [(1 - \delta_1)(r_1 - a_1^*(m_2, \rho_1))^{\rho_1'}$$

$$+ \delta_1 \pi(a_1^*(m_2, \rho_1), m_2, \beta)(r_1 + r_2 - c)^{\rho_1'}]^{\rho_1/\rho_1'}.$$

Given that $\rho_1/\rho_1' < 1$, the function $f(y) = y^{\rho_1/\rho_1'}$ is strictly concave downward. Using this fact and noting that $(1 - \delta_1)^{\rho_1/\rho_1'} > (1 - \delta_1)$ and $\delta_1^{\rho_1/\rho_1'} > \delta_1$, then the preceding inequality holds if

$$(r_1 - i_1(m_2, \rho_1))^{\rho_1} \leq (1 - \delta_1)(r_1 - a_1^*(m_2, \rho_1))^{\rho_1}$$

$$+ \delta_1 \pi(a_1^*(m_2, \rho_1), m_2, \beta)(r_1 + r_2 - c)^{\rho_1}.$$

But this inequality is simply $P_1(i_1(m_2, \rho_1)) \leq A_1^*(m_2, \rho_1)$, which the definition of i_1 ensures is true.

Establishing the third comparative-static result is trivially easy but is included for the sake of completeness. If one of the state's stake in the status quo goes up, both states' military allocations decline. Suppose that S_1 and S_2 respectively gain g_1 and g_2 from international cooperation. Then $i_1(m_2, g_1)$ solves $(r_1 + g_1 - i_1(m_2, g_1))^{\rho_1}/(1 - \delta_1) = A_1^*(m_2)$ where, by assumption, S_1's payoff to attacking is independent of g_1. (This supposition reflects the presumption that S_1 would impose its optimal policy on S_2 whether or not the states were cooperating before the war.) Clearly, i_1 is increasing in g_1. Thus, if S_1's stake in the status quo goes up, i_1 shifts to the right, and both states' military allocations rise.

Appendix 3

The Formalities of Bargaining in the Shadow of Power

This appendix presents the formal analysis underlying the discussion in chapter 3 of the relation between the distribution of power and the likelihood that bargaining will break down in an imposed settlement. How, that is, do changes in the distribution of power affect the probability that one of the bargainers will become so pessimistic about the prospects of reaching a mutually acceptable settlement that that bargainer resorts to the use of power to try to impose a resolution? The next section describes two variants of a bargaining game between a satisfied and a potentially dissatisfied bargainer. The satisfied bargainer makes the first offer in the first variant, and the potentially dissatisfied bargainer makes the first offer in the second. The second section characterizes the equilibria of the asymmetric-information game when the satisfied bargainer moves first. The third section describes the equilibria of the game when the potentially dissatisfied bargainer moves first. That section also shows that the probability that the bargaining will break down is the same regardless of which bargainer moves first as long as the bargainers do not discount the future too much. There follows a discussion of the relation among the distribution of power, the status quo distribution of benefits, and the probability of breakdown. A final section provides the details of the proofs.

The Model

Two actors are bargaining about how to reallocate a flow of benefits. One actor begins the game by proposing a division of the flow to the other actor who can accept the offer, reject it in order to make a counter-offer, or impose a settlement. If the second actor accepts the first's proposal, the flow is divided as agreed and the game ends. If the second actor imposes a settlement, the game also ends with one bargainer winning the entire flow with probability p and the other bargainer winning the entire flow with probability $1 - p$. In effect, p represents the distribution of political power: the larger p, the greater one actor's expected payoff to trying to impose a solution and the lower the other actor's expected payoff. Finally, if the second actor makes a counter-offer, then the first actor can accept the offer, counter it, or impose a settlement. Play continues in this way with offers alternating back and forth until one of the players accepts an offer or imposes a settlement.

To specify the model more precisely, suppose the flow of benefits equals one in each period; the two bargainers are called D and S; and the existing division of benefits is q, i.e., D receives q in each period as long as the status quo continues and S receives $1 - q$. If the bargainers agree to a new distribution of benefits x at time t, then D's utility to having q from the zero-th to the t-th period and having x thereafter is the average payoff $(1 - \delta^t)U_D(q) + \delta^t U_D(x)$ where δ is the bargainers' common discount factor. D's utility, U_D, is also assumed to be increasing and to have a nondecreasing marginal utility: $U_D' > 0$ and $U_D'' \leq 0$. Similarly, S's payoff is $(1 - \delta^t)U_S(1 - q) + \delta^t U_S(1 - x)$ where $U_S' > 0$ and $U_S'' \leq 0$.

To define the payoffs if the players fail to agree and one of them tries to impose a settlement, suppose that someone forces the issue at time t. Then D is assumed to win the entire flow of benefits with probability p and to obtain no benefits with probability $1 - p$. The use of power, however, is costly, and D and S pay costs d and s, respectively. D's utility is therefore $(1 - \delta^t)U_D(q) + \delta^t(pU_D(1) + (1 - p)U_D(0) - d) = (1 - \delta^t)U_D(q) + \delta^t(p - d)$ where $U_D(1)$ and $U_D(0)$ have been normalized to be one and zero, respectively. Similarly, S's utility is $(1 - \delta^t)U_S(b - q) + \delta^t(1 - p - s)$.[1]

Each player has private information about its cost of imposing a settlement. In particular, D believes that S's costs or types are distributed over the interval $[\underline{s}, \bar{s}]$ where $\underline{s} > 0$ and the distribution function $F_S(s)$ is assumed to have a monotone hazard rate and a bounded and continuous density function $f_S(s)$ such that $f_S(s) > 0$ over $(\underline{s}, \bar{s})$.[2] The smaller s, the lower the cost to S of trying to impose a settlement and, less formally, the "tougher" or more willing S is to impose a settlement. Analogously,

---

[1] Assuming that an attempt to impose a settlement can end in only two ways simplifies the exposition by providing a natural way to formulate the distribution of power, namely as the probability that one of the states prevails. However, this simplification is unimportant analytically. What is crucial is that the outcome of an imposed settlement is Pareto inefficient.

[2] A monotone hazard rate means the hazard rate, $F_S'(s)/(1 - F(s))$, is nondecreasing. Many common distributions satisfy this condition (see Fudenberg and Tirole 1991, 267).

S believes that D's costs are distributed over $[\underline{d}, \bar{d}]$ according to $F_D(d)$ where $\underline{d} > 0$ and $F_D(d)$ has a monotone hazard rate and a bounded and continuous density function $f_D(d)$ such that $f_D(d) > 0$ over $(\underline{d}, \bar{d})$. The distributions F_D and F_S are common knowledge.

A player-type is *dissatisfied* if it strictly prefers an imposed settlement to the status quo. If a player-type is not dissatisfied, then it is *satisfied*. A bargainer is *potentially dissatisfied* if one its types is dissatisfied. Accordingly, D is potentially dissatisfied if the toughest type of D, $\underline{d}$, is dissatisfied, and S is potentially dissatisfied if $\underline{s}$ is dissatisfied. In symbols, d is dissatisfied if $p - d > U_D(q)$ and s is dissatisfied if $1 - p - s > U_S(1 - q)$.

At most only one player can be potentially dissatisfied. To see this, suppose that both bargainers are potentially dissatisfied. Then $p - \underline{d} > U_D(q)$ and $1 - p - \underline{s} > U_S(1 - q)$. Concavity implies $U_D(q) \geq q$ and $U_S(1 - q) \geq 1 - q$. Combining the previous inequalities gives $0 > \underline{d} + \underline{s}$, which contradicts the assumption that there is a positive cost to using power.

Without loss of generality, let D denote the potentially dissatisfied bargainer if there is one. Then the equilibria of two games must be characterized. The satisfied bargainer makes the initial offer in the first game, and the potentially dissatisfied bargainer makes the initial offer in the second. Let Γ_S and Γ_D denote these two games respectively.

To specify the players' strategies and beliefs more fully in these games, let h_n be an n-period history composed of a series of offers and rejections and ending with a rejection. Let H_n be the set of all h_n. Take h'_n to be the history h_n followed by a proposed division and let H'_n be the set of all h'_n. Assuming for notational convenience that the first offer occurs in the zero-th period, then D makes offers in even-numbered periods in Γ_D and S accepts, rejects, or imposes a resolution. Similarly, S makes offers in odd-numbered periods. Accordingly, a pure strategy for player D in Γ_D is a family of measurable functions $\{\sigma_D^n\}_{n=0}^{\infty}$ such that: if n is even, $\sigma_D^n : H_n \times [\underline{d}, \bar{d}] \to [0, 1]$ where $\sigma_D^n(h_n, d)$ is the share of benefits D will receive. If n is odd, $\sigma_D^n : H'_n \times [\underline{d}, \bar{d}] \to \{Y, N, I\}$ where Y, N, and I respectively denote accepting the offer, rejecting the offer in order to make a counter-offer, and trying to impose a resolution. Pure strategies for S in Γ_D and for D and S in Γ_S are defined analogously.

To specify the players' beliefs in Γ_D, let G_D and G_S denote the set of probability distributions over $[\underline{d}, \bar{d}]$ and $[\underline{s}, \bar{s}]$, respectively. Let $\mu_D^n(d)$ for n even and $\mu_S^n(s)$ for n odd denote D's and S's beliefs at the start of the n-th round at which point the players are making an offer. Let

$\mu_D^n(d)$ for n odd and $\mu_S^n(s)$ for n even denote D's and S's beliefs when deciding how to answer an offer. Then, $\mu_D^n : H_n \to G_S$ for n odd and $\mu_D^n : H_n' \to G_S$ for n even and similarly for μ_S^n. A player's beliefs will also be assumed to be unaffected by its decision to reject an offer in order to make a counter-offer: $\mu_D^n = \mu_D^{n+1}$ for n odd and $\mu_S^n = \mu_S^{n+1}$ for n even. Beliefs are defined analogously in Γ_S.

A perfect Bayesian equilibrium (PBE) of Γ_D or Γ_S is a strategy profile (σ_D, σ_S), which is sequentially rational and a system of beliefs (μ_D, μ_S) that satisfies Bayes's rule whenever possible. That is, a player's beliefs after receiving an offer must be consistent with Bayes's rule applied to that player's beliefs just prior to the offer and the other player's behavioral strategy for making the offer.

The Asymmetric-Information Equilibria When the Satisfied Bargainer Makes the First Offer

As a first step in characterizing the equilibrium of the game in which there is asymmetric information and S makes the first offer, it will be useful to describe S's equilibrium offers in the complete-information versions of Γ_S and Γ_D. If neither bargainer is potentially dissatisfied, then neither bargainer can credibly threaten to overturn the status quo by imposing a settlement. In these circumstances, neither bargainer has any incentive to revise the status quo in favor of the other bargainer and the status quo remains in place. It is also clear that if D is dissatisfied, then S offers D just enough to make D indifferent between imposing a settlement and accepting the proposal. Offering more only means a less favorable agreement when D accepts the offer, while offering less than D's certainty equivalent of imposing a settlement results in D's imposing a settlement. This result is stated as proposition 3.1 in chapter 3.[3]

The asymmetric-information equilibrium of the game is very simple if the satisfied bargainer makes the first offer. S makes its optimal take-it-or-leave-it offer in Γ_S given its prior beliefs F_D and subject to the constraint that this offer is at least as large as D's status quo share q. The potentially dissatisfied bargainer D either accepts this offer or imposes a settlement.

---

[3] Alternatively, one can think of the present bargaining game as a Rubinstein bargaining game in which there are no joint gains and there are outside options. Osborne and Rubinstein (1990) characterize the equilibria of the outside-option Rubinstein game, and modifying that analysis for the present game is straightforward.

Lemmas A3.1 and A3.2 are the keys to this result. Lemma A3.1 puts bounds on what the satisfied bargainer would offer or accept starting at any information set at which this bargainer is making an offer. As will be seen, these bounds hold in both Γ_S and Γ_D and will play an important role in the analysis of both of these games. Lemma A3.2, which is a more formal statement of lemma 3.1 in chapter 3, uses these bounds to show that no dissatisfied type ever rejects an offer in order to make a counter-offer. It either accepts the offer on the table or imposes a settlement.

The intuition underlying lemma A3.1 is straightforward. Suppose that S is at any information set in either Γ_S or Γ_D at which it is making an offer to D. Suppose further that d^t is the toughest type that S might be facing, i.e., d^t is the minimum of the support of S's beliefs at this information set. Then the most pessimistic beliefs that S could have about D are that S is facing d^t for sure. Lemma A3.1 shows that no s would ever offer more or accept less than it would in the complete-information game in which s faces d^t for sure. If d^t is satisfied, then it cannot credibly threaten to impose a settlement and s will not make any concessions, i.e., S can offer any $x \leq q$ and will reject any demand of more than q. (Since s's offer has no effect on the outcome as long as $x \leq q$, we will assume as a matter of convenience that s offers q.) If d^t is dissatisfied, s offers d^t its certainty equivalent of imposing a settlement, which will be denoted by $\tilde{x}(d^t)$, and rejects anything leaving it with less than the present value of countering with d^t's certainty equivalent. That is, s would never accept less than $1 - z$ where s is indifferent between accepting $1 - z$ now and countering with d^t's certainty equivalent; i.e., z solves $U_S(1 - z) = (1 - \delta)U_S(1 - q) + \delta U_S(1 - \tilde{x}(d^t))$. In sum, s would never offer more than $\max\{q, \tilde{x}(d^t)\}$ or accept less than $\min\{1 - q, 1 - z\}$. Since these bounds do not depend on s, the satisfied bargainer, regardless of type, would never offer more than $\max\{q, \tilde{x}(d^t)\}$ or accept less than $\min\{1 - q, 1 - z\}$. Stating this result more formally,

Lemma A3.1: *Consider any PBE of Γ_S or Γ_D and any information set at which the satisfied bargainer is making an offer. Take d^t to be the toughest type that S might be facing, i.e., d^t is the minimum of the support of S's beliefs at this information set. Then S never offers more than $\max\{q, \tilde{x}(d^t)\}$. Nor does S ever accept any offer of less than $\min\{1 - q, 1 - z\}$ where $\tilde{x}(d^t)$ is the certainty equivalent to d^t of imposing a settlement, i.e., $U_D(\tilde{x}(d^t)) = p - d^t$, and z solves $U_S(1 - z) = (1 - \delta)U_S(1 - q) + \delta U_S(1 - \tilde{x}(d^t))$.*

Proof: The proof is an adaptation of the argument establishing lemma 3.1 in Ausubel and Deneckere (1992) and is sketched in the final section below.

The bounds on S's offers and acceptances imply that no dissatisfied type would reject an offer in order to make a counter-offer. To see this, suppose that a dissatisfied type did make a counter-offer by demanding some x. Let d^t be the toughest type that demands x, i.e., d^t is the minimum of the set of types demanding x. It is straightforward to show that d^t would have done strictly better by imposing a settlement rather than countering with x. This contradiction implies that no dissatisfied type makes a counter-offer.

To show that d^t can do strictly better by not making a counter-offer, note that d^t obtains $p - d^t$ if it imposes a settlement. If, alternatively, d^t foregoes the present opportunity to impose a settlement in order to counter with x, the game can subsequently end in only one of three ways. First, the game might end in an imposed settlement in a future period. Discounting ensures that d^t strictly prefers imposing a settlement now to an imposed settlement in the future. The second way the game can end is that d^t accepts a future offer. But d^t is the toughest type facing S conditional on x. As shown in lemma A3.1, S never offers more than d^t's certainty equivalent to imposing a resolution. Discounting again means that d^t would strictly prefer imposing a settlement now to accepting the certainty equivalent of imposing a resolution later. Third, the game might end with the satisfied bargainer's accepting d^t's demand. Lemma A3.1, however, implies that S never accepts a demand that leaves d^t with more than $\max\{q, z\}$. If, therefore, d^t foregoes an opportunity to impose a settlement in order to make an offer that S accepts, d^t's payoff is bounded above by $(1 - \delta)U_D(q) + \delta U_D(\max\{q, z\})$, which is d^t's payoff if it does not impose a settlement, demands $\max\{q, z\}$ instead, and S accepts this demand immediately. But z solves $U_S(1 - z) = (1 - \delta)U_S(1 - q) + \delta U_S(1 - \tilde{x}(d^t))$ and $\tilde{x}(d^t) > q$ because d^t is, by assumption, dissatisfied. Thus, $1 - z > 1 - \tilde{x}(d^t)$ and, therefore, $\tilde{x}(d^t) > \max\{q, z\}$. Consequently, d^t's payoff to imposing a settlement immediately, $U_D(\tilde{x}(d^t))$, is strictly larger than the upper bound to d^t's payoff to countering x if its counter is subsequently accepted. Thus, d^t strictly prefers imposing a settlement now to any of the ways that the game might end if it did make a counter-offer. This contradiction means that no dissatisfied type ever makes a counter-offer and leaves:

Lemma A3.2: *Consider any perfect Bayesian equilibrium of Γ_S or Γ_D. If d is dissatisfied, i.e., if $p - d > U_D(q)$, then d never rejects an offer in order to make a counter-offer.*

Proof: The result follows directly from the previous discussion and the proof is omitted.

If a dissatisfied type would never reject an offer in order to make a counter-offer, then a dissatisfied type must either accept the offer on the table or impose a settlement. Lemma A3.3 formalizes this.

Lemma A3.3: *Consider any perfect Bayesian equilibrium of Γ_S or Γ_S. If d is dissatisfied and the current offer to d is x, then d accepts x if $U_D(x) > p - d$ and imposes a resolution if $U_D(x) < p - d$.[4]*

Proof: The lemma follows directly from lemmas A3.1 and A3.2, and the proof is omitted.

Lemma A3.3 implies that a counter-offer unambiguously signals that d is satisfied, because only these types might make a counter-offer in equilibrium. In symbols, d's making a counter-offer reveals that $\tilde{x}(d) \leq q$ where $\tilde{x}(d) = p - d$. This signal effectively transforms the game into one of complete information, because both players now know that neither is willing to impose a settlement. The outcome of this complete-information game is the continuation of the status quo q. If, therefore, d is satisfied and the current offer x is better than the status quo q, d will accept. If S "offers" q or less, d counters, thereby revealing that it is satisfied and the status quo goes unchanged. Lemma A3.4 states this decision more formally.

Lemma A3.4: *Consider any perfect Bayesian equilibrium of Γ_S or Γ_D. Suppose further that d is satisfied and the current offer to d is x. Then d accepts any $x > q$. If $q \leq x$, d does not impose a settlement, thereby signaling that it is satisfied and ensuring that the status quo will not be revised.*

Proof: The lemma follows directly from the preceding lemmas and the proof is omitted.

---

[4] If d is indifferent, then d's actions affect the satisfied player's payoff and the equilibrium outcome only if there is an atom at the value d_0 in the distribution characterizing the satisfied bargainer's beliefs where d_0 satisfies $U_D(x) = p - d_0$. If there is an atom at d_0, then d_0 must accept in equilibrium. For, if d_0 imposes a solution with positive probability, then the satisfied state can always do strictly better by offering slightly more than x, which ensures that d_0 will accept.

The previous lemmas describe the dissatisfied bargainer's behavioral strategy at an arbitrary information set in both Γ_S and Γ_D at which this bargainer is considering how to respond to an offer from S. In equilibrium, S must play a best response to this strategy when making an offer, and this best reply turns out to be S's optimal take-it-or-leave-it offer given its beliefs and subject to the constraint that this offer is at least as large as the status quo q. To describe S's best response more precisely, consider a simple ultimatum game in which S makes an offer which D either accepts or rejects by imposing a settlement. Let $\beta_D[a, b]$ denote the satisfied bargainer's beliefs about the dissatisfied bargainer's type where $\beta_D[a, b]$ is the distribution of d conditional on $d \in [a, b]$ given a prior distribution of F_D. In symbols, $\beta_D[a, b](d)$ equals zero if $d < a$, $(F_D(d) - F_D(a))/(F_D(b) - F_D(a))$ if $d \in [a, b]$, and one if $d > b$. Because d rejects x if $p - d > U_D(x)$ in this ultimatum game, the probability that x will be rejected is $\beta_D[a, b](p - U_D(x))$. Consequently, s's expected utility to offering x conditional on beliefs $\beta_D[a, b]$ and given that D either accepts x or imposes a settlement is:

$$T(x, s, \beta_D[a, b]) = U_S(1 - x)\left(1 - \frac{F_D(p - U_D(x)) - F_D(a)}{F_D(b) - F_D(a)}\right)$$

$$+ (1 - p - s)\frac{F_D(p - U_D(x)) - F_D(a)}{F_D(b) - F_D(a)}.$$

It follows that s's payoff to offering x in Γ_S is $T(x, s, \beta_D[\underline{d}, \bar{d}])$ if $x > q$ as those d for which $p - d > U_D(x)$ impose a settlement and the other d accept. If $x \leq q$, then all dissatisfied d impose a settlement. Satisfied d either accept q or, by countering it, signal that they are satisfied. In either case, the distribution of benefits remains at q. Accordingly, s's payoff to offering $x \leq q$ is $T(q, s, \beta_D[\underline{d}, \bar{d}])$.

Therefore, s's optimal offer $x^*(s, \beta_D[a, b])$ is the value of $x \in [0, 1]$, which maximizes $T(x, s, \beta_D[\underline{d}, \bar{d}])$ for $x > q$ and $T(q, s, \beta_D[\underline{d}, \bar{d}])$ for $x \leq q$. This problem has a simple solution. Let $t^*(s, \beta_D[a, b])$ maximize $T(x, s, \beta_D[a, b])$ for $x \in [0, 1]$ where the assumption that F_D has a montone hazard rate ensures that t^* is unique. Consequently, $x^*(s, \beta_D[a, b]) = t^*(s, \beta_D[a, b])$ if $t^* > q$. If $t^* \leq q$, then any $x \in [0, q]$ maximizes s's payoffs, as any proposal in this range leads to the same outcome, namely an imposed settlement with probability $F_D(p - U_D(q))$ and a continuation of the status quo distribution q with probability $1 - F_D(p - U_D(q))$. Summarizing this analysis:

Proposition A3.1: *Consider any PBE of Γ_S:*

(i) *If $t^*(s, \beta_D[\underline{d}, \bar{d}]) > q$, the satisfied bargainer initially proposes its optimal bounded take-it-or-leave-it offer $x^*(s, \beta_D[\underline{d}, \bar{d}]) = \max\{q, t^*(s, \beta_D[\underline{d}, \bar{d}])\} = t^*(s, \beta_D[\underline{d}, \bar{d}])$. Dissatisfied types accept x^* if $U_D(x^*) > p - d$ and impose a settlement if $U_D(x^*) < p - d$. Satisfied types accept x^*.*

(ii) *If $t^*(s, \beta_D[\underline{d}, \bar{d}]) \leq q$, the satisfied bargainer can propose any $x \leq q$. Dissatisfied types impose a settlement. Satisfied types do not impose a settlement, thereby signaling their satisfaction and ensuring that the status quo q will not be changed.*[5]

Proof: Follows immediately from the preceding discussion and is omitted.

The Equilibria When the Dissatisfied Bargainer Makes the First Offer

This section characterizes the equilibria of the game when the dissatisfied bargainer makes the initial offer and then shows that which bargainer makes the first offer has no effect on the probability that bargaining breaks down in an imposed settlement. That is, the probabilities of an imposed settlement in Γ_D and Γ_S are equal in the limit as the discount factor goes to one.

D makes the first offer in Γ_D, and lemmas A3.1–A3.4 imply that S either accepts this offer or rejects it by countering with its optimal bounded take-it-or-leave-it offer given its updated beliefs. D then either accepts this offer or imposes a settlement. The problem of characterizing the equilibria of Γ_D therefore reduces to describing D's initial offer.

There are three cases to be considered depending on S's prior beliefs, and two further assumptions are need to facilitate the analysis of these cases. The first assumption is that D's demands are monotonic in D's type. That is, if two types, say d_1 and d_2, make a demand following the same history and if d_1 is at least as willing to impose a settlement as d_2 (i.e., if $d_1 \leq d_2$), then d_1 must demand at least as much as d_2.

The second assumption imposes a restriction on a bargainer's beliefs following an equilibrium demand made by a nonempty but measure-zero

---

[5] Since the outcome of the game is unaffected by the particular $x \leq q$ that s proposes, s will be assumed to propose q.

set of types. Suppose that a set of types of D makes a common demand x in equilibrium and that this set, although nonempty, has probability zero. Then the support of S's beliefs conditional on x is assumed to be contained in the set of types that made this demand and that were in the support of S's beliefs when this demand was made. That is, let $\mathcal{D}_x$ be the set of types that demand x and suppose that this set is nonempty but has measure zero. Then, the support of S's beliefs following x must be in the intersection of $\mathcal{D}_x$ and the support of S's beliefs just prior to receiving x. D's beliefs are similarly restricted. Finally, note that this assumption places *no* restriction on the bargainers' beliefs following an out-of-equilibrium demand, i.e., a demand that no type would make in equilibrium.

To begin to see the significance of this restriction, suppose there were a separating equilibrium in which each type of D makes a distinct demand. (Just such an equilibrium will be constructed below.) Because there are no atoms in the distribution of types, the probability that any particular demand is made is zero. Bayes's law, therefore, places no restriction on what S should believe following an equilibrium demand even though only one type of D would make that demand in equilibrium. The restriction on beliefs defined above eliminates this possibility by requiring that S believe that it is facing the one type that might have made that demand.

Turning to the equilibrium of Γ_D, the first case occurs when S's prior beliefs are such that S is so confident that D is dissatisfied that all s offer D the certainty equivalent of D's toughest type. In symbols, $t^*(s, \beta_D[\underline{d}, \bar{d}]) = \tilde{x}(\underline{d})$ for all s. This offer is large enough to ensure that all d accept. In the context of Γ_S, these prior beliefs imply that all s initially offer $\tilde{x}(\underline{d})$. In the context of Γ_D, these beliefs will be shown to imply that essentially all d pool on a common demand in any PBE of Γ_D if the discount factor δ is sufficiently close to one.

The second case that needs to be examined is at the other extreme. S's prior beliefs make S so confident that D is actually satisfied that S makes no concessions. That is, all types s propose the status quo q. These priors mean that S's initial offer in Γ_S would be q, and d imposes a settlement if it is dissatisfied and accepts if it is satisfied. If S has these priors in Γ_D, then proposition A3.2 shows that all d that are sufficiently "tough," i.e., those d that have a low enough cost, pool on a non-serious demand, i.e., a demand that is sure to be rejected. S then counters this demand with q. Those d that do not pool on the non-serious demand signal that they are satisfied and the status quo q continues.

In the third and intermediate case, S's priors are such that S, depending on its type, does make concessions to D by offering something between the q and $\tilde{x}(\underline{d})$. In these circumstances, all d pool on a common, high demand in any PBE of Γ_D if δ is sufficiently close to one. Because the demand is high, S generally rejects it and makes a counteroffer. Because of pooling, updating does not change S's priors, and S's counter in Γ_D is the same as its initial offer in Γ_S.

All types pool in the intermediate case above, and there are substantial amounts of pooling in the extreme cases. Figure A3.1 helps make the reason for the complete pooling in the intermediate case clear and helps develop the intuition underlying the proof of this case in proposition A3.2. Suppose that there are at least two distinct demands in Γ_D. The assumption that D's demands are monotonic in D's type implies that there exists a $\underline{d}^w \leq \overline{d}^t$ such that the set $[\underline{d}, \underline{d}^w)$ makes one demand, say x, and the $(\overline{d}^t, \overline{d}]$ makes another demand y where $x \neq y$. (The pneumonic

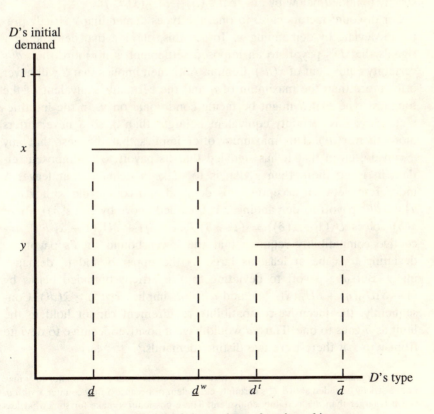

Figure A3.1 D's initial demand as a function of its type

here is that $\overline{d^t}$ is the "toughest" type—hence the superscript t—that makes the same demand as $\overline{d}$, whereas $\underline{d}^w$ is the "weakest" type that demands what $\underline{d}$ does.) Given that $\underline{d}^w$ is the weakest type that might have demanded x, S would never counter x by offering D less than $\underline{d}^w$'s certainty equivalent of imposing a settlement. Such an offer would surely be rejected and, as shown below, is always strictly dominated by offering slightly more than $\underline{d}^w$'s certainty equivalent. S's counter, therefore, will be strictly bounded below by $\underline{d}^w$'s certainty equivalent, which is denoted by $\tilde{x}(\underline{d}^w)$. Accordingly, $\underline{d}^w$'s payoff to demanding x is strictly bounded below by $(1 - \delta)U_D(q) + \delta U_D(\tilde{x}(\underline{d}^w))$, which is $\underline{d}^w$'s payoff if S counters x with $\tilde{x}(\underline{d}^w)$.

Because $\underline{d}^w$ is offered more than its certainty equivalent of imposing a settlement, it accepts S's counter. Because $\underline{d}^w$ accepts, any other type can costlessly mimic $\underline{d}^w$. In particular, any d demanding y can costlessly mimic $\underline{d}^w$ by demanding x instead of y and thereby obtain a payoff strictly bounded below by $(1 - \delta)U_D(q) + \delta U_D(\tilde{x}(\underline{d}^w))$.

For discount factors close to one, the types demanding y strictly prefer to deviate by demanding x. To see this, observe that demanding y signals that D's payoff to an imposed settlement is no more than $\overline{d^t}$'s certainty equivalent of $\tilde{x}(\overline{d^t})$. Lemma A3.1 then implies that S will never offer more than the maximum of q and the certainty equivalent of the toughest type that S might be facing conditional on y. In the intermediate case, this certainty equivalent is larger than q, so S never offers more than $\tilde{x}(\overline{d^t})$. This maximum offer implies that the best that any d can do, given that it has signaled that its payoff to an imposed settlement is no more than $\tilde{x}(\overline{d^t})$, is to make a demand that leaves S indifferent between accepting this demand and countering with $\tilde{x}(\overline{d^t})$. Thus, $\overline{d^t}$'s payoff to demanding y is bounded above by $U_D(z(\delta))$ where $z(\delta)$ solves $U_S(1 - z(\delta)) = (1 - \delta)U_S(1 - q) + \delta U_S(1 - \tilde{x}(\overline{d^t}))$. Incentive compatibility requires that the lower bound to $\overline{d}$'s payoff to deviating to x be at least as large as the upper bound to demanding y. But $\overline{d^t}$'s payoff to deviating to x is strictly bounded below by $(1 - \delta)U_D(q) + \delta U_D(\tilde{x}(\underline{d}^w))$, and $\underline{d}^w \leq \overline{d^t}$ implies $\tilde{x}(\underline{d}^w) \geq \tilde{x}(\overline{d^t})$. Consequently, the incentive-compatibility requirement cannot hold in the limit as δ goes to one. Thus, $\overline{d}$ would have a positive incentive to deviate from y to x if there were two distinct demands.[6]

---

[6] This argument does not work in the two extreme cases because S's counter to y may not be strictly bounded above $\underline{d}^w$'s certainty equivalent or because S may counter x with q, which is larger than $\overline{d^t}$'s certainty equivalent. These possibilities make for somewhat less pooling.

Proposition A3.2 formalizes this discussion:

Proposition A3.2: *For any $\epsilon > 0$, there exists a $\underline{\delta} < 1$ such that:*

(i) *If $t^*(\underline{s}, \beta_D[\underline{d}, \bar{d}]) = \tilde{x}(\underline{d}) > q$, then all $d \in (\underline{d} + \epsilon, \bar{d}]$ pool on a common demand in any PBE of Γ_D whenever $\delta > \underline{\delta}$.[7]*

(ii) *If $t^*(\bar{s}, \beta_D[\underline{d}, \bar{d}]) \leq q$, then all $d \in [\underline{d}, \hat{d})$ pool on a non-serious demand in any PBE of Γ_D whenever $\delta > \underline{\delta}$ where $\hat{d}$ is sufficiently large that all s offer q conditional on S's beliefs $\beta_D[\underline{d}, \hat{d}]$: $x^*(s, \beta_D[\underline{d}, \hat{d}]) = q$ for all s. By not pooling on the non-serious demand, $d \in (\hat{d}, \bar{d}]$ signals that it actually is satisfied and the game degenerates into a complete-information bargaining game in which d's demand is irrelevant and the status quo distribution q remains unchanged.*

(iii) *If $\tilde{x}(\underline{d}) > t^*(\underline{s}, \beta_D[\underline{d}, \bar{d}])$ and $t^*(\bar{s}, \beta_D[\underline{d}, \bar{d}]) > q$, then all $d \in [\underline{d}, \bar{d}]$ pool on a common demand in any PBE of Γ_D whenever $\delta > \underline{\delta}$.*

Proof: See the final section below.

Two remarks about proposition A3.2 are in order. The first focuses on the restriction put on beliefs at information sets following an offer made by a nonempty but zero-measure set of types. Recall that if a nonempty set of types in the support of S's beliefs at some information set makes a demand x, then the support of S's beliefs conditional on x must be contained in the nonempty set that might have demanded x even if this nonempty set has probability zero. Without this restriction, quite pathological equilibria may exist and the equilibrium outcomes of Γ_S and Γ_D may be quite different even in the limit as δ goes to zero.

To illustrate this possibility, suppose, as in the first case above in proposition A3.2, that S's prior beliefs, F_D, are such that s offers the certainty equivalent of the toughest type in order to ensure that a settlement will not be imposed by offering. That is, all s offer $\tilde{x}(\underline{d})$. Assume further that all types of D but $\bar{d}$ are dissatisfied, i.e., $\tilde{x}(\bar{d}) = q$. Proposition A3.1 implies that all s offer $\tilde{x}(\underline{d})$ in Γ_S. This offer is accepted and the probability of breakdown equals zero.

Without some restriction on what S can believe after an offer from a nonempty, measure-zero set of types, it is easy to construct an equilibrium of Γ_D in which the probability of breakdown is one. Suppose

---

[7] If $\tilde{x}(\underline{d}) = q$, then D is satisfied and d's demands are irrelevant as the status quo remains unchanged with probability one.

each d makes the largest possible demand that s would accept conditional on being sure of facing d. That is, d demands $z(d)$ where $U_S(1 - z(d)) = (1 - \delta)U_S(1 - q) + \delta U_S(1 - \tilde{x}(d))$. Although each type makes a distinct demand, the probability that any particular demand is actually made is zero. If no restriction is put on S's beliefs, S may be assumed to put probability one on facing the weakest type, $\bar{d}$. But this type is satisfied, so these beliefs imply that s will never agree to less than $1 - q$ and will counter any larger demand with q. These strategies form an equilibrium: No matter what d demands, that demand will be countered with q, so any demand is a best-reply to S's counter and, in particular, demanding $z(d)$ is a best reply. And, given D's separating strategy and S's pessimistic beliefs, s's countering with q is a best response. Moreover, the probability of breakdown is one, as all $d \in [\underline{d}, \bar{d})$ are sure to reject this counter and impose a settlement. Therefore, it is easy to construct a pathological example unless there is some restriction on what S can believe following a demand by a zero-measure set of types. The restriction defined above eliminates the kind of pathological example just described by requiring S to infer from a demand of $z(d)$ that it is facing the type that might have made this demand, namely d.

The second remark focuses on D's participation constraint in Γ_D. The extensive form of Γ_D does not permit a player to try to impose a settlement in the same round in which it is making an offer. When making an offer, a player's next opportunity to impose a resolution comes in the next round if its offer is rejected. Consequently, D cannot impose a settlement in the first round of Γ_D, and $\underline{d}$ generally obtains less in the pooling equilibria of Γ_D described in proposition A3.2 than what it would receive if it could impose a settlement at the outset of the game. Depending on the substantive interpretation underlying the model, this would seem to violate $\underline{d}$'s participation constraint. The idea here is that there is some positive but arbitrarily small cost to not entering the negotiations. For example, it may be costly in terms of public support to be seen as unwilling to give diplomacy a chance. If there is a positive but arbitrarily small cost, then as long as the discount factor is close enough to one, $\underline{d}$ strictly prefers making even a non-serious demand to forcing the issue without having been at the table.

Propositions A3.1 and A3.2, respectively, characterize the equilibria when the satisfied bargainer moves first or second. The substantial pooling that takes place in Γ_D ensures that S's update beliefs when it makes its first offer in Γ_D are "almost" the same as its prior beliefs in Γ_S. This implies that S makes roughly the same offers in Γ_D as in Γ_S and therefore that the probability of breakdown is approximately equal in these games. Indeed, they are equal in limit as the time between offers goes to zero (i.e., the discount factor goes to one) as proposition A3.3 shows. Thus, the order of play has no significant effect on the probability of breakdown if the discount factor is sufficiently close to one.

Proposition A3.3: *For any distribution of power p and any $\epsilon > 0$, there exists a $\underline{\delta} < 1$ such that the probabilities of breakdown in any PBE of Γ_S and Γ_D differ by less than ϵ whenever $\delta > \underline{\delta}$.*

Proof: See the final section below.

Proposition A3.3 means that the relation between the probability of breakdown and the distribution of power can be examined solely in terms of the much simpler equilibrium of Γ_S where the probability of breakdown is just the probability that S's bounded take-it-or-leave-it offer is rejected.

The Distributions of Power and Benefits and the Probability of Breakdown

The disparity between the status quo distribution q and the allocation expected to result from an imposed settlement is crucial to the relation between the distribution of power and the probability of an imposed settlement. Neither bargainer can credibly threaten to impose a settlement if they both prefer the status quo to the expected outcome, and the status quo remains unchanged. In symbols, the status quo continues if $U_D(q) \geq p - \underline{d}$ and $U_S(1 - q) \geq 1 - p - \underline{s}$. Concavity implies $U_D(q) \geq q$ and $U_S(1 - q) \geq 1 - q$, so the status quo is sure to persist as long as $q > p - \underline{d}$ and $1 - q > 1 - p - \underline{s}$. The latter two inequalities hold whenever $|p - q| < \min\{\underline{d}, \underline{s}\}$. Hence, the probability of an imposed settlement is zero as long as the disparity between the distributions of power and benefits is not too large.

Detailed Proofs

Proof of Lemma A3.1

The proof is an adaptation of the argument establishing lemma 3.1 in Ausubel and Deneckere (1992, 606) and so will only be sketched here. Let h be any information set at which s is making an offer and let d^t

denote the minimum of the support of s's beliefs about the dissatisfied bargainer at that information set. Less formally, d^t is the toughest type that s believes it might be facing at h. Assume further that z satisfies $U_S(1 - z) = (1 - \delta)U_S(1 - q) + \delta U_S(1 - \tilde{x}(d^t))$, where $\tilde{x}(d^t)$ is the certainty equivalent of d^t for imposing a settlement, i.e., $U_D(\tilde{x}(d^t)) = p - d^t$.

To see that s will never offer more than $\max\{q, \tilde{x}(d^t)\}$ or agree to give the dissatisfied bargainer more than $\max\{q, z\}$ in a perfect Bayesian equilibrium given that h has been reached, let $\bar{x}$ be the supremum of s's offers or acceptances. Now consider d's decision at any information set following h, which is reached with positive probability from h. The payoff to d to rejecting s's offer or forcing the issue is bounded above by $\max\{(1 - \delta)U_D(q) + \delta U_D(\bar{x}), U_D(\tilde{x}(d^t))\}$. The first element is the best that the potentially dissatisfied bargainer can do if it rejects s's offer and the bargainers subsequently reach an agreement. The second element is the upper bound on d's payoff if S or D ultimately compels a resolution. This bound means that d accepts any offer x such that $x > \max\{y, \tilde{x}(d^t)\}$ where y solves $U_D(y) = (1 - \delta)U_D(q) + \delta U_D(\bar{x})$. But, s will never offer more than the minimal amount required to induce the potentially dissatisfied actor to accept. That is, s will only make offers x such that $x \leq \max\{y, \tilde{x}(d^t)\}$.

Given that s never offers more than $\max\{y, \tilde{x}(d^t)\}$, lemma A3.1 holds if $\max\{y, \tilde{x}(d^t)\} \leq \max\{q, \tilde{x}(d^t)\}$. This relation will be established by showing that a contradiction ensues if it does not hold. Assume $y > \max\{q, \tilde{x}(d^t)\}$. Because $\bar{x}$ is the supremum of s's offers and acceptances, s either accepts or proposes a $v \in (\bar{x} - \epsilon, \bar{x}]$ for any $\epsilon > 0$. Furthermore, y solves $U_D(y) = (1 - \delta)U_D(q) + \delta U_D(\bar{x})$ and $y > q$, so $\bar{x} > y$. Thus, ϵ can be taken small enough to ensure that $v > y$. Because $v > y$ and y is an upper bound on s's offers, d must have proposed v and s must have accepted v.

However, s could have done better by countering v. If S accepts v, it receives $U_S(1 - v)$. But if s counters with $y + \eta$, then D accepts this offer because $y > \max\{q, \tilde{x}(d^t)\}$ and D accepts any offer larger than $\max\{q, \tilde{x}(d^t)\}$. Therefore, s's payoff to countering with $y + \eta$ is $(1 - \delta)U_S(1 - q) + \delta U_S(1 - (y + \eta))$. But $U_S(1 - v) < (1 - \delta)U_S(1 - q) + \delta U_S(1 - y)$ because $v > y > q$. It follows that $U_S(1 - v) < (1 - \delta)U_S(1 - q) + \delta U_S(1 - (y + \eta))$ for η small enough. Thus, s's payoff to accepting v, which is $U_S(1 - v)$, is less than its payoff to countering with $y + \eta$. This contradiction means that s will never offer more than $\max\{q, \tilde{x}(d^t)\}$, from which it immediately follows that s would never agree to more than $\max\{q, z\}$.

Proof of Proposition A3.2

Before considering the three cases defined in the statement of the proposition, it will be useful to introduce some notation and establish two lemmas.

Consider any perfect Bayesian equilibrium $(\sigma(\delta), \mu(\delta))$ of Γ_D. Let $x(\underline{d}, \delta)$ be $\underline{d}$'s equilibrium demand at the start of the game and, roughly, take $\underline{d}^w(\delta)$ to be the weakest type demanding $x(\underline{d}, \delta)$. More formally, $\underline{d}^w(\delta) = \sup\{d : x(d) = x(\underline{d}, \delta)\}$. The assumption that D's demands are monotonic in its type implies that all types $d \in [\underline{d}, \underline{d}^w(\delta))$ propose $x(\underline{d}, \delta)$. (Type $\underline{d}^w(\delta)$ may or may not demand $x(\underline{d}, \delta)$.) Similarly, $x(\bar{d}, \delta)$ is $\bar{d}$'s equilibrium demand at the beginning of Γ_D in $(\sigma(\delta), \mu(\delta))$, and $\overline{d}^t(\delta)$ is the toughest type that might demand $x(\bar{d}, \delta)$, i.e., $\overline{d}^t(\delta) = \inf\{d : x(d) = x(\bar{d}, \delta)\}$. Accordingly, all types in $(\overline{d}^t(\delta), \bar{d}]$ demand $x(\bar{d}, \delta)$. Table A3.1 summarizes these definitions as well as some additional notation which will be introduced as needed.

The first lemma shows that if s is uncertain of the type it is facing, then it never makes a proposal that is sure to be rejected. More formally, s's optimal take-it-or-leave-it offer t^* is always strictly greater than the certainty equivalent of the weakest type it might be facing. The second lemma shows that no $d > \underline{d}^w(\delta)$ imposes a settlement with positive probability.

Lemma A3.5: $t^*(s, \beta_D[a, b]) > \tilde{x}(b)$ *for all s whenever $b > a$.*

Proof: Suppose s offers $\tilde{x}(b) + \eta$. This offer is accepted with positive probability because the distribution of d is assumed to have a posi-

TABLE A3.1

Useful Notation

$x(d, \delta) = d$'s initial demand in the equilibrium $(\sigma(\delta), \mu(\delta))$ when the discount factor is δ.

$\overline{d}^t(\delta) = $ the "toughest" type to demand what $\bar{d}$ does, i.e., $\inf\{d : x(d, \delta) = x(\bar{d}, \delta)\}$.

$\underline{d}^w(\delta) = $ the "weakest" type to demand what $\underline{d}$ does, i.e., $\sup\{d : x(d, \delta) = x(\underline{d}, \delta)\}$.

$\underline{d}^{w*} = $ a lower bound on $d^w(\delta)$ for δ in a neighborhood of one.

$\tilde{x}(d) = d$'s certainty equivalent for fighting, i.e., $p - d = U_D(\tilde{x}(d))$.

$\beta_D[a, b] = s$'s updated beliefs if all d in $[a, b]$ make the same initial offer.

$T(x, s, \beta_D[a, b]) = s$'s expected payoff to making the take-it-or-leave-it offer x given beliefs $\beta_D[a, b]$.

$t^*(s, \beta_D[a, b]) = $ the offer that maximizes $T(x, s, \beta_D[a, b])$.

$x^*(s, \beta_D[a, b]) = \max\{q, t^*(s, \beta_D[a, b])\}$.

---

tive density over $(\underline{d}, \bar{d})$. Let $\alpha > 0$ be this probability. Then s's payoff to making this offer is $(1 - p - s)(1 - \alpha) + \alpha U_S(1 - (\tilde{x}(b) + \eta))$, whereas the payoff to offering $\tilde{x}(b)$ is $1 - p - s$. Thus, s strictly prefers to offer $\tilde{x}(b) + \eta$ whenever $U_S(1 - (\tilde{x}(b) + \eta)) > 1 - p - s$. But, $U_S(1 - \tilde{x}(b)) > U_S(1 - \tilde{x}(a)) \geq U_S(1 - \tilde{x}(\underline{d}))$ because $b > a \geq \underline{d}$. And, $U_S(1 - \tilde{x}(\underline{d})) \geq 1 - p - s$ because S is satisfied. Consequently, $U_S(1 - \tilde{x}(b)) > 1 - p - s$. Because the previous inequality is strict, there exists an $\eta > 0$ such that $U_S(1 - (\tilde{x}(b) + \eta)) > 1 - p - s$.

Lemma A3.6: *If $d > \underline{d}^w(\delta)$, then the probability that d imposes a settlement is zero.*

Proof: Suppose the contrary. Then there exists an $e > \underline{d}^w$ such that e imposes a settlement with positive probability. (Arguments like the δ in $\underline{d}^w(\delta)$ will be suppressed in order to simplify the notation whenever this can be done unambiguously.) Because $e > \underline{d}^w$, $\underline{d}^w$'s cost of trying to impose a resolution is strictly less than e's. Thus, $\underline{d}^w$'s payoff to mimicking e's initial demand of $x(e)$ is strictly greater than e's payoff, for both $\underline{d}^w$ and e obtain the same payoff if the game ends in an agreed settlement and $\underline{d}^w$ obtains a higher payoff than e if the game ends in an imposed settlement, which it does with positive probability since e imposes a settlement with positive probability. Letting $\mathcal{U}_D(d, x)$ denote d's expected payoff to demanding x and playing optimally thereafter, then $\mathcal{U}_D(\underline{d}^w, x(e)) > \mathcal{U}_D(e, x(e)) + \epsilon$ where ϵ is some small positive number.

Because $e > \underline{d}^w$, e's demand of $x(e)$ is distinct from $\underline{d}$'s demand of $x(\underline{d})$. Incentive compatibility also implies that e cannot benefit by demanding $x(\underline{d})$ instead of $x(e)$. This gives $\mathcal{U}_D(e, x(e)) \geq \mathcal{U}_D(e, x(\underline{d}))$. Lemma A3.5, however, implies that any s rejecting $x(\underline{d})$ will offer strictly more than $\tilde{x}(\underline{d}^w)$. Thus, the probability that $\underline{d}^w$ will subsequently impose a settlement if it demands $x(\underline{d})$ is zero. Hence, e can mimic $\underline{d}^w$ and obtain the same payoff that $\underline{d}^w$ obtains by demanding $x(\underline{d})$. So, $\mathcal{U}_D(e, x(\underline{d})) = \mathcal{U}_D(\underline{d}^w, x(\underline{d}))$. These relations yield the contradiction $\mathcal{U}_D(e, x(e)) \geq \mathcal{U}_D(e, x(\underline{d})) = \mathcal{U}_D(\underline{d}^w, x(\underline{d})) \geq \mathcal{U}_D(\underline{d}^w, x(e)) > \mathcal{U}_D(e, x(e)) + \epsilon$.

Turning to the three cases defined in the statement of proposition A3.2:

Case (i): $\underline{s}$ and, therefore all s, are so confident that the dissatisfied bargainer is tough that they offer the certainty equivalent of the toughest type: $t^*(\underline{s}, \beta_D[\underline{d}, \bar{d}]) = \tilde{x}(\underline{d}) > q$.

Assume the claim made in the proposition does not hold. Then it is possible to construct a sequence of PBEs $\{\mu(\delta_n), \sigma(\delta_n)\}_{n=0}^{\infty}$ of Γ_D such that δ_n converges to one and the $\overline{d^i}(\delta_n)$ are bounded away from $\underline{d}$. As will be seen, $\bar{d}$ prefers to deviate from $x(\bar{d}, \delta_n)$ to $x(\underline{d}, \delta_n)$ in the limit as δ_n goes to one, and this contradiction establishes the claim.

Three observations ensure that any d demanding $x(\underline{d}, \delta_n)$ receives a payoff of at least $(1 - \delta_n)U_D(q) + \delta_n U_D(\tilde{x}(\underline{d}))$. First, $\underline{d}$'s payoff to demanding $x(\underline{d}, \delta_n)$ is bounded below by $(1 - \delta_n)U_D(q) + \delta_n U_D(\tilde{x}(\underline{d}))$, which is what $\underline{d}$ could unilaterally assure itself of by making a non-serious offer and then imposing a resolution.

Second, s's optimal offer conditional on beliefs $\beta_D[\underline{d}, \underline{d}^w(\delta_n)]$ is the certainty equivalent of the toughest type; i.e., $x^*(s, \beta_D[\underline{d}, \underline{d}^w(\delta_n)]) = \tilde{x}(\underline{d})$ for all s. This follows from the Envelope Theorem, which ensures $t^*(s, \beta_D[\underline{d}, e])$ is nonincreasing in e and nondecreasing in s. Hence, $x^*(s, \beta_D[\underline{d}, e]) = \max\{q, t^*(s, \beta_D[\underline{d}, e])\}$ is nonincreasing in e and nondecreasing in s. Thus, $\tilde{x}(\underline{d}) = x^*(\underline{s}, \beta_D[\underline{d}, \bar{d}]) \leq x^*(s, \beta_D[\underline{d}, \underline{d}^w(\delta_n)]) \leq \tilde{x}(\underline{d})$ for all s where the last inequality simply says that s would never offer more than the certainty equivalent of the toughest type it might be facing.

Finally, any d that demands $x(\underline{d}, \delta_n)$ would obtain what $\underline{d}$ receives. If this demand is accepted, both d and $\underline{d}$ receive $U_D(x(\underline{d}, \delta_n))$. If this demand is rejected, then all s counter with $\tilde{x}(\underline{d})$ as was just shown. But the payoffs to both d and $\underline{d}$ of receiving this counter are $(1 - \delta_n)U_D(q) + \delta_n U_D(\tilde{x}(\underline{d}))$. Thus any d can obtain the same payoff as $\underline{d}$ does by demanding just what $\underline{d}$ demands. Consequently, any d can obtain at least $(1 - \delta_n)U_D(q) + \delta_n U_D(\tilde{x}(\underline{d}))$, which the first observation shows to be a lower bound on $\underline{d}$'s payoff.

Turning to $\bar{d}$'s payoff to demanding $x(\bar{d}, \delta_n)$, lemma A3.1 implies those demanding $x(\bar{d}, \delta_n)$ can do no better than $U_D(\max\{q, z(\delta_n)\})$ where $z(\delta_n)$ solves $U_S(1 - z(\delta_n)) = (1 - \delta_n)U_S(1 - q) + \delta_n U_S(1 - \tilde{x}(\overline{d^i}(\delta_n)))$. Incentive compatibility then requires that $\bar{d}$ cannot benefit by demanding $x(\underline{d}, \delta_n)$ instead of $x(\bar{d}, \delta_n)$, which means $U_D(\max\{q, z(\delta_n)\}) \geq (1 - \delta_n)U_D(q) + \delta_n U_D(\tilde{x}(\underline{d}))$. Since $\{\overline{d^i}(\delta_n)\}_{n=0}^{\infty}$ is bounded away from $\underline{d}$, it contains a subsequence $\overline{d^i}(\delta_m)$, which converges to a $\overline{d^{i*}}$ which is strictly larger than $\underline{d}$. Taking the limit of the incentive compatibility condition gives $U_D(\max\{q, \tilde{x}(\overline{d^{i*}})\}) = U_D(\tilde{x}(\overline{d^{i*}})) \geq U_D(\tilde{x}(\underline{d}))$, which contradicts the fact that $\underline{d} < \overline{d^{i*}}$.

Case (ii): In this case, the satisfied state is so confident that D is also satisfied that S never makes any concessions even if it has the highest cost of fighting: $t^*(\bar{s}, \beta_D[\underline{d}, \bar{d}]) \leq q$.

There are five steps to the demonstration of this case. The first shows that the weakest type that demands $x(\underline{d})$, namely $\underline{d}^w(\delta)$, is bounded away from $\underline{d}$. This means that s is unsure of the dissatisfied bargainer's type if $x(\underline{d})$ is demanded. As lemma A3.5 shows, this uncertainty implies that any s that counters $x(\underline{d})$ offers strictly more than the certainty equivalent of the weakest type. Thus, this weakest type, $\underline{d}^w(\delta)$, always accepts this offer instead of imposing a settlement. The second and third steps demonstrate that all those d that do not demand $x(\underline{d})$ are satisfied, i.e., $U_D(q) \geq p - d$. Thus an equilibrium demand of $x \neq x(\underline{d})$ reveals that the demander is satisfied, and the game effectively degenerates into a complete-information game in which the status quo goes unchanged. The fourth step establishes that $x(\underline{d})$ is non-serious in that it is sure to be rejected. Finally, the fifth step shows that S's response to this non-serious demand is not to make any concessions and to "offer" the status quo q instead.

Step 1: There exists a $\underline{\delta} < 1$ and a $\underline{d}^{w*} > \underline{d}$ such that $\underline{d}^w(\delta) > \underline{d}^{w*}$ in any PBE of Γ_D whenever $\delta > \underline{\delta}$.

Suppose the contrary. Then there exists a sequence of PBEs such that δ_n converges to one and, looking along the appropriate subsequences if necessary, $\underline{d}^w(\delta_n)$ converges to $\underline{d}$, $\overline{d}^i(\delta_n)$ converges to some type $\overline{d}^{i*} \geq \underline{d}$, and $\overline{d}$'s demands $x(\overline{d}, \delta_n)$ converge to x^0.

It follows that $\overline{d}^{i*} = \underline{d}$, i.e., that $\overline{d}^i(\delta_n)$ must converge to $\underline{d}$. Lemma A3.1 implies that $\overline{d}$'s payoff to making its equilibrium demand of $x(\overline{d}, \delta_n)$ is bounded above by $U_D(\max\{q, z(\delta_n)\})$ where $z(\delta_n)$ solves $U_S(1 - z(\delta_n)) = (1 - \delta_n)U_S(1 - q) + \delta_n U_S(1 - \tilde{x}(\overline{d}^i(\delta_n)))$. Lemma A3.5 also implies that $\overline{d}$'s payoff to demanding $x(\underline{d}, \delta_n)$ is bounded below by $(1 - \delta_n)U_D(q) + \delta_n U_D(\tilde{x}(\underline{d}^w(\delta_n)))$. Incentive compatibility then requires that $\overline{d}$ cannot benefit by demanding $x(\underline{d}, \delta_n)$ instead of $x(\overline{d}, \delta_n)$, which leaves $U_D(\max\{q, z(\delta_n)\}) \geq (1 - \delta_n)U_D(q) + \delta_n U_D(\tilde{x}(\underline{d}^w(\delta_n)))$. Taking the limit gives $U_D(\max\{q, \tilde{x}(\overline{d}^{i*})\}) \geq U_D(\tilde{x}(\underline{d}))$. But $\tilde{x}(\underline{d}) > q$ by assumption, so $\overline{d}^{i*}$, which is bounded below by $\underline{d}$, must in fact equal $\underline{d}$.

Because $\overline{d}^i(\delta_n)$ converges to $\underline{d}$, $x(\overline{d}, \delta_n)$ must be accepted with positive probability for δ_n close enough to one. To see this, suppose the contrary. If $x(\overline{d}, \delta_n)$ is rejected for sure, then the weakest type must at least be indifferent to rejecting this demand and countering with $x^*(\overline{s}, \beta_D[\overline{d}^i(\delta_n), \overline{d}]) = \max\{q, t^*(\overline{s}, \beta_D[\overline{d}^i(\delta_n), \overline{d}])\}$. But $t^*(\overline{s}, \beta_D[d, \overline{d}])$ is nonincreasing in d, so $t^*(\overline{s}, \beta_D[\overline{d}^i(\delta_n), \overline{d}]) \leq t^*(\overline{s}, \beta_D[\underline{d}, \overline{d}]) \leq q$, where the last inequality is what defines case (ii). Thus, $\overline{s}$ counters with $x^*(\overline{s}, \delta_n, \beta_D[\overline{d}^i(\delta_n), \overline{d}]) = q$. However, $\underline{d}$, strictly prefers an imposed settlement to q, i.e., $p - d > U_D(q)$. Because this inequality is strict and d has a positive density over $(\underline{d}, \bar{d})$, there must exist an $\epsilon > 0$ such that $d \in [\underline{d}, \underline{d} + \epsilon]$ also strictly prefer an imposed settlement to q. The fact that $\bar{d}^i(\delta_n)$ converges to $\underline{d}$ then means that there must also exist a $\bar{d}^i(\delta_n)$ close enough to $\underline{d}$ such that some $e > \bar{d}^i(\delta_n)$ also prefers an imposed settlement to accepting q. Type e therefore rejects the counter-offer of q and imposes a settlement. But $e > \underline{d}^w(\delta_n)$ because $\bar{d}^i(\delta_n) \geq \underline{d}^w(\delta_n)$, and this contradicts lemma A3.6, which says that no $d > \underline{d}^w(\delta_n)$ imposes a settlement. This contradiction means that $x(\bar{d}, \delta_n)$ is accepted with positive probability if δ_n is close enough to one.

The fact that $x(\bar{d}, \delta_n)$ is accepted with positive probability implies that the limit of $\bar{d}$'s demands as δ_n goes to 1 is strictly less than $\underline{d}$'s certainty equivalent for fighting, i.e., $x^0 < \tilde{x}(\underline{d})$. To see that this is so, observe that $\bar{s}$'s payoff to agreeing to $x(\bar{d}, \delta_n)$ must also be at least as large as its payoff to countering this demand: $U_S(1 - x(\bar{d}, \delta_n)) \geq (1 - \delta_n)U_S(1 - q) + \delta_n T(x^*(\bar{s}, \beta_D[\bar{d}^i(\delta_n), \bar{d}]), \bar{s}, \beta_D[\bar{d}^i(\delta_n), \bar{d}])$. But $x^*(\bar{s}, \beta_D[\bar{d}^i(\delta_n), \bar{d}]) = \max\{q, t^*(\bar{s}, \beta_D[\bar{d}^i(\delta_n), \bar{d}])\} = q$, where the last equality holds because $t^*(\bar{s}, \beta_D[\underline{d}, \bar{d}])$ is nonincreasing in d and, by definition, $t^*(\bar{s}, \beta_D[\underline{d}, \bar{d}]) \leq q$ in case (ii). Thus, $U_S(1 - x(\bar{d}, \delta_n)) \geq (1 - \delta_n)U_S(1 - q) + \delta_n T(q, \bar{s}, \beta_D[\bar{d}^i(\delta_n), \bar{d}])$, which in the limit gives $U_S(1 - x^0) \geq T(q, \bar{s}, \beta_D[\underline{d}, \bar{d}])$. However, $x^*(\bar{s}, \beta_D[\underline{d}, \bar{d}]) = q$ is the unique maximizer of T over $x \in [q, 1]$. Accordingly, $T(q, \bar{s}, \beta_D[\underline{d}, \bar{d}]) > T(\tilde{x}(\underline{d}), \bar{s}, \beta_D[\underline{d}, \bar{d}])$, where the inequality is strict because $q \neq \tilde{x}(\underline{d})$. Finally, $T(\tilde{x}(\underline{d}), \bar{s}, \beta_D[\underline{d}, \bar{d}]) = U_S(1 - \tilde{x}(\underline{d}))$ because an offer of $\tilde{x}(\underline{d})$ is accepted for sure. Putting these inequalities together gives $U_S(1 - x^0) > U_S(1 - \tilde{x}(\underline{d}))$ or $\tilde{x}(\underline{d}) > x^0$.

The facts that $\tilde{x}(\underline{d}) > x^0$ and that $x(\bar{d}, \delta_n)$ is accepted with positive probability lead to the contradiction that $\bar{d}$ prefers deviating to $x(\underline{d}, \delta_n)$ for δ_n sufficiently close to one. The positive probability of acceptance implies that $\bar{d}^i(\delta_n)$'s payoff if this demand is accepted must be at least as large as its payoff to making a non-serious demand and then imposing a settlement: $U_D(x(\bar{d}, \delta_n)) \geq (1 - \delta_n)U_D(q) + \delta_n U_D(\tilde{x}(\bar{d}^i(\delta_n)))$. Taking the limit yields $U_D(x^0) \geq U_D(\tilde{x}(\underline{d}))$ or $x^0 \geq \tilde{x}(\underline{d})$, which contradicts the inequality $\tilde{x}(\underline{d}) > x^0$. This contradiction establishes the claim made in step 1 that $\underline{d}^w(\delta)$ is bounded away from $\underline{d}$.

Step 2: Let λ be the type such that $\bar{s}$'s optimal offer conditional on $\beta_D[\underline{d}, \lambda]$ is to offer q; i.e., λ solves $t^*(\bar{s}, \beta_D[\underline{d}, \lambda]) = q$. Then the weakest type demanding $x(\underline{d})$ is in the limit at least as large as λ. In symbols, for any $\epsilon > 0$, there exists a $\underline{\delta} < 1$ such that $\underline{d}^w(\delta) > \lambda - \epsilon$ in any PBE of Γ_D whenever $\delta > \underline{\delta}$.

The Intermediate Value Theorem ensures that such a λ exists because t^* is continuous and $t^*(\bar{s}, \beta_D[\underline{d}, \underline{d}]) = \tilde{x}(\underline{d}) > q \geq t^*(\bar{s}, \beta_D[\underline{d}, \bar{d}])$ where the last inequality is what defines case (ii). Now suppose that the claim made in this step does not hold. Then there must exist an $\epsilon' > 0$ and a sequence of PBEs of Γ_D such that δ_n converges to one, $\underline{d}^w(\delta_n) < \lambda - \epsilon'$, and $\underline{d}^w(\delta_n)$ converges to some $\underline{d}^{w*}$. Step 1 also ensures that $\underline{d} < \underline{d}^{w*}$.

The payoff to $\underline{d}^w(\delta_n)$ of demanding $x(\underline{d}, \delta_n)$ is bounded below by $(1 - \delta_n)U_D(q) + \delta_n \int_{\underline{s}}^{\bar{s}} U_D(x^*(s, \beta_D[\underline{d}, \underline{d}^w(\delta_n)]))dF_S$. This is clearly so if this demand is rejected with probability one, for s would then counter with $x^*(s, \beta_D[\underline{d}, \underline{d}^w(\delta_n)])$. If $x(\underline{d}, \delta_n)$ is accepted with positive probability, then $\underline{d}$'s payoff if this demand is accepted must be at least as large as its payoff to making a non-serious demand and then imposing a settlement. That is, $U_D(x(\underline{d}, \delta_n)) \geq (1 - \delta_n)U_D(q) + \delta_n U_D(\tilde{x}(\underline{d}))$. But no s ever offers more than $\tilde{x}(\underline{d})$, so $U_D(\tilde{x}(\underline{d})) \geq U_D(x^*(s, \beta_D[\underline{d}, \underline{d}^w(\delta_n)]))$ for all s. Thus, $\underline{d}^w(\delta_n)$'s payoff is also bounded below by $(1 - \delta_n)U_D(q) + \delta_n \int_{\underline{s}}^{\bar{s}} U_D(x^*(s, \beta_D[\underline{d}, \underline{d}^w(\delta_n)]))dF_S$ if $x(\underline{d}, \delta_n)$ is accepted with positive probability.

This lower bound is in turn strictly greater than and bounded away from $(1 - \delta_n)U_D(q) + \delta_n U_D(\max\{q, \tilde{x}(\underline{d}^w(\delta_n))\})$. This follows by observing first that $t^*(\bar{s}, \beta_D[\underline{d}, \underline{d}^{w*}]) > q$ because $\underline{d}^{w*} \leq \lambda - \epsilon'$. Furthermore, lemma A3.5 shows that $t^*(\bar{s}, \beta_D[\underline{d}, \underline{d}^{w*}]) > \tilde{x}(\underline{d}^{w*})$. Thus, there exists a $\phi > 0$ such that $t^*(\bar{s}, \beta_D[\underline{d}, \underline{d}^{w*}]) > \max\{q, \tilde{x}(\underline{d}^{w*})\} + \phi$. Continuity then ensures that there exist $\xi > 0$ and $\zeta > 0$ such that $t^*(\bar{s} - \xi, \beta_D[\underline{d}, \underline{d}^{w*} + \zeta]) > \max\{q, \tilde{x}(\underline{d}^{w*})\} + \phi$ if δ_n is close enough to one. Now if need be choose a still tighter bound on δ_n sufficient to ensure that $|\underline{d}^w(\delta_n) - \underline{d}^{w*}| < \zeta$. Then $t^*(s, \beta_D[\underline{d}, \underline{d}^w(\delta_n)]) \geq t^*(\bar{s} - \xi, \beta_D[\underline{d}, \underline{d}^{w*} + \zeta]) > \max\{q, \tilde{x}(\underline{d}^{w*})\} + \phi$ for all $s \geq \bar{s} - \xi$ because $t^*(s, \beta_D[\underline{d}, d])$ is nondecreasing in s and nonincreasing in d. Thus, $x^*(s, \beta_D[\underline{d}, \underline{d}^w(\delta_n)]) \geq \max\{q, \tilde{x}(\underline{d}^w(\delta_n))\} + \phi$ for all $s \geq \bar{s} - \xi$ and $x^*(s, \beta_D[\underline{d}, \underline{d}^w(\delta_n)]) = \max\{q, t^*(s, \beta_D[\underline{d}, \underline{d}^w(\delta_n)])\} \geq \max\{q, \tilde{x}(\underline{d}^w(\delta_n))\}$ for all $s < \bar{s} - \xi$. Accordingly, the lower bound on $\underline{d}^w(\delta_n)$'s payoff to demanding $x(\underline{d}, \delta_n)$ is bounded below by $(1 - \delta_n)U_D(q) + \delta_n[\int_{\underline{s}}^{\bar{s} - \xi} U_D(\max\{q, \tilde{x}(\underline{d}^w(\delta_n))\})dF_S + \int_{\bar{s} - \xi}^{\bar{s}}[U_D(\max\{q, \tilde{x}(\underline{d}^w(\delta_n))\}) + \gamma]dF_S]$ for some small $\gamma > 0$. This expression is in turn at least as large as $(1 - \delta_n)U_D(q) + \delta_n[U_D(\max\{q, \tilde{x}(\underline{d}^w(\delta_n))\}) + \gamma(1 - F_S(\bar{s} - \xi))]$.

This lower bound for $\underline{d}^w(\delta_n)$'s payoff to demanding $x(\underline{d}, \delta_n)$ is also a lower bound to $\bar{d}$'s payoff to demanding $x(\underline{d}, \delta_n)$. This follows because $\underline{d}^w(\delta_n)$ never imposes a settlement if it demands $x(\underline{d}, \delta_n)$, as all s counter with at least $\tilde{x}(\underline{d}^w(\delta_n))$, which $\underline{d}^w(\delta_n)$ accepts. And because

$\underline{d}^w(\delta_n)$ accepts, $\bar{d}$ can costlessly mimic $\underline{d}^w(\delta_n)$ and obtain the same payoff that $\underline{d}^w(\delta_n)$ does by demanding $x(\underline{d}, \delta_n)$.

Lemma A3.1, however, implies that the best that $\bar{d}$ can do by demanding $x(\bar{d}, \delta_n)$ is bounded above by $\max\{q, z(\delta_n)\}$ where $z(\delta_n)$ solves $U_S(1 - z(\delta_n)) = (1 - \delta_n)U_S(1 - q) + \delta_n U_S(1 - \tilde{x}(\overline{d^i}(\delta_n)))$. Incentive compatibility then requires $\bar{d}$'s payoff to demanding $x(\bar{d}, \delta_n)$ to be at least as large as the lower bound on its payoff to demanding $x(\underline{d}, \delta_n)$: $U_D(\max\{q, z(\delta_n)\}) \geq (1 - \delta_n)U_D(q) + \delta_n[U_D(\max\{q, \tilde{x}(\underline{d}^w(\delta_n))\}) + \gamma(1 - F_S(\bar{s} - \xi))]$. Taking the limits of both sides of the inequality shows that this inequality must break down for δ_n close enough to one. This contradiction ensures that there exists a $\underline{\delta} < 1$ such that $\underline{d}^w(\delta) \geq \lambda - \epsilon$ whenever $\delta > \underline{\delta}$.

Step 3: There exists a $\underline{\delta} < 1$ such that d is satisfied if $d > \underline{d}^w(\delta)$, i.e., $\tilde{x}(d) \leq q$ whenever $d > \underline{d}^w(\delta)$ and $\delta > \underline{\delta}$.

Let $\tilde{d}$ be the type with certainty equivalent q, i.e., $\tilde{x}(\tilde{d}) = q$. Now $\tilde{d}$ is sure to exist, because $\underline{d}$ is dissatisfied by assumption and, therefore, $U_D(\tilde{x}(\underline{d})) = p - \underline{d} > U_D(q)$. Thus, $\tilde{x}(\underline{d}) > q$. Further, $q \geq t^*(\bar{s}, \beta_D[\underline{d}, \bar{d}]) > \tilde{x}(\bar{d})$ where the first inequality is what defines case (ii) and the second inequality follows from lemma A3.5. Continuity then ensures that $\tilde{d}$ exists.

Clearly, $\tilde{d} < \lambda$ where, recall, λ is given by $t^*(\bar{s}, \beta_D[\underline{d}, \lambda]) = q$. This inequality follows by observing that $\tilde{x}(\tilde{d}) = q = t^*(\bar{s}, \beta_D[\underline{d}, \lambda]) > \tilde{x}(\lambda)$ where the last inequality follows from lemma A3.5.

Step 3 follows immediately from $\tilde{d} < \lambda$. With $\tilde{d} < \lambda$, step 2 guarantees that δ can be chosen close enough to one to ensure that $\underline{d}^w(\delta) > \tilde{d}$. If, therefore, $d > \underline{d}^w(\delta)$, then $\tilde{x}(d) < \tilde{x}(\underline{d}^w(\delta)) < \tilde{x}(\tilde{d}) = q$.

Step 4: There exists a $\underline{\delta} < 1$, such that $\underline{d}^w(\delta)$ is at least as large as λ whenever $\delta > \underline{\delta}$.

This follows immediately from incentive compatibility. Step 3 shows that all d that do not demand $x(\underline{d}, \delta)$ reveal that they are satisfied: $d > \underline{d}^w(\delta) \Rightarrow \tilde{x}(d) \leq q$. Once a set of types reveals this information, the game effectively degenerates into a complete-information game and the distribution of benefits remains q. Hence, $d > \underline{d}^w(\delta)$ receives $U_D(q)$ by making an equilibrium demand that differs from $x(\underline{d}, \delta)$. Incentive compatibility requires that $\bar{d}$ cannot do better by demanding $x(\underline{d}, \delta)$. This is true only if $\underline{d}^w(\delta)$ satisfies $U_D(q) \geq (1 - \delta)U_D(q) + \delta \int_{\underline{s}}^{\bar{s}} U_D(x^*(s, \beta_D[\underline{d}, \underline{d}^w(\delta)]))dF_S$, which leaves $U_D(q) \geq \int_{\underline{s}}^{\bar{s}} U_D(x^*(s, \beta_D[\underline{d}, \underline{d}^w(\delta)]))dF_S$. But, $x^*(s, \beta_D[\underline{d}, \underline{d}^w(\delta)])$ is continuous in s and bounded below by q. Thus, $x^*(\bar{s}, \beta_D[\underline{d}, \underline{d}^w(\delta)])$ must equal q, and therefore, $\underline{d}^w(\delta) \geq \lambda$.

Step 5: It only remains to be shown that there exists a $\underline{\delta} < 1$ such that $\underline{d}$'s demand is non-serious in all PBEs of Γ_D whenever $\delta > \underline{\delta}$.

Suppose the contrary. Then there exists a sequence of PBEs such that δ_n converges to one, $\underline{d}^w(\delta_n)$ converges to some $\underline{d}^{w*} > \underline{d}$, and $\underline{d}$'s demands are serious. Step 2 shows that $\underline{d}^w(\delta_n)$ is bounded below by $\lambda - \epsilon$ for any $\epsilon > 0$ if δ is close enough to one. The supposition that the demands $x(\underline{d}, \delta_n)$ are serious will be seen to imply that $\underline{d}^w(\delta_n)$ has an upper bound that is strictly less than the lower bound implied by step 2. This contradiction will establish step 5.

To determine the upper bound on $\underline{d}^w(\delta_n)$ if the $x(\underline{d}, \delta_n)$ are serious, let v be the largest d such that $\bar{s}$'s optimal take-it-or-leave-it offer conditional on $\beta_D[\underline{d}, d]$ is $\tilde{x}(\underline{d})$: $v = \max\{d : t^*(\bar{s}, \beta_D[\underline{d}, d]) = \tilde{x}(\underline{d})\}$. And v is well defined because the set is closed and contains $\underline{d}$.

Then for any $\epsilon > 0$, there exists a $\underline{\delta} < 1$ such that $\underline{d}^w(\delta_n) < v + \epsilon$ whenever $\delta > \underline{\delta}$. To establish this bound, it suffices to show that $\bar{s}$'s optimal offer of $t^*(\bar{s}, \beta_D[\underline{d}, \underline{d}^w(\delta_n)])$ equals $\tilde{x}(\underline{d})$ in the limit. That is, $t^*(\bar{s}, \beta_D[\underline{d}, \underline{d}^{w*}]) = \tilde{x}(\underline{d})$. If so, then $\underline{d}^{w*} \leq v$ and, thus, for any $\epsilon > 0$, there exists a $\underline{\delta} < 1$ such that $\underline{d}^w(\delta_n) \leq v + \epsilon$ whenever $\delta_n > \underline{\delta}$.

To see that $t^*(\bar{s}, \beta_D[\underline{d}, \underline{d}^{w*}]) = \tilde{x}(\underline{d})$, suppose the contrary: $t^*(\bar{s}, \beta_D[\underline{d}, \underline{d}^{w*}]) < \tilde{x}(\underline{d})$. A contradiction follows. Because $x(\underline{d}, \delta_n)$ is accepted with positive probability, $\underline{d}$'s payoff to having $x(\underline{d}, \delta_n)$ must be at least as large as its payoff to making a non-serious demand and then imposing a settlement. That is, $U_D(x(\underline{d}, \delta_n)) \geq (1 - \delta)U_D(q) + \delta U_D(\tilde{x}(\underline{d}))$. So, S's payoff to accepting $x(\underline{d}, \delta_n)$, $U_S(1 - x(\underline{d}, \delta_n))$, is bounded above by $U_S(1 - U_D^{-1}((1 - \delta)U_D(q) + \delta U_D(\tilde{x}(\underline{d}))))$.

Moreover, the fact that the $x(\underline{d}, \delta_n)$ are accepted with positive probability means that a small neighborhood of $\bar{s}$ must prefer agreeing to this demand rather than countering it. Thus, $\bar{s}$'s payoff to accepting $x(\underline{d}, \delta_n)$ is bounded below by $(1 - \delta_n)U_S(1 - q) + \delta_n T(x^*(\bar{s}, \beta_D[\underline{d}, \underline{d}^w(\delta_n)]), \bar{s}, \beta_D[\underline{d}, \underline{d}^w(\delta_n)]))$.

Combining the bounds on $U_S(1 - x(\underline{d}, \delta_n))$ and taking the limit shows that for any $\epsilon > 0$, there exists a $\underline{\delta} < 1$ such that $U_S(1 - \tilde{x}(\underline{d})) + \epsilon > T(x^*(\bar{s}, \beta_D[\underline{d}, \underline{d}^{w*}]), \bar{s}, \beta_D[\underline{d}, \underline{d}^{w*}])$. But $x^*(\bar{s}, \beta_D[\underline{d}, \underline{d}^{w*}])$ is the unique offer that maximizes $T(x, \bar{s}, \beta_D[\underline{d}, \underline{d}^{w*}])$ subject to $x \in [q, 1]$ and $x^*(\bar{s}, \beta_D[\underline{d}, \underline{d}^{w*}]) = \max\{q, t^*(\bar{s}, [\underline{d}, \underline{d}^{w*}])\} < \tilde{x}(\underline{d})$. Because $x^*(\bar{s}, \beta_D[\underline{d}, \underline{d}^{w*}]) \neq \tilde{x}(\underline{d})$, $\bar{s}$'s payoff to its unique optimal offer is strictly larger than its payoff to proposing $\tilde{x}(\underline{d})$: $T(x^*(\bar{s}, \beta_D[\underline{d}, \underline{d}^{w*}]), \bar{s}, \beta_D[\underline{d}, \underline{d}^{w*}]) >$

$T(\tilde{x}(\underline{d}), \bar{s}, \beta_D[\underline{d}, \underline{d}^{w*}])$. Moreover, $T(\tilde{x}(\underline{d}), \bar{s}, \beta_D[\underline{d}, \underline{d}^{w*}]) = U_S(1 - \tilde{x}(\underline{d}))$ because an offer of $\tilde{x}(\underline{d})$ is accepted. Combining these inequalities leaves $U_S(1 - \tilde{x}(\underline{d})) + \epsilon > U_S(1 - \tilde{x}(\underline{d}))$, and this contradiction leaves $t^*(\bar{s}, [\underline{d}, \underline{d}^{w*}]) = \tilde{x}(\underline{d})$, which implies $\underline{d}^{w*} \leq v$.

Finally, v is less than λ since $t^*(\bar{s}, \beta_D[\underline{d}, d])$ is nonincreasing in d and $t^*(\bar{s}, \beta_D[\underline{d}, v]) = \tilde{x}(\underline{d}) > q = t^*(\bar{s}, \beta_D[\underline{d}, \lambda])$. Taking $\epsilon = (\lambda - v)/4$, there must exist a $\underline{\delta} < 1$ such that $\underline{d}^w(\delta_n) < v + (\lambda - v)/4$ and, by step 2, $\underline{d}^w(\delta_n) > \lambda - (\lambda - v)/4$. This contradiction establishes that $\underline{d}$'s demands must be non-serious for δ close enough to one.

Case (iii): In this intermediate case, S's priors are such that the toughest type of S does not offer the toughest type of D enough to satisfy it, but the weakest type of S does offer the weakest type of D enough to satisfy it. More precisely, $t^*(\underline{s}, \beta_D[\underline{d}, \bar{d}]) < \tilde{x}(\underline{d})$ and $t^*(\bar{s}, \beta_D[\underline{d}, \bar{d}]) > q$.

The proof takes three steps. Assuming that there are two distinct demands in a PBE for δ arbitrarily close to one, the first step shows that $\underline{d}^w(\delta)$ is bounded away from $\underline{d}$ as in case (ii). With $\underline{d}^w(\delta) > \underline{d}^{w*}$ for some $\underline{d}^{w*} > \underline{d}$, the second step uses lemma A3.5 to put a lower bound on $\underline{d}^w(\delta)$'s payoff to demanding $x(\underline{d}, \delta)$. The final step then relies on this lower bound to show that $\bar{d}$ prefers to deviate to $x(\underline{d})$.

Step 1: There exists a $\underline{d}^{w*} > \underline{d}$ and a $\underline{\delta} < 1$ such that $\underline{d}^w(\delta) > \underline{d}^{w*}$ whenever $\delta > \underline{\delta}$.

Suppose the contrary. Then there is a sequence of PBEs of Γ_D such that δ_n converges to one, $\underline{d}^w(\delta_n)$ converges to $\underline{d}$, $\overline{d}^i(\delta_n)$ converges to a $\overline{d}^{i*}$, and the sequence of demands $x(\bar{d}, \delta_n)$ also converges to some x^0. The argument in step 1 of case (ii) then shows that $\overline{d}^{i*} = \underline{d}$.

The convergence of $\overline{d}^i(\delta_n)$ to $\underline{d}$ implies that $x(\bar{d}, \delta_n)$ must be accepted with probability one if δ is sufficiently close to one. Suppose the contrary. Then there exists a subsequence $\{\delta_m\}$ converging to one such that a small neighborhood of $\underline{s}$ rejects this demand for each δ_m. Lemma A3.6, however, shows that no $d > \underline{d}^w(\delta_m)$ can impose a settlement with positive probability. If, therefore, a small neighborhood of $\underline{s}$ rejects $x(\bar{d}, \delta_m)$, then each s in this neighborhood must counter with $\tilde{x}(\overline{d}^i(\delta_m))$. Otherwise, some d slightly larger than $\overline{d}^i(\delta_m)$ and therefore larger than $\underline{d}^w(\delta_m)$ would impose a settlement rather than accept the counter-offer. In particular, $\underline{s}$ must counter with $\tilde{x}(\overline{d}^i(\delta_m))$: $x^*(\underline{s}, \beta_D[\overline{d}^i(\delta_m), \bar{d}]) = \tilde{x}(\overline{d}^i(\delta_m))$. Taking the limit along this subsequence then gives $x^*(\underline{s}, \beta_D[\underline{d}, \bar{d}]) = \tilde{x}(\underline{d})$. This, however, is a contradiction, because the condition defining case (iii) implies $x^*(\underline{s}, \beta_D[\underline{d}, \bar{d}]) = \max\{q, t^*(\underline{s}, \beta_D[\underline{d}, \bar{d}])\} < \tilde{x}(\underline{d})$. This contradiction establishes that $x(\bar{d}, \delta_n)$ is accepted with probability one.

Because $x(\bar{d}, \delta_n)$ is accepted for sure, $\underline{s}$ cannot strictly prefer to counter $x(\bar{d}, \delta_n)$ and this implies $\tilde{x}(\underline{d}) > x^0$. The fact that $\underline{s}$'s payoff to accepting $x(\bar{d}, \delta_n)$ must be at least as large as its payoff to countering means that $U_S(1 - x(\bar{d}, \delta_n)) \geq (1 - \delta_n)U_S(1 - q) + \delta_n T(x^*(\underline{s}, \beta_D[\bar{d}^i(\delta_n), \bar{d}]), \underline{s}, \beta_D[\bar{d}^i(\delta_n), \bar{d}])$. Taking the limit then gives $U_S(1 - x^0) \geq T(x^*(\underline{s}, \beta_D[\underline{d}, \bar{d}]), \underline{s}, \beta_D[\underline{d}, \bar{d}])$. But $x^*(\underline{s}, \beta_D[\underline{d}, \bar{d}]) = \max\{q, t^*(\underline{s}, \beta_D[\underline{d}, \bar{d}])\} < \tilde{x}(\underline{d})$, where the inequality is from the condition defining case (iii). Moreover, $x^*(\underline{s}, \beta_D[\underline{d}, \bar{d}])$ is the unique x that maximizes $T(x, \underline{s}, \beta_D[\underline{d}, \bar{d}])$ for all $x \in [q, 1]$. So, $T(x^*(\underline{s}, \beta_D[\underline{d}, \bar{d}]), \underline{s}, \beta_D[\underline{d}, \bar{d}]) > T(\tilde{x}(\underline{d}), \underline{s}, \beta_D[\underline{d}, \bar{d}])$ where the inequality is strict because $x^*(\underline{s}, \beta_D[\underline{d}, \bar{d}]) \neq \tilde{x}(\underline{d})$. Finally, $T(\tilde{x}(\underline{d}), \underline{s}, \beta_D[\underline{d}, \bar{d}]) = U_S(1 - \tilde{x}(\underline{d}))$ because an offer of $\tilde{x}(\underline{d})$ is accepted. Putting these inequalities together gives $U_S(1 - x^0) > U_S(1 - \tilde{x}(\underline{d}))$ or $\tilde{x}(\underline{d}) > x^0$.

The previous inequality and the fact that $x(\bar{d}, \delta_n)$ is accepted for sure lead to the contradiction that $\bar{d}$ prefers deviating to $x(\underline{d}, \delta_n)$ for δ_n sufficiently close to one. The payoff to $\bar{d}$'s demanding $x(\bar{d}, \delta_n)$ is $U_D(x(\bar{d}, \delta_n))$ because this offer is sure to be accepted. But this payoff must be at least as large as $\bar{d}$'s payoff to demanding $x(\underline{d}, \delta_n)$, which by lemma A3.5, is bounded below by $(1 - \delta_n)U_D(q) + \delta_n U_D(\tilde{x}(\bar{d}^i(\delta_n)))$. This leaves $U_D(x(\bar{d}, \delta_n)) \geq (1 - \delta_n)U_D(q) + \delta_n U_D(\tilde{x}(\bar{d}^i(\delta_n)))$, and taking the limit yields the contradiction $U_D(x^0) \geq U_D(\tilde{x}(\underline{d}))$ or $x^0 \geq \tilde{x}(\underline{d})$. This contradiction leaves $\underline{d}^w(\delta)$ bounded away from $\underline{d}$.

> *Step* 2: $\underline{d}^w(\delta)$'s payoff to demanding $x(\underline{d}, \delta)$ is strictly greater than and bounded away from its status quo payoff and its certainty equivalent, i.e., there exists a $\underline{\delta} < 1$ and an $\epsilon > 0$ such that $\underline{d}^w(\delta)$'s payoff to demanding $x(\underline{d}, \delta)$ is at least $U_D(\max\{q, \tilde{x}(\underline{d}^w(\delta))\}) + \epsilon$ whenever $\delta > \underline{\delta}$.

As shown in step 2 of case (ii), $\underline{d}^w(\delta)$'s payoff to demanding $x(\underline{d}, \delta)$ is bounded below by $(1 - \delta)U_D(q) + \delta \int_{\underline{s}}^{\bar{s}} U_D(x^*(s, \beta_D[\underline{d}, \underline{d}^w(\delta)]))dF_S$. It suffices, therefore, to show that the previous expression is strictly greater than and bounded away from $U_D(\max\{q, \tilde{x}(\underline{d}^w(\delta))\})$ for δ close enough to one.

Suppose the contrary. Then there must exist a sequence of PBEs of Γ_D such that δ_n converges to one, $\underline{d}^w(\delta_n)$ converges to some $\underline{d}^{w*} > \underline{d}$, and $\lim_{n \to \infty}[(1 - \delta_n)U_D(q) + \delta_n \int_{\underline{s}}^{\bar{s}} U_D(x^*(s, \beta_D[\underline{d}, \underline{d}^w(\delta_n)]))dF_S] \leq U_D(\max\{q, \tilde{x}(\underline{d}^{w*})\})$. The functions $U_D(x^*(s, \beta_D[\underline{d}, \underline{d}^w(\delta_n)]))$ are bounded, measurable, and converge to $U_D(x^*(s, \beta_D[\underline{d}, \underline{d}^{w*}]))$ as n goes to infinity. So, it must be that the limit of the previous inequality is $\int_{\underline{s}}^{\bar{s}} U_D(x^*(s, \beta_D[\underline{d}, \underline{d}^{w*}]))dF_S \leq U_D(\max\{q, \tilde{x}(\underline{d}^{w*})\})$.

Because t^* is continuous and $t^*(\bar{s}, \beta_D[\underline{d}, \bar{d}]) > q$, there exists a $\xi > 0$ such that $t^*(s, \beta_D[\underline{d}, \bar{d}]) \geq t^*(\bar{s} - \xi, \beta_D[\underline{d}, \bar{d}]) > q$ for all $s \geq \bar{s} - \xi$ where the first inequality reflects the fact that t^* is nondecreasing in s. Lemma A3.5 implies further $t^*(s, \beta_D[\underline{d}, \underline{d}^{w*}]) > \tilde{x}(\underline{d}^{w*})$ for all s. Thus, $x^*(s, \beta_D[\underline{d}, \underline{d}^{w*}]) = \max\{q, t^*(s, \beta_D[\underline{d}, \underline{d}^{w*}])\} \geq \max\{q, \tilde{x}(\underline{d}^{w*})\}$ with the inequality strict for $s \in [\bar{s} - \xi, \bar{s}]$ as long as $\delta > \underline{\delta}$. Hence, $\int_{\underline{s}}^{\bar{s}} U_D(x^*(s, \beta_D[\underline{d}, \underline{d}^w]))dF_S > U_D(\max\{q, \tilde{x}(\underline{d}^w)\})$. This contradiction establishes the claim.

Step 3: If there are two distinct demands, i.e., if $x(\underline{d}, \delta) \neq x(\bar{d}, \delta)$, then $\bar{d}$ strictly prefers to deviate to $x(\underline{d}, \delta)$ for δ close enough to one.

Suppose the contrary. Then there exists a sequence of PBEs of Γ_D for $\delta_n \to 1$ such that $x(\underline{d}, \delta_n) \neq x(\bar{d}, \delta_n)$, $\overline{d^t}(\delta_n) \to \overline{d^{t*}}$, and $\underline{d}^w(\delta_n) \to \underline{d}^{w*}$. Step 1 ensures that $\underline{d}^{w*} > \underline{d}$ and the fact that $\overline{d^t}(\delta_n) \geq \underline{d}^w(\delta_n)$ implies $\overline{d^{t*}} \geq \underline{d}^{w*}$. Incentive compatibility also requires that $\bar{d}$'s payoff to demanding $x(\bar{d}, \delta_n)$ be at least as large as the payoff to demanding $x(\underline{d}, \delta_n)$. Step 2 in turn says that there exists a $\underline{\delta} < 1$ and an $\epsilon > 0$ such that $\underline{d}^w(\delta_n)$'s payoff to demanding $x(\underline{d}, \delta_n)$ is at least $U_D(\max\{q, \tilde{x}(\underline{d}^w(\delta_n))\}) + \epsilon$. But $\underline{d}^w(\delta_n)$ never imposes a settlement if it demands $x(\underline{d}, \delta_n)$, so $\bar{d}$ can costlessly mimic $\underline{d}^w(\delta_n)$. Thus $\bar{d}$'s payoff to demanding $x(\underline{d}, \delta_n)$ is at least $U_D(\max\{q, \tilde{x}(\underline{d}^w(\delta_n))\}) + \epsilon$.

Lemma A3.1 implies that $\bar{d}$'s payoff to demanding $x(\bar{d}, \delta_n)$ is bounded above by $U_D(\max\{q, z(\delta_n)\})$ where $z(\delta_n)$ solves $U_S(1 - z(\delta_n)) = (1 - \delta_n)U_D(q) + \delta_n U_D(\tilde{x}(\overline{d^t}(\delta_n)))$. Incentive compatibility then gives $U_D(\max\{q, z(\delta_n)\}) \geq U_D(\max\{q, \tilde{x}(\underline{d}^w(\delta_n))\}) + \epsilon$. As δ_n goes to one, the left side becomes arbitrarily close to $U_D(\max\{q, \tilde{x}(\overline{d^{t*}})\})$ and the right side approaches $U_D(\max\{q, \tilde{x}(\underline{d}^{w*})\}) + \epsilon$. The previous inequality must therefore breakdown for δ_n close enough to one. This contradiction means $x(\underline{d}, \delta) = x(\bar{d}, \delta)$ and establishes case (iii).

Proof of Proposition A3.3

Let π_S and π_D denote the probabilities of breakdown in any PBE of Γ_S and Γ_D, respectively. Recalling that the probability that D will reject an offer of $x \geq q$ in order to impose a settlement is $F_D(p - U_D(x))$. Then, $\pi_S = \int_{\underline{s}}^{\bar{s}} F_D(p - U_D(x^*(s, \beta_D[\underline{d}, \bar{d}])))dF_S$.

In case (i) of proposition A3.2, $t^*(\underline{s}, \beta_D[\underline{d}, \bar{d}]) > q$ and all $d \in (\underline{d} + \eta, \bar{d}]$ pool for any $\eta > 0$ if δ is close enough to one. So, δ can be chosen close enough to one to ensure that $t^*(\underline{s}, \beta_D[\underline{d} + \eta, \bar{d}]) > q$ and all $d \in [\underline{d} + \eta, \bar{d}]$ pool on a common demand. Then $x^*(s, \beta_D[\underline{d} + \eta, \bar{d}]) = t^*(s, \beta_D[\underline{d} + \eta, \bar{d}])$. Accordingly, π_D is bounded below by $\int_{\underline{s}}^{\bar{s}} [F_D(p - U_D(t^*(s, \beta_D[\underline{d} + \eta, \bar{d}]))) - F_D(d + \eta)]dF_S$, which is the probability of breakdown if all $d \in [\underline{d}, \underline{d} + \eta]$ settle without trying to impose a solution. π_D is bounded above by $\int_{\underline{s}}^{\bar{s}} [F_D(p - U_D(t^*(s, \beta_D[\underline{d} + \eta, \bar{d}]))) - F_D(d + \eta)]dF_S + F_D(\underline{d} + \eta)$, which is the probability of breakdown if the $d \in [\underline{d}, \underline{d} + \eta]$ are assumed to impose a solution. The integrand is measurable and bounded, and $t^*(s, \beta_D[\underline{d} + \eta, \bar{d}])$ converges to $t^*(s, \beta_D[\underline{d}, \bar{d}])$ as η goes to zero. So the upper and lower bounds of π_D converge to $\int_{\underline{s}}^{\bar{s}} F_D(p - t^*(s, \beta_D[\underline{d}, \bar{d}]))dF_S = \pi_S$ as η goes to zero.

In case (ii), all s offer q in Γ_S regardless of the value of δ. The probability of breakdown is therefore the prior probability that D is dissatisfied: $\pi_S = F_D(p - U_D(q))$.

In Γ_D, $[\underline{d}, \hat{d}(\delta))$ pool on a non-serious demand, and all $d \in (\hat{d}(\delta), \bar{d}]$ reveal that they are satisfied. So, $\pi_D = \int_{\underline{s}}^{\bar{s}} F_D(p - U_D(x^*(s, \beta_D[\underline{d}, \hat{d}(\delta)])))dF_S$. If δ is close enough to one, then $\hat{d}(\delta)$ satisfies $x^*(s, \beta_D[\underline{d}, \hat{d}(\delta)]) = q$, which leaves $\pi_D = \int_{\underline{s}}^{\bar{s}} F_D(p - U_D(q))dF_S = F_D(p - U_D(q))$.

Turning to case (iii), if the common demand is non-serious, then all s reject $x(\underline{d}, \delta)$ and counter with $x^*(s, \beta_D[\underline{d}, \bar{d}])$. π_S and π_D are identical.

Suppose $x(\underline{d}, \delta)$ is serious. Let $\tilde{s}$ be the type whose optimal take-it-or-leave-it offer t^* is $\underline{d}$'s certainty equivalent: $t^*(\tilde{s}, \beta_D[\underline{d}, \bar{d}]) = \tilde{x}(\underline{d})$. (If no such type exists, define $\tilde{s}$ to be $\bar{s}$.) Because t^* is nondecreasing in s, all $s > \tilde{s}$ offer $\tilde{x}(\underline{d})$ in Γ_S and reach agreement with probability one. This leaves $\pi_S = \int_{\underline{s}}^{\tilde{s}} F_D(p - x^*(s, \beta_D[\underline{d}, \bar{d}]))dF_S$.

Now take $\hat{s}(\delta)$ to be the infimum of the set of s that accept $x(\underline{d}, \delta)$ in Γ_D. If $\tilde{s} \leq \hat{s}(\delta)$, then all $s > \hat{s}(\delta)$ accept $x(\underline{d}, \delta)$ in Γ_D and all $s \in [\tilde{s}, \hat{s}(\delta)]$ counter with $\tilde{x}(\underline{d})$, which D accepts. Thus the probability of breakdown in Γ_D is $\int_{\underline{s}}^{\tilde{s}} F_D(p - x^*(s, \beta_D[\underline{d}, \bar{d}]))dF_S$, which is just π_S.

Now assume that $\tilde{s} > \hat{s}(\delta)$ along a sequence of PBEs as $\delta_n \to 1$. Looking along a subsequence if necessary, then $x(\underline{d}, \delta_n)$ converges to some x^0 and $\hat{s}(\delta)$ converges to some $\hat{s}$. Because $\tilde{s} > \hat{s}(\delta)$, $\pi_D = \int_{\underline{s}}^{\hat{s}(\delta)} F_D(p - x^*(s, \beta_D[\underline{d}, \bar{d}]))dF_S$. Then to show that $|\pi_S - \pi_D|$ can be made arbitrarily small by taking δ close enough to one, it suffices to show that $\hat{s}(\delta)$ can be made arbitrarily close to $\tilde{s}$ for δ sufficiently close to one. Assume the contrary, i.e., $\hat{s}(\delta) \to \hat{s} < \tilde{s}$.

Because $x(\underline{d}, \delta_n)$ is serious, $\underline{d}$'s payoff if $x(\underline{d}, \delta_n)$ is accepted must be at least as large as its payoff to making a non-serious offer and then imposing a settlement in the second period: $U_D(x(\underline{d}, \delta_n)) \geq (1 - \delta_n)U_D(q) + \delta_n U_D(\tilde{x}(\underline{d}))$. This leaves $x^0 \geq \tilde{x}(\underline{d})$ and, accordingly, $U_S(1 - \tilde{x}(\underline{d})) \geq U_S(1 - x^0)$. Furthermore, s's acceptance for $s > \hat{s}(\delta)$ implies $U_S(1 - x(\underline{d}, \delta_n)) \geq (1 - \delta_n)U_S(b - q) + \delta_n T(x^*(\hat{s}(\delta_n), \beta_D[\underline{d}, \bar{d}]), \hat{s}(\delta_n), \beta_D[\underline{d}, \bar{d}])$. Letting δ_n go to one leaves $U_S(1 - x^0) \geq T(x^*(\hat{s}, \beta_D[\underline{d}, \bar{d}]), \hat{s}, \beta_D[\underline{d}, \bar{d}])$. But $\hat{s} < \tilde{s}$, so $x^*(\hat{s}, \beta_D[\underline{d}, \bar{d}]) = \max\{q, t^*(\hat{s}, \beta_D[\underline{d}, \bar{d}])\} < \tilde{x}(\underline{d}) = x^*(\tilde{s}, \beta_D[\underline{d}, \bar{d}])$. Since x^* is the unique offer that maximizes T and $\hat{s}$ could propose $\tilde{s}$'s optimal offer, $\hat{s}$ must strictly prefer to offer $x^*(\hat{s}, \beta_D[\underline{d}, \bar{d}])$ instead of $x^*(\tilde{s}, \beta_D[\underline{d}, \bar{d}])$: $T(x^*(\hat{s}, \beta_D[\underline{d}, \bar{d}]), \hat{s}, \beta_D[\underline{d}, \bar{d}]) > T(x^*(\tilde{s}, \beta_D[\underline{d}, \bar{d}]), \hat{s}, \beta_D[\underline{d}, \bar{d}])$. The fact that $\hat{s} < \tilde{s}$ also means that $\hat{s}$'s cost of an imposed settlement is strictly less that $\tilde{s}$'s cost and, therefore, $\hat{s}$'s payoff to making any offer is at least as large as $\tilde{s}$'s payoff to making this offer. Accordingly, $T(x^*(\tilde{s}, \beta_D[\underline{d}, \bar{d}]), \hat{s}, \beta_D[\underline{d}, \bar{d}]) \geq T(x^*(\tilde{s}, \beta_D[\underline{d}, \bar{d}]), \tilde{s}, \beta_D[\underline{d}, \bar{d}])$. Moreover, $\tilde{s}$'s maximum payoff is at least $U_S(1 - \tilde{x}(\underline{d}))$, which $\tilde{s}$ could obtain by offering $\tilde{x}(\underline{d})$. Combining the bounds on $U_S(1 - x^0)$ leaves $U_S(1 - \tilde{x}(\underline{d})) \geq U_S(1 - x^0) > T(x^*(\tilde{s}, \beta_D[\underline{d}, \bar{d}]), \tilde{s}, \beta_D[\underline{d}, \bar{d}]) \geq U_S(1 - \tilde{x}(\underline{d}))$. This contradiction ensures $|\pi_S(\delta) - \pi_D(\delta)|$ can be made arbitrarily small.

Appendix 4

The Formalities of Bargaining in the Shadow of Shifting Power

The model of bargaining in the shadow of shifting power modifies the game introduced in chapter 3 in three ways. First, only the declining state makes offers. The offers do not alternate back and forth as they did in chapter 3. Second, there is only one-sided asymmetric information. The declining state does not know the rising state's cost to fighting, but the rising state does know the declining state's cost. These two technical modifications simplify the formal analysis of the game. The third modification is substantive. The distribution of power changes over time. This appendix formalizes these modifications and characterizes the equilibria of the complete- and incomplete-information versions of the game. It also discusses the finding that the probability that a shift in power breaks down in war is independent of the speed of the shift.

A Model

A declining state, D, and a rising state, R, are bargaining about revising the distribution of territory or, more generally, about changing the existing international order and the distribution of benefits associated with that order. The set of feasible distributions is represented by the interval $[0, 1]$ where $x \in [0, 1]$ represents the rising state's share of the total benefits. The distribution of benefits at the outset of the game is q_0.

The declining state begins the game by either attacking or making a proposal $x_0 \in [0, 1]$. If D attacks, the game ends. If D makes a proposal, the rising state can accept it, reject it, or attack. If R attacks, the game ends. If R rejects the proposal, the first round ends, the distribution of benefits remains q_0, and play moves on to the second round. If R accepts the proposal, the first round also ends, the distribution of benefits changes to x_0, and play moves on to the second round. This sequence of moves is illustrated in figure 4.2 and is repeated in the second and all subsequent rounds. The game continues as long as neither side attacks.

To specify the states' payoffs, suppose the states never fight and let $q_0, q_1, q_2, \ldots$ be the distribution of benefits in each period. Then the rising and declining states' payoffs to this stream of benefits are $\sum_{k=0}^{\infty} \delta^k U_R(q_k)$ and $\sum_{k=0}^{\infty} \delta^k U_D(1 - q_k)$, respectively, where δ is the states' common discount factor. The utility functions U_R and U_D are also assumed to be increasing and concave, i.e., $U_R' > 0$, $U_D' > 0$, $U_R'' \leq 0$, and $U_D'' \leq 0$.[1]

Now suppose the states fight in round w. If the rising state prevails, which it does with probability p_w, it imposes its optimal distribution of benefits ($x = 1$), which it will enjoy forever. If R loses, D imposes its optimal distribution, which leaves R with zero forever. Thus, R's expected payoff to fighting at time w is:

$$\sum_{k=0}^{w-1} \delta^k U_R(q_k) + p_w \left(\sum_{k=w}^{\infty} \delta^k (U_R(1) - r) \right)$$

$$+ (1 - p_w) \left(\sum_{k=w}^{\infty} \delta^k (U_R(0) - r) \right)$$

where r is the rising state's cost of fighting and $q_0, q_1, \ldots, q_{w-1}$ is the distribution of benefits in the periods preceding the war. (This expression simply generalizes equation 4.1 by replacing x^{ρ_R} with $U_R(x)$.) Normalizing U_R so that $U_R(0) = 0$ and $U_R(1) = 1$ leaves:

$$\sum_{k=0}^{w-1} \delta^k U_R(q_k) + \frac{\delta^w(p_w - r)}{1 - \delta}$$

Similarly, the declining state's payoff to fighting in round w is:

$$\sum_{k=0}^{w-1} \delta^k U_D(1 - q_k) + \frac{\delta^w(1 - p_w - d)}{1 - \delta}$$

where d is the declining states' cost of fighting.

The declining state is uncertain about the rising state's willingness to use force to revise the status quo. In particular, D is unsure of the rising state's cost of fighting, r. The lower r, the lower the rising state's cost of fighting and the more willing it is to use force to overturn the status quo. Although D unsure of R's cost of fighting, D believes that r is distributed over the interval $[\underline{r}, \bar{r}]$ according to the cumulative probability distribution $Z(r)$. This distribution is assumed to have a nondecreasing hazard rate $H(r)$ and to be common knowledge.

---

[1] Chapter 3 focused on the specific example in which $U_R(x) = (1 - x)^{\rho_R}$ and $U_D(x) = x^{\rho_D}$.

To model a shift in the distribution of power, the probability that the rising state would prevail against the declining state will start out small and then rise throughout a shift in power, which lasts T periods. After the T-period shift, the distribution of power remains constant. More formally, assume that the distribution of power starts at $\underline{p}$ in the first round, rises by Δ in each of the next T periods, and then remains constant. In symbols, $p_k = \underline{p} + k\Delta$ for $0 \leq k \leq T$ and $p_k = \overline{p} = \underline{p} + T\Delta$ for $k > T$.

The Complete-Information Equilibrium

The game can be solved by backward programing if there is complete information, and doing so establishes proposition 4.1. To solve the game, consider the declining state's decision at time T. The distribution of power remains constant at $p = \overline{p} = \underline{p} + T\Delta$ for all future periods. Thus, results of appendix 3 can be used to solve the current game from time T forward. To wit, the satisfied state's optimal offer at T and in all future periods is to give the rising state just enough to ensure that it will not fight. R's payoff to fighting at any $t \geq T$ is $(\overline{p} - r)/(1 - \delta)$, so the declining state's optimal offer at all $t \geq T$ is $x_t^* = U_R^{-1}(\overline{p} - r)$.[2]

Now consider the declining state's decision at time $t < T$. If D is going to induce the rising state not to attack, then the declining state must offer the rising state just enough to make it indifferent between fighting in period t or waiting. The rising state's payoff to attacking is $(p_t - r)/(1 - \delta)$. R's payoff to waiting is the payoff to accepting D's offer in period t, $U_R(x_t^*)$, plus the discounted value of R's continuation payoff in the subgame starting in period $t + 1$. But in round $t + 1$, the declining state will offer just enough to leave the rising state indifferent between attacking and continuing. This indifference implies that R's continuation payoff in period $t + 1$ is just the payoff to attacking in that period. Thus, R's payoff to waiting in period t is $U_R(x_t^*) + \delta(p_{t+1} - r)/(1 - \delta)$. Equating

---

[2] There are, of course, two differences between the game in chapter 3 and the bargaining game that begins at time T. First, the satisfied or declining state makes all of the offers in the latter. Second, the current game continues as long as neither state attacks, whereas the game in chapter 3 ends as soon as an offer is accepted or one of the states attacks. It is easy to see, however, that these two differences have no effect on the solution to the game once p_t levels out at T, and the results derived in appendix 3 still apply. (Whether or not a game ends when an offer is accepted is discussed in more detail in appendix 5, where it is more consequential.)

R's payoff to attacking and waiting at $t < T$ gives:

$$x_t^* = U_R^{-1}\left(p_t - r - \frac{\delta(p_{t+1} - p_t)}{1 - \delta}\right)$$

$$= U_R^{-1}\left(p_t - r - \frac{\delta\Delta}{1 - \delta}\right)$$

Of course, x_t^* is the minimal amount R has to have at time t in order to be willing not to attack at that time. If, therefore, the rising state already controls more than x_t^* because its status quo share q_0 is larger than x_t^*, then the declining state does not have to offer anything more in that period. In this case D "offers" q_0. (As will be seen below, q_0 is typically larger than x_t^* at the outset of the shift, i.e., for t small. The intuition is that early in a shift, the rising state's incentive to wait until it is stronger is so large that the declining state does not have to make any concessions in order to induce R to wait.)

Thus, the complete-information shift will be peaceful if the declining state always prefers offering $\max\{q_0, x_t^*\}$ to attacking. That is, the shift passes peacefully if the following holds for $t < T$:

$$\frac{1 - p_t - d}{1 - \delta} \leq \sum_{j=t}^{\infty} \delta^{j-t} U_D(1 - \max\{q_0, x_j^*\}) \qquad (A4.1)$$

Proposition 4.1 claims that the complete-information shift is peaceful if the per-period shift is no larger than the cost of fighting ($\Delta \leq d + r$) and if the initial distribution of benefits favors the declining state. To formalize this latter condition, note that if the status quo were to remain fixed at q_0, then the declining state would be indifferent between fighting and living with the status quo if $U_D(1 - q_0) = 1 - \underline{p} - d$. Accordingly, we will define the declining state's stake, σ, to be the difference between its payoffs to the status quo and to fighting $\sigma = U_D(1 - q_0) - (1 - \underline{p} - d)$.

The larger D's stake, the lower R's status quo share and payoff. The assumption that both states are satisfied with the initial distribution of benefits given the initial distribution of power therefore puts an upper bound on D's stake. In particular, R is satisfied only if $U_R(q_0) \geq \underline{p} - r$, and this implies that D's stake is bounded above by $U_D(1 - U_R^{-1}(\underline{p} - r)) - (1 - \underline{p} - d)$.

In order to establish that expression A4.1 holds, it will be useful to describe the pattern of concessions x_t^*. Note first that the sequence x_t^* is strictly increasing for $t = 0, 1, \ldots, T$. R, moreover, is assumed to be dissatisfied at $\overline{p}$ if the distribution of benefits remains at q_0. (Otherwise

R could never credibly threaten to impose a new distribution and the status quo would never be revised.) Accordingly, $x_T^* > q_0$. Observe also that $x_0^* = p - r - \Delta\delta/(1 - \delta)$ may be less than q_0 if the rising state has a small stake in the status quo (e.g., if $U_R(q_0) = p - r$). Thus, x_t^* can be less than q_0 for t small. If $q_0 \geq x_0^*$, take m to be the integer that satisfies $x_{T-m}^* \leq q_0 < x_{T-m+1}^*$. If $q_0 < x_0^*$, take m to be $T + 1$. Then, we have $q_0 < x_t^*$ for all $t \geq T - m + 1$ and $q_0 \geq x_t^*$ for all $0 \leq t \leq T - m$.

Backward programming shows that expression A4.1 holds. The analysis in appendix 3 ensures that the declining state prefers offering x_T^* to fighting for all $t \geq T$. Working backward from time T, D prefers conceding x_{T-1}^* to fighting if:

$$\frac{1 - p_{T-1} - d}{1 - \delta} \leq U_D(1 - x_{T-1}^*) + \sum_{k=1}^{\infty} \delta^k U_D(1 - x_T^*)$$

Note, however, that $U_D(x) \geq x$ and $x \geq U_R^{-1}(x)$, because U_D and U_R are concave and have been normalized so that $U_D(0) = U_R(0) = 0$ and $U_D(1) = U_R(1) = 1$. Substituting for $x_{T-1}^* = U_R^{-1}(p_{T-1} - r - \delta\Delta)/(1 - \delta)$ and $x_T^* = U_R^{-1}(p_{T-1} + \Delta - r)$ then shows that the previous inequality is sure to hold if:

$$\frac{1 - p_{T-1} - d}{1 - \delta} \leq 1 - \left(p_{T-1} - r - \frac{\delta\Delta}{1 - \delta}\right) + \frac{\delta(1 - (p_{T-1} + \Delta - r))}{1 - \delta}$$

This holds as long as $0 \leq d + r$, which is true by assumption. Thus, D offers x_{T-1}^*.

Arguing by induction, suppose that D prefers conceding x_t^* to fighting for all t larger than some N where $N \geq T - m + 1$. Because $N \geq T - m + 1$, D's optimal offer is $x_N^* = \max\{q_0, x_N^*\}$ because $x_N^* > q_0$. To see that D prefers conceding x_N^* to fighting, note that if D attacks at time N, it obtains $(1 - p_N - d)/(1 - \delta)$. If it offers x_N^*, it obtains $U_D(1 - x_N^*)$ in the current period and can ensure itself of at least $\delta(1 - (p_N + \Delta) - d)/(1 - \delta)$ by attacking in the next period. D, therefore, prefers to offer x_N^* as long as:

$$\frac{1 - p_N - d}{1 - \delta} \leq U_D(1 - x_N^*) + \frac{\delta(1 - (p_N + \Delta) - d)}{1 - \delta}$$

which also holds as long as $0 \leq d + r$. In sum, the declining state always prefers conceding x_t^* to fighting as long as the $x_t^* > q_0$, i.e., for all $t \geq T - m + 1$.

Now consider D's decision at time $T - m$. Since $x_{T-m}^* \leq q_0$, D does not have to concede anything in this period in order to induce R not to fight. Consequently, D prefers living with the status quo in this period and conceding $x^*_{T-m+1}, x^*_{T-m+2}, \ldots, x^*_T$ in the future to fighting if

$$\frac{1 - p_{T-m} - d}{1 - \delta} \leq U_D(1 - q_0) + \sum_{k=1}^{m-1} \delta^k U_D(1 - x^*_{T-m+k})$$

$$+ \sum_{k=m}^{\infty} \delta^k U_D(1 - x^*_T)$$

Because of concavity and normalizations of U_D and U_R, the previous inequality is sure to hold whenever:

$$\frac{1 - p_{T-m} - d}{1 - \delta} \leq U_D(1 - q_0) + \sum_{k=1}^{m-1} \delta^k \left[1 - \left(p_{T-m} + k\Delta - r - \frac{\delta\Delta}{1 - \delta}\right)\right]$$

$$+ \sum_{k=m}^{\infty} \delta^k [1 - (p_{T-m} + m\Delta - r)]$$

Simplifying this inequality using the fact that $\sum_{k=1}^{m-1} \delta^k k = \sum_{k=1}^{m-1} \sum_{j=k}^{m-1} \delta^j = \sum_{k=1}^{m-1} [\delta^k (1 - \delta^{m-k})/(1 - \delta)] = \delta(1 - \delta^{m-1})/(1 - \delta)^2 - (m - 1)\delta^m/(1 - \delta)$ gives:

$$\frac{1 - p_{T-m} - d}{1 - \delta} \leq U_D(1 - q_0) + \frac{\delta(1 - p_{T-m} + r)}{1 - \delta} - \frac{\delta\Delta}{1 - \delta}$$

Rewriting this expression in terms of terms of the declining state's stake in the status quo yields $\delta\Delta \leq (1 - \delta)\sigma + \delta(d + r) + (1 - \delta)(T - m)\Delta$. This surely holds as long as $\delta\Delta \leq (1 - \delta)\sigma + \delta(d + r)$. (If the shift in power only lasts one period, i.e., if $T = 1$, then $m = T$ and the upper bounds on $\delta\Delta$ in the last two inequalities are the same.) Finally, D's stake is bounded above by $U_D(1 - U_R^{-1}(p - r)) - (1 - p - d)$, which is at least as large as $d + r$. If, therefore, D's stake is at least $d + r$, then D prefers to offer x^*_{T-m} as long as $\delta\Delta \leq d + r$.

The only decisions that remain to be considered are those that D makes at $t < T - m$. If D attacks at t it receives $(1 - p_t - d)/(1 - \delta)$, whereas it obtains $U_D(1 - q_0) + \delta(1 - (p_t + \Delta) - d)/(1 - \delta)$ if it does not make any concessions and attacks in the next period. The latter is at least as large as the former if $\sigma \geq \delta\Delta$, which also holds as long as $d + r \geq \delta\Delta$ and $\sigma \geq d + r$.

Thus, D prefers to appease R throughout the shift in power in the complete-information game if its initial stake in the status quo is at least $d + r$ and if the total per-period cost of fighting is at least as large as Δ (and therefore $\delta\Delta$).

The Asymmetric-Information Equilibrium

In the unique equilibrium, the declining state makes a nondecreasing sequence of offers $x_0^*, x_1^*, \ldots x_{T-1}^*, x_T^*$ during the shift. A rising state of type r accepts x_t^* and the distribution of benefits becomes $q_t = x_t^*$ if r's payoff to accepting x_t^* and continuing on to the next period is larger than its payoff to fighting. These strategies create a series of cut-points $\tilde{r}_0 \leq \tilde{r}_1 \leq \tilde{r}_2 \leq \tilde{r}_3 \leq \cdots \leq \tilde{r}_T$ where $\tilde{r}_t$ is just indifferent between accepting x_t^* and fighting.

Although the game has asymmetric information, it turns out that it can be solved by backward programming. Consider the declining state's decision at time T when the support of D's beliefs is $[\tilde{r}_{T-1}, \bar{r}]$. The distribution of power levels out at $\bar{p}$ at time T, and the argument made in appendix 3 implies that D will make its optimal take-it-or-leave-it offer.

To characterize this offer, note that $r \in [\tilde{r}_{T-1}, \bar{r}]$ rejects x_T if the payoff to fighting is greater than the payoff to accepting, i.e., if $\bar{p} - r = p_T - r > U_R(x_T)$. Therefore, the probability that R rejects x_T is $\Pr\{r : r \in [\tilde{r}_{T-1}, p_T - U_R(x_T)]\} / \Pr\{r : r \in [\tilde{r}_{T-1}, \bar{r}]\} = (Z(p_T - U_R(x_T)) - Z(\tilde{r}_{T-1})) / (1 - Z(\tilde{r}_{T-1}))$. Accordingly, D's expected payoff to offering x_T given a lower bound of $\tilde{r}_{T-1}$ on the support of D's beliefs is:

$$V_T(x_T | \tilde{r}_{T-1}) = \left(\frac{U_D(1 - x_T)}{1 - \delta} \right) \frac{1 - Z(p_T - U_R(x_T))}{1 - Z(\tilde{r}_{T-1})}$$

$$+ \left(\frac{1 - p_T - d}{1 - \delta} \right) \frac{Z(p_T - U_R(x_T)) - Z(\tilde{r}_{T-1})}{1 - Z(\tilde{r}_{T-1})}$$

The assumption that Z has a nondecreasing hazard rate ensures that V_T is concave and thus a unique value of x_T maximizes V_T. Letting x_T^* denote this maximizing value, then x_T^* is defined implicitly by the expression:

$$U_D'(1 - x_T^*)$$
$$= [U_D(1 - x_T^*) - (1 - p_T - d)]H(p_T - U_R(x_T^*))U_R'(x_T^*) \tag{A4.2}$$

where $H(r)$ is the hazard rate $Z'(r)/(1 - Z(r))$.

Three things should be noted about this equation. First, $\tilde{r}_T$ follows immediately from x_T^* since $\tilde{r}_T$ is just indifferent between accepting x_T^* and fighting. Consequently, $\bar{p} - \tilde{r}_T = U_R(x_T^*)$, which leaves $\tilde{r}_T = \bar{p} - U_R(x_T^*)$. Second, expression A4.2 presumes an "interior" solution in that the x_T^* that satisfies the first order condition $\partial V_T(x_T | \tilde{r}_{T-1}) / \partial x_T = 0$ must be at least as large as the existing status quo, which is x_{T-1}^*. This requirement is equivalent to saying that $\tilde{r}_T$ must be at least as large as $\tilde{r}_{T-1}$. The presumption of an interior solution will be discussed below. Finally, note that x_T^* does not depend on the lower bound of the support, $\tilde{r}_{T-1}$. This independence is the key that makes it possible to backwards program the game.

To determine D's optimal offer x_{T-1}^*, suppose the declining state offers x_{T-1} and let $\tilde{r}_{T-2}$ be the type that was just indifferent between accepting x_{T-2}^* and fighting. This means $\tilde{r}_{T-2}$ is the lower bound of the support of D's beliefs when D offers x_{T-1}. Then the probability that R rejects x_{T-1} is $(Z(\tilde{r}_{T-1}(x_{T-1}) - Z(\tilde{r}_{T-2})))/(1 - Z(\tilde{r}_{T-2}))$ where $\tilde{r}_{T-1}(x_{T-1})$ is the type that is just indifferent between accepting x_{T-1} and fighting. This implies that D's expected payoff to offering x_{T-1} is:

$$V_{T-1}(x_{T-1}|\tilde{r}_{T-2})$$
$$= \left(\frac{1 - p_{T-1} - d}{1 - \delta}\right) \frac{Z(\tilde{r}_{T-1}(x_{T-1})) - Z(\tilde{r}_{T-2})}{1 - Z(\tilde{r}_{T-2})}$$
$$+ \left[U_D(1 - x_{T-1}) + \delta V_T(x_T^*|\tilde{r}_{T-1}(x_{T-1}))\right] \frac{1 - Z(\tilde{r}_{T-1}(x_{T-1}))}{1 - Z(\tilde{r}_{T-2})}$$

The first step in solving for the optimal offer x_{T-1}^* is eliminating $\tilde{r}_{T-1}(x_{T-1})$ from the previous expression. If $\tilde{r}_{T-1}(x_{T-1})$ attacks, it obtains $(p_{T-1} - \tilde{r}_{T-1}(x_{T-1}))/(1 - \delta)$. If, however, $\tilde{r}_{T-1}(x_{T-1})$ continues, it receives $U_R(x_{T-1})$ in round $T - 1$ plus the discounted value of its continuation payoff in the subgame beginning in period T.

This continuation payoff is just $\tilde{r}_{T-1}(x_{T-1})$'s payoff to fighting in round T, which is $(p_T - \tilde{r}_T(x_{T-1}))/(1 - \delta)$. To see that this is in fact the continuation payoff, note that the declining state never offers more in period T than the certainty equivalent of the toughest type that it might be facing. (Offering the certainty equivalent of the toughest type ensures that D's proposal is accepted whereas offering any more than this only lowers D's payoff when the offer is accepted.) Thus, D either offers $\tilde{r}_{T-1}(x_{T-1})$ its certainty equivalent to fighting or D offers less than $\tilde{r}_{T-1}(x_{T-1})$'s certainty equivalent, in which case $\tilde{r}_{T-1}(x_{T-1})$ attacks. In either case, $\tilde{r}_{T-1}(x_{T-1})$ obtains its payoff to fighting.

But $\tilde{r}_{T-1}(x_{T-1})$ is by definition indifferent between fighting and accepting x_{T-1}. This yields:

$$\frac{p_{T-1} - \tilde{r}_{T-1}(x_{T-1})}{1 - \delta} = U_R(x_{T-1}) + \frac{\delta}{1 - \delta}(p_T - \tilde{r}_{T-1}(x_{T-1}))$$

$$\tilde{r}_{T-1}(x_{T-1}) = \overline{p} - U_R(x_{T-1}) - \frac{\Delta}{1 - \delta}$$

Substituting the expression for $\tilde{r}_{T-1}(x_{T-1})$ in $V_{T-1}(x_{T-1}|\tilde{r}_{T-2})$ and differentiating with respect to x_{T-1} yields D's optimal offer in period $T-1$. This offer, x^*_{T-1}, solves:

$$U'_D(1 - x^*_{T-1}) = [U_D(1 - x^*_{T-1}) - (1 - p_T - d) + \Delta/(1 - \delta)]$$
$$\times H(p_T - U_R(x^*_{T-1}) - \Delta/(1 - \delta))U'_R(x^*_{T-1})$$

This expression also presumes an interior solution. Such a solution exists as long as the type that is just indifferent between accepting x^*_{T-1} is larger than the lower bound of the support of D's beliefs, i.e., as long as $\tilde{r}_{T-2} \leq \tilde{r}_{T-1}(x^*_{T-1})$. This requirement will be discussed further below. Finally, note that x^*_{T-1} does not depend on the lower bound of D's support, $\tilde{r}_{T-2}$, just as x^*_T did not depend on the lower bound $\tilde{r}_{T-1}$.

Continuing in this way generates a nondecreasing sequence of offers that forms the basis of the unique equilibrium of the game. Let $\pi_t = p_t - \delta\Delta/(1 - \delta)$ for $t < T$, then x^*_t solves:

$$U'_D(1 - x^*_t) = [U_D(1 - x^*_t) - (1 - \pi_t - d)]$$
$$\times H(\pi_t - U_R(x^*_t))U'_R(x^*_t) \tag{A4.3}$$

(This equation is equivalent to equation 4.3, which defines the optimal offers in proposition 4.2.) Differentiating expression A4.3 implicitly and recalling that the hazard rate H is nondecreasing then gives $\partial x^*_t/\partial \pi_t > 0$. Thus, the sequence $x^*_0, x^*_1, \ldots, x^*_T$ is strictly increasing.

Since this sequence is strictly increasing, there exists a smallest T' such that $x^*_{T'}$ is at least as large as the initial status quo distribution q_0. In equilibrium, D offers q_0 for $0 \leq t \leq T' - 1$, x^*_t for $T' \leq t \leq T - 1$, and x^*_T for $T \geq t$. The cut-points are given by $\tilde{r}_t = \max\{\underline{r}, \pi_t - U_R(x^*_t)\}$ for $1 \leq t \leq T - 1$ and $\tilde{r}_t = p_T - U_R(x^*_T)$ for $t \geq T$.

The construction of the sequence of offers $\{x^*_t\}$ and cut-points $\{\tilde{r}_t\}$ has been based on the assumption that maximizing the continuation payoff $V_t(x_t|\tilde{r}_{t-1})$ yields an interior solution. This is sure to be the case if the type that is just indifferent between accepting x^*_t and fighting, namely $\tilde{r}_t$, is contained in the support of types actually facing D at that time. That is, there will be an interior solution if $\tilde{r}_{t-1} \leq \tilde{r}_t$. But, $\tilde{r}_t$ is also endogenous. So, all of the maximization problems will have interior solutions if the sequence of cut-points generated by the sequence of offers $\{x^*_t\}$ is nondecreasing, i.e., if $\tilde{r}_0 \leq \tilde{r}_1 \leq \tilde{r}_2 \leq \tilde{r}_3 \leq \cdots \leq \tilde{r}_T$. Now let expression A4.3

define x_t^* implicitly as a function of π_t. Then, $\tilde{r}_t = \max\{\underline{r}, \pi_t - U_R(x_t^*)\}$ is sure to be nondecreasing and the maximization problem is certain to have an interior solution if $\partial(\pi - U_R(x^*(\pi)))/\partial\pi \geq 0$. A shift in power that satisfies this condition will be said to be *regular*.

This completes the derivation of the asymmetric-information equilibrium for regular shifts, which is all that will be done here. However, two final remarks are in order. The first provides a less formal, more intuitive description of what it means for a shift to be regular. To see the substantive significance of the assumption that $\partial(p - U_R(x^*(p)))/\partial p \geq 0$, consider the situation in which D and R are bargaining about revising the territorial status quo in a strategic setting in which the distribution of power remains constant at a level p. Let $x^*(p)$ denote D's optimal offer in this "degenerate" game. This degenerate game is essentially the same as that studied in chapter 3, and $x^*(p)$ solves expression A4.2 when p is substituted for p_T. Then the probability of war if D offers $x^*(p)$ is the probability that r satisfies $p - r > U_R(x^*(p))$, which is $Z(p - U_R(x^*(p)))$. Let $w(p)$ denote this probability.

In a comparative-statics analysis of the game in which the distribution of war remains fixed throughout the bargaining, one might like to know how the probability of war, $w(p)$, varies with the distribution of power p. (In fact, this was precisely what we asked when we considered the relation between the distribution of power and the probability of war in chapter 3.) Suppose, for example, p increases to p'. How does this affect the risk of war?

If D did not alter its offer at all, then the probability of war would go up by $Z(p' - U_R(x^*(p))) - Z(p - U_R(x^*(p)))$, which is certainly nonnegative and is strictly positive if Z is increasing. D, however, does increase its offer when p increases as $\partial x^*(p)/\partial p > 0$. Indeed, D's offer $x^*(p')$ could at least in principle be so much larger than $x^*(p)$ that this larger offer more than offsets the increase in risk. That is, D could offer so much more that the risk of war actually declines when p increases from p to p'. In symbols, $p' - U_R(x^*(p')) < p - U_R(x^*(p))$ even though $p' > p$.

Although this is analytically possible, it seems substantively implausible and the assumption that $\partial(p - U_R(x^*(p)))/\partial p \geq 0$ rules out this possibility. More formally, the assumption $\partial(p - U_R(x^*(p)))/\partial p \geq 0$ implies that the probability of war is nondecreasing in p, i.e., $\partial w/\partial p = Z'(p - U_R(x^*(p))) \cdot \partial(p - U_R(x^*(p)))/\partial p \geq 0$. Accordingly, a regular shift in the distribution of power is one in which D does not fully offset the risk caused by an increase in p.

The second remark focuses on the finding that faster shifts are no more likely to break down in war than slower shifts. The overall probability of breakdown is the probability that R rejects an offer at some point in the shift in power. This is just $Z(\tilde{r}_T)$. But $\tilde{r}_T = \bar{p} - U_R(x_T^*)$, so the probability of breakdown is a function of D's final offer x_T^*. Expression A4.2 however, formally establishes that this offer is independent of the speed of the shift Δ.

Appendix 5

The Formalities of the Alignment

This appendix formally specifies the alignment game that was discussed informally in chapter 5. The appendix then establishes a claim made in that chapter: If the distribution of power mirrors the distribution of benefits and the potential attacker actually attacks one of the other states, then the third state's payoff to aligning with the larger of the other two states is greater than its payoff to aligning with smaller of the other two states (see page 182 above). More concretely, if A attacks S_1 when the distributions of power and benefits are the same, then S_2's payoff to aligning with the larger of A and S_1 is greater than its payoff to aligning with the smaller of the two states.

The Alignment Game

The alignment model is a two-stage game among the three players A, S_1, and S_2. The first stage determines which two of these states survives the first stage and move on to the second. The outcome of the first stage also determines what the distributions of power and benefits are between the two surviving states at the outset of the second stage.

Figure 5.1 describes the sequence of moves in the first stage. The states also begin the game with a distribution of territory q_A, q_1, q_2 where $q_A + q_1 + q_2 = 1$, and a distribution of power p_1^A and p_2^1 where $p_{\text{subscript}}^{\text{superscript}}$ is the probability that the state or coalition denoted in the superscript defeats and thereby eliminates the state or coalition in the subscript. (The probability that A defeats S_2, which is p_2^A, is not a primitive and is derived below from p_1^A and p_2^1.) Given these preliminaries, two things must be done to complete the specification of the first stage.

First, the probabilities of the random moves (i.e., the moves Nature makes) must be defined as a function of the initial distribution of power p_1^A and p_2^1. To derive these probabilities from p_1^A and p_2^1, it is convenient to think of each state as having some underlying military capability. Let k_A, k_1, and k_2 denote these capabilities where $k_A + k_1 + k_2 = 1$. Then the probability that state i defeats j is $p_j^i = k_i/(k_i + k_j)$, and the probability that state i prevails over the coalition composed of j and n is $p^i_{j,n} = k_i/[k_i + g(k_j + k_n)]$ where g measures the extent to which military capabilities cumulate.

To solve for p^A_2 in terms of p^A_1 and p^1_2, note that $p^i_j = k_i/(k_i + k_j)$ implies $k_i/k_j = p^i_j/(1 - p^i_j)$. Then eliminating k_A and k_2 from $p^A_2 = k_A/(k_A + k_2)$ yields:

$$p^A_2 = \frac{p^A_1 p^1_2}{p^A_1 p^1_2 + (1 - p^A_1)(1 - p^1_2)}.$$

It is also easy to find $p^i_{j,n}$ (and therefore $p^{j,n}_i$ as $p^{j,n}_i = 1 - p^i_{j,n}$). To wit,

$$p^i_{j,n} = \left[\frac{k_i + g(k_j + k_n)}{k_i}\right]^{-1}$$

$$= \left[1 + g\left(\frac{k_j}{k_i} + \frac{k_n}{k_i}\right)\right]^{-1}$$

$$= \left[1 + g\left(\frac{p^j_i}{1 - p^j_i} + \frac{p^n_i}{1 - p^n_i}\right)\right]^{-1}$$

$$= \left[1 + g\left(\frac{1 - p^i_j}{p^i_j} + \frac{1 - p^i_n}{p^i_n}\right)\right]^{-1}$$

$$= \frac{p^i_j p^i_n}{p^i_j p^i_n + g(p^i_j p^i_n + (1 - p^i_j)(1 - p^i_n))}.$$

The last task to be done in defining the first stage is to describe the possible outcomes of this stage. There are two kinds of outcomes. If the game ends in the first stage because A does not attack or because one state eliminates the other two states, then the states' payoffs have to be specified. If, by contrast, two states survive the first stage, then the distributions of power and benefits between these two states must be characterized. These distributions constitute the initial conditions under which the second-stage bargaining occurs. It will be convenient to represent this outcome by the four-tuple $(n, m, \hat{q}_n, \hat{p}_n)$ where n and m are the two surviving states, $\hat{q}_n$ is state n's share of the territory at the outset of bargaining ($\hat{q}_m = 1 - \hat{q}_n$), and $\hat{p}_n$ is the probability that n prevails if the bargaining breaks down in war.

If A does not attack, the game ends and the distribution of benefits is unchanged. The states' payoffs in this case are q_A, q_1, and q_2. Now suppose that A attacks both S_1 and S_2. If A prevails, it eliminates both S_1 and S_2 and the game ends. A obtains all of the territory and receives a payoff of one less the cost of fighting, i.e., $1 - c_A(q_1 + q_2)$. S_1, by contrast, retains control of nothing and pays the cost of fighting. Its payoff is

$-p_2^1(c_1 q_A)$ where $c_1 q_A$ is the total cost S_1 would bear if it fought A alone. Similarly, S_2's payoff if A eliminates it is $-(1 - p_2^1)c_2 q_A$.

If, by contrast, A loses when it attacks both S_1 and S_2, the first stage ends and S_1 and S_2 move on to the second. By assumption, when two states fight together and eliminate a third, the distribution of power between the two victors after the war is presumed to be the same as it was before the war. Consequently, the distribution of power between S_1 and S_2 at the start of the second stage is p_2^1. We also assume that the fighting that eliminates one state divides that state's territory in proportion to the distribution of power between the two victorious states. Consequently, S_1's share of the territory at the end of the first stage is its original share plus what it captures from A: $q_1 + p_2^1 q_A$. S_2's share is $q_2 + (1 - p_2^1)q_A$. If, therefore, A attacks both S_1 and S_2 and loses, then the four-tuple $(S_1, S_2, q_1 + p_2^1 q_A, p_2^1)$ defines the conditions for the subsequent bargaining.

If A attacks only one of the other states, say S_i, then the outcome of the first stage depends on what S_j $(j \neq i)$ does. If S_j waits and A wins, then A obtains all of S_i's territory and acquires all of its military capabilities. The resulting outcome is the four-tuple $(A, S_j, q_A + q_i, p_j^{A,i})$. If S_j waits and S_i prevails, the outcome is $(S_i, S_j, q_A + q_i, p_j^{A,i})$.

Suppose instead that S_j aligns with A when A strikes S_i. Then the game ends if S_i prevails, and S_i captures all of the territory at cost $c_i(q_A + q_j)$. If the coalition of A and S_j prevails, then A and S_j divide S_i's territory and the distribution of power between them remains p_j^A. The outcome is $(A, S_j, q_A + p_j^A q_i, p_j^A)$.

Finally, assume A attacks S_i and S_j aligns with S_i. If A prevails, the game is over. If S_i and S_j triumph, then the second stage begins with $(S_i, S_j, q_i + p_j^i q_A, p_j^i)$.

If two states survive the first stage, then their payoffs depend on the outcome of the bargaining, which depends on the initial distributions of power and benefits between the bargainers. Suppose that the alignment stage results in the four-tuple $(n, m, \widehat{q}_n, \widehat{p}_n)$. Then in keeping with the bargaining model discussed in chapter 3, n is dissatisfied if its payoff to fighting is greater than its payoff to living with the status quo: $\widehat{p}_n - c_n \widehat{q}_m > \widehat{q}_n$. Similarly, m is dissatisfied if $\widehat{p}_m - c_m \widehat{q}_n > \widehat{q}_m$. (As before, both states cannot be dissatisfied at the same time.)

The payoffs associated with $(n, m, \widehat{q}_n, \widehat{p}_n)$ depend on whether or not one of the states is dissatisfied. If n is dissatisfied, then we assume that m concedes just enough territory to n to make it indifferent between attacking and accepting the offer. In symbols, n offers x where $x =$

$\widehat{p}_n - c_n\widehat{q}_m$. The payoffs associated with $(n, m, \widehat{q}_n, \widehat{p}_n)$ if n is dissatisfied therefore are $\widehat{p}_n - c_n\widehat{q}_m$ for n and $1 - (\widehat{p}_n - c_n\widehat{q}_m)$ for m. If, by contrast, m is dissatisfied, then m's payoff is $\widehat{p}_m - c_m\widehat{q}_n$ and n's payoff is $1 - (\widehat{p}_m - c_m\widehat{q}_n)$. If both states are satisfied, neither can credibly threaten to use force to revise the status quo. In this case, n's payoff is $\widehat{q}_n$ and m's is $1 - \widehat{q}_n$.

The definitions of the payoffs associated with $(n, m, \widehat{q}_n, \widehat{p}_n)$ complete the specification of the alignment game. This perfect-information game is readily solved by backward programming, and the results of doing so for different parameter values are reported in chapter 5. However, two related remarks about different ways of thinking about the payoffs associated with $(n, m, \widehat{q}_n, \widehat{p}_n)$ are in order.

First and most directly, we can simply take these payoffs to be part of the definition of the game. In this interpretation, there is no formally specified bargaining game in the second stage. Rather, the bargaining game discussed in chapter 3 is only used informally to motivate the definition of the states' payoffs.

Alternatively, we may conceive of the payoffs associated with $(n, m, \widehat{q}_n, \widehat{p}_n)$ as those that actually do result from solving a well-defined bargaining game. Indeed, we might use the bargaining game discussed in chapter 3 and formally analyzed in appendix 3 in this way. Although this can be done, there is an important difference between the assumptions underlying that game and those underlying the alignment game. The former assumed that the cost of fighting was constant, whereas the cost of fighting in the alignment game depends on an adversary's size. Because of this difference, the bargaining game in chapter 3 provides an unnatural model of the bargaining in the alignment game.

In chapter 3, the bargaining and the game end as soon as one of the states accepts an offer. There are no further opportunities to revise the distribution of territory. This assumption simplifies the model and the characterization of the equilibria. But, we can easily imagine a more complicated bargaining game in which offers and counter-offers can continue as long as no state has attacked. In this formulation, the distribution of territory could be revised multiple times.

As it happens, the solutions to the simple game and to the more complicated one are the same if the cost of fighting remains constant.[1] Recall what happens in the simple game in which the bargaining ends as soon as

---

[1] This equivalence also presumes that the satisfied state makes the first offer. Matters are somewhat more complicated but essentially the same if the dissatisfied state makes the first offer and the discount factor is close to one.

a proposal is accepted. With complete information, the satisfied state offers the dissatisfied state its certainty equivalent for fighting, and the dissatisfied state accepts. This revision in the distribution of territory leaves both states satisfied. Accordingly, the distribution of territory would not be amended any further even if the bargaining could continue.

If there were asymmetric information in the simple game, then the satisfied state would make its optimal take-it-or-leave-it offer. The dissatisfied state then either attacks or accepts depending on whether or not its payoff to fighting is greater than its payoff to accepting the offer. Because the only types that accept an offer are those that prefer it to fighting, neither state would be willing to use force to change the distribution of territory again if the first proposal is accepted. Thus there would be no subsequent revisions even if the states could continue to negotiate. It does not matter whether the bargaining can continue or not if the cost of fighting (or more generally the payoff to fighting) remains constant.

But it does matter whether or not the bargaining can continue if the cost of fighting depends on an adversary's size. If the bargaining ends as soon as a proposal has been accepted, then the status quo will be revised only once. If, by contrast, the bargaining can continue as long as neither state attacks, then the status quo will be revised infinitely often.

To see that this is so, suppose the bargaining ends as soon as one state accepts an offer. Then the satisfied state in this formulation again offers the dissatisfied state its certainty equivalent. In symbols, the satisfied state grants the dissatisfied state $x^* = p - d(1 - q)$ where p is the probability that the dissatisfied state prevails, d is its marginal cost of fighting, and $1 - q$ is the status quo size of the satisfied state.

Now assume that the bargaining can continue until one of the states attacks. The satisfied state no longer makes one large concession equal to x^*. Rather, it makes a series of concessions $x_0, x_1, x_2, \ldots$ where the first offer x_0 is smaller than x^* and the series of concessions converges in the limit to $(p - d)/(1 - d)$. It is easy to verify that this limit is larger than x^* as long as the dissatisfied state is actually dissatisfied (i.e., as long as $p - d(1 - q) > q$). Thus the initial offer x_0 is less than what would have been offered if the bargaining stopped after one revision (i.e., $x_0 < x^*$) and the latter offers are larger than what would have been offered if the bargaining stopped after one revision (i.e., $x^* < (p - d)/(1 - d)$).

To derive these concessions, consider the satisfied state's first offer x_0. If the dissatisfied state rejects this offer and fights, it obtains $[p - d(1 - q)]/(1 - \delta)$. If, however, the dissatisfied state accepts x_0, it can always fight in the next period when its cost will be less because its adversary will be smaller. The payoff to doing so is $x_0 + \delta[p - d(1 - x_0)]/(1 - \delta)$. The satisfied state can therefore induce the dissatisfied state to postpone an attack for at least the current period by offering an x_0 such that

$$\frac{p - d(1 - q)}{1 - \delta} = x_0 + \frac{\delta(p - d(1 - x_0))}{1 - \delta}$$

$$x_0 = \frac{(1 - \delta)(p - d) + dq}{1 - \delta + \delta d}$$

More generally, the satisfied state can get the dissatisfied state not to attack at time t when the distribution of territory is x_{t-1} by conceding $x_t = [(1 - \delta)(p - d) + dx_{t-1}]/(1 - \delta + \delta d)$. A straightforward application of the proof of proposition 1 in Fearon (1996) shows that x_t is in fact the equilibrium offer of an underlying bargaining game in which the satisfied state makes all of the offers and the bargaining continues as long as neither state attacks.[2]

Thus, whether or not the bargaining can continue after a proposal has been accepted affects the pattern of concessions when the payoff to fighting is a function of past concessions. But, interestingly, it does not affect the states' payoffs in the game. The dissatisfied state's payoff to receiving $x_0, x_1, x_2, \ldots$ is just $\sum_{t=0}^{\infty} \delta^t x_t$. It is easy, if tedious, to solve for x_t recursively for q to show:

$$x_t = \sum_{j=0}^{t}\left[\left(\frac{d}{1 - \delta + \delta d}\right)^j \frac{(1 - \delta)(p - d)}{1 - \delta + \delta d}\right] + \left(\frac{d}{1 - \delta + \delta d}\right)^{t+1} q$$

$$= \frac{p - d}{1 - d}\left[1 - \left(\frac{d}{1 - \delta + \delta d}\right)^{t+1}\right] + \left(\frac{d}{1 - \delta + \delta d}\right)^{t+1} q$$

Substituting this expression for x_t in $\sum_{t=0}^{\infty} \delta^t x_t$ gives

$$\sum_{t=0}^{\infty} \delta^t x_t = \frac{p - d(1 - q)}{1 - \delta}.$$

But this payoff is just what the dissatisfied state would have received if the bargaining had ended as soon as a state accepted an offer. As we have seen, the satisfied state would offer $x^* = p - d(1 - q)$ in those circumstances, and the dissatisfied state's payoff would be $[p - d(1 -$

---

[2] Fearon studies a model in which the distribution of power is a function of the distribution of territory. Thus, a concession to an adversary in the current period makes that adversary stronger in the next, and this increases the adversary's payoff to attacking. The analysis of that model carries over to the present situation in which a concession in the current period reduces an adversary's cost of fighting in the next and thereby raises its payoff to attacking.

$q)]/(1-\delta)$. (An intuition for the equivalence of these payoffs is that regardless of whether or not the bargaining continues, the satisfied state obtains all of the surplus saved by not fighting. Whether or not the bargaining continues only affects the way that this surplus is collected.)

In sum, we can think of the payoffs associated above with the outcome $(n, m, \widehat{q}_n, \widehat{p}_n)$ as the average payoffs of the states in the rather unnatural bargaining game in which the interaction stops as soon as an offer is accepted. Or, we can take the payoffs associated with $(n, m, \widehat{q}_n, \widehat{p}_n)$ to be the average payoffs of a bargaining game in which the bargaining can continue as long as no state attacks.

Aligning with Larger States

Consider now the claim that if the distribution of power mirrors the distribution of benefits and the potential attacker actually attacks one of the other states, then the third state's payoff to aligning with the larger and therefore more powerful of the other two states is greater than its payoff to aligning with smaller of the other two states. To establish this, suppose A attacks S_1. Then the claim asserts that S_2's payoff to aligning with the larger of A and S_1 is greater than the payoff to aligning with the smaller of those two states.

Because the distribution of power mirrors the distribution of benefits, S_2 and its coalition partner will be satisfied with each other if they move on to the bargaining stage. This means that S_2's payoff to aligning with A is $p_1^{A,2}(q_2 + p_A^2 q_1) - c_2 p_A^2 q_1$. Similarly, S_2's payoff to aligning with S_1 is $p_A^{1,2}(q_2 + p_1^2 q_A) - c_2 p_1^2 q_A$.

The fact that the distributions of power and benefits mirror each other also means that we can treat each state's territory as a measure of its military capability, i.e., $k_A = q_A$, $k_1 = q_1$, $k_2 = q_2$. Substituting these into the expression for S_2's payoff to aligning with A gives:

$$\frac{g(q_A + q_2)}{q_1 + g(q_A + q_2)}\left(q_2 + \frac{q_2 q_1}{q_A + q_2}\right) - \frac{c_2 q_2 q_1}{q_A + q_2}$$

Substituting the expressions for the states' capabilities into the expression for S_2's payoff to aligning with S_1 and recalling that $q_A + q_1 + q_2 = 1$ show that the difference between S_2's payoff to aligning with S_1 and A is:

$$(q_1 - q_A)\left[\frac{g(1-g)}{[q_A + g(1-q_A)][q_1 + g(1-q_1)]} + \frac{c_2}{(1-q_A)(1-q_1)}\right]$$

Thus, S_2's payoff to aligning with S_1 is larger than its payoff to aligning with A if and only if $q_1 > q_A$.

References

Allen, H. C. 1955. *Great Britain and the United States*. New York: St. Martin's Press.

Altfeld, Michael. 1984. "The Decision to Ally." *Western Political Quarterly* 37:523–44.

Anderson, M. S. 1995. *The War of the Austrian Succession, 1740–1748*. New York: Longman.

Aron, Raymond. 1966. *Peace and War*. Garden City, NY: Doubleday.

Art, Robert, and Robert Jervis. 1992. *International Politics*, 3^d ed. New York: Harper Collins.

Ausubel, Lawrence, and Raymond Deneckere. 1992. "Bargaining and the Right to Remain Silent." *Econometrica* 60:627–50.

Axelrod, Robert. 1984. *The Evolution of Cooperation*. New York: Basic Books.

Axelrod, Robert, and Robert Keohane. 1985. "Achieving Cooperation under Anarchy." *World Politics* 38:226–54.

Baldwin, David. 1985. *Economic Statecraft*. Princeton: Princeton University Press.

Barbieri, Katherine. 1996. "Economic Interdependence," *Journal of Peace Research* 33:29–49.

Barlow, Ima. 1971. *The Agadir Crisis*. Hamden, CT: Archon.

Barnhart, Michael. 1987. *Japan Prepares for Total War*. Ithaca, NY: Cornell University Press.

Barraclough, Geoffrey. 1982. *From Agadir to Armageddon*. New York: Holmes and Meier.

Bean, Richard. 1973. "War and the Birth of the Nation-State." *Journal of Economic History* 33:201–21.

Betts, Richard. 1993/94. "Wealth, Power, and Instability." *International Security* 18:34–77.

Blainey, Geoffrey. 1973. *The Causes of War*. New York: Free Press.

Borg, Dorothy. 1964. *The United States and the Far Eastern Crisis of 1933–38*. Cambridge, MA: Harvard University Press.

Bourne, Kenneth. 1967. *The Balance of Power in North America*. Berkeley: University of California Press.

Brewer, John. 1990. *The Sinews of Power*. Cambridge, MA: Harvard University Press.

Brodie, Bernard. 1946. *The Absolute Weapon*. New York: Harcourt Brace.

———. 1959. *Strategy in the Missile Age*. Princeton: Princeton University Press.

Brooks, Stephen. 1997. "Dueling Realisms." *International Organization* 51:445–78.

Browning, Reed. 1993. *The War of the Austrian Succession*. New York: St. Martin's Press.

Brzezinski, Zbigniew. 1997. *The Grand Chessboard*. New York: Basic Books.

Bueno de Mesquita, Bruce. 1981. *The War Trap*. New Haven: Yale University Press.

Bueno de Mesquita, Bruce, and David Lalman. 1988. "Systemic and Dyzdic Explanations of War." *World Politics* 41:1–20.

———. 1992. *War and Reason*. New Haven: Yale University Press.

Bueno de Mesquita, Bruce, James Morrow, and Ethan Zorick. 1997. "Capabilities, Perception, and Escalation." *American Political Science Review* 91:15–27.

Bueno de Mesquita, Bruce, James Morrow, Randolph Siverson, and Alastair Smith. 1997. "Inside-Out: A Theory of Domestic Political Institutions and the Issues of International Conflict." Manuscript, Hoover Institution, Stanford University.

———. 1998. "An Institutional Explanation of the Democratic Peace." Manuscript, Hoover Institution, Stanford University.

Bull, Hedley. 1977. *The Anarchical Society*. New York: Columbia University Press.

Butow, Robert. 1960. "The Hull-Nomura Conversations." *American Historical Review* 65:822–36.

———. 1961. *Tojo and the Coming of War*. Stanford: Stanford University Press.

Butterfield, Herbert. 1950. "The Tragic Element in Modern International Conflict." *Review of Politics* 12:147–64.

———. 1951. *History and Human Relations*. London: Collins.

———. 1966. "The Balance of Power." In Herbert Butterfield and Martin Wight, eds. *Diplomatic Investigations*. London: Allen and Unwin.

Campbell, Charles. 1974. *From Revolution to Rapprochement*. New York: John Wiley.

Carr, E. H. [1939], 1954. *The Twenty Years' Crisis*. 2d ed. London: Macmillan.

Christensen, Thomas, and Jack Snyder. 1990. "Chain Gains and Passed Bucks." *International Organization* 44:137–66.

Claude, Innis. 1962. *Power and International Relations*. New York: Random House.

Conybeare, John. 1985. "Trade Wars." *World Politics* 38:147–172.

———. 1987. *Trade Wars*. New York: Columbia University Press.

Cooter, Robert, Stephen Marks, and Robert Mnookin. 1982. "Bargaining in the Shadow of the Law." *Journal of Legal Studies* 11:225–51.

Cooter, Robert, and Daniel Rubinfeld. 1989. "Economic Analysis of Legal Disputes and Their Resolution." *Journal of Economic Literature* 27:1067–97.

Cox, Gary, and Matthew McCubbins. 1993. *Legislative Leviathan*. Berkeley: University of California Press.

Dallek, Robert. 1979. *Franklin Roosevelt and American Foreign Policy, 1932–1945*. New York: Oxford University Press.

Dessler, David. 1991. "Beyond Correlations: Toward a Causal Theory of War." *International Studies Quarterly* 35:337–55.

Doran, Charles, and Wes Parsons. 1980. "War and the Cycle of Relative Power." *American Political Science Review* 74:947–65.

Dorn, D. B. 1957. "The Diplomatic Revolution." In J. O. Lindsay, ed. *The New Cambridge Modern History*. Vol. 7. New York: Cambridge University Press.

Downing, Brian. 1992. *The Military Revolution and Political Change*. Princeton: Princeton University Press.

Downs, George, and David Rocke. 1990. *Tacit Bargaining, Arms Races, and Arms Control*. Ann Arbor: University of Michigan Press.

———. 1994. "Conflict, Agency, and Gambling for Resurrection." *American Journal of Political Science* 38:362–80.

———. 1995. *Optimal Imperfection*. Ann Arbor: University of Michigan Press.

Downs, George, David Rocke, and Peter Barsoom. 1996. "Is the Good News about Compliance Good News about Cooperation?" *International Organization* 50:379–406.

Downs, George, David Rocke, and Randolph Siverson. 1985. "Arms Races and Cooperation." *World Politics* 38:116–46.

Doyle, Michael. 1997. *Ways of War and Peace*. New York: Norton.

Eggertsson, Thrainn. 1990. *Economic Behavior and Institutions*. New York: Cambridge University Press.

Eisenhower, Dwight. 1953. *Public Papers of the Presidents, 1953*. Washington, D.C.

Elster, Jon. 1989. *Nuts and Bolts*. New York: Cambridge University Press.

Fearon, James. 1992. "Threats to Use Force." Ph.D. diss., University of California, Berkeley.

———. 1993. "Ethnic War as a Commitment Problem." Unpublished manuscript, Department of Political Science, University of Chicago.

———. 1994. "Signaling versus the Balance of Power and Interests." *Journal of Conflict Resolution* 38:236–69.

———. 1995a. "The Offense-Defense Balance and War since 1648." Manuscript, Department of Political Science, University of Chicago.

———. 1995b. "Rationalist Explanations for War." *International Organization* 39:379–414.

———. 1996. "Bargaining over Objects That Influence Future Bargaining Power." Manuscript, Department of Political Science, University of Chicago.

———. 1998. "Bargaining, Enforcement, and International Cooperation." *International Organization* 52:269–306.

Feis, Herbert. 1950. *The Road to Pearl Harbor*. Princeton: Princeton University Press.

Ferris, Wayne. 1973. *The Power Capabilities of Nation States*. Lexington, MA: Lexington Books.

Finer, Samuel. 1975. "State- and Nation-Building in Europe." In Charles Tilly, ed. *The Formation of Nation States in Western Europe*. Princeton: Princeton University Press.

Fischer, Fritz. 1975. *War of Illusions*. New York: Norton.

———. 1988. "The Miscalculation of British Neutrality." In Soloman Wank et. al., eds. *The Mirror of History*. Santa Barbara, CA: ABC-Clio.

Frank, Philipp. 1947. *Einstein: His Life and Times*. New York: Knopf.

Freedman, Lawrence. 1981. *The Evolution of Nuclear Strategy*. London: Macmillan.

Friedberg, Aaron. 1988. *The Weary Titan*. Princeton: Princeton University Press.

Fudenberg, Drew, and Jean Tirole. 1991. *Game Theory*. Cambridge, MA: MIT Press.

Gaddis, John. 1982. *Strategies of Containment*. New York: Oxford University Press.

Garfinkel, Michelle, and Stergios Skaperdas. 1996. *The Political Economy of Conflict and Appropriation*. New York: Cambridge University Press.

Gasiorowski, Mark. 1986. "Economic Interdependence and International Conflict." *International Studies Quarterly* 30:23–38.

Gasiorowski, Mark, and Soloman Polacheck. 1982. "Conflict and Interdependence." *International Organization* 26:708–29.

Gates, Robert. 1996. *From the Shadows*. New York: Simon and Schuster.

Geiss, Imanuel. 1976. *German Foreign Policy, 1871–1914*. London: Routledge.

Geller, Daniel, and J. David Singer. 1998. *Nations at War*. New York: Cambridge University Press.

Gilbert, Martin. 1966. *The Roots of Appeasement*. London: Nicolson.

Gillespie, John, Dina Zinnes, and G. Tahim. 1977. "Deterrence as Second Attack Capability." In John Gillespie and Dina Zinnes, eds. *Mathematical Systems in International Relations Research*. New York: Praeger.

Gillespie, John, Dina Zinnes, G. Tahim, and Philip Schrodt. 1977. "An Optimal Control Theory of Arms Races." *American Political Science Review* 71:226–51.

Gilpin, Robert. 1981. *War and Change in World Politics*. Cambridge: Cambridge University Press.

———. 1987. *The Political Economy of International Relations*. Princeton: Princeton University Press.

Glaser, Charles. 1992. "Political Consequences of Military Strategy." *World Politics* 44:497–538.

———. 1994/95. "Realists as Optimists." *International Security* 19:50–90.

———. 1997. "The Security Dilemma Revisited." *World Politics* 50:171–210.

Glaser, Charles, and Kaufmann, Chaim. 1998. "What Is the Offense-Defense Balance and Can We Measure It?" *International Security* 22:44–82.

Goldstein, Avery. 1997/98. "Great Expectations." *International Security* 22:36–73.

Gould, John. 1973. "The Economics of Legal Conflicts." *Journal of Legal Studies* 2:279–300.

Gowa, Joanne. 1986. "Anarchy, Egoism, and Third Images." *International Organization* 40:167–86.

———. 1989. "Bipolarity, Multipolarity, and Free Trade." *American Political Science Review* 83:1245–56.

———. 1994. *Allies, Adversaries, and International Trade*. Princeton: Princeton University Press.

Gowa, Joanne, and Edward Mansfield. 1993. "Power Politics and International Trade." *American Political Science Review* 87:408–20.

Grieco, Joseph. 1988a. "Anarchy and the Limits of Cooperation." *International Organization* 42:485–507.

———. 1988b. "Realist Theories and the Problem of Cooperation." *Journal of Politics* 50:600–624.

———. 1990. *Cooperation among Nations*. Ithaca, NY: Cornell University Press.

———. 1993. "Understanding the Problem of International Cooperation." In David Baldwin, ed. *Neorealism and Neoliberalism*. New York: Columbia University Press.

Grieco, Joseph, Robert Powell, and Duncan Snidal. 1993. "The Relative Gains Problem for International Cooperation." *American Political Science Review* 87:729–43.

Grossman, Sanford, and Oliver Hart. 1986. "The Costs and Benefits of Ownership." *Journal of Political Economy* 94:691–719.

Gulick, Edward. 1955. *Europe's Classical Balance of Power.* Ithaca, NY: Cornell University Press.

Haas, Ernst. 1953. "The Balance of Power." *World Politics* 5:442–77.

Hale, J. R. 1985. *War and Society in Renaissance Europe, 1450–1620.* Baltimore: Johns Hopkins University Press.

Herken, Gregg. 1985. *Counsels of War.* New York: Knopf.

Herz, John. 1950. "Idealist Internationalism and the Security Dilemma." *World Politics* 2:157–180.

———. 1959. *International Politics in the Atomic Age.* New York: Columbia University Press.

Hinsley, F. H. 1963. *Power and the Pursuit of Peace.* New York: Cambridge University Press.

Hinsley, F. H., E. E. Thomas, C. F. G. Ransom, and R. C. Knight. 1979–90. *British Intelligence in the Second World War.* New York: Cambridge University Press.

Hirshleifer, Jack. 1988. "The Analytics of Continuing Conflict." *Synthese* 76:201–33.

———. 1995. "Anarchy and Its Breakdown." *Journal of Political Economy.* 103:26–52.

Hobbes, Thomas. 1991. *Leviathan.* New York: Cambridge University Press.

Hoffman, Stanley. 1987. *Janus and Minerva.* Boulder, CO: Westview Press.

Horn, D. B. 1957. "The Diplomatic Revolution." In J. O. Lindsay, ed, *The New Cambridge Modern History.* Vol. 7. New York: Cambridge University Press.

Houweling, Henk, and Jan Siccama. 1988. "Power Transitions as a Cause of War." *Journal of Conflict Resolution* 31:87–102.

Howard, Michael. 1972. *The Continental Commitment.* London: Temple Smith.

———. 1984. *The Causes of War.* Cambridge, MA: Harvard University Press.

Hume, David. [1752]/1898. *Essays. Moral, Political and Literary.* New York: Longmans, Green, and Co.

Huntington, Samuel. 1961. *The Common Defense.* New York: Columbia University Press.

———. 1996. *The Clash of Civilizations.* New York: Simon and Schuster.

Huth, Paul, and Bruce Russett. 1988. "Deterrence Failure and Crisis Escalation." *International Studies Quarterly* 32:29–46.

Jehiel, Philippe, and Benny Moldovanu. 1995. "Negative Externalities May Cause Delay in Negotiation." *Econometrica* 63:1321–35.

Jervis, Robert. 1977. *Perception and Misperception in International Politics.* Princeton: Princeton University Press.

———. 1978. "Cooperation under the Security Dilemma." *World Politics* 30:167–214.

———. 1979. "Deterrence Theory Revisited." *World Politics* 31:289–346.

———. 1984. *The Illogic of American Nuclear Strategy*. Ithaca, NY: Cornell University Press.

———. 1985. "From Balance to Concert." *World Politics* 38:58–79.

Kagan, Donald. 1969. *The Outbreak of the Peloponnesian War*. Ithaca, NY: Cornell University Press.

———. 1974. *The Archidamian War*. Ithaca, NY: Cornell University Press.

———. 1981. *The Peace of Nicias and the Sicilian Expedition*. Ithaca, NY: Cornell University Press.

———. 1987. *The Fall of the Athenian Empire*. Ithaca, NY: Cornell University Press.

Kaplan, Morton. 1957. *System and Process in International Politics*. Chicago: University of Chicago Press.

Kaplan, Morton, Arthur Lee Burns, and Richard Quandt. 1960. "Theoretical Analysis of the Balance of Power. *Behavioral Science* 5:240–52.

Kaufman, Chaim, and Charles Glaser. 1998. "What Is the Offense-Defense Balance and How Can We Measure It?" *International Security* 22:44–82.

Kaufman, Robert. 1992. "To Balance or to Bandwagon." *Security Studies* 1:417–47.

Kaufmann, William. 1956. "The Requirements of Deterrence." In William Kaufmann, ed. *Military Policy and National Security*. Princeton: Princeton University Press.

Kennan, George. 1979. *The Decline of Bismarck's European Order*. Princeton: Princeton University Press.

———. 1984. *The Fateful Alliance*. New York: Pantheon.

Kennan, John, and Robert Wilson. 1993. "Bargaining with Private Information." *Journal of Economic Literature* 31:45–104.

Kennedy, Paul. 1976. *The Rise and Fall of British Naval Mastery*. New York: Scribner.

———. 1980. *The Rise of the Anglo-German Antagonism, 1860–1914*. Boston: Allen and Unwin.

———. 1983. "Strategy *versus* Finance in Twentieth-Century Britain." In Paul Kennedy, ed., *Strategy and Diplomacy, 1870–1945*. London: Allen and Unwin.

———. 1987. *The Rise and Fall of the Great Powers*. New York: Random House.

Keohane, Robert. 1984. *After Hegemony*. Princeton: Princeton University Press.

———. 1990. "International Liberalism Reconsidered." In John Dunn, ed. *The Economic Limits to Modern Politics*. Cambridge: Cambridge University Press.

———. 1993. "Institutionalist Theory and the Realist Challenge after the Cold War." In David Baldwin, ed. *Neorealism and Neoliberalism*. New York: Columbia University Press.

Keohane, Robert, and Joseph Nye. 1977. *Power and Interdependence*. Boston: Little Brown.

Kim, Woosang. 1989. "Power, Alliance, and Major Wars, 1816–1975," *Journal of Conflict Resolution* 33:255–73.

———. 1991. "Alliance Transitions and Great Power War." *American Journal of Political Science* 35:833–50.

———. 1992. "Power Transitions and Great Power War from Westphalia to Waterloo." *World Politics* 45:153–72.

Kim, Woosang, and James Morrow. 1992. "When Do Power Shifts Lead to War?" *American Journal of Political Science* 36:896–922.

Kindleberger, Charles. 1996. *World Economic Primacy*. New York: Oxford University Press.

King, Gary, Robert Keohane, and Sidney Verba. 1994. *Designing Social Inquiry*. Princeton: Princeton University Press.

Kissinger, Henry. 1957a. *Nuclear Weapons and Foreign Policy*. New York: Harper.

———. 1957b. *A World Restored*. Boston: Houghton Mifflin.

Knutsen, Torbjorn. 1997. *A History of International Relations Theory*. 2d. ed. New York: Manchester University Press.

Kreps, David. 1990. *Game Theory and Economic Modeling*. New York: Oxford University Press.

———. 1997. "Economics—The Current Position." *Daedalus* 126:59–86.

Krugman, Paul. 1995. *Development, Geography, and Economic Theory*. Cambridge, MA: MIT Press.

Kugler, Jacek, and David Lemke. 1996. *Parity and War*. Ann Arbor: University of Michigan Press.

Kuhn, Thomas. 1970. *The Structure of Scientific Revolutions*. 2d ed. Chicago: University of Chicago Press.

Kydd, Andrew. 1997. "Game Theory and the Spiral Model." *World Politics* 49:371–400.

Labs, Eric. 1992. "Do Weak States Balance?" *Security Studies* 1:383–416.

———. 1997. "Offensive Realism and Why States Expand Their War Aims." *Security Studies* 6:1–49.

Laffont, Jean-Jacques, and Jean Tirole. 1993. *A Theory of Incentives in Procurement and Regulation*. Cambridge, MA: MIT Press.

Lakatos, Imre. 1970. "Falsification and the Methodology of Scientific Research Programmes." In Imre Lakatos and Alan Musgrave, eds. *Criticism and the Growth of Knowledge*. Cambridge: Cambridge University Press.

Lake, David. 1999. *Entangling Relations*. Princeton: Princeton University Press.

Landes, William. 1971. "An Economic Analysis of the Courts." *Journal of Law and Economics* 14:61–107.

Lebow, Richard. 1981. *Between Peace and War*. Baltimore: Johns Hopkins University Press.

Levy, Jack. 1983. "Misperception and the Causes of War." *World Politics* 36:76–99.

———. 1984. "The Offense/Defense Balance of Military Technology." *International Studies Quarterly* 28:219–38.

———. 1987. "Declining Power and the Preventive Motivation for War." *World Politics* 40:87–107.

———. 1989. "The Causes of War: A Review of Theories and Evidence." In Philip Tetlock, Jo Husbands, Robert Jervis, Paul Stern, and Charles Tilly, eds. *Behavior, Society, and Nuclear War*. Vol 1. New York: Oxford University Press.

———. 1990/91. "Preferences, Constraints, and Choices in July 1914." *International Security* 15:151–86.

Liberman, Peter. 1996. "Trading with the Enemy." *International Security* 21:147–75.

Lipson, Charles. 1984. "International Cooperation in Economic and Security Affairs." *World Politics* 37:1–23.

———. 1985. "Bankers' Dilemmas." *World Politics* 38:200–225.

Mansfield, Edward. 1992. "The Concentration of Capabilities and the Onset of War." *Journal of Conflict Resolution* 36:3–24.

———. 1994. *Power, Trade, and War.* Princeton: Princeton University Press.

Maoz, Zev. 1983. "Resolve, Capabilities, and the Outcomes of Interstate Disputes, 1815–1976." *Journal of Conflict Resolution* 27:195–229.

Mastanduno, Michael. 1991. "Do Relative Gains Matter?" *International Security* 16:73–113.

Matthews, John. 1996. "Current Gains and Future Outcomes." *International Security* 21:112–46.

Mattingly, Garrett. 1955. *Renaissance Diplomacy.* Boston: Houghton Mifflin.

McKay, Derek, and H. M. Scott. 1983. *The Rise of the Great Powers, 1648–1815.* New York: Longman.

McNeill, Robert. 1982. *The Pursuit of Power.* Chicago: University of Chicago Press.

Mearsheimer, John. 1990. "Back to the Future." *International Security* 15:5–56.

———. 1994/95. "The False Promise of International Institutions." *International Security* 19:5–49.

The Military Balance, 1985–86. 1985. London: Institute for International and Strategic Studies.

Miller, Richard. 1987. *Fact and Method.* Princeton: Princeton University Press.

Modelski, George. 1987. *Long Cycles in World Politics.* London: Macmillan.

Moravcsik, Andrew. 1997. "A Liberal Theory of International Politics." *International Organization* 51:513–54.

Morgenthau, Hans. 1967. *Politics among Nations.* 4th ed. New York: Alfred Knopf.

Morrow, James. 1989. "Capabilities, Uncertainty, and Resolve—A Limited Information Model of Crisis Bargaining." *American Journal of Political Science* 33:941–72.

———. 1993. "Arms versus Allies." *International Organization* 47:207–34.

———. 1994a. "Alliances, Credibility, and Peacetime Costs." *Journal of Conflict Resolution* 38:270–97.

———. 1994b. *Game Theory for Political Scientists.* Princeton: Princeton University Press.

———. 1997. "When Do 'Relative Gains' Impede Trade?" *Journal of Conflict Resolution* 41:12–37.

Most, Benjamin, and Randolph Siverson. 1987. "Substituting Arms and Alliances, 1870–1914." In Charles Hermann, Charles Kegley, and James Rosenau, eds. *New Directions in the Study of Foreign Policy.* Boston: Unwin Hyman.

Most, Benjamin, and Harvey Starr. 1984. "International Relations Theory, Foreign Policy Substitutability and Nice Laws." *World Politics* 36:383–406.

Moul, William. 1988. "Balances of Power and the Escalation to War of Serious International Disputes among the European Great Powers, 1815–1939." *American Journal of Political Science* 32:241–75.

Mueller, Dennis. 1989. *Public Choice II*. New York: Cambridge University Press.

Murray, Williamson. 1984. *The Change in the European Balance of Power, 1938–39*. Princeton: Princeton University Press.

Myerson, Roger. 1992. "On the Value of Game Theory in Social Science." *Rationality and Society* 4:62–73.

Nalebuff, Barry. 1986. "Brinkmanship and Nuclear Deterrence." *Conflict Management and Peace Science* 9:19–30.

———. 1987. "Credible Pretrial Negotiation." *Rand Journal of Economics* 18:189–210.

———. 1991. "Rational Deterrence in an Imperfect World." *World Politics* 43:313–35.

Neary, Hugh. 1997. "A Comparison of Rent-Seeking Models and Economic Models of Conflict." *Public Choice* 93:373–88.

Niou, Emerson, and Peter Ordeshook. 1990. "Stability in Anarchic International Systems." *American Political Science Review* 84:1207–34.

———. 1991. "Realism versus Neorealism." *American Journal of Political Science* 35:481–511.

Nish, Ian. 1985. *The Origins of the Russo-Japanese War*. New York: Longman.

Nixon, Richard. 1978. *The Memoirs of Richard Nixon*. New York: Grosset and Dunlap.

Nye, Joseph. 1988. "Neorealism and Neoliberalism." *World Politics* 40:235–51.

———. 1998. "As China Rises, Must Others Bow." *The Economist* (June 27).

Organski, A. F. K. 1968. *World Politics*. 2d. ed. New York: Knopf.

Organski, A. F. K., and Jacek Kugler. 1980. *The War Ledger*. Chicago: University of Chicago Press.

Osborne, Martin, and Areil Rubinstein. 1990. *Bargaining and Markets*. New York: Academic Press.

Oye, Kenneth. 1985. "Explaining Cooperation under Anarchy." *World Politics* 38:1–24.

Pareto, Vilfredo. 1935. *The Mind and Society*. Vol. 1. New York: Harcourt, Brace and Company.

Parker, Geoffrey. 1988. *The Military Revolution.* New York: Cambridge University Press.

Parker, R. A. C. 1981. "British Rearmament 1936–39." *English Historal Review* 96:305–43.

———. 1993. *Chamberlain and Appeasement*. New York: St. Martins.

Peden, G. P. 1979. *British Rearmament and the Treasury, 1932–39*. Edinburgh: Scottish Academic Press.

Polachek, Soloman. 1980. "Conflict and Trade." *Journal of Conflict Resolution* 24:55–78.

Pollins, Brian. 1989a. "Does Trade Still Follow the Flag." *American Review of Political Science* 83:465–80.

———. 1989b. "Conflict, Cooperation, and Commerce." *American Journal of Political Science* 33:737–61.

Popper, Karl. 1959. *The Logic of Scientific Discovery*. New York: Basic Books.

Porter, Bruce. 1994. *War and the Rise of the State*. New York: Free Press.

Post, Gaines. 1993. *Dilemmas of Appeasement*. Ithaca, NY: Cornell University Press.

Powell, Robert. 1987. "Crisis Bargaining, Escalation, and MAD." *American Political Science Review* 81:717–35.

———. 1988. "Nuclear Brinkmanship with Two-Sided Incomplete Information." *American Political Science Review* 82:155–78.

———. 1989. "Nuclear Deterrence Theory and the Strategy of Limited Retaliation." *American Political Science Review* 83:503–19.

———. 1990. *Nuclear Deterrence Theory: The Search for Credibility*. New York: Cambridge University Press.

———. 1991. "Absolute and Relative Gains in International Relations Theory." *American Political Science Review* 85:1303–20.

———. 1993. "Guns, Butter, and Anarchy." *American Political Science Review* 87:115–32.

———. 1994. "Anarchy in International Relations Theory." *International Organization* 48:313–44.

———. 1996a. "Bargaining in the Shadow of Power." *Games and Economic Behavior* 15:255–89.

———. 1996b. "Stability and the Distribution of Power." *World Politics* 48:239–67.

———. 1996c. "Uncertainty, Shifting Power, and Appeasement." *American Political Science Review* 90:749–64.

Prange, Gordon. 1981. *At Dawn We Slept*. New York: Penguin.

Priest, George, and Benjamin Klein. 1984. "The Selection of Disputes for Litigation." *Journal of Legal Studies* 13:1–55.

Quester, George. 1977. *Offense and Defense in the International System*. New York: John Wiley.

Ray, James. 1995. *Democracy and International Politics*. Columbia: University of South Carolina Press.

Reinganum, Jennifer, and Louis Wilde. 1986. "Settlement, Litigation, and the Allocation of Litigation Costs." *Rand Journal of Economics* 17:557–66.

Reynolds, David. 1985. "Churchill and the British 'Decision' to Fight on in 1940." In Richard Langhorne, ed. *Diplomacy and Intelligence during the Second World War*. New York: Cambridge University Press.

Richardson, James. 1994. *Crisis Diplomacy*. New York: Cambridge University Press.

Richardson, Lewis. 1960. *The Statistics of Deadly Quarrels*. Chicago: Quadrangle.

Robson, Eric. 1957. "The Seven Years' War." In J. O. Lindsay, ed. *The New Cambridge Modern History*. Vol. 7. New York: Cambridge University Press.

Rosecrance, Richard, and Chin-Cheng Lo. 1996. "Balancing, Stability, and War." *International Studies Quarterly* 40:479–500.

Rousseau, David, Christopher Gelpi, Dan Reiter, and Paul Huth. 1996. "Assessing the Dyadic Nature of Democratic Peace, 1918–88." *American Political Science Review* 90:512–33.

Roy, Denny. 1994. "Hegemon on the Horizon?" *International Security* 19:149–68.

Rubinstein, Ariel. 1982. "Perfect Equilibrium in a Bargaining Model." *Econometrica* 50:97–109.

Russett, Bruce. 1993. *Grasping the Democratic Peace*. Princeton: Princeton University Press.

Ryan, Alan. 1996. "Hobbes' Political Philosophy." In Tom Sorell, ed. *The Cambridge Companion to Hobbes*. New York: Cambridge University Press.

Salanie, Bernard. 1997. *The Economics of Contracts*. Cambridge, MA: MIT Press.

Sandler, Todd and Keith Hartley. 1995. *The Economics of Defense*. New York: Cambridge University Press.

Schelling, Thomas. 1966. *Arms and Influence*. New Haven: Yale University Press.

Schroeder, Paul. 1994a. "Historical Reality vs. Neo-realist Theory." *International Security* 19:108–38.

———. 1994b. *The Transformation of European Politics, 1763–1848*. Oxford: Clarendon Press.

———. 1995. "History versus Neorealism." *International Security* 20:193–95.

Schultz, Kenneth. 1996. "Domestic Opposition and Signaling in International Crises." Manuscript, Woodrow Wilson School, Princeton University.

Schweizer, Urs. 1989. "Litigation and Settlement under Two-Sided Incomplete Information." *Review of Economic Studies* 18:163–78.

Schweller, Randall. 1994. "Bandwagoning for Profit." *International Security* 19:72–107.

———. 1996. "Neorealism's Status-Quo Bias." *Security Studies* 5:90–121.

Shay, Robert. 1977. *British Rearmament and the Treasury, 1932–39*. Princeton: Princeton University Press.

Shepsle, Kenneth, and Barry Weingast. 1987. "The Institutional Foundations of Committee Power." *American Political Science Review* 81:85–104.

Simaan, Marwan, and Jose Cruz. 1975. "Formulation of Richardson's Model of the Arms Race from a Differential Game Viewpoint." *Review of Economic Studies* 42:67–77.

Singer, J. David, and Melvin Small. 1972. *The Wages of War, 1816–1965*. New York: John Wiley.

Singer, J. David, Stuart Bremer, and John Stuckey. 1972. "Capabilities Distribution, Uncertainty, and Major Power Wars, 1820–1965." In Bruce Russett, ed. *Peace, War, and Numbers*. Beverly Hills, CA: Sage.

Siverson, Randolph, and Michael Tennefoss. 1984. "Power, Alliance, and the Escalation of International Conflict, 1815–1965." *American Political Science Review* 78:1057–69.

Small, Melvin, and J. David Singer. 1982. *Resort to Arms*. Beverly Hills, CA: Sage.

Smith, Alastair. 1995. "Alliance Formation and War." *International Studies Quarterly* 39:405–25.

———. 1997. "The Nature of Warfare." Manuscript, Department of Political Science, Washington University.

———. 1998. "Extended Deterrence and Alliance Formation." *International Interactions* 24:151–79.

Snidal, Duncan. 1991. "Relative Gains and the Pattern of International Cooperation." *American Review of Political Science* 85:701–26.

Snyder, Glenn. 1984. "The Security Dilemma in Alliance Politics." *World Politics* 36:461–95.

———. 1997. *Alliance Politics*. Ithaca, NY: Cornell University Press.

Snyder, Jack. 1984a. "Civil-Military Relations and the Cult of the Offensive, 1914 and 1984." *International Security* 9:108–46.

———. 1984b. *The Ideology of the Offensive*. Ithaca, NY: Cornell University Press.

———. 1991. *Myths of Empire*. Ithaca, NY: Cornell University Press.

Sorokin, Gerald. 1994. "Arms, Alliances, and Security Tradeoffs in Enduring Rivalries." *International Studies Quarterly* 38:421–46.

Spier, Kathryn. 1992. "The Dynamics of Pretrial Negotiation." *Review of Economics Studies*. 59:93–108.

Stein, Arthur. 1982. "When Misperception Matters." *World Politics* 34:505–26.

———. 1990. *Why Nations Cooperate*. Ithaca, NY: Cornell University Press.

———. 1993. "Governments, Economic Interdependence, and International Co-operation." In Philip Tetlock, Jo Husbands, Robert Jervis, Paul Stern, and Charles Tilly, eds. *Behavior, Society, and Nuclear War*. Vol 3. New York: Oxford University Press.

Stevenson, David. 1996. *Armaments and the Coming of War*. Oxford: Clarendon Press.

Stoye, John. 1969. *Europe Unfolding, 1648–1688*. London: Collins.

Tallett, Frank. 1992. *War and Society in Early Modern Europe, 1495–1715*. New York: Routledge.

Taylor, A. J. P. 1962. *The Origins of the Second World War*. New York: Atheneum.

———. 1963. *The Struggle for the Mastery of Europe*. London: Oxford University Press.

Taylor, Telford. 1979. *Munich: The Price of Peace*. Garden City, NY: Doubleday.

Thompson, William. 1988. *On Global War*. Columbia: University of South Carolina Press.

Thomson, Mark. 1957. "The War of the Austrian Succession." In J. O. Lindsay, ed. *The New Cambridge Modern History*. Vol. 7. New York: Cambridge University Press.

Thucydides. 1954. *History of the Peloponnesian War*. Trans. by Rex Warner. New York: Penguin Books.

Tilly, Charles. 1975. "War Making and State Making as Organized Crime." In Peter Evans, Dietrich Rueschemeyer, and Theda Skocpol, eds. *Bringing the State Back In*. Cambridge: Cambridge University Press.

———. 1990. *Coercion, Capital and European States, AD 990–1990*. Cambridge: Basil Blackwell.

Tirole, Jean. 1988. *The Theory of Industrial Organization*. Cambridge, MA: MIT Press.

Trachtenberg, Marc. 1991. *History and Strategy*. Princeton: Princeton University Press.

Utley, Jonathan. 1985. *Going to War with Japan*. Knoxville: University of Tennessee Press.

Van Creveld, Martin. 1977. *Supplying War*. New York: Cambridge University Press.

Van Evera, Stephen. 1984. "The Cult of the Offensive and the Origins of the First World War." *International Security* 9:58–107.

———. 1985. "Why Cooperation Failed in 1914." *World Politics* 38:80–117.

———. 1998. "Offense, Defense, and the Causes of War." *International Security* 22:5–43.

Wagner, R. Harrison. 1986. "The Theory of Games and the Balance of Power." *World Politics* 38:546–76.

———. 1994. "Peace, War, and the Balance of Power," *American Political Science Review* 88:593–607.

———. 1997. "Bargaining and War." Manuscript, Department of Government, University of Texas at Austin.

Walt, Stephen. 1987. *The Origins of Alliances*. Ithaca, NY: Cornell University Press.

———. 1988. "Testing Theories of Alliance Formation." *International Organization* 43:275–316.

———. 1992. "Alliance, Threats, and U.S. Grand Strategy." *Security Studies* 1:448–82.

———. 1996. *Revolution and War*. Ithaca, NY: Cornell University Press.

Walter, Barbara. 1997. "The Critical Barrier to Civil War Settlement." *International Organization* 51:335–64.

Waltz, Kenneth. 1959. *Man, the State and War*. New York: Columbia University Press.

———. 1979. *Theory of International Politics*. Reading, MA: Addison-Wesley.

———. 1990. "Nuclear Myths and Political Realities." *American Political Science Review* 84:731–45.

———. 1993. "The Emerging Structure of International Politics." *International Security* 18:44–79.

Wark, Wesley. 1985. *The Ultimate Enemy*. Ithaca, NY: Cornell University Press.

Wayman, Frank. 1996. "Power Shifts and the Onset of War." In Jacek Kugler and Douglas Lemke, eds. *Parity and War*. Ann Arbor: University of Michigan Press.

Weede, Erich. 1976. "Overwhelming Preponderance as a Pacifying Condition among Contiguous Asian Dyads, 1950–1969." *Journal of Conflict Resolution* 20:395–411.

Weingast, Barry, and William Marshall. 1988. "The Industrial Organization of Congress." *Journal of Political Economy* 96:132–63.

Wells, Samuel. 1979. "Sounding the Tocsin." *International Security* 4:116–58.

White, John. 1964. *The Diplomacy of the Russo-Japanese War*. Princeton: Princeton University Press.

Wight, Martin. 1946. "Power Politics." *Looking Forward*. No. 8. London: Royal Institute of International Affairs.

———. 1979. *Power Politics*. London: Pelican Books.

Williamson, Oliver. 1985. *Economic Organization*. New York: New York University Press.

Williamson, Samuel. 1969. *The Politics of Grand Strategy*. Boston: Harvard University Press.

Wittman, Donald. 1979. "How a War Ends." *Journal of Conflict Resolution* 23:743–63.

Wohlforth, William. 1987. "The Perception of Power." *World Politics* 39:353–81.

Wolfers, Arnold. 1962. *Discord and Collaboration*. Baltimore: Johns Hopkins University Press.

World Military Expenditures and Arms Transfers, 1967–1976. 1978. Washington, D.C.: United States Arms Control and Disarmament Agency.

——, *1968–77*. 1979.

——, *1970–79*. 1980.

——, *1971–80*. 1982.

——, *1971–80*. 1983.

——, *1972–82*. 1984.

——, *1985*. 1985.

——, *1986*. 1986.

——, *1987*. 1987.

——, *1988*. 1988.

——, *1989*. 1990.

——, *1990*. 1991.

Wright, Quincy. [1942], 1965. *A Study of War*. 2nd ed. Chicago: University of Chicago Press.

Yarbrough, Beth, and Robert Yarbrough. 1992. *Cooperation and Governance in International Trade*. Princeton: Princeton University Press.

Zakaria, Fareed. 1992. "Realism and Domestic Politics." *International Security* 17:177–98.

Index

accounting standard. *See* formal models

Agadir crisis, 10–11

aggressive realism. *See* offensive realism

alignment decisions: asymmetric resolve and, 188–94; balancing, 22, 149–56, 169–70, 176–84, 188–96; bandwagoning, 22, 149–56, 174–76, 188–96; chain-ganging in, 177, 180–84; costs of fighting and, 161–62, 166–67, 170, 286–89; effects of distribution of power on, 162–67, 176–84; passing the buck in, 177, 180–84; returns to scale and, 151–52, 163–64, 165–66, 170, 172–76; waiting, 22, 149–52, 170–73, 176–84, 188–96. *See also* alignment decisions, model of

alignment decisions, model of: decision to attack in, 184–88; decision to balance, bandwagon, or wait in, 176–84; limitations of, 201–4, 211–13; payoffs to balancing, bandwagoning, and waiting in, 168–76; specification of, 156–68, 296–303; summary of results, 200–201

Allen, H. C., 4, 21

Altfeld, Michael, 28

anarchy, 4, 197, 216–22. *See also* international system, stylization of

appropriative behavior, 221

Anderson, M. S., 149

arms races, 7, 204–5

Aron, Raymond, 5

Art, Robert, 216–17

asymmetric information: as bridge linking international relations theory to political science and economics, 221–22; defined, 9–10; examples of, 10–12; risk-return trade-off induced by, 14, 97, 101, 117, 133–34, 199, 206, 217; shifting power and, 19–21, 117, 133–41, 147–48; strategic problems caused by, 12–14, 197, 199, 218, 221. *See also* bargaining

Ausubel, Lawrence, 248, 257

Axelrod, Robert 5, 42, 72

balance-of-power school, 18, 83–85, 104–10, 199

balance-of-power theory, 152–56

balance-of-threat theory, 154–55

balancing. *See* alignment decisions

Baldwin, David, 79

bandwagoning. *See* alignment decisions; alignment decisions, model of

Baraclough, Geoffrey, 9

Barbieri, Katherine, 79

bargaining: asymmetric information and, 12–14, 18–21, 83–86, 116–18, 199; cost of fighting and, 91, 98–99, 110–11, 207–8; in international politics and in the shadow of the law, 217–19; offense-defense balance and, 85, 111–13. *See also* bargaining, model of with fixed distribution of power; bargaining, model of with shifting distribution of power

bargaining, model of with fixed distribution of power: equilibrium of with asymmetric information, 101–4, 251, 255; equilibrium of with complete information, 96–97; formal analysis of with asymmetric information, 99–104, 246–56; formal analysis of with complete information, 90–97; limitations of 202–4, 206–9, 213–16; specification of, 86–90, 97–99, 243–46; summary of results, 199. *See also* bargaining

bargaining, model of with shifting distribution of power: equilibrium of with complete information, 132; equilibrium of with asymmetric information, 139–40; formal analysis of with asymmetric information, 133–41, 278–82; formal analysis of with complete information, 123–33, 274–77; limitations of, 202–4, 209–11, 213–16; specification of, 118–23, 272–74; summary of results, 200. *See also* bargaining

Barlow, Ima, 10

Barnhart, Michael, 82

Barraclough, Geoffrey, 10